CRITICAL INSIGHTS

Harlan Ellison

CRITICAL INSIGHTS

Harlan Ellison

Editor
Joseph Francavilla
Columbus State University

Salem Press
Pasadena, California   Hackensack, New Jersey

Cover photo: ©Mark Hanauer/CORBIS Outline

Copyright © 2012 by Salem Press,
a Division of EBSCO Publishing, Inc.

Editor's text © 2012 by Joseph Francavilla
"The *Paris Review* Perspective" © 2012 by Sam Costello for *The Paris Review*

All rights in this book are reserved. No part of this work may be used or reproduced in any manner whatsoever or transmitted in any form or by any means, electronic or mechanical, including photocopy, recording, or any information storage and retrieval system, without written permission from the copyright owner except in the case of brief quotations embodied in critical articles and reviews or in the copying of images deemed to be freely licensed or in the public domain. For information address the publisher, Salem Press, at csr@salempress.com

∞ The paper used in these volumes conforms to the American National Standard for Permanence of Paper for Printed Library Materials, Z39.48-1992 (R1997).

Library of Congress Cataloging-in-Publication Data
Harlan Ellison / editor, Joseph Francavilla.
   p. cm. — (Critical insights)
Includes bibliographical references and index.
ISBN 978-1-58765-828-0 (alk. paper) — ISBN 978-1-58765-821-1 (set for Critical insights : alk. paper) — ISBN 978-1-58765-822-8 (set-Pack A : alk. paper)
 1. Ellison, Harlan—Criticism and interpretation. 2. Ellison, Harlan. 3. Authors, American—20th century—Biography. I. Francavilla, Joseph.
 PS3555.L62Z64 2011
 813'.54—dc22
                                                            2011019021

PRINTED IN CANADA

Contents

About This Volume, Joseph Francavilla   vii

Career, Life, and Influence

On Harlan Ellison, Joseph Francavilla	3
Biography of Harlan Ellison, Larisa Mikhaylova	23
The *Paris Review* Perspective, Sam Costello for *The Paris Review*	30

Critical Contexts

Harlan Ellison: *Deathbird Stories*, George Edgar Slusser	37
Allegories of Injustice: Social Engagement in Harlan Ellison's Short Fiction of the 1950s, 1960s, and 1970s, Rob Latham	60
All Roads Lead to Hell: Harlan Ellison, Cormac McCarthy, and the Bitter End of the American Dream, Andrew J. Wilson	75
Harlan Ellison's Critical Reception, Darren Harris-Fain	90

Critical Readings

The Annihilation of Time: Science Fiction, Ellen Weil and Gary K. Wolfe	107
Consumed by Shadows: Ellison and Hollywood, Ellen Weil and Gary K. Wolfe	141
The Computer as a Symbol of God: Ellison's Macabre Exodus, Charles J. Brady	171
Myth, George Edgar Slusser	181
The Concept of the Divided Self in Harlan Ellison's "I Have No Mouth and I Must Scream" and "Shatterday," Joseph Francavilla	194
Created in the Image of God: The Narrator and the Computer in Harlan Ellison's "I Have No Mouth, and I Must Scream," Darren Harris-Fain	214
Mythic Patterns in Ellison's *A Boy and His Dog*, John Crow and Richard Erlich	230
The Ellison Personae: Author, Storyteller, Narrator, Ellen R. Weil	237

Descents into Private Hells: Harlan Ellison's "Psy-Fi," Philip M. Rubens	248
Stripped Down Naked: The Short Stories of Harlan Ellison, Paul Di Filippo	258
The Fractured Whole: The Fictional World of Harlan Ellison, Peter Malekin	286
Afterword to *The Fantasies of Harlan Ellison*, Robert Thurston	293
Clogging Up the (In)Human Works: Harlan Ellison's Apocalyptic Postmodern Visions, Oscar De Los Santos	310
The Self on Trial: Fragmentation and Magic Realism, Ellen Weil and Gary K. Wolfe	333

Resources

Chronology of Harlan Ellison's Life	365
Works by Harlan Ellison	369
Bibliography	371
About the Editor	377
About *The Paris Review*	377
Contributors	379
Acknowledgments	382
Index	384

About This Volume

Joseph Francavilla

This volume is unique in the third round of the Salem Press Critical Insights series. It is one of the few books of the series that collects criticism on a popular author who is usually identified as writing popular fiction and genres and is part of the popular culture. Unlike the other volumes on authors such as James Baldwin, F. Scott Fitzgerald, T. S. Eliot, Isabel Allende, and Arthur Miller, who tend to be viewed as part of the mainstream literary establishment, Harlan Ellison is generally considered a popular author of science fiction, speculative fiction, fantasy, mystery, and horror. One of the few other volumes in the series similar in this respect is that on author Stephen King, although, unlike Ellison, King is a "best-seller" author, a popular "genre" author who has many times put several books on the important best-seller lists, each book selling at least a few million copies. Despite the "opening" of the canon of works taught in colleges in the late 1960s and 1970s, and a postmodern mixing of "high" and "low" art, there is currently something of a backlash, and suspicions still linger about the status and merit of "genre" fiction, "popular" fiction, and "best sellers." This concern was recently sounded when Stephen King in 2003 received the National Book Foundation's Medal for Distinguished Contribution to American Letters. As King mentioned in his acceptance speech, many had publicly voiced opposition to such a "best-seller" genre author's receiving this award.

Ellison, like virtually all science fiction and fantasy writers, is not such a "best-seller" writer. And although the occasional author has achieved a "singular" best seller (such as Vladimir Nabokov with *Lolita* in 1955), Ellison is not one of them despite his wide readership base. Ellison is part of an equivocal field (science fiction and fantasy) as seen by the mainstream literary community, but he is also seen by the science fiction and fantasy community itself as an equivocal member, often because he lashes out at what he sees as genre limitations and shortcomings—one of the main reasons for his famous *Dangerous Visions* anthologies.

In the United States this split between the "literary" novel and the popular "best seller" began when the public found the high modernist aesthetics of many authors of the 1920s, 1930s, and 1940s too challenging, and consequently too difficult to read. The "shock of the new" and the radical stylistic dislocations of authors such as T. S. Eliot, James Joyce, William Faulkner, and Franz Kafka forced the popular readership to seek and fashion their own cheap "pulp" magazines (and sometimes book lines), usually in digest form, almost always dedicated to specific genres or combinations of genres. *Weird Tales* in 1923 published dark fantasy and horror, *Amazing Stories* in 1926 dealt in science fiction, and in the 1940s and 1950s *Ellery Queen's Mystery Magazine* and *Alfred Hitchcock Mystery Magazine* specialized in crime and mystery stories, and *Harlequin Romances* exclusively published love and romance novels. An awful lot of bad writing in the early days filled these venues when the only requirement for someone to be a writer sometimes appeared to be merely that he or she owned a typewriter and sufficient postage. As science fiction writer Theodore Sturgeon famously remarked when someone complained to him about the poor quality of science fiction writing, "Of course 95 percent of science fiction is crap—but then 95 percent of *everything* is crap." The segregation of "genre" writing from the "mainstream" generated a "separate but unequal" lasting prejudice by the mainstream literary establishment—no matter how many talented and innovative writers, such as Ellison, reshaped and reinvigorated the genres in which they wrote.

Another misconception about Ellison is that since he has written some science fiction (and because science fiction today in film and television is incredibly popular), he must be a best-selling author like Stephen King. But in fact (with two or perhaps three main exceptions), virtually no science fiction author has often been on the best-seller lists with works based on his or her own original conceptions. Discounting novelizations and merchandising media tie-ins (*Star Trek*, *Star Wars*, *Alien*, and so on), and going back half a century, Robert A. Heinlein's 1961 *Stranger in a Strange Land* was the first major postwar science fiction novel to "cross over" to best-sellerdom, perhaps because of its sexual suggestiveness and its descriptions of unusual cult rituals that appealed to the emerging youth counterculture. (It is said that Charles Manson often carried a copy around and that it was the only book that Manson allowed his cult followers to read.) In 1965 Frank Herbert's *Dune* made an even stronger mark on the best-seller list, perhaps again appealing to the youth counterculture with its Campbellian monomyth hero's rise to power and its ecological themes. But Herbert, for the rest of his career, was forced within the confines of the genre to write *Dune* sequels, none of which achieved the impact of the original novel.

A similar fate awaited Arthur C. Clarke, who, after collaborating with director Stanley Kubrick on the landmark 1968 film *2001: A Space Odyssey*, had a best seller with a sequel in book form in 1982; Clarke primarily wrote sequels to *2001* for the rest of his career, none of which measured up, critically or commercially, to the original.

With romances and love stories, often colored with the exotic and the rich and famous, books by Judith Krantz, Jackie Collins, Danielle Steel, and Jacqueline Susann have frequently been on best-seller lists through the years. For horror, Anne Rice and Dean Koontz have made the lists, though Stephen King is likely the king of the heap. For suspense thrillers, John le Carré, Tom Clancy, John Grisham, Ian Fleming, Ken Follet, and Robert Ludlum have all had their share of best sellers. But for science fiction, only two writers, both now dead, often wrote best sellers: Kurt Vonnegut achieved best-sellerdom with *Slaughterhouse-Five* in 1969, *Breakfast of Champions* in 1973, and *Slapstick* in 1976. Michael Crichton used his medical background to write science fiction/techno-thrillers, such as the best sellers *The Andromeda Strain* (1969), *The Terminal Man* (1972), *Jurassic Park* (1990), *The Lost World* (1995), *Timeline* (1999), *State of Fear* (2004), and *Next* (2006), among others. Despite the enormous, record-breaking box-office success of science fiction films directed by George Lucas, Stephen Spielberg, and James Cameron, science fiction writers in general have not been likely to appear repeatedly on best-seller lists.

In a new essay written for this volume, Darren Harris-Fain addresses Ellison's push-pull relationship with the science fiction and fantasy community, Ellison's sense that mainstream critics have slighted his work because it is identified with genre fiction or popular fiction (and he has been so labeled), Ellison's easy postmodern accommodation of popular-culture references and images, and his ambiguous standing in the literary establishment. Given that he is not a best-seller author, why do so many people read Ellison's work—and not just science fiction and fantasy fans? One possible reason is the readers' sense that Ellison's works are often moral parables, with strong social concerns and cautionary themes about technology. These ideas are expanded on in Larisa Mikhaylova's biography of Ellison, Sam Costello's "*Paris Review* Perspective," and Rob Latham's longer survey of Ellison's short fiction. Costello and Latham see Ellison's work as not located in the general fiction section of most bookstores, but housed in the science fiction or fantasy areas, using the metaphors and images of such genres to examine social concerns of the day. As Latham's title indicates ("Allegories of Injustice: Social Engagement in Harlan Ellison's Short Fiction of the 1950s, 1960s, and 1970s"), Ellison can be viewed as producing a Sartre-like "engaged literature" in which the "authentic" individual strives to fight oppression, accept responsibility for his actions, and steer toward freedom in a social context, with an eye toward moral responsibility. The Promethean rebels and rebellious trickster figures in Ellison's fiction often fail to achieve their ultimate goals, but they are willing to put their lives on the line for important ideas, against all odds, and, if necessary, to die trying to resist oppression.

Many young readers may not recognize the exact historical references or allegorical points that have generated Ellison's fiction; the social/historical moments of origin (civil rights protests, abortion debates, the Kitty Genovese murder in New York, and so on) may well be long gone. It could be, then, that readers still recognize the overall general feelings or ideas of rebellion against conformity, revolt against constrictive authority, and imagination of disaster that fit their new historical context. The old specific context that generated a given story slips away, but the new universal frame slides into a contemporary context.

Ellison once described his intentions for writing stories to writer Joanna Russ as trying to "grab readers by the throat." Another reason young readers and students today, who may have no notion of the underlying social or activist debates that originated the fiction, still have such strong reactions to Ellison's fiction may lie in its sheer postmodern newness. Andrew J. Wilson's new essay in this volume pointedly compares and contrasts Ellison's vision of dystopian hell with that of Cormac McCarthy. It may be that the bleak, minimalist, Beckett-like vista of the inferno shakes a person up and appeals to the apocalyptic imagination. Ellison's fiction may also have other postmodern appeals: unconventional typographical and lexical innovations; edgy satire, black humor, and parody; magical realism and metafiction; experiments with alternate ways of storytelling and of using points of view; pop-culture references; fragmented narrative; and a general sense of freedom and improvisation in the stories. All of these elements of mainstream postmodernism seem to have, at one point or another, filtered into Ellison's landmark fiction. Young readers may enjoy his tone of comic absurdism and edgy satire (as in, say, Kurt Vonnegut's work as well), even if they do not fully recognize the references.

Another way to explain the appeal of Ellison's work is to examine the underlying mythological and psychological themes, as my essays and George Edgar Slusser's do. In a new essay, Slusser examines the consciously designed mythic structures of Ellison's collection *Deathbird Stories*, which relates urban tales of gods and devils, ancient and modern. The Promethan rebels, sacrificing trickster figures, and vengeful demons are all here, as the heroes set off on their quests, ultimately to escape themselves, their own identity. My new essay, "On

Harlan Ellison," compares Edgar Allan Poe and Ellison in regard to the alienated outsider figure, both as author and as character, who attempts to reach the supreme, sublime moment of transcendence, the terrible wonder that infuses the best speculative fiction. My other essay, reprinted here, looks at the ancient mythological figure of the doppelgänger or double as it plays out in a central way in two of Ellison's famous stories, and the psychological effect the doubling has on the characters.

There may be other explanations for the appeal of Ellison's fiction, but the new essays offered here, in addition to the reprints of classic essays on Ellison's most famous stories, provide a sufficient starting place for appreciating the work of Harlan Ellison—an author who has published for more than half a century and has certainly paid his dues.

CAREER, LIFE, AND INFLUENCE

On Harlan Ellison[1]

Joseph Francavilla

For more than a half century Harlan Ellison has produced an astonishing array of fiction, screenplays, essays, and criticism. He has written or edited more than seventy-six books. His fiction (more than seventeen hundred stories) covers many genres, including crime stories, realistic stories, comic books, horror, fantasy, postmodern vignettes, and science fiction. Though he is best known for his work in the last of these genres, he prefers the broader term "speculative fiction," coined by Robert A. Heinlein, to describe his fiction of the fantastic.

For decades Ellison has made a very successful living from his writing, and a wide group of Ellison readers faithfully buy his books, read his stories, listen to his convention speeches and readings, and watch him on television shows. The many honors he has received include four awards for outstanding teleplay from the Writers Guild of America, three Nebula Awards from the Science Fiction and Fantasy Writers of America, eight and a half Hugo Awards from the World Science Fiction Society,[2] two Edgar Allan Poe Awards from the Mystery Writers of America, six Bram Stoker Awards from the Horror Writers Association, the British Fantasy Award, the World Fantasy Award, and the inclusion of his short story "The Man Who Rowed Christopher Columbus Ashore" in the 1993 volume of *The Best American Short Stories*. In 2006, the Science Fiction and Fantasy Writers of America named Ellison a Damon Knight Memorial Grand Master, an honor "bestowed upon a living author for a lifetime's achievement in science fiction and/or fantasy." He is also notorious for his thorny personality, his abusive talk and insults, and his "take no crap" attitude—he is a self-defined *enfant terrible* in his seventies, a "troublemaker" who, committed ethically to a certain course, will unabashedly say unpopular things to those who don't want to hear them. This, too, is part of the charismatic public persona who will do the unexpected, the Ellison mystique, that suffuses his writings and attracts people to him and his works.

Yet despite his popularity, his longevity as a writer, and the many awards he has received, with a very few exceptions Ellison has not yet been recognized by or accepted into the larger literary establishment and community, has not been published or reviewed regularly in the elite literary journals and magazines, and has not crossed over from the ghetto of "genre" fiction into the palatial region of canonical literature, the Celestial City. Why should this be? With the help of an extended comparison of the neoromantic author Harlan Ellison and the romantic writer Edgar Allan Poe, as well as an examination of the nature and origin of the science fiction genre itself, I would like to suggest some reasons.

Andrew J. Wilson's fine essay in this volume compares and contrasts the postmodern elements of the postapocalyptic worlds in the writings of Harlan Ellison and 2010 Nobel Prize nominee and Pulitzer Prize winner Cormac McCarthy, highlighting hitherto unseen connections. Ellison and Poe certainly have numerous differences. Ellison's career spans more than half a century, while Poe wrote fiction for little more than fifteen years in his four-decade life span. Ellison has been commercially successful at writing for decades, while Poe lived in virtual poverty until the last few years of his life. Ellison's degree of popular success and recognition contrasts with Poe's relative obscurity as an author of fiction until he published his poem "The Raven" in 1845, four years before his death. Ellison's presentation of overt ethical messages in the themes of his parables is quite the converse of Poe's strong belief in the "heresy of the didactic."

Unlike Wilson, I will highlight in this essay only some of the similarities between Ellison and Poe, in order more pointedly to illuminate the genre elements (specifically related to science fiction) that may have contributed to Ellison's being denied entrance into the celestial palace of canonical literature. After all, it is important to recall that, as a teenager in the late 1940s, Ellison discovered science fiction through fandom, then wrote science fiction as his first batch of professional sales in the mid-1950s. He continued to make his name and reputation in the field (with both fiction and teleplays) throughout the 1960s and 1970s, until in 2006 the Science Fiction and Fantasy Writers of America recognized him by naming him a Damon Knight Memorial Grand Master, an honor given by the organization to living authors in recognition of lifetime achievement in science fiction or fantasy. (Ironically, as Weil and Wolfe point out in their book *Harlan Ellison: The Edge of Forever*, many of Ellison's award-winning stories are not usually considered science fiction, and in recent decades Ellison has written few bona fide science fiction stories, concentrating instead on fantasy, horror, postmodern collage pieces, and what might be called a homegrown kind of magical realism.) Nevertheless, to understand Ellison's dilemma, it is crucial to examine how Poe developed the science fiction genre and how Ellison, more than a century later, still follows in that tradition.

For decades, Ellison has been vitally concerned with his literary legacy, with what will be valued in his work by generations to come. For example, in the 2008 film documentary about Ellison's life and work, *Dreams with Sharp Teeth*, one of Ellison's protégés, Dan Simmons, remarks that the only time he saw Ellison at a loss for words was when he was asked in an interview of a group of writers what he thought about his literary posterity. Ellison said nothing and passed the question on to others. But after the show was over, Ellison admitted he was overwhemingly obsessed with the question. Unlike the Woody Allen joke about achieving immortality not through his work, but "by not dying," Ellison broods about what his literary legacy will be through his work.

Like Ellison, Poe, too, considered what an author's literary afterlife would be. In his 1843 review of *Wyandotté: Or, The Hutted Knoll*, by one of the most popular novelists of the time (James Fenimore Cooper, author of *The Deerslayer* and *The Last of the Mohicans*), Poe suggests that certain works, regardless of their deficiencies in style, composition, or structure, could win popular appeal simply if their subjects or themes are life in the wilderness or on the ocean, if they present minutely detailed accounts, and if they portray exotic Native Americans as characters. In the science fiction of a century later this formula might be transformed to involve a ship journeying through space to another planet, a realistic veneer of technobabble and pseudoscience, and extraterrestrials and artificial intelligences. Poe goes on to divide the stories and their writers into two distinct groups in terms of the works' impacts on generations of readers after the author has died:

> There are two great classes of fictions,—a popular and widely circulated class, read with pleasure, but without admiration, in which the author is lost or forgotten; or remembered, if at all, with something very nearly akin to contempt; and then, a class not so popular, nor so widely diffused, in which, at every paragraph, arises a distinctive and highly pleasurable interest, springing from our perception and appreciation of the skill employed, of the genius evinced in the composition. After perusal of the one class, we think solely of the book; after reading the other, chiefly of the author. The former class leads to popularity—the latter to fame. In the former case, the books sometimes live, while the authors usually die; in the latter, even when the works perish, the man survives. Among American writers of the less generally circulated, but more worthy and more artistical fictions, we may mention Mr. Brockden Brown, Mr. John Neal, Mr. Simms, Mr. Hawthorne; at the head of the more popular division we may place Mr. Cooper. (205-6)

Early on, then, Poe foresaw the ever-widening gap between what we would call today best sellers or popular literature and the soon-to-be canonical literary texts taught in universities and revered by the literary establishment: in the twentieth century, Jacqueline Susann, Danielle Steele, and Harold Robbins on one hand, and Franz Kafka, William Faulkner, and Jorge Luis Borges on the other. In 1920, F. Scott Fitzgerald's first novel, *This Side of Paradise*, was perhaps what we could call a "best seller," but the continuing modernist challenges to popular audience expectations became ever more pronounced until in the 1920s, 1930s, and 1940s "pulp" and "digest" specialty magazines (publishing science fiction, horror, fantasy, detective, and other genre fiction) were designed with the popular audience in mind, while practitioners of the "New Criticism" championed the modernist writers in the little magazines and literary journals, as well as in the universities, for an elite, specialized audience. An irrevocable split occurred between best-selling popular literature and "serious," canonical, literary works—a split that grew to Grand Canyon proportions with the coming of television and other mass media. Pulp fiction ("pulp" designated rough, cheap, unfinished paper) was predominantly denigrated by the "literary" audience; in fact, some thought that to be a "popular" novelist was de facto to be an author of bad literature. Hence, to be known to much of the literary establishment as a "science fiction writer" was to be forever tarred and feathered or, worse, to be invisible. (Curiously, this split did not happen in Britain, where an Aldous Huxley could write a *Brave New World* or a George Orwell could produce a *1984* without any damage to his literary reputation or status.)

It seems that Harlan Ellison did not believe what science fiction writer Robert A. Heinlein had stated he believed: that such genre writers were simply competing for people's "beer money," and that was an end to it. And Ellison has repeatedly said that he sees no real differences among the items on his reading list, consisting, say, of comics, Dostoevski, a fantasy novel, and Kafka. In a 1990 interview, I asked him about popular and critical success. His answer, which he has since repeated in other places, was that he wants to be a popular *and* a critical success, to have literary immortality in the canon but also to have great commercial achievement today. But such ambitions come at a price. In a 1988 keynote address at the International Conference on the Fantastic, Ellison ruefully meditated on the genre writer trapped in popular-fiction marketplaces like a snail inside a chambered nautilus: "Once in a while a Bradbury can escape; once in a while a Vonnegut can escape, but not even a Heinlein, not even an Asimov, not even a Clarke—for all the money they get—manages to escape. . . . We are condemned to a very strange Gulag . . . we are all bent by the marketplace" (qtd. in Weil and Wolfe 4-5).

Poe is usually thought of as a key developer of the American gothic horror tale, the mystery story, and the detective story. Sir Arthur Conan Doyle's Sherlock Holmes is acknowledged as a direct descendant of Poe's C. Auguste Dupin, and H. P. Lovecraft's New England nightmares bear the unmistakable imprints of Poe's terrifying visions. In fact, most people do not realize that half of Poe's stories are comic—satires, parodies, and jeux d'esprit. Poe, like Ellison, followed the marketplace; for Poe, the trail started with poetry, parodies, then essays and reviews, and stories imitating the sensational outlets such as *Blackwood's Magazine*, including crime stories, horror, fantasy, science fiction, mystery, and detective stories. For Ellison, the marketplace journey early on involved fiction about juvenile delinquents, confessional stories, realistic crime stories, pieces in the men's magazines, then science fiction and fantasy and, when the magazine market began to wither, television scripts. Poe, like Ellison, managed to make a living from his writing, though Poe, unlike Ellison, could eke out only (at best) subsistence wages.

While of Poe's sixty-odd stories only five can conceivably be considered detective stories and more than a baker's dozen can be classed as science fiction, Poe is still not often thought by the public to have originated science fiction and is not ordinarily given credit in many surveys and histories of science fiction for the foundation of that genre. Instead, everyone and anyone is named the progenitor, from Lucian of Samosata, Plato, and anonymous authors of myths such as the story of Daedalus and Icarus to Thomas More's *Utopia* (1516), Jonathan Swift's *Gulliver's Travels* (1726), and Mary Wollstonecraft Shelley's *Frankenstein* (1818). Thus, for example, in his standard and authoritative work *Billion Year Spree: The True History of Science Fiction* (1973), British author Brian W. Aldiss names his countrywoman Mary Shelley as writing the "first real novel of science fiction" (29). To be sure, finding originators of science fiction depends on one's definition of that genre, and there are at least as many definitions of science fiction as there are definers.

It is also important to note that editor Hugo Gernsback's tongue-tying term "scientifiction" first appeared in his 1926 pulp magazine *Amazing Stories*, a designation that he fortunately changed a few years later in another of his pulp magazines to the more palatable name "science fiction." He described the newly christened infant genre as "that Jules Verne, H. G. Wells and Edgar Allan Poe type of story—a charming romance intermingled with scientific fact and prophetic vision" (qtd. in Broderick 7). The use of the word "romance," the older term for the fantastic narrative in opposition to the realistic novel, is understandable. But to describe Poe's stories (full of putrification, gore, corpses, and necrophilia) as "charming" is like describing Charles Manson as "cuddly."

Because Poe hopped from genre to genre and from venue to venue, he learned to write short stories, which were easier to finish and quicker to submit. His only completed novel, *The Narrative of Arthur Gordon Pym*, urged on him early in his career by his publishers at Harper & Brothers, was a complete financial and critical disaster when it debuted in 1838. Similarly, Harlan Ellison early in his career tried a novel about juvenile gangs (*Rumble*, 1958; later retitled *Web of the City*) and another novel about rock and roll (*Spider Kiss*, 1961). However, publishers' changes to his material and the need to find outlets quickly caused him to stay with short-fiction markets and, when he moved to Los Angeles in 1962, with screenplays for the lucrative television arena. In fantastic fiction he is known primarily as a short-story writer. The general literary prejudice for novels as worthier than collections of short stories has been around at least since Dorothy Parker's 1927 *New Yorker* review of Ernest Hemingway's second story collection, *In Our Time*, in which Parker described people's reactions to story collections as feeling cheated and viewing them as "just a lot of those short things" (qtd. in Baker 305). That persistent prejudice, however, may have hindered *both* Ellison and Poe, at least at first, from being accepted into the canonical literary establishment.

Though science fiction has often been described as "the literature of change," "the literature of the future," "the literature of technology," and "the literature of ideas," Aldiss's fairly well-accepted definition (from his revised *Trillion Year Spree: The History of Science Fiction*) bears repeating: "Science fiction is the search for a definition of man and his status in the universe which will stand in our advanced but confused state of knowledge (science), and is characteristically cast in the Gothic or post-Gothic mode" (25). The last part of this definition neatly severs premodern works from those written after the Industrial Revolution. For example, if myths look to the past to explain the origins of the world, then science fiction tends to look toward the future and speculate on the end of the world. Modern science developed when technology began to have direct impacts on people's everyday lives and when scientists (such as those belonging to the Royal Society of London, first founded in 1660) began publishing papers and reports on their experiments for both other scientists and the general pubic to read. Modern fiction in English started with the experiments in the novel during the early 1700s by Daniel Defoe, Laurence Sterne, and Samuel Richardson, among others. It thus would seem likely that the origins of modern science fiction stem from the confluence of these two vital forces in Western society.

It is interesting to note that Poe wrote many more stories that fit Aldiss's genre definition than did Mary Shelley with her two novels on which Aldiss dwells (*Frankenstein* and *The Last Man*). About Poe, Aldiss asserts that although he uses "scientific flavouring" (59), he is not really a science fiction writer predominantly and that if "Poe had conceived a science fictional form more clearly, he could have cast the story [*Arthur Gordon Pym*] more effectively; and this applies to most of his few other gestures towards the genre" (63). Aldiss goes on to conclude that "far from being the Father of Science Fiction, this genius botched it when he confronted its themes directly" (63). Other, later surveys of science fiction, such as Carl Freedman's *Critical Theory and Science Fiction* (2000), echo this traditional view of placing Poe's "science fiction" in some other genre, though Aldiss puts Poe's tales in the gothic or the nonfictional journal or dialogue genre, whereas Freedman classifies them as travel or geographic narratives.

Ellison, as a neoromantic writer, follows Poe in several distinctive ways: the fascination with revolt and rebellion, the valuing of the individual and antiauthoritarian nonconformity, the doppelgänger theme, the fondness for shocking gothic horror effects (often at the ends of scenes or stories), the reverence for the imagination as one of the highest human faculties (and frequently testing the limits of imagination), and, most significant, the virtually constant striving in fiction for the grotesque and the sublime. In *The Seven Beauties of Science Fiction*, Istvan Csicsery-Ronay, Jr., explores in detail two key elements (the grotesque and the sublime) among others in science fiction. I will concentrate on the sublime as reflecting the movement toward mystical transcendence and, for Ellison, the sacrifice of the Promethean-like, antiauthoritarian rebel amid hellish circumstances.

When science fiction fans are asked to define science fiction, they almost inevitably spout the cliché that a work of science fiction provides a "sense of wonder." That is, a special astonishment, a "sense of wonder and awe," ensues after a reader of science fiction has followed Samuel Taylor Coleridge's dictum involving a "willing suspension of disbelief," often aided by what H. G. Wells terms the author's ingenious use of "scientific patter." This "wonder and awe" tentatively link the special pleasure of reading or viewing science fiction to the notion of the romantic sublime as discussed by Edmund Burke or Immanuel Kant. But when pressed to expand on their definitions, science fiction fans are likely just to hide behind Damon Knight's amusingly circular definition of the genre: "[Science fiction] means what we point to when we say it."

Poe's stories of extraordinary voyages in space, mesmerism, and apocalypse virtually always evoke the romantic notion of the "sublime," a term with which Poe was familiar, as shown in his use of the term in his reviews and criticism, as well as his reference in both his criticism and stories to one of the key theorists, German philosopher Immanuel Kant. Edmund Burke, in his 1757 work *A Philosophical En-*

quiry into the Origin of Our Ideas of the Sublime and Beautiful, set forth the influential notion of the sublime in romantic thought for the succeeding decades. He contrasted the beautiful, which evokes feelings of calmness, restfulness, and tenderness, with the sublime, which evokes the ecstasy of terror, especially the terrible wonder and awe of witnessing potentially dangerous events such as natural storms or raging floods, or viewing vast vistas. Kant revised Burke's theory of the mingling of pleasure with pain to add the notion of the "incomparably great," or of the mind's inability to contemplate the "infinity" in the scene experienced, as well as dynamic natural forces and processes that exert such power that it seems they may overcome us.

In a number of Poe's tales, such as "MS. Found in a Bottle," *The Narrative of Arthur Gordon Pym*, "The Facts in the Case of M. Valdemar," and "The Conversation of Eiros and Charmion," Poe generates this sense of awe and wonder, this quasi-religious or mystical vision, this idea of the terrible ecstasy of contemplating the infinite or of vast changes of scale. But rather than rely on scenes of nature alone to create this effect, Poe mixes in his perverse sense of an absurd hoax and what David E. Nye calls the "technological sublime," the sublime feelings evoked by the contemplation of technological devices, or states arrived at by technological means. Nye asserts that the technological object or process overwhelms the imagination of the ordinary person: "While the natural sublime is related to eternity, the technological sublime aims at the future and is often embodied in instruments of speed, such as the railway, the airplane, and the rocket, that annihilate time and distance" (61). Other examples include great bridges, skyscrapers, dams, and the atom bomb. In addition, dynamic and sudden changes of state or scale produced by technological means generate the technological sublime. Dynamic, shifting changes of scale of elements such as speed, location, size, telecommunication, time, power, and motion are central to science fiction. This in fact may be the origin of what science fiction writers and scholars term the "sense of wonder" or awe that is universally seen at the heart of science fiction.

Poe, an amateur astonomer and reviewer of many popularized scientific books, was always searching for terra incognita, especially those places that cross borders, those realms "out of space and out of time." If Poe could simultaneously pull his readers' legs while hoaxing them and making them believe the fantastic situations he created, he was all the more pleased with his stylistic attempts at verisimilitude. He wrote stories and sketches about machines ("Maezel's Chess Player"), aliens ("The Balloon-Hoax" and "Hans Pfaall"), paranormal hypnotic powers and mesmerism ("A Tale of the Ragged Mountains," "The Facts in the Case of M. Valdemar," "Some Words with a Mummy"), the apocalypse ("The Colloquy of Monos and Una," "The Conversation of Eiros and Charmion"), space travel and travel between dimensions or parallel worlds, including the popular nineteenth-century theory of holes at the earth's poles ("MS. Found in a Bottle," *The Narrative of Arthur Gordon Pym*), the future ("Mellonta Tauta"), and immortality or the afterlife ("The Facts in the Case of M. Valdemar" and "Some Words With a Mummy"). Both Arthur Conan Doyle ("Captain of the Polestar") and Jules Verne (*Le Sphinx des glaces*, translated into English as *An Antarctic Mystery*) wrote works imitating (and perhaps trying to "finish") Poe's *The Narrative of Arthur Gordon Pym*, a sea voyage turned cannibalistic catastrophe turned metaphysical disaster. Verne could not have created his series known as the Voyages Extraordinaires, including such works as the 1865 *De la terre à la lune* (*From the Earth to the Moon*, 1873), without Poe's "Hans Pfaall," or invented his 1863 *Cinq Semaines en ballon* (*Five Weeks in a Balloon*, 1876) without Poe's "The Balloon Hoax." Why is it, then, that the bad boy of American literature, the "genius wonder boy" of imaginative stories, has been expelled from the school of science fiction? It would seem that if one wants to be credited with inventing or reinventing a genre—and usually finding the riches and popular fame Poe was never able to find during his lifetime—all one needs to do is finish what Poe started: Arthur Conan Doyle with his detective stories, Jules Verne with his Voyages Extraordinaires, Stephen King with his modern American gothic horror, and Ray Bradbury with his early science fiction and dark psychological fantasies or "weird tales."

Ellison, like Poe, is attracted to those sublime elements of wonder and awe in his fiction, even if, Ellison admits, he doesn't know much about science except what he happens to read. Ellison has expressed astonishment at the way some science fiction writers (such as, say, Frederik Pohl) have immense catalogs of scientific information and knowledge in their heads in order to achieve in fiction the "verisimilitude" Ellison believes is important in any genre. The early stories Ellison published in the science fiction magazines of the mid- to late 1950s all feature the standard science fiction tropes, props, and icons of the technological sublime, involving vast changes of scale, location, speed, power, dynamism, shape, and so on. The stories thus include faster-than-light space travel, time travel, alien invasions and earth-alien wars, robots, immortality, and telepathy, but these are simply convenient, commercial devices Ellison uses to tell entertaining stories fitting popular-fiction formulas. Such magazines, Ellison reflects in the documentary *Dreams with Sharp Teeth*, were so disreputable in the early days that people would hide them within the covers of *National Geographic* or other "respectable" magazines. (How, most people then thought, could any sane and decent person prefer to read about renegade robots, ray guns, bug-eyed monsters, and big-headed aliens?) For certain elite elements of the literary establishment, the bone-deep "stink" of that pulp genre ghetto is, evidently, extremely hard to remove—even if for decades an author has not written that type of story and has composed mostly outstanding "general" fiction. In addition, the breakthrough in the 1960s and 1970s of opening up the literary canon toward popular fiction, has, like feminism, experienced a backlash and reversal in recent decades. It is no wonder that Poe, writing in the gothic mode about such bizarre pseudoscience and cult fashions of his day, was also for so long resisted by the established literary and academic world (and in some corners still is).

Following up hints regarding the centrality of Poe's "science fictional" gothic in Leslie Fiedler's *Love and Death in the American Novel* (1960) and of Poe's "apocalyptic imagination" in David Ketterer's *New Worlds for Old: The Apocalyptic Imagination, Science Fiction, and American Literature* (1974), Thomas M. Disch (a longtime American writer of science fiction and fantasy, sometimes identified with the "New Wave" SF of the 1960s) moves Mary Shelley to the edges and Poe, fellow American, to the center of the science fiction egg. In his history, *The Dreams Our Stuff Is Made Of: How Science Fiction Conquered the World*, Disch asserts that Aldiss errs in attributing influence to Shelley when she was not read very widely after publication while ignoring Poe, who was a market-driven "magazinist" whose stories have always been influential and read widely around the world. Regarding *Frankenstein*, Disch argues that after Shelley presents a weakly explained conceit that a human being could be engineered, the novel "becomes a Model-T melodrama with philosophic interludes" (33). In contrast, Poe's use of scientific verisimilitude, his extensive borrowings from the language of science and technology (for example, nautical terms in *Arthur Gordon Pym* and "MS. Found in a Bottle," medical terms in "The Facts in the Case of M. Valdemar," and astonomical terms in "The Conversation of Eiros and Charmion"), and his blending of mystical visionary elements with dry, scientific, factual reportage all make him, according to Disch, "the source" of science fiction.

But, Disch continues, science fiction, as with Poe, is not without its defects, its glitzy "so bad it's good" traits. This may explain why critics often have failed to acknowledge both the genre and Poe, as the title of Disch's chapter on Poe—an allusion to Allen Tate's piece on Poe—may indicate: "Poe: Our Embarrassing Ancestor." Disch quotes T. S. Eliot on Poe to show the utter contempt certain highbrows have for lowbrow Poe—though ironically Poe would become the high priest of modernism to the French symbolists—and their feeling that "Poe's work was considered most suitable for intellectually hyperkinetic teenagers" (35). As Eliot puts it, "That Poe had a powerful intellect is undeniable: but it seems to me the intellect of a highly gifted young person before puberty" (35). The equation, says Disch, is more than perfect; as the cliché goes concerning when science fiction was in its golden age: "The golden age of science fiction is twelve." He continues by listing traits Poe first developed in the establishment of science fiction: using as the basis for a story a popular, fuzzy pseudoscience such as mesmerism (a contemporary equivalent would be demonic possession, channeling, or alien abduction); offering at least a glimpse of wish fulfillment (immortality, escaping death, traveling freely in time or space or dimension); taking a superior, "chip on the shoulder" attitude while preemptively attacking those who doubt unusual notions; and displaying genuine visionary power.

Disch concludes with two final traits Poe established for science fiction: great special effects and sophomoric humor: "Poe was a prophetic and exemplary popular artist in the sense that he refused to recognize the boundaries of good taste. He delighted in going over the top and grossing people out, and his readers delighted in this side of his work" (45). He attempted to get a "gasp" of astonishment, horror, wonder, and burlesque—all at once—out of his reader. As Disch notes, "The Facts in the Case of M. Valdemar" "offers a good example of Poe at his gore-blimiest (a special form of the sublime)" (45). In this story, the tubercular Valdemar is hypnotized at the point of death. In his suspended state eventually there is a deterioration: a swollen, blackened tongue and a putrid "yellowish ichor" oozing from the eyes. Eventually Valdemar begs to be either put to sleep or wakened. As the victim is unhypnotized, the narrator describes what happens: "His whole frame at once . . . shrunk—crumbled—absolutely *rotted* away beneath my hands. Upon the bed, before that whole company, there lay a nearly liquid mass of loathesome—of detestable putridity" (203).

Similarly, Ellison ends stories with such shocking gothic images, mixing the sublime and the grotesque—frequently heightened by ramped-up rhetoric, meant to grab the reader by the throat—and, like

Poe, doing away with or minimizing denouement and epilogue. Ellison also follows the suggestion in Poe's essay "The Philosophy of Composition" concerning why Poe, in composing "The Raven," put the raven in the room with the student: the "close circumscription of space"—what Weil and Wolfe have called in Ellison the persistent theme of entrapment or enclosure (3-4)—allows the incident to have the predetermined desired effect.

A good example of this combined effect is found at the end of Ellison's famous story "I Have No Mouth, and I Must Scream" (which has generated more parody titles than dogs have fleas). Ted, the narrator, has been trapped with the handful of other surviving humans after a world war inside the supercomputer AM, which tortures them forever. In outmaneuvering AM and sacrificing the others so they can no longer be tortured, Ted brings AM's wrath upon himself and is transformed into a huge "soft jelly thing" with pulsing, fog-filled holes instead of eyes, incapable of killing himself and subject to AM's tortures forever. The unforgettable, horrific image, both sublime and grotesque, essentially ends the tale, without a denouement. (The rhetorical overdrive, however, is contained in earlier sections such as AM's telepathic, raging rant against Ted.) Ellison wrote this particular story around a painting that inspired the key image, but the same sort of strategy can be seen in other Ellison works, including "Demon with a Glass Hand," a teleplay he wrote for the television program *The Outer Limits*, in which the hero, Trent (and the viewer), finally discovers that Trent is a robot and must live and wait among humanity for thousands of years; or *A Boy and His Dog*, where in the final scene Vic and Blood devour Quilla June in order to survive in the aboveground wasteland; or "The Deathbird," where eventually the "God" is defeated and Earth is euthanized.

This type of final effect can be seen in the climaxes of most of Poe's best stories, a cutting off (so to speak) of the last, denouement, leg of Freytag's pyramid, so that the tale ends with an image associated with a shock, a gasp of horror and revulsion, an element of the ludicrous, and a glimpse of sensational astonishment or terrible awe. Poe first tried this kind of trick of ending, with a climax and eliding the denouement, in his early 1833 story "MS. Found in a Bottle." After a terrible storm, the narrator in this sea adventure finds himself hurled onto a weird and ancient ghost ship and writes a journal of his adventure. The story may be a version of the Flying Dutchman legend, or it may depict a voyage to a parallel dimension involving Spanish galleons of the past, a journey into one of the holes in the center of the earth at the South Pole, or a hallucination. The final vision is one of awe and terror, of possible discovery and seeming destruction, of fear mingled with excitement (yet tinged with the ludicrous); that is, it is the sublime generated by the vast whirlpool into which the large ship is being sucked:

> The ship is at times lifted bodily from out the sea . . . and we are whirling dizzily, in immense concentric circles . . .—the circles rapidly grow small—we are plunging madly within the grasp of the whirlpool—and amid a roaring, and bellowing, and thundering of ocean and of tempest, the ship is quivering, oh God! and—going down. (11)

While the vastness of the scale of the storm and the whirlpool create a sense of the infinite and dynamic power that Kant suggests is key to the feeling of the sublime, that feeling is also supercharged with rhetorical flourishes, mixed with a sense of the narrator's ludicrous situation: journal writing to the last minute while being sucked into a gigantic whirlpool. In creative-writing classes, this is usually called the "and then I died" story. Poe in later stories learned to have a witness survive and describe such cataclysms.

In Poe's one and only completed novel, *The Narrative of Arthur Gordon Pym*, a lengthy subtitle actually announces the tabloid sensational events to follow. There will be "details of a Mutiny and atrocious butchery on board the American brig Grampus, on her way to the South Seas," "shipwreck and subsequent horrible sufferings from famine [and cannibalism]," and a "massacre of her crew," "together with the incredible adventures and discoveries still farther south to which that distressing calamity gave rise" (41). Along the way, the teenage narrator's good friend Augustus will be lifted up, and his leg will fall off from disease and wounds and into the sea, to the delight of waiting sharks.

In the novel, which is often seen as proto-science fiction, Poe makes use of the sublime but complicates it with perverseness, constant hoaxing, and an abrupt ending without extensive explanation. This complexity may be why critics have overlooked its science fictional elements touching on the sublime. The final image is again the most enigmatic, mystical, and sublime: as the two last living men in a canoe are about to plunge into a cataract, the narrator's journal describes their last vision: "But there arose in our pathway a shrouded human figure, very far larger in its proportions than any dweller among men. And the hue of the skin of the figure was of the perfect whiteness of snow" (239). No explanation is provided after the journal stops short, but we know the narrator, Pym, survives to write the tale.

The final white "shrouded human figure" could be interpreted as practically anything, from the abominable snowman to a divinity, to Titans guarding the holes at the earth's poles, to the white at the end of the page, to a sail or figurehead of a ship seen by a deluded narrator. If the final figure turns out to be simply a sail or a figurehead, then its apparent sublimity transforms into a bad, ironic joke. Still, critics have explained this image as the ultimate metaphysical enigma, or as an emblem of epistemological questioning of perception, reality, or language itself.

Through the lens of Poe, then, we may begin to understand Harlan Ellison's dilemma of aspiring to attain both popular and critical success. Fighting prejudices against science fiction itself, pulp genre fiction, popular or commercial fiction, short stories as a primary medium, neogothicism, the grotesque, and the sublime, Ellison for decades has constantly been denied access to the literary immortality he so craves.

Sometimes a critic will accuse him of "overwriting," of using a "baroque" style, of "writing at the top of his lungs," but when Ellison writes a "quiet," moving story such as "Jeffty Is Five" in reply, only silence ensues. Poe, too, was attacked for his "overwrought" style, his vulgar "bad taste" (by Aldous Huxley, William Butler Yeats, and T. S. Eliot, among others), and his persistent love of the macabre and the supernatural.

Both Ellison and Poe have sometimes been accused of showing bad taste in the content of their writing. On April 30, 1835, about three years after Poe's career in fiction began, he wrote a letter to editor Thomas W. White. White had complained about the "bad taste" that Poe displayed in a story submission titled "Berenice." In this story, a man is about to marry his cousin as she is dying of a disease. He becomes entranced and obsessed with her teeth just before she dies. Then, lost in meditation, he awakens to find that he has forgotten that, in a sort of trance, he has just dug up her body from the grave and taken out her teeth with dental instruments. In his letter, Poe agrees that White may be correct in his assessment of "Berenice," but he notes also that the tale is similar in nature to the kinds of popular stories then being published in the magazines: "You ask me in what does this nature consist? In the ludicrous heightened into the grotesque: the fearful coloured into the horrible: the witty exaggerated into the burlesque: the singular wrought out into the strange and mystical. You may say all this is bad taste. I have my doubts about it" (*Letters* 1:57-58).

Ellison must also have his doubts about "bad taste," though his creative-writing professor at Ohio State University in the early 1950s bluntly told Ellison he had no writing talent, had poor taste in subject matter (science fiction), and should stop attempting to be a writer to avoid frustration. (And Ellison likes to quote science fiction critic and writer James Blish, who said Ellison's first sale, "Glowworm," was "the single worst story ever published in the field of science fiction"; qtd. in Weil and Wolfe 51.) Ironically, many years later, after Ellison had become an established author, J. Michael Straczynski (eventually creator of the television series *Babylon 5* and friend of Ellison) called Ellison on the phone out of the blue to ask him why Straczynski's writing wasn't selling. Without knowing Straczynski or his work, Ellison almost echoed the professor's comments in an eerie way by replying, "Stop writing crap." If it weren't crap, Ellison continued, it would sell.

In the avowed attempt to shock and schlock the reader, to bring the reader up short, and to go "over the top" for effect with rhetorical overdrive, Poe and Ellison prefigure the awesome "growl" of the ape given knowledge by the alien monolith in *2001: A Space Odyssey*, the sublime "gasp" of the chest-busting scene in Ridley Scott's film *Alien*, and the unforgettable and bizarre image of the upside-down severed head sprouting alien "legs" and walking across the floor in John Carpenter's film *The Thing*. Poe or Ellison can be seen as the film equivalent of a combination John Waters/Alfred Hitchcock/Roger Corman/Edward Wood director—who provides us with pink flamingos and other shocking birds, with "I Was a Teenage Caveman" exposés, and "Plan Nines from Outer Space" in all their B-movie glory: part ghouls, part monsters, part abductors and grave robbers from outer space, which nevertheless grab us by the throat, make us think and feel deeply, and are sometimes wholly ludicrous, grotesque, and sublime simultaneously.

Notes

1. As I write this essay, I am saddened by the news that, because of severe health problems leading Harlan Ellison to believe he is dying, he has publicly declared that he will not write another new book and he will not lecture at another major convention. This is a great loss to speculative fiction and imaginative literature in general. A unique voice has been stilled, a voice the like of which we will never hear again.

2. When in 1976 the L. Q. Jones film *A Boy and His Dog* (based on Ellison's 1969 novella) won a Hugo for Best Dramatic Presentation, Ellison complained that he was being left out as the writer of the source material. To appease him, the awards committee gave him the bottom half, the base, of the Hugo Award, and the filmmaker was presented with the other half. Since that time, on television shows such as the 1990s series *Sci-Fi Buzz*, Ellison has proudly displayed his eight and a half Hugo Awards, among his many other awards.

Works Cited

Aldiss, Brian W. *Billion Year Spree: The True History of Science Fiction*. Garden City, NY: Doubleday, 1973.

Aldiss, Brian W., with David Wingrove. *Trillion Year Spree: The History of Science Fiction*. New York: Avon, 1986.

Baker, Sheridan. *The Practical Stylist with Readings*. 5th ed. New York: Harper & Row, 1982.

Broderick, Damien. *Reading by Starlight: Postmodern Science Fiction*. New York: Routledge, 1995.

Csicsery-Ronay, Istvan, Jr. *The Seven Beauties of Science Fiction*. Middletown, CT: Wesleyan UP, 2008.

Disch, Thomas M. *The Dreams Our Stuff Is Made Of: How Science Fiction Conquered the World*. New York: Free Press, 1998.

Dreams with Sharp Teeth. Documentary. Dir. Erik Nelson. Prod. Erik Nelson and Randall M. Boyd. Creative Differences, 2008.

Ellison, Harlan. "Ellison Wonderland: Harlan Ellison Interviewed." Interview by Joseph Francavilla. *Post Script: Essays in Film and the Humanities* 10.1 (Fall 1990): 9-20.

Freedman, Carl. *Critical Theory and Science Fiction*. Hanover, NH: Wesleyan UP, 2000.

Nye, David E. *American Technological Sublime*. Cambridge: MIT Press, 1994.

Poe, Edgar Allan. "The Conversation of Eiros and Charmion." *The Science Fiction of Edgar Allan Poe*. Ed. Harold Beaver. New York: Penguin, 1976. 65-72.

_____. "The Facts in the Case of M. Valdemar." *The Science Fiction of Edgar Allan Poe*. Ed. Harold Beaver. New York: Penguin, 1976. 194-205.

_____. *The Letters of Edgar Allan Poe*. 2 vols. Ed. John Ward Ostrom. New York: Gordian, 1966.

_____. "MS. Found in a Bottle." *The Science Fiction of Edgar Allan Poe*. Ed. Harold Beaver. New York: Penguin, 1976. 1-12.

_____. *The Narrative of Arthur Gordon Pym of Nantucket*. Ed. Harold Beaver. New York: Penguin, 1975.

_____. Rev. of *Wyandotté, or the Hutted Knoll*, by James Fenimore Cooper. 1843. *Complete Works of Edgar Allan Poe*. Vol. 11. Ed. James A. Harrison. 1902. New York: AMS Press, 1965.

Weil, Ellen, and Gary K. Wolfe. *Harlan Ellison: The Edge of Forever*. Columbus: Ohio State UP, 2002.

Biography of Harlan Ellison

Larisa Mikhaylova

Harlan Jay Ellison was born on May 27, 1934, in Cleveland, Ohio, into the Jewish American family of dentist Louis Laverne Ellison and his wife Serita Ellison (née Rosenthal). Ellison has always been grateful for the parental support he received while growing up with his sister, Beverly, in the aggressively anti-Semitic town of Painesville, Ohio. Eventually, however, he ran away from home several times, when the pressure and bullying of his schoolmates grew too much, as he recollects in the 2008 biographical documentary film *Dreams with Sharp Teeth*.[1] The smallest in his class, he was beaten up almost every day, which only served to make him tougher and more determined to become a writer. After his father died in 1949, the family moved back to Cleveland.

In his teens Ellison worked a number of odd jobs, which he thought of as a true writer's education on the road: he picked crops in New Orleans, drove a nitroglycerine truck in North Carolina, and worked on a tuna fishing boat near Galveston, Texas; at various times he was a lumberjack, a short-order cook, a cab driver, a lithographer, and a door-to-door salesman of books and of brushes. Having appeared as a child in minstrel shows, Ellison has never stopped paying tribute to the performing arts—first as an actor in several productions at the Cleveland Play House, then as a screenplay writer for television and film, as inimitable reader of both his own stories and those by other writers (including twenty-six one-hour installments of the radio series "2000^x," produced by the Hollywood Theatre for the Ear, which aired in 2000-2001 and won a Ray Bradbury Award for drama series), and as an occasional performer in films based on his stories.

Ellison never graduated from Ohio State University, which he entered in 1951. He was expelled after eighteen months when he punched his English professor in the nose for making contemptuous remarks about science fiction in general and Ellison's ability to write in particular. For decades afterward, whenever Ellison published a new story he sent his old professor a copy. Ellison has expressed his belief that the expanding knowledge of the writer comes from constant self-education rather than formal schooling. An avid reader who had a library card before he was ten years old, he became closely involved with the Cleveland Science Fiction Society, acting in 1952-54 as editor of its fanzine, the *Bulletin of the Cleveland Science Fiction Society*, later renamed *Dimensions*. For Ellison, fandom served as a way to allow him to come into contact with kindred souls.

In 1955 Ellison moved to New York to become a science fiction writer. Over the next two years, he published more than one hundred short stories and articles, starting with the story "Glowworm" in early 1956. Also in 1956 he married for the first time, but the marriage—to Charlotte Stein—was short-lived. The couple separated in 1957 and divorced in 1959.

Ellison has noted that writing, in addition to being an act of "self-performed exorcism," has always been much more for him. From his youth onward it has been an act of preservation of humanity, of always reaching out—whether he was composing letters for the semiliterate soldiers in his regiment during his military service (1957-59) or writing fiction. He wrote his first book, *Rumble* (later retitled *Web of the City*), about youth street gangs, while he was in the U.S. Army. He had briefly joined a Brooklyn gang to get the inside story, and, while the other soldiers slept after exhausting marches, he typed the novel in the barracks latrine. The anguish Ellison feels for misspent human potential is clearly expressed in the 1977 story "Jeffty Is Five," about a television salesman who meets a strange five-year-old boy in whose presence all that was good about the 1950s continues to manifest itself: science fiction, radio shows, innocent camaraderie, and so on. Ellison refuses to be labeled a "sci-fi author" because he feels that the term is derogatory and diminishes the scope of artistic possibilities inherent in science fiction. Once, during a 1980 interview in a New York television studio, Ellison abruptly left when, despite his prior warning, the inteviewer called him that.

In 1960, following his military service, Ellison first returned to New York and then soon moved to Chicago, where he worked for William Hamling's men's magazine *Rogue* and as a book editor for Hamling's Regency Books. In 1961, Ellison married Billie Joyce Sanders, but this marriage also ended in divorce, in 1962. With a move to Los Angeles in 1962, Ellison began his most productive writing period.

Life's Work

Ellison has garnered a mountain of prizes throughout his creative life by weaving a "love-hate relationship with human race." He came to the field of science fiction with the intention of exploding it from within, to make people aware of its potential, and the original anthology *Dangerous Visions* (1967), which he edited, became such a breakthrough. The volume broke numerous "taboos" by presenting stories with themes of violence, religion, and sex; the authors included Robert Silverberg, Theodore Sturgeon, Damon Knight, Philip K. Dick, Brian W. Aldiss, and J. G. Ballard. This anthology and its sequel, *Again, Dangerous Visions* (1972), put Ellison in the limelight, although by then he had already become quite well-known.

The social activism of the 1960s was a perfect environment for Ellison's talent. Remembering those years (approximately 1961-75) in the more complacent 1980s, Ellison noted that it became fashionable for people fearful of change to ignore the nobility of the times and exaggerate the follies: "People were weighing and evaluating . . . they were taking all the parts of the society that we had lived with for over two hundred years and . . . sort of jostling them and shaking them up, seeing which ones would fall through the cultural sieve and which ones had enough weight and substance to stay." The societal changes most important to him concerned the civil rights struggles of African Americans, Native peoples, and feminists. Ellison takes particular pride in the fact that he marched with more than fifty thousand people, led by the Reverend Martin Luther King, Jr., from Selma to Montgomery, Alabama, in 1965. Many of what people consider to be Ellison's "eccentricities" spring from his belief that all battles are worth fighting. As the guest of honor at the 1978 World Science Fiction Convention (Worldcon) in Phoenix, Arizona, Ellison attended but refused to spend any money in the state because it had not ratified the Equal Rights Amendment; he slept in an RV rather than in a room at the convention hotel.

Despite the many violent, bleak, and desperate scenes depicted in his works, Ellison remains a humanist, akin to the most prominent American satirist of the twentieth century, Kurt Vonnegut. Ellison's opinion on the improbability of God's existence mirrors that of another satirist—Mark Twain. Ellison never wavers from his atheist position. He has noted that an experience from his childhood influenced his view of fanatical religious beliefs: at five years of age he was thrown out of Sunday school for heresy, and subsequently someone burned a cross on the front lawn of his family's home. If the universe does not care that we exist, Ellison has repeatedly stated, it is up to human beings to create life worthy of our abilities, built with the help of a "toolbox" containing "ethics, courage, kindness, friendship, ratiocination—[the] ability to think, to work problems out logically, dreams, imagination, things that make us to want to go to the stars, things that make us to want ourselves to become better." The ultimate sign of humanity for Ellison is a person's responsibility for his or her own actions.

Ellison's love-hate relationship with the human race encompasses the medium with which people have become increasingly enthralled—television. During the late 1960s, Ellison wrote a column about TV for the *Los Angeles Free Press* titled "The Glass Teat" (the essays were subsequently collected and published in two volumes). His foray into the world of feature films was close to a disaster, and having written in 1965 a screenplay for *The Oscar* (the film was released in 1966), he never returned to writing for the big screen, although some of his stories have been adapted for films by other writers, such as *A Boy and His*

Dog in 1975. Ellison's television writing career was constantly growing, however. He sold scripts for episodes of many different shows, including *Burke's Law, Route 66, The Outer Limits, Star Trek, The Man from U.N.C.L.E.*, and *The Alfred Hitchcock Hour.* Later Ellison was a creative consultant for the critically acclaimed SF shows *The New Twilight Zone* (early 1980s version) and *Babylon 5* (1993-98).

Two marriages—the third with Lory Patrick in 1965, and the fourth with Lori Horowitz in 1976—each lasted less than a year. On September 7, 1986, Ellison married Susan Toth, whom he had met in Scotland the year before. This fifth marriage proved to be stable.

As part of a campaign to fight illiteracy and to demonstrate that writers need not be distanced from their readers, Ellison has let people witness his creative process more than forty times. In 1981 he wrote a story while sitting in the window of a bookstore on Fifth Avenue in New York City, and in 1986 he created the story "Hitler Painted Roses" live on the Friday-night radio program *Hour 25*, broadcast on Pacifica Radio station KPFK-FM, Los Angeles. He has stated that he considers radio to be a significantly better medium for fiction than television, as it activates the imaginations of listeners instead of providing "a full audiovisual package."

During the 1970s and 1980s, in addition to writing scripts and stories, Ellison lectured extensively at universities and taught at various writing workshops, such as Clarion. Ellison would shame those workshop participants who were not performing at their best while unreservedly promoting the outstanding—notably Dan Simmons, whom he singled out among workshop participants in 1988 and whose works' popularity skyrocketed internationally in the next decade. Recognition of the excellence of Ellison's own work has spread gradually beyond the field of science fiction: his 1992 story "The Man Who Rowed Christopher Columbus Ashore" was selected from more than six thousand entries for inclusion in the 1993 edition of *The Best American Short Stories*.

Since 1966 Ellison has resided in the same Los Angeles house, built to his design and decorated with sculptures and bas-reliefs of fantastic creatures. He considers himself to be a contented man with a loving wife, who is also a trusted companion, living in a wonderful California valley and continuing to write.

Ellison never switched to writing on a computer; he still types on an Olympia manual typewriter. One of the sayings that has adorned Ellison's typewriter the longest is "I am an artist and should be exempt from shit," credited to rock singer P. J. Proby; this was later accompanied by the Latin proverb *Sat ci sat bene*—It is done quickly enough if it is done well. The importance of performing at his best has often brought Ellison into conflicts with publishers over deadlines.

The dignity of an author, in Ellison's opinion, includes being paid fairly for doing his job, whether it is a story, an article, or an interview. Throughout the 1990s he fought and won on his own behalf and on behalf of authors in general a number of legal cases: in 1997 he sued filmmaker James Cameron for "providing inspiration for his *Terminator*"—Ellison's name is now included in all the credits for the film; in 2000 he sued AOL to protect writers' intellectual property from online theft and won the case in 2004.

Over the course of his career, Ellison has written or edited seventy-six books; more than seventeen hundred stories, essays, articles, and newspaper columns; and more than twenty teleplays. He has received the Writers Guild of America's award for most outstanding teleplay four times, and the list of his other honors includes three Nebula Awards (given by the Science Fiction and Fantasy Writers of America); eight and a half Hugo Awards (from the World Science Fiction Society); two Edgar Allan Poe Awards (from the Mystery Writers of America); six Bram Stoker Awards (from the Horror Writers Association), including an award for lifetime achievement in 1996; the Silver Pen from PEN Center USA for his writings "in defense of the First Amendment"; the World Fantasy Award; the British Fantasy Award; the American Mystery Award; and a Distinguished Skeptic Award (presented by the Committee for the Scientific Investigation of Claims of the Paranormal). In 2006, the Science Fiction and Fantasy Writers of America named Ellison a Damon Knight Memorial Grand Master, an honor given to living authors for lifetime achievement in science fiction or fantasy. In May 2009, he turned down the Cleveland Arts Prize for Lifetime Achievement, refusing to be "appropriated by Cleveland." In early 2011, Ellison agreed to accept the J. Lloyd Eaton Lifetime Achievement Award in Science Fiction, which is presented to authors who have made contributions "of lasting significance to the field."

Note

1. All quotations from Ellison, unless otherwise noted, are taken from this film.

Works Consulted

Dreams with Sharp Teeth. Documentary. Dir. Erik Nelson. Prod. Erik Nelson and Randall M. Boyd. Creative Differences, 2008.

Slusser, George Edgar. *Harlan Ellison: Unrepentant Harlequin*. San Bernardino, CA: Borgo Press, 1977.

Weil, Ellen, and Gary K. Wolfe. *Harlan Ellison: The Edge of Forever*. Columbus: Ohio State UP, 2002.

the PARIS REVIEW

The *Paris Review* Perspective
Sam Costello for *The Paris Review*

You won't find Harlan Ellison's books in the fiction section in most bookstores. Instead, you will have to venture to a place seen by many as the home of less-than-serious writing: the section devoted to science fiction/fantasy. Ellison writes fantasy, but not about elves; he writes science fiction, but not space opera. Peel away the fantastic elements—God-like computers in a postapocalyptic world; a trickster defying punctuality in a hyperefficient future; the worship of terrifying, modern gods in soulless cities; a five-year-old time traveler—and you reveal stories about how people should behave toward each other. Ellison's stories, speculative though they may be, are parables. And, like much social criticism, Ellison's parables both reflect the concerns and attitudes of the eras from which they arose and reject the homilies those eras held dear.

Born in the thick of the Great Depression in 1934, Ellison gained his first sustained writing success with the publication of two socially engaged books attuned to *The Blackboard Jungle* era's concerns about youth crime. The first, 1958's *Rumble* (later retitled *Web of the City*), chronicles a New York City youth gang, the Barons, which Ellison joined for research. The short-story collection *The Deadly Streets*, published in 1958 as well, also drew material from his experiences in the gang.

Ellison's work flourished in the 1960s, a decade in which he produced thirteen books, three in 1967 alone. Without lionizing a period that is excessively scrutinized, it may be said that the sixties were perhaps the decade of the twentieth century most concerned with questions of how people should treat one another, making Ellison's work of a piece with his times. In addition to the moral and ethical examinations in his stories, Ellison took part in the activism of the era, participating in Martin Luther King, Jr.'s march from Selma to Montgomery, Alabama, in 1965.

As Ellison continued to write fiction, he also expanded to other forms, both television (among his credits are episodes of *Star Trek*, *The Outer Limits*, the 1980s *Twilight Zone*, *Route 66*, and *Babylon 5*) and nonfiction, including a stint with the pioneering underground newspaper the *Los Angeles Free Press*. But Ellison was most provocative in his fiction.

Unlike other writers of speculative fiction, for whom the possibility and promise of the fantastic are paramount, Ellison's stories focus resolutely on the people confronting the actuality of those promises. "Jeffty Is Five" (1977) concerns a child forever stuck at age five, who simultaneously lives in the modern world and sustains a nostalgia-soaked alternative reality. Though "Jeffty Is Five" evokes *Slaughterhouse-Five*-style time travel, like that Kurt Vonnegut novel, the story is not *about* its speculative elements. A writer most interested in the fantastic might see Jeffty's problems with time as the beginning of an adventure or a gift. Instead, the quiet horrors that Jeffty's stasis visits on his parents undercut the story's Bradbury-esque nostalgia. Ellison never leaves the human scale, never considers adventure: the story focuses on how Jeffty's parents are affected by their son's strangeness, and how they struggle to live with it.

Ellison's stories often feature technology, but, unusually, they rarely locate salvation, or even hope, there. In Ellison's conception, because humans create technology, and humans are flawed, our technology is flawed as well. These flaws are manifest in "I Have No Mouth, and I Must Scream" (1967), which posits a future where a few Cold War supercomputers gain sentience and merge, killing all but five humans and making the world their playground. That same technology allows the computer, AM, to take revenge on Ted, the humans' leader, by making him literally less than human:

> I am a great soft jelly thing. Smoothly rounded, with no mouth, with pulsing white holes filled by fog where my eyes used to be. Rubbery appendages that were once my arms . . . a thing whose shape is so alien a travesty that humanity becomes more obscene for the vague resemblance.

Ellison's suspicion of technology makes his parables antidotes to midcentury utopian, progress-will-solve-everything science fiction. He cannot accept that technology will save us: only people can save each other, "only kindness and rational thinking permit us to weather the plague," as he writes in the introduction to his 1988 collection *Angry Candy*.

Faced with irrationality, with suffering caused by callous or casual disregard, Ellison's stories rage (and not just his stories; Ellison is known for a Vesuvian temper) and reject traditional science fiction heroics. "The ones we are asked to relate to, in SF and fantasy, the ones we are urged to see as the Good Folks, are usually the ones who say excuse me and thank you ma'am," he writes in "Xenogenesis" (1984), an examination of SF fandom.

But Ellison doesn't ally himself or his work with those anodyne Good Folks. As he says in his introduction to the 1996 edition of his essay collection *An Edge in My Voice*:

> I am an enemy of the people. The ones who don't want to get involved, and the ones who don't want to risk a dime of their money; the ones who permit evil to walk unchecked, the ones who abet the monsters because "if I didn't do it, someone else would."

With such restless focus on the effects on our shared world of how we treat each other, Ellison's parables leave us like the self-absorbed Billy in "Night of Black Glass," stranded in limbo, unable to live a life that honors those who died in Vietnam instead of him, realizing that "his crime was not in surviving; it was that he felt no guilt or shame at having survived. He could not pay the price for his life." In asking us to examine how we behave toward each other, Ellison's stories force us to confront the question: *Can we*?

Copyright © 2012 by Sam Costello.

Works Consulted

Ellison, Harlan. *Angry Candy*. New York: Plume Books, 1989.
_____. *Deathbird Stories*. New York: Collier Books, 1993.
_____. *Edgeworks 1*. Clarkston, GA: White Wolf, 1996.
_____. *Edgeworks 2*. Clarkston, GA: White Wolf, 1996.
_____. *Edgeworks 3*. Clarkston, GA: White Wolf, 1997.
_____. *The Essential Ellison: A Thirty-five Year Retrospective*. 1987. Ed. Terry Dowling, with Richard Delap and Gil Lamont. Beverly Hills, CA: Morpheus International, 1991.

CRITICAL CONTEXTS

Harlan Ellison:
Deathbird Stories

George Edgar Slusser

Although the short story seems the ideal form for science fiction extrapolations, it is curious that very few SF writers have persisted as *exclusively* short-story writers. There is of course Ray Bradbury. And one can only speculate what would have happened had Robert A. Heinlein continued to write in short forms after those miraculous years 1939-42. A writer such as William Tenn wrote only short stories; Robert Silverberg reinvented his art with a series of brilliant short stories in the late 1980s. A highly talented new writer such as Ted Chiang produces stories that, in the context of modern publishing, are worth twenty novels each. But perhaps the most extraordinary, and persistent, writer of short fiction in the SF community is Harlan Ellison.

Ellison began his writing career with a novel, *Rumble* (1958; later retitled *Web of the City*), which he touts as a "new-journalistic" exercise, running with the gangs in order to tell their true story. If this is fiction, its distant model is Ernest Hemingway. It looks forward to Hunter Thompson and Joan Didion. The point is that Ellison's longer fictions are works of journalism and activist social commentary. In his *Memos from Purgatory* (1961), for example, Ellison offers a diptych: the first section is another account of the author's ten weeks with the gangs of the Red Hook; the second section is a sociological essay that comments on the cultural implications of this ten-week "experiment." After this work, Ellison turns his fictional efforts almost exclusively to the short story. However, on a parallel track, he continues to use the longer form for works of activist social commentary, such as his famous running commentary on television in *The Glass Teat* (1969) and *The Other Glass Teat* (1975). These works are important for our concern, for it is here, in this running commentary, that Ellison develops the persona "Ellison"—commentator, activist, friend, enemy, teller of anecdotes—who will become the central character in his writing and, more important, the voice that will tie together his many stories as these are edited and reedited in various story collections. The links between stories in any given collection (as in Ray Bradbury's collections) are less thematic than personal.

Ellison's career as a short-story writer takes off with the publication of such stunning (and award-winning) tales as "'Repent, Harlequin!' Said the Ticktockman" (1965) and "I Have No Mouth, and I Must Scream" (1967). The nature of these stories (indeed of their titles) raises the question: In what recognizable genre, if any, is Ellison writing? As we have seen, Ellison's model for tough-guy writing is Hemingway; for activist social commentary it is H. L. Mencken. He often mentions Mark Twain. Increasingly, in his work, he cites (and/or mentions) writers such as Herman Melville, Franz Kafka, and Jorge Luis Borges. He later characterizes his stories as examples of "magic realism," "literary" fantasy, anything but science fiction. And yet, Ellison was an early SF fan, eventually fan editor of the *Bulletin of the Cleveland Science Fiction Society*. He used the fan network to forge lifelong relationships with SF writers as diverse as Philip José Farmer, Isaac Asimov, Philip Klass (William Tenn), and Robert Silverberg. "'Repent, Harlequin!'" was published by H. L. Gold in *Galaxy Science Fiction*, and "I Have No Mouth" appeared in the very pulpy *If: Worlds of Science Fiction*. Whatever genre Ellison claims for his stories, it is clear their creative matrix is the world of SF, which was, at the time Ellison entered the literary world, the most dynamic literary milieu that existed. Ellison's energy and eclectic vision, shaped in the general cauldron of post-World War II popular culture, found in the SF world its creative path. This is important for an understanding of what remains his masterwork—the story collection *Deathbird Stories: A Pantheon of Modern Gods* (1975). If what Ellison is writing in these stories does not fit everyone's definition, it would never have existed without SF. It represents a highly personal, and creative, synthesis of the various elements that compose this major literary form of the American (and in fact global) twentieth century.

Ellison's previous story collections simply grouped the most recent batches of stories, for the most part previously published in SF magazines (or other "genre" publications, such as mystery or horror magazines). The cohesive thread in these collections was the "Ellison" persona, which placed each story and its genesis in the readers' minds through anecdotes, comments about reception good or bad, judgments, and other offhand remarks, the purpose of which was to keep a given story "alive" as it was being recycled. For *Deathbird Stories*, however, Ellison makes a claim to a thematic thread. In his "Introduction: Oblations at Alien Altars," the author (who signs his comments as author, and dates them 1 November 1973) describes his themes as gods ancient and modern: "This group of stories deals with the new gods, with the new devils, with the modern incarnations of the little people, and the wood sprites and the demons" (14). Ellison gives proof of vast readings into world deities. His gods, however, are chthonic (Greek *khthon*—earth), gods of the underworld, blood, human sacrifice. Their modern avatars—gods of the freeway, the machine, paingod, rock god, gods of smog and the slot machine—arise to avenge an Earth blighted by cities and consumer societies. Ellison asks us to witness, in the stories to follow, the always violent resurgence of these new gods. His message: in a world ruled by material violence, the only ones who survive are those who learn to worship at these alien altars.

This is the ostensible message. And given what follows, many have seen it as little more than an excuse to revel in some of the most violent prose ever written. Indeed, Ellison prefaces the volume with a "caveat lector" in which he cautions the reader that "the emotional content of these stories, taken without break, may be extremely upsetting." The collection in fact does not proceed to a crescendo of emotional violence. But there is a high point, the story "Bleeding Stones," in which the stones and gargoyles of a New York cathedral react to a century of smog and human pollution by cutting loose from their moorings and wreaking total destruction on the falsely worshipping humans below. The resulting prose is sustained wallowing in ultraviolence:

Deathbird Stories

Two demi-devils . . . land on the roof of a Fifth Avenue bus, slash it open with their clawed feet. Screams fill the air as the bus fills with bloody pulp. A window is smashed as an old man tries to escape and one of the demi-devils saws his neck across the jagged glass, spraying the street outside with a geyser from the carotid artery. (197)

If the prose here were not so compelling, this would read like a parody of a gory horror novel. In other stories, however, this violent prose is put to powerful effect. The high point is "Basilisk," which, because of its uncompromising and honest violence, is possibly the quintessential Vietnam War story. Here uncomprehending Lance Corporal Vernon Lestig steps on pungi stakes and explodes into the underworld of pain and torture: "Every circuit shorted out, every light bulb blew . . . snakes shed their skins, wagon wheels creaked, plate-glass windows shattered, dentist drills ratcheted across nerve ends, vomit burned tracks up through throats" (94). Surviving this, he returns to Kansas, only to be hunted down as a "traitor" by the bigots who sent him to war in the first place. But in his pain he has become one with the primeval Basilisk, a paingod capable of wreaking the same unimaginable physical mayhem on Lestig's tormentors: "They jumped him and beat him, and he flailed up through a mass of bodies and was staring directly into a wild-eyed mandrill face, and he *looked* at him. *Looked* at him. As the deathbeast struck. The man screamed, clawed at his face, and his face came away in handfuls, the rotting flesh dripping off his fingers" (110). There is no moral here, just pain for pain, violence for violence, a pure cathartic effect for those of us who experience this most stupid and hypocritical of wars.

But there is more to *Deathbird Stories* than just a vague theme, and a tone or style of violent prose. One sees here, as in the best American short-story cycles, from Sherwood Anderson's *Winesburg, Ohio* to Bradbury's *Martian Chronicles*, a thematic *structure*, a formal construction whereby stories respond to each other, presenting the reader with a developing construct that contains the true meaning of the book.

We notice first of all that a number of stories here were previously published. For example, the story "Paingod," first published in 1964 and reprinted in the 1965 Pyramid Books collection *Paingod and Other Delusions*, is placed here in a context where pain is no delusion. Three stories are transplanted here from the 1969 collection *The Beast That Shouted Love at the Heart of the World*: "Along the Scenic Route," "The Place with No Name," and "Shattered Like a Glass Goblin." It becomes clear, in the new context of *Deathbird Stories*, that there is no beast to shout love at the heart of any of these stories' worlds. But it also becomes clear, in the new collection, that there are contrasting stories where love is still possible, even in the darkest depths of world violence, blight, mass destruction of all that is human at the hands of the death beasts our greed, stupidity, and cowardice have unleashed. Ellison imports elements, creates new ones, but with the clear purpose of generating a rhythm that alternates between despair and redemption. What he announces as unrelenting pain and violence will open out to the possibility of recovery and surcease.

Let us look at some of the interlocking structures of *Deathbird Stories*. First, there is the overarching structure. Here a series of earlier stories—whose common theme is the city as inhuman place and purveyor of inhuman gods—find their respondents in a set of later stories in which urban humankind's god quests open out, through magic doors into nowhere, into the inhuman landscapes of natural myth, where human inadequacies are shattered like glass goblins. Within this frame, however, there is no straight-line progression from human-made violence to cosmic violence. Instead there are ripples, where stories respond to stories, moments of redemption to moments of despair. And in all of this often imperceptible dialectic, this interplay of humankind and its gods, there is a subtle, and hopeful, sea change. All of Ellison's stories appear to be about those who survive and those who do not. But on what terms do we survive? In the first story in the volume, "The Whimper of Whipped Dogs," the protagonist survives by becoming one with the god of urban violence, a watcher at the blood feast. The final story, "The Deathbird," is again a story of human survival. The survivor here outlasts—indeed, defeats—the tyrant gods. The cost of defeating all our false gods, however, is the death of the Earth.

"The Whimper of Whipped Dogs" fictionalizes the brutal murder of Kitty Genovese in the courtyard of a New York City apartment building, which took place as a number of people looked on from their windows and did nothing. The protagonist, Beth, is a Bennington graduate recently arrived in the city, and one of the watchers. This is her initiation into the city, a place where (in the words of her male friend) conditions are so inhuman that they summon forth inhuman things: "You can't expect to jam as many people into this stone thing as we do . . . you can't do it without making the time right for some god-forsaken other kind of thing to be born!" (29). This "thing" is the presence she felt watching the spectacle as the young woman was stabbed to death. When she is brutally attacked in turn, she realizes that this presence is the new god that reigns over the city: "God! A new God. . . . A God who needed worshipers and offered the choices of death as a victim or life as an eternal witness to the deaths of *other* chosen victims. A God to fit the times, a God of streets and people" (34-35). The choice is clear, and Beth, who came from civilized rural Vermont, decides to survive, to side with and worship this new God: "Him! Take him! Not me! I'm yours! . . . Take him, I'm yours! And the black man was suddenly lifted away, wrenched off her, and off the balcony . . . as Beth sank to her knees on the ruined flowers" (35).

A number of subsequent stories deal with similar human-created gods of the city. "Along the Scenic Route" moves us to Los Angeles's road-city congestion and the god of the freeway: "God, in the latest, chrome-plated, dual-carb, chopped and channeled, eight-hundred-horsepowered incarnation" (39). The new "scenic route" is a place of unregulated duels to the death. The protagonist is a family man, taunted into a duel by a Billy the Kid of the highways, who becomes a raging maniac in a lethal contest, which he wins. Survival, however, means only more challenges, this time from more "professional" gladiators: "He would have to fight. In the world of the Freeway, there was no place for a walking man" (51). There is the Smog God in "Bleeding Stones," who, after long suffering at the hands of city pollution, unleashes its horde of stone gargoyles to massacre a crowd gathered before the New York cathedral: "Finally, nothing moves in the city but the creatures that were once stone, and they fly up, circling the stainless steel and glass towers of industrial magic. They look down with the hungry eyes of those who have slept too long and now, rested, seek exercise" (199). The story "Rock God" takes us back to Stonehenge and an early awakening of the Rock God Dis (Dis Pater, a Roman god of the underworld, the City of Dis is Lower Hell in Dante's *Inferno*). The story segues to modern New York and a new aspirant, the developer Frank Stierman. But Stierman has betrayed his god, he has built his skyscrapers on sand, and they are collapsing. His domain violated, the Rock God comes to take his apostate, incorporate him into his "flesh," and rule over the city of stone: "All this was rock. All this was flesh of his flesh. All this belonged to Dis, to be absorbed, to permit him to grow as he had never grown before. To feed Dis" (271).

These are all stories of modern humankind violating the natural, unleashing the vengeance of ancient gods. The age of innocence is gone. Ellison the midwesterner can no longer visit the City from Meadowville and sing, "New York, New York, it's a wonderful town." In this place of filth, smog, violence, among the brutal gods, one's only hope is survival: worship or perish. But in these stories, not all of the urban gods are brutal. Amid the stories of survival there are stories of redemption. In "Neon," for example, protagonist Roger Charna has been the victim of an accident that has mangled his body. Doctors put him back together with some strange appendages: "They bestowed on him three special gifts.... A collapsible metal finger.... A vortex spiral of neon tubing in his chest, it glowed bright red when activated; and a right eye that came equipped with sensors that fed informational load from both the infrared and ultraviolet ends of the spectrum" (82). Charna, a freak in the city, finds himself "spoken to" by some presence that lights up neon signs, with corresponding flashing in his chest. The neon "voice" declares love for him. He thinks he is going insane. The neon, however, urges him to trust and believe: "ROGER, WILL YOU HAVE A LITTLE TRUST. . . . I'M PART OF THE REPAYMENT FOR WHAT'S HAPPENED TO YOU. ALL IT TAKES IS A LITTLE BELIEF AND A COUPLE OF STEPS" (88). If he believes, Roger is offered escape from the city. Climbing high above Times Square, he answers the call of the neon sign—"TAKE ME! TAKE ME NOW!"— and "slams himself against the love message" (91). His death in this tawdry world leads to apotheosis in another: "Every neon sign in Times Square had a new color added to its spectrum. It seemed to reside somewhere between silver and orange. . . . It smelled like a forest of silver pines just after the rain. . . . Someone said it was the exact color of caring" (91-92). Ellison's Neon God allows the maimed of the city to recover the lost world of the virgin land. We come full circle, from Beth's loss of Vermont innocence to Charna's ascension through the neon jungle of Times Square, to a new heaven of fresh smells and colors.

An ironic twist on giving oneself to a "god of love" is found in a second story, "Corpse." In this story, an act of faith does not lead to redemption, but rather to the instauration of a new form of deity, who is in the process of gathering its worshippers from the night streets of the metal and neon jungle. The city milieu here is that of college teachers and phony intellectuals, who look down on this world from theoretical heights. The protagonist, an assistant professor at City College about to be denied tenure, walks the night streets and sees juveniles stripping abandoned cars: "They reminded me of grave robbers stripping corpses" (143). The cynical protagonist taunts the politically correct wife of a colleague with a theory of how our society treats the "largest single minority in our country today"—the automobile: "We use them as beasts of burden, we drive them into one another . . . we abandon them by roadsides, unburied, unloved" (144).

Despite the banter, our assistant professor becomes obsessed with cars. He sees them as a "group mind," capable of making a quantum leap to sentience. They are "a society within a society.... The world of the wheeled," able suddenly to "big-bang into existence" (145). He begins to mount comparisons between the wrecking yard and Cortez's slaughter of Aztecs coming to pay homage to the return of a "white god" who is possibly the Jesus of the "lost years." As it turns out, however, the wreckers of cars are not the apostates to this new machine god. They are the worshippers at its altar. One night, returning home, he again sees black youths smashing a car. In his sympathy for this "race" of beings that "dream as their motors idle," he reaches into the car and snatches away a plastic figure of the Virgin Mary: "For the first time in my life, I felt I must perform an act of selfless commitment.... I wanted to save the figure from the depredations of the grave robbers" (148). But he has things turned around. His is the act of desecration, and for it the Car God imprisons him in stone: "He is a young God, and a jealous one. He does not like his graves robbed.... But the children *believe*, you see; and I did not." Here in the city the old god-system is "downtrending." The forces of anarchy and violence are forming their own gods. Order returns, although, as with the god Cortez brought with him, it may not be the order we the gullible Indians want.

The stories described above are essentially stories of victims of the city and of the gods reawakened by the conditions within. Corresponding to these are a sequence of stories, found primarily in the second part of *Deathbird Stories*, that deal with fugitives from the city, insignificant city dwellers suddenly propelled on a god quest for which their means prove inadequate. "O Ye of Little Faith" is the story of Jerry Niven. Niven is a disillusioned city dweller who has taken his girlfriend to Tijuana for an abortion. Niven is a man who cannot commit himself to any person or god: "You see before you the last of cynics.... I look out on a landscape littered with the refuse of misspent youth. All my gods and goddesses had feet of shit, and there they lie, like Etruscan statuary, the noses bashed off" (76). The couple enter a Mexican soothsayer's shop, and the soothsayer tells Niven "all the dark and tongueless things Niven had never been able to say of himself." Niven beats the old man violently and instantly finds himself facing the Minotaur in some unknown place: Niven is now "*all* the men who had forsaken their gods. Who had allowed the world to tell them they were alone, and believed it" (78). Niven now is doomed to wander among gods forgotten because no one still believes in them, "in a land without a name; and *his* name was Niven, but it was no more important a name than Apollo or Vishnu or Baal" (80). Escape means wandering forever "in this terrible Coventry where old gods went to die. . . . For as he had believed in no god. . . . No god believed in him" (80). Niven is a fugitive from commitment to others.

"Delusion for a Dragon Slayer" is the story of Warren Glazer Griffin, a forty-one-year-old accountant accidentally crushed to death by a giant "headache ball" as he walks down an alley near a demolition site in New York City. As with the Mexican's shop, here it is the ball that propels Griffin from seedy mediocrity to a land of his own fantasies. His puny body and acne are replaced by rippling muscles, bronze skin, Aryan features. A wizard tells Griffin he is in this land because of his dreams; all he has to do is live up to those dreams. His task is to pilot his boat through clashing rocks, to seek out a beautiful maiden and kill the "dust-devil" who is guarding her. This is precisely what he cannot do: he loses his crew, kills the dust-devil from behind, then rapes the woman with disgusting lust. He dies ground under the teeth of a dragon, at the moment the wrecking ball crushes him. The story has a moral: "A man may truly live in his dreams, his noblest dreams, but only if he is worthy of those dreams" (179).

A third variation on this scenario is found in "The Place with No Name." We have here another brutal and senseless murder, as in the collection's opening story, but now seen from the point of view of the perpetrator. A small-time drug dealer, Norman Mogart, beats a woman with a pipe. Seeking to escape, he enters another "magic" store, with an illuminated sign: ESCAPE INSIDE. He can either be caught or accept the terms of some agreement he does not understand. He is at once transported to the South American jungle, on a quest for a Place with No Name. For a cocaine dealer, this appears a psychedelic journey, until he comes upon Prometheus chained to his rock and learns that he is to replace Prometheus. On his rock, Mogart has a dream: Prometheus and Christ had been lovers, both punished by "the Justice" for bringing compassion to us primitive mortals. "So the Justice had selected two. One was even now exchanging places with the other, and Norman Mogart had taken the place of the one called Prometheus" (226). However grim the punishment, apotheosis of the little man, the down-and-out city man, has taken place: "He thought of himself, and was in pain, and could not be entirely unhappy. How long it would last, he had no idea, but it was not a completely unsatisfactory way to mark out eternity" (226).

Mogart in a sense survives the city, even if it is to dwell forever in this place with no name. Moreover, there is the promise (from his own experience) that his "eternity," however horrible, will end: there will be reconciliation. We look forward to the final story in the volume, "The Deathbird," where the action of a questing hero now unfolds on the broadest possible mythic plane: that of cosmic order and the death of the Earth. This is the Earth we have been reading about, a place blighted by the tyrant gods who rule the city, by chthonic forces perverted into machine and rock gods. From the depths of this rock, a man named Nathan Stack is literally resurrected. He is led on a journey, by a certain Dira who becomes Snake, across a blighted wasteland over which the Deathbird circles. The mythic journey of Stack, through the valley of the shadow of death, enduring all the trials and tribulations—physical and psychical—of the Man with a Thousand Faces, is interspersed with fictitious "episodes" from Stack's life and with a story that appears to be told by the author himself. The latter is about a man's love for his dog and the agony he feels upon the dog's death. Contrasted with the abstraction of mythic narrative, this simple story is moving. It bears a lesson: one must have the courage to use the needle oneself, one cannot confide this final act to strangers. And so it is that

Stack, at the end of his mythic ordeal, finds himself wielding the same power of mercy over a terminally ill Earth as he supposedly did with his mother. It is the same ruined Earth we have experienced in the previous stories: "Across the dead centuries he heard his mother pleading with him to set her free. . . . *Use the needle.* Her voice mingled with the voice of the Earth crying out in endless pain at her flesh that had been ripped away . . . at her rolling hills and green fields slagged to greenglass and ashes" (343). Stack is no longer a Prometheus, or any such figure punished by the gods; he has defeated these tyrants; the Earth belongs to him now, and his is the power to put his friend and companion Snake out of his misery: "Then they worked together and Nathan Stack used the needle with a wave of his hands, and the Earth could not sigh with relief as its endless pain was ended . . . but it did sigh" (345). Ellison concludes his story: "This is for Mark Twain." And indeed, in the end, Ellison's panorama of modern gods and their victims, of urban humankind's crime- and drug-induced quests to delusions of no name—all of this comes to rest on the American self-reliant man, for whom institutions, myths, earthscapes, are nothing more than its lengthened shadows. Ellison presents this story as a college course, possibly in creative writing, which means that any person can, potentially, write the script.

 The discussion above addresses the main line of development in *Deathbird Stories*, but it should be noted that the collection contains at the same time important side currents, pairings of stories where opposites seem to balance, where violence and despair are answered by hope, however muted. We find, for example, in "Pretty Maggie Moneyeyes," we have victim Maggie, "twenty three, and determined as hell never to abide in that vale of poverty her mother had called purgatory for her entire life" (119). Pouring out all of her desire for money and her hatred of her life as a cheap prostitute, Maggie dies while pulling the handle of a Las Vegas slot machine, the Chief: "The wheels cycled and spun and whirled and whipped . . . as Maggie blue-eyed Maggie hated and hated and thought of hate and all the days and nights of swine behind her and ahead of her" (126). Her fate is fatally intertwined with that of Kostner, who comes to Vegas down and out from a failed love affair. He puts his last dollar in the Chief and hits a jackpot: "But the three bars did not say JACKPOT. They were three gray bars . . . with a blue eye directly in the center of each bar" (121). Kostner plays the machine over and over, each time hitting a jackpot. All at once, the machine speaks to him, "inside his skull, where no one had ever lived but himself, now someone else moved and spoke to him: *I've been waiting for you . . . Kostner. . . . You'll win all the jackpots. Because I want you, I need you. Love me, I'm Maggie, I'm so alone, love me*" (129). In this strange love affair, lovelorn Kostner gives his trust—"*She met him on a windswept plain of thought, and he made love to her more completely than he had known any passion before*"—and Maggie betrays him. As Kostner pulls the handle one last time, he hears terrible shrieking, a tortured metal voice (paraphrasing Baudelaire) crying, "*Free! Free! Heaven or Hell it doesn't matter!*"—he dies, the final loneliness. The machine is scrapped. Now, however, in the jackpot bars there are three sad brown eyes—Kostner's eyes.

In this story Maggie loves too little and Kostner too much. Her selfish strength wins, his weakness loses. Ellison, however, reverses this outcome in a corresponding story, which in fact is placed before "Maggie" in order of presentation. This story, "On the Downhill Side," pairs up two suicides who are freed from their graves for a nocturnal excursion through the streets of New Orleans. One is modern architect Paul Ordahl, the other Lizette Charbonnet, a member of nineteenth-century Creole aristocracy. Paul had apparently committed suicide out of excess of love, Lizette because she was unable to love. In the story, both are given this last chance to find love before they are forever consigned to oblivion. The old scenario seems to play out once again: "We talked across each other, our conversations at right angles, only meeting in the intersections of silence at story's end" (59). The "downhill side" refers to the hours before dawn, when these souls will be whisked away forever. Paul pleads with Lizette: "Listen to me. . . . Our time's almost gone. This is our last chance. You've lived in stone for a hundred years; I've heard you cry, I've come there to that place. . . . You've paid enough, God knows. So have I. We can *do* it" (61). In the end the two prove unable to save themselves: "Lizette and I were the two sides of the same coin, devalued and impossible to spend" (62). It is, however, not Paul nor his love that saves Lizette from the circle of "claimers"; it is Paul's familiar spirit, a unicorn, who in a selfless act passes the barrier and takes her place: "Old friend. . . . We took a step toward him but could not pass the barrier. Lizette clung to me, Paul held me tight as I trembled with terror and the cold of that inner circle still frosting my flesh" (67). The unicorn is gone, the two remain, syntactically entwined: "This time love would not destroy us. This time out we would have luck. The luck of silken mane and rainbow colors . . . and spiral horn" (70). Echoing across the volume to the boy and his dog in "The Deathbird," it is love as animal devotion that saves them.

Another such pairing in which hope seems to trump despair, at least for "this time out," is that of "Basilisk" and the story "Paingod." In "Basilisk," the discovery of raw pain only begets more pain, in a world without redemption. "Paingod," however—this time placed toward the end of the collection, inverting the movement from the conciliatory "On the Downhill Side" to the despairing geometry of "Pretty Maggie Moneyeyes"—not only explores the uses of pain but also proves to be a learning experience for the god of pain itself. We have the god Trente, and we have two tortured beings on Earth, both of whom are again castaways of the modern city, skid-row bums. One is Colin Marshack, a failed sculptor whose hands shake so badly he can no longer create. Trente was responsible for sending the pain that created the shaking hands. Now he tries a further experiment: "He drew forth the mind of Marshack . . . and fled with it. Out there. . . . He showed it all to Colin Marshack, drenched him in wonder, filled him like the most vital goblet . . . poured him full of love and life and the staggering beauty of the cosmos" (235). This done, he returns Marshack to his studio. There Marshack "does it," creates a work that is his. He does so not despite the pain but because of it. And Trente now fully understands his own being: "I am Paingod, and it is my life . . . to treat them to the finest they will ever know. To give them pain, that they may know pleasure."

We have here the case of a god—in a sense the greatest of all of Ellison's new and reawakened gods—who is "converted" to the contradictory nature of the *human* condition. We remain Pascal's creatures, incomprehensible monsters both to God and to ourselves. And so Ellison's world, in this collection, gradually, imperceptibly, changes focus, until we come to rest, not on God's ways to humankind but on humankind's ways to itself. Most, if not all, of our quests to find ourselves in some external god or force fail. The true direction of our quest should be inward. But how can modern humanity, product of cities and overpopulation, and all the ills Ellison displays, find the way back to its soul? The good thing, perhaps, is that in Ellison's materialist world there is no Christian or Cartesian "soul" left. In this world, therefore, a soul *has* coordinates, a material location. The problem is to find it. This is the quest undertaken in the penultimate story in the collection, "Adrift Just Off the Islets of Langerhans: Latitude 38° 54′ N, Longitude 77° 00′ 13″ W." If many of the other pieces in *Deathbird Stories* appear to move into mythico-fantastical territory, "Adrift" anchors myth and fantasy squarely in a realm of SF. It would not be possible to dedicate this story to Mark Twain, or to any other writer. It is sui generis, the apotheosis of science fiction, a masterpiece of world short fiction.

Ellison's epigraph tips this story back into the realm of reality, in this case the hyperreality of SF: "Reality has become fantasy; fantasy has become reality. 35mm constructs have more substance than your senior congressman, but Martha Nelson is real, no matter what you think. And the search for your soul in a soulless world requires special maps." The Islets of Langerhans are indeed "special," but not in the sense of the conventional imaginary or mythical voyage. The Islets of Langerhans are a real place, and they are inside our physical bodies. We would not—perhaps could not—go there physically; yet we have, as with maps for buried treasure, material coordinates for the place. "X" marks the spot. Martha Nelson too sounds like a real person. If she does exist "in there," as flesh and blood, not as a memory or mental image, then perhaps she is "really" alive. Ellison asks us to kick the stone, to verify the reality of this object by going and physically finding it, "no matter what you think." This is an SF response to a fantastic situation.

The first lines of the story are significant. At first they seem surreal ravings: "When Moby Dick awoke one morning from unsettling dreams, he found himself changed in his bed of kelp into a monstrous Ahab" (274). This is a fanciful paraphrase of the opening sentence of Franz Kafka's *The Metamorphosis*. Kafka's Gregor has *really* become a giant bug, but neither he nor his world sees this fact. So enter Ahab and Moby Dick, where the fantastic quest is rendered material in the great white whale. But why a "monstrous" Ahab? The being who arises from this morning bed is none other than Larry Talbot, alias the Wolfman. Talbot's personal "Moby Dick" is a "terrible fish" that whistles like a blue jay. Like the fish, Talbot-Ahab cannot die, his changes tied to the blind rhythms of the "moon"—the chthonic world of Ellison's gods. The Wolfman is the incarnation of Ellison's city dweller, who anonymously walks the city's gritty streets by day but by night sows random violence in its parks and courtyards. In one of the earlier stories, "Ernest and the Machine God," a manipulative woman has a car breakdown in rural North Carolina. Her car is fixed by a young "machine god," Ernest, who simply reaches in and revives the dead motor. When she later initiates Ernest into love, he seemingly does the opposite to her. Standing over her dead body, one of the locals remarks: "Looks like somethin' stopped her pump" (258). This seems the most Talbot can do when he finds his "soul": stop the mechanical cycle of life and death to which he seems—machine and Prometheus alike— forever chained.

The means of Talbot's quest will be, as in Heinlein's "Waldo," the engineering sciences. If Talbot's split existence is a material incarnation of the Cartesian mind-matter duality, then like Waldo he hopes to close the gap by locating a material bridge between these opposites *inside* his own body. Waldo's place of connection is the physical brain; Talbot's will be an organ deep in the folds of the body, where the metaphor "islets" is now the clusters of cells that control the endocrine or hormone-producing function of the body. Thus, if Talbot begins his quest in the realm of myth, it must end within the compass of his own material existence. If he turns to Demeter, this time it is not the Earth God but a *Mr.* Demeter, CEO of "Information Associates," who gives him the coordinates. Needing scientific help to accomplish his journey, he turns to none other than Frankenstein. But this time it is Victor Frankenstein *fils*, now a respected scientist in Eastern Europe, naturally, for here is where Frankenstein will again meet Dracula.

In this story, Ellison's mythic figures mutate from Demeter and Ahab to myths of the popular culture of fantasy and SF. In this process, these myths are essentially demythified. As Talbot seeks to free himself from his mythic destiny, the mythic figures he meets are rendered literal. An example is Talbot's journey across the river of the dead with Victor. The river, however, is the modern-day Danube, and the "corpse barge" nothing more than a garbage scow, filled with the detritus of lives in progress: "The corpse barge cut through the invisible water, silent, fog-shrouded, without Charon, without Styx, merely a public service, a garbage scow of unfinished sentences, uncompleted errands, unrealized dreams" (285). As Talbot travels to the yet-unfound portal to himself, myths collapse into one another, and we are finally left with the brute fact of the particle accelerator. Here, for example, is the description of Talbot's journey to Victor's laboratory in the Carpathians:

> Expectedly, like the most suspenseful chapter of a cheap Gothic novel, a fierce electrical storm suddenly erupted out of the mountains when the ancient touring car was within a few miles of Talbot's destination. It rose up through the steep mountain pass, hurtling out of the sky, black as the grave, and swept across the road, obscuring everything. (287)

Frankenstein conflates with Dracula's Borgo Pass, and only scraps of book and film remain, as the obligatory electrical storm hovers over Victor's journey.

To find his soul, on its treasure island, Talbot must enter his own body. He can do this only if he sheds all reflections and shadows, all vestiges of the mind-body split, even those present in the dark mirror of death. Victor at first thinks he can use

> micro-telemetry, either through direct microminiaturizing techniques or by shrinking a servomechanism package containing sensing, remote control, and guidance-manipulative-propulsion hardware. Use a saline solution to inject it into the bloodstream. Knock you out with "Russian sleep" and/or tap into the sensory nerves so you'd perceive or control the device as if you were there . . . conscious transfer of point of view. (285)

This is nice techno-mumbo jumbo, but it will not do. The "trail" marked by Information Associates must be one that merges "shadow with substance, reality with fantasy." What is needed is a homunculus in the literal sense, a little body. Victor first must make "a perfect simulacrum of you," then "*actualize* it, turn an image into something corporeal, material, something that exists. . . . A miniature *you* with all the reality you possess" (295).

Talbot's life until now has been one of mirror dispersion of self. This life confronts him when, as he examines Frankenstein's machine, he sees himself iterated to infinity in its gallery of glasses: "The remaining three monitors showed research areas in the underground lab complex, the final one of which was the main hall itself, where Talbot stood looking into twelve monitors, in the twelfth screen of which could be seen Talbot looking into twelve" (292). Mirrored here is the cycle of the moon, endless images and alternating blank moments, such as his awakening "in the botanical garden next to the Minneapolis Museum of Art, lying beside something bloody and still." This iterated memory belongs to Talbot's "nightside," to the terrible repetition of Wolfman images in his dark mirror of self. Now, made to look into this mirror, Talbot must begin the process that he hopes will free him from himself, from the curse of his dual existence, reflecting endlessly in these glasses of science.

This union of image and flesh occurs as Talbot takes total possession of the mirror as place of physical activity. At first, Talbot sees nothing but a "sheet of photographic glass." Victor, however, teaches him to see himself through the blankness:

> "Not this," Victor said . . . , "*this*!" He put his finger on a spot in the center of the glass and Talbot leaned to look. He saw nothing at first, then detected a faint ripple; and when he put his face as close as possible to the imperfection he perceived a light *moiré* pattern. . . . "Microholographic plate," Victor said. . . . "That's where we capture your spirit." (296)

Leaning into this mirror, Talbot is physically blasted into its surface by a "graser" beam, made to become this "minute imperfection in the glass." Then, by a reverse blast, this spot in the glass is set before him as a "life-size hologram of himself, standing naked as he had been a few moments before" (297). In this holographic plate, we have nothing less than the literal death and resurrection of Talbot's physical being. As a result, Talbot can now confront himself, in the same space-time continuum, on a different size scale: "Talbot walked to the phantasm, passed his hand through it, stood close and looked into the clear brown eyes, noted the wide pore patterns in the nose, studied himself more closely than he had ever been able to do in a mirror. He felt as if someone had walked over his grave" (297). This "someone" is himself, and the "grave" it walks over is his own body. Of the fantasy double, the shadow and the act, Ellison creates a science fiction double. By means of this double, Talbot can enter the only place to which a human being can never have access—its own physical body. Once this small self enters its own body, that body has already recaptured its "soul."

In order for the quest to continue, there must be a literal transfer from Talbot to this mite. Ellison does this through the same sort of narrative shift in focus we see in "On the Downhill Side":

> Lawrence Talbot went to the microscope, adjusted the knob . . . and saw himself in infinitely reduced perfection. . . . [here there is a physical gap in the text] staring up at himself. He recognized himself, though all he could see was a cyclopean eye staring down from the smooth glass satellite that dominated his sky. He waved. The eye blinked. *Now it begins*, he thought. (298-99)

The opacity of his own flesh is the final barrier here: "He went down on his stomach and cupped his hands around his eyes, putting his face against the dead flesh. It was like looking through a pane of isinglass" (300). The "atrophied" umbilical cord is the physical marker of his isolation, of his being forever separated from his biological origins and ends. Its rupture makes him, physically, an "outsider" to himself, a being forever subject to the mind-body duality. At this moment, Talbot realizes that "monsterdom" is the condition of all men, whose minds are forever separated from their bodies. This revelation frees the Wolfman to use his famous teeth to tear his way into his own body. The hole he crawls through opens into a place of light without images or shadows: "It was quite light, the interior of the world called Lawrence Talbot suffused with a golden luminescence" (301). Outside, all men remain islands; here, inside, on his own internal islet, he discovers the possibility that the simulacrum can again become one with the self, a self now in perfect control of its entire being: "He would find that which had been stolen from him one full-mooned night of horror so very long ago. And having found it, having assured himself of eternal sleep, not merely physical death from a silver bullet, he would stop his heart" (301). No longer thrall to external gods, he can achieve "surcease," the ending of things of their own accord.

Talbot reaches the shore of the pancreatic sea and finds a hoard of things he had given away as a child, such as his "cardboard detective kit with fingerprint dusting powder." But, as with Citizen Kane's Rosebud, something is missing, the key piece in the puzzle of self. He sets sail on the sea and becomes becalmed at the exact coordinates of the story's title. Here he turns on an old radio from his hoard and hears broadcaster Graham MacNamee tell the story of Martha Nelson, a woman who has spent ninety-eight years in an insane asylum for no apparent reason, most likely the victim of the "eugenics alarm" of the late 1800s. It is at this moment of stasis, "the sail hanging like a forlorn ornament from its single centerpole," that epiphany comes. Here Talbot, released from perpetual mutability, can weep for the wasted life of another, a stranger "of whom he *never* would have heard had it not been by chance by chance by chance he had heard by chance, by chance thoughts of her skirled through his mind like cold winds. And the cold winds rose, and the sail filled, and he was no longer adrift" (306).

As he sails his inner sea, he seems sheltered from the Deathbird. The winds blow him to a place where he rediscovers a personal God—the missing piece from his existence, a Howdy Doody button: "the little metal button with the sly innocent face of a mythical creature painted on its surface" (311). Howdy Doody is the god of lost and found, the missing piece in everyone's life, which, once found, allows the individual to turn his or her quest away from self, toward another. Talbot had to go into himself in order to free self from self. Like Browning's Childe Roland, he sets out for a dark tower that rises above the islet. In its depths, the depths of his material being, he is suddenly able to see in the darkness. As per Eliot's epigraph, he knows the place which is himself for the first time. Here he finds frail Martha Nelson—"It was like lifting a sack of dead flowers"—and carries her physically "back up the long stairway to the golden sky."

Talbot awakens, but the dream is now literal reality. Now "activating" the myth, Talbot, who has become a god unto himself, asks Victor *fils* to make him the bride Victor *père* refused his creature ancestor. Talbot's body-as-world will remain in cryonic suspension. Victor will make another "mite," that of old Nadja the laboratory lady, and send this other "wasted life" into the golden realm where he and Martha are waiting. Talbot now realizes he does not need to die, for he has repossessed his self as a *place* of wholeness:

> "I want you to create her mite, the same way you created mine, and send her inside. He's waiting for her. . . . He can be—I can be—her father when she's a baby, her playmate when she's a child, her buddy when she's maturing, her boy friend when she's a young girl, her suitor when she's a young woman, her lover, her husband, her companion as she grows old. Let her be all the woman she was never permitted to be. . . . And when it's over, it will start again. . . ." (310)

Most of the stories in this collection are about people who cannot "get out of themselves." These people create gods in their own images, selfish and lonely gods. In "Adrift" Larry Talbot the Wolfman is allowed to get out of himself, to abolish his condition as being chained to the Promethean rock, by literally getting into himself, creating within his physical being a sort of bodily millennium, where there is no change, no wolf, no shadows or mirrors that prevent him from embracing another being: "I've been there, Victor, I was there for months, maybe years, and I never changed. . . . There's no moon there . . . no night and day, just golden light and warmth" (310). Some may see this place as a womb reconstructed by Frankenstein's science, presided over by the child-god Howdy Doody, who in the end allows its "sly" but "innocent" face to give way to the sound of a *single baby* crying. I want to return to my initial question: Is this story, insofar as it stands for the stories in Ellison's collection, a fantasy—in this case a self-indulgent fantasy? Or can it make claim to being science fiction, and as such offering a coherent statement as to what humankind in general might become in the future?

The question is hard to answer. But many SF classics deal with gods and godlike forces, and the individuals who deal with them and become their avatars. Examples are Frank Herbert's Paul Atreides and Isaac Asimov's Hari Seldon, men who hold together the forces of contending gods. What is more, the apotheosis of self, and specifically of one's own physical body, such as we have in "Adrift," is a constant theme in the work of Heinlein, considered SF's grand master of all grand masters. Heinlein's Lazarus Long uses Frankensteinian science across his long career to expand the perimeter of his own physical body until it becomes coextensive with the known universe. Ellison's venue is more modest. The body of the violent Wolfman—incarnation of all the violent gods and their worshippers in *Deathbird Stories*—becomes the sheltered place where all of modern blight and violence can be reversed, death defeated, love restored. This is the beast that shouted love at the heart of *its own world*. Real-life particle physics may not bring this scenario about, but nanotechnology is already letting parts enter the whole, and, who knows, someday this fantastic voyage may be routine. In any case, this story, and the stories in this collection, are consummate works of human speculation.

Work Cited

Ellison, Harlan. *Deathbird Stories: A Pantheon of Modern Gods*. New York: Dell, 1975.

Allegories of Injustice:
Social Engagement in Harlan Ellison's Short Fiction of the 1950s, 1960s, and 1970s_____
Rob Latham

Over the course of his five-decade career, Harlan Ellison has published pathbreaking work in a number of different media and genres, including not only the science fiction for which he is best known but also fantasy and horror, crime fiction, critical essays and reviews, memoirs, and film and television scripts.[1] He has won three Nebula Awards and eight and a half Hugo Awards, as well as an Edgar Award from the Mystery Writers of America, and an unprecedented four Writers Guild of America awards for outstanding teleplay. He is one of only three authors—the others being Fritz Leiber and Michael Moorcock—to receive lifetime achievement awards from the Science Fiction Writers of America, the Horror Writers of America, and the World Fantasy Association. This remarkable record of success is due not only to the range and power of Ellison's writing but also to the author's unparalleled willingness to grapple with concerns of public moment, to engage charged social issues and cultural debates that other writers might shy away from as too dangerous or potentially inflammatory. Though writing largely in genres perceived by some as "escapist," Ellison has produced work that fearlessly confronts the darkest and most disturbing of historical realities, such as political repression, racial discrimination, urban conflict, and war. His handling of these themes, while often displaying a fury born of despair, has also consistently manifested an undaunted commitment to social justice.

Ellison's most successful early work, during the late 1950s and early 1960s, was "social problem" fiction that addressed widespread public concerns about juvenile delinquency and gang violence. Some of this material was frankly "exploitational"—that is, it sensationalized and exaggerated the topic for popular markets dealing in cheap shocks—but most of it was strong, honest reportage based on a lengthy and hazardous "undercover" stint with a Brooklyn street gang. The novel *Web of the City* (originally published as *Rumble*, 1958), the stories gathered in *The Deadly Streets* (1958) and *Children of the Streets* (originally published as *The Juvies*, 1961), and the memoir *Memos from Purgatory* (1961), while clearly apprentice work, have an immediacy and emotional vivacity that one recognizes in Ellison's later, mature fiction. All four books mine the author's personal experiences for powerful tales of angry, alienated children desperately seeking some form of belonging—recognition, if not redemption.

"Kid Killer," which ran in the March 1957 issue of *Guilty Detective Story Magazine* and was gathered into *The Deadly Streets*, encapsulates the basic themes of this early body of work. A puny Polish teenager, Petey Cosnakof, moves to New York City from Detroit with his weak, unemployed father and mentally disturbed mother. Given no guidance by these neglectful parents, whom he despises, Petey is at a loss as to how to deal with the ethnic slurs and casual beatings he suffers from members of a local youth gang. Finally he arms himself with a pistol and, cornered in an alley, shoots and kills their leader, Snake. Filled with crazed bravado, he then confronts the gang and demands to be made their new "president"; a melee ensues, the police arrive, and Petey is shot dead while trying to escape. Bullied, harassed, filled with frustrated machismo and a longing for vengeance, this misguided boy convinces himself that in order to be respected—to prove himself a "cool stud"—he has to have "guts enough to kill" (117). Yet all this ersatz courage earns him is a mean death in the street. In an introduction to the collection, titled "Some Sketches of the Damned," Ellison bemoans the plight of these lost kids who have learned only to "get your stomps before they stomp *you*" (19). Yet he affirms that, underneath the tattered leather jackets and jaded tough-guy poses, they are "basically honest and decent. . . . All they need is a chance" (20).

These early "juvie" tales, published in hard-boiled detective digests and as paperback originals by small presses such as Ace and Pyramid Books, show how open such down-market venues were to fiction that engaged pressing social issues, albeit often in a caricatured way or with a moralizing tone. Ellison's work does not always escape these pitfalls, but it possesses an undeniable dynamism and a sincere note of humane outrage that would become characteristic of all his output. It is only a short step from these stark, depressing, if admittedly sometimes hackneyed stories to such later classics of urban violence as "The Whimper of Whipped Dogs" (1973). Based on the true story of Kitty Genovese, a young woman stabbed to death by a maniac on a New York street in front of dozens of uncaring neighbors who made no move to help her, this Edgar-winning effort transmutes the basic crime-story materials of Ellison's early fiction into something altogether more horrific and profound. Its graphically naturalistic opening shades into a tale of the ambiguously supernatural, with the girl's seemingly random murder serving to feed the appetite of a callous urban deity, "a deranged blood God of fog and street violence. A God who needed worshipers and offered the choices of death as a victim or life an an eternal witness to the deaths of *other* chosen victims" (19). The rough-and-ready materials of Ellison's youthful work here give way to a more polished and subtle treatment, which the author would select to head up probably his most accomplished single collection, *Deathbird Stories: A Pantheon of Modern Gods*.

Ellison's socially conscious work of the early 1960s included some brave approaches to the fraught issue of racial conflict, forces then in the process of rending American society. A strong proponent of civil rights, Ellison participated in a freedom march in Alabama to protest segregation, where he was confronted firsthand with naked racist hatred on the part of white southerners, "the frenzied and hideous *doppelgangers* of Hitler's storm troopers" ("From Alabamy" 111). As Ellen Weil and Gary K. Wolfe observe, his fiction from the period depicts this ugly reality with a "visceral documentary power" (97). "The Night of Delicate Terrors" (1961), for example, is a compelling story of an African American family traveling from Georgia to Chicago during a dangerous blizzard. The father, McKinley Hooker, finds himself exhausted after long hours of driving, but he is unable to stop for rest because all the restaurants and motels along the route serve whites only. The festering irrationality of racial prejudice is captured in literally chilling terms, as the desperate family is turned away from a diner that won't even let them use the bathrooms. Back on the highway, battling blowing snow that threatens to upend the car, Hooker finally reconciles himself to his decision to join a secret black militia group—his destination in Chicago, as it turns out. "He had been uncertain before, because he was not a man of violence . . . but suddenly, it was right. It was the way it would be, because they had forced it this way" (255). Here the yearning for vengeance that characterizes little Petey Cosnakof is given a broader, more apocalyptic twist, since the bully in the story is institutionalized racism itself and the put-upon protagonist a representative of an entire downtrodden community.

The ideological complexity of racial struggle during the civil rights era is the theme of "Daniel White for the Greater Good" (1961), probably Ellison's most sophisticated take on the topic. The eponymous character is a young black man entirely lacking in conscience who, after raping a white girl and now faced with the prospect of a lynch mob, is smugly certain a representative from the Georgia NAACP will protect him. But as the mob violence starts to spread and target the larger African American community, this representative advises the local black leaders to allow White to be lynched, arguing that in death he will be more useful to his people than he had ever been in life, as a martyr whose grim fate will rally supporters to the cause. "It was a double-edged sword that slicing one way would tame the wrath of the mob beast, and slicing the other would make a path for more understanding, by use of shame and example" (69-70). According to Weil and Wolfe, "Daniel White for the Greater Good" stands out from most of Ellison's early social-problem stories in depicting such a "tangled moral parable" that it is impossible to discern what the correct decision should be: to save the individual and sacrifice the community, or vice versa (96).

It was likely this ethical complexity that led Dorothy Parker, in her review of the 1961 collection *Gentleman Junkie, and Other Stories of the Hung-Up Generation* in *Esquire* magazine, to single out "Daniel White" as "the best presentation I have ever seen of present racial conditions in the South and of those who try to alleviate them." This review gave Ellison a much-needed boost at a critical juncture in his career, convincing him that his work, though published in obscure outlets far from the arenas of literary respectability ("Daniel White" had appeared in the men's magazine *Rogue* before being collected in *Gentleman Junkie*), were reaching serious readers and critics. As a result, Ellison's fiction of the mid-1960s began to grow markedly more ambitious: rather than producing stories to accommodate existing markets, he sought instead to transform those markets to fit his own artistic and social vision. Specifically, he returned with renewed vigor to his earliest literary love, science fiction (SF), a genre that had significantly atrophied during the late 1950s and early 1960s, when hosts of magazines died off and major talents fled the field.

Just beginning to recover in the mid-1960s, as paperback publishers discovered the genre in earnest, SF nonetheless remained artistically stalled, the intellectual energy that fueled the boom of the 1950s spent and that decade's major themes played out to exhaustion. Sensing an opportunity, Ellison leaped into the breach with typical flamboyance, releasing a story in the December 1965 issue of *Galaxy* magazine, "'Repent, Harlequin!' Said the Ticktockman," that almost certainly could not have been published a decade earlier, given its almost surreal tone and fragmentary form. The tale went on to win both the Hugo and Nebula awards, Ellison's first major recognitions within the genre, and has since been translated into most major languages and anthologized more frequently than any other modern SF story.

Most interestingly, what "'Repent, Harlequin!'" accomplished, aside from helping to refresh a moribund field, was to extrapolate the theme of ideological conflict so pronounced in the author's earlier social-problem fiction in such a way that it converted mere topical relevance, the congruence with contemporary headlines, into a universal allegory of rebellion against tyrannical authority. Set in a totalitarian dystopia where time is regulated with brutal efficiency, the story pits the dour, rigid Ticktockman, agent of this remorseless order, against the Harlequin, a mercurial prankster whose persistent acts of surreal sabotage undermine the well-oiled precision of the state. Opening with a long quotation from Henry David Thoreau's 1849 essay "Civil Disobedience," the tale manages to combine a didactic antiauthoritarian message with a freewheeling, anarchic atmosphere; at one point, the Harlequin drops a load of candy onto the express slidewalk that takes commuters to and from their work shifts: "Everyone was summarily dumped thisawayaandthataway in a jackstraw tumble, still laughing and popping little jelly beans of childish color into their mouths. It was a holiday, and a jollity, an absolute insanity, a giggle. . . . The shift was delayed seven minutes" (134). As this passage suggests, Ellison's prose, released from the constraints of the hard-boiled crime genre, achieves a fresh lyrical energy, and the tale delights in coining strange words: "swizzleskid," "minee," "Flash-O," "fallaron." Though the Harlequin is captured and compelled to repent, the story ends on an enigmatic note of hope, as the Ticktockman is apparently infected with the trickster's wayward spirit, showing up late for work while humming a merry tune.

Ellison wrote "'Repent, Harlequin!'" while attending a writers' workshop in Milford, Pennsylvania, hosted by SF author and editor Damon Knight, and he has reported that response to the story at the workshop split right down the middle: one group deplored its outright daffiness and seeming formlessness while the other appreciated its whimsical brilliance and clever skewering of autocratic pretensions. Among the latter crowd was Frederik Pohl, then editor of *Galaxy*, who bought the manuscript on the spot (see Ellison, "A Time" 29), but Ellison would come to have problems with Pohl as well, when his later story "I Have No Mouth, and I Must Scream"—another scathing denunciation of tyrannical power—was censored, upon its appearance in *Galaxy*'s sister magazine, *If*, in 1967, because of its sexual frankness and religious irreverence. "I Have No Mouth" is a much darker tale than "'Repent, Harlequin!'": gone is the airy lightness of tone, replaced by the cynical, desperate, brutalized voice of a nuclear-war survivor trapped, by a despotic artificial intelligence, in a computer-generated hell. The story fuses the fantastic imagery of Ellison's SF with the stark violence of his crime stories in a savage commentary on the unfeeling brutality of a technocratic system that suppresses freedom and punishes individuality, "with the innate loathing that all machines had always held for the weak, soft creatures that built them" (26). Despite Pohl's peremptory edits, Ellison was vindicated when "I Have No Mouth" won him his second Hugo Award for best short story; however, the push-back against his efforts to expand SF's thematic and stylistic repertoire on the part of the field's major editors convinced him that a more radical intervention was in order.

In a combative speech delivered at the Nineteenth Annual West Coast SF Convention in San Diego, California, on Independence Day, 1966 (later published as "A Time for Daring"), Ellison declared his own independence from the genre's hidebound rules and blinkered sense of its own possibilities. Decrying the elitist snobbery that had kept science fiction segregated from the literary mainstream, Ellison also lambasted SF writers and fans for falling into a compensatory "ghetto" mentality that rationalized this marginalization. Refusing to change and adapt, they clung to familiar subcultural rituals and formula stories while the larger world passed them by. "We've been leaching the vitality out of our best writers," he proclaimed, or else forcing them to flee the field because "they're too big and too talented to be constrained by our often vicious, often ungrateful little back water eddy" (33). While postmodern authors such as Kurt Vonnegut and William Burroughs were already pushing the borders of speculative fiction into surprising terrain, SF fans remained content to read "the hacks" who "give us a nice technological thing that we can play with and toy with and masturbate with.... we like that a lot. But when they really demand something from us, when they write something really new and fresh and different and inventive, we don't know where they are" (33). With this pugnacious speech (which featured snippy banter with a cantankerous audience), along with similarly polemical pieces published in professional and fan magazines, Ellison sought to build the constituency for a more experimental, more adventurous brand of science fiction, of the sort that he was currently producing himself. But in order to give this kind of work a prestigious showplace, the author was compelled to become an editor, shepherding into print the publishing event of the decade, the anthology *Dangerous Visions* (1967).

A compendium of thirty-three mind-bending stories by SF writers both old and new, *Dangerous Visions* was nonetheless unmistakably an Ellison production: every story came complete with a breathless editorial preface, and the book also featured a lengthy, barn-burning introduction that trumpeted the volume's "new horizons and styles and forms and challenges," its "fresh and daring ideas," and its fearless trampling of taboos surrounding sex, politics, and religion ("Introduction" xxi). "No one has ever told the speculative writer, 'Pull out all the stops, no holds barred, get it said!' Until this book came along" (xxiv). *Dangerous Visions* was one of the first, and was certainly the largest and most visible, all-original anthologies ever published within the genre, and its purpose was to compel the magazines to liberalize their editorial policies by showing what could be possible absent traditional constraints on idea and expression. If Ellison's calculated rabble-rousing—his aggressive flaunting of stories of atheism, "deviant" sexuality, and ultraviolence—may seem a bit dated today, this is testimony to just how effective his editorial program was in shaking up and helping to transform the field, since these themes no longer seem so unthinkable, quite so beyond the pale.

While the volume was unsurprisingly controversial among hardcore Old Guard types (fan author Ted White called it "an ugly book, and a disaster" [34]), it sold extremely well and was showered with awards: two Hugos and two Nebulas for its fiction, and a special Hugo plaque to Ellison for editing it. In a response to his critics, Ellison claimed that *Dangerous Visions* "accomplished *everything* I intended": it "forc[ed] the closet reactionaries to voice their musty opinions in an undisguised manner that revealed them for what they are" while simultaneously "creat[ing] a more liberal atmosphere in which the stylistic innovators emergent these last few years could have their work accepted" ("Final").[2]

Dangerous Visions has been described as "the starting gun of the War of the New Wave in America" (Dozois 13), a conflict that had already been raging for several years in Great Britain. The so-called New Wave was a loosely affiliated movement of writers, editors, and fans who, like Ellison, were convinced that SF of the early to mid-1960s had grown embarrassingly stale and needed an invigorating jolt of creative and intellectual energy.[3] Ellison himself has dismissed the term as misleading, declaring that there was "no conscious 'movement' by any one group of writers"; rather, if the New Wave refers to anything meaningful, it signals "a reflection of what was happening in the world during the Sixties. A dawning social consciousness, the youth rebellion, the civil rights movement, the rise of Third World powers, a reaction to the repressiveness of established governments, a time of involvement and turmoil" filtered into the seemingly sealed-off world of SF, setting off "tremblors that shocked our younger writers and our more adaptable older writers" ("A Few" 42). Another way to put this, of course, is that the genre had finally managed to catch up with Harlan Ellison, since his work had been addressing many of those concerns since the late 1950s. However one formulates the issue, there is no question that, once the furious debates over the New Wave—and the countercultural trends it reflected—erupted in the United States, Ellison threw himself into the fray with gusto, churning out a prodigious stream of fiction, essays, reviews, and letters to editors that cheerfully grappled with some of the most contentious questions of the times. Indeed, the period of the mid-1960s to mid-1970s was the most productive of the author's career, and there can be little doubt that the ardor and intensity that marked the struggles of that era served as galvanizing forces for his best, most vital work.

Some of Ellison's voluminous output during this decade continued the social-problem emphasis of his earlier fiction, now extrapolated to countercultural concerns. "Shattered Like a Glass Goblin" (1968), for example, is a tale of lost youth similar to those gathered in *The Deadly Streets*, though hippies and psychotropic drugs have supplanted juvenile delinquents and gang violence. Set in an urban crash pad amid a tatterdemalion crew of wasted stoners, the tale centers on the efforts of a recently discharged serviceman, Rudy, to save his former girlfriend, Kris, from a hideous descent into addiction. As he is drawn into her weird twilight world, Rudy feels himself metamorphosing into a fabulous creature, the eponymous glass goblin, surrounded by much more fearsome and dangerous beasts that represent the terrors of uncontrollable dependency. With its psychedelic haunted-house imagery, "Shattered" is much more aligned in tone with horror fiction than with SF, giving voice to the author's lifelong abstinence from drug and alcohol use in a forthright and (it must be admitted) rather heavy-handed way. Still, it stands apart from his earlier "juvie" stories in the greater expressiveness of Ellison's mature style: baroque as opposed to spare, lyrical instead of hard-boiled.

Much more successful, in its fusing of social-problem fiction with the modalities of the fantastic genres, is "Basilisk" (1972), an antiwar story of considerable subtlety and power. After being seriously injured by a pungi stake, American corporal Vern Lestig is captured by a nameless Asian enemy that is clearly a stand-in for the Vietnamese. Discovered in the ruined enemy camp, his captors butchered by some mysterious agency, Vern is rescued by his countrymen, but the fact that he confessed to the enemy under torture leads to a court martial and dismissal from the Army. Returning to his Kansas town as a pariah, he is shunned by his former girlfriend and persecuted by the locals, who despise his "treasonous" cowardice. As thus summarized, the tale would seem like a straightforward, realistic effort to depict the manifold injustices of the Vietnam conflict, but Ellison adds a characteristic twist: the pungi stake that wounded Vern had been anointed with the blood of a basilisk, a "great black gap-mawed beast . . . stepping down through mists of potent barriers erected to separate men from their masters" (81). Like this mythical monster, Vern now possesses the ability to kill with a look or a breath, as his Vietnamese captors discovered to their horror. Now goaded beyond endurance, Vern lashes out at his Kansas neighbors in an orgy of bloodletting that achieves, albeit in a grimly ironic way, the antiwar movement's goal of "bringing the war home." The basilisk, we discover at the end, is the tamed pet of Mars, Roman god of war, who is much pleased to see the carnage expanding to the American heartland.

Ellison's depiction of the Kansas denizens as a mob of angry, benighted "patriots" lashing out at a convenient scapegoat echoes his earlier portraits of racist southerners, smug in their moral superiority and eager to prove it through recourse to righteous violence. An even more scathing treatment of Middle American bigotry and closed-mindedness can be found in the novella *A Boy and His Dog* (1969), another Nebula winner and perhaps the author's single finest story. It is certainly one of his most science fictional, set in the aftermath of a nuclear conflagration that has driven whole communities underground while gangs of survivors wander the shattered wastelands. The narrator, Vic, a "solo" unaffiliated with any of the "roverpaks," is partnered with Blood, a telepathic dog descended from brain-boosted animals adapted for the battlefield. Vic hooks up with Quilla June, a young woman from "Topeka" (one of the subsurface cities), and after defending her from a band of marauders in a pitched battle that severely wounds Blood, he follows her underground. There he finds a sealed-off world living a dead fantasy of 1950s normalcy: "Neat little houses, and curvy little streets, and trimmed lawns, and a business section" (243); as one of the town leaders affirms, "It's nice down here. Quiet, orderly, nice people who respect each other, no crime, respect for the elders, and just all around a good place to live. We're growin' and we're prosperin'" (243-

44). Unfortunately, after a generation underground, the population is no longer reproductively viable, and they need outsiders like Vic to infuse their stagnant gene pool with new energy. Horrified by this claustrophobic false utopia, Vic escapes, choosing a dangerous, rootless freedom with Blood over the bleak, reactionary stasis of "Topeka." One is left to conclude that the real-world Topeka was no less sterile and soul-killing, and atomic armageddon history's just verdict on its vacuous inanity.

While many of Ellison's stories from this period display a similarly barbed satirical thurst, skewering the sacred cows of American middle-class life, some of his most powerful and searching efforts are more elusive allegories that, while still offering sharp commentary on the social realities of the day, do so with a distanced irony and in a highly symbolic fashion. Probably the most brilliant of these is "The Deathbird" (1973), a Hugo-winning tale that provides the title for Ellison's most thematically cohesive collection. Like several of his most ambitious stories from this era, such as "The Beast That Shouted Love at the Heart of the World" (1968) and "Adrift Just Off the Islets of Langerhans" (1974), "Deathbird" is a conflation of generic tropes culled from science fiction, fantasy, and postmodernist literature that strain for—and at their best achieve—the potency of a kind of pop-cultural myth.

An assemblage of fragments of narrative, autobiography, and quotations from the Bible and Friedrich Nietzsche, framed as a "test" for the reader complete with topics for discussion and a multiple-choice exam, "Deathbird" retells Genesis as a science fiction fable in which the snake who led humankind astray is actually the hero, while the villain is an insane, petulant, vindictive, patriarchal God. Impossible to summarize neatly, the story shifts through a range of rhetorical voices with dizzying virtuosity, by turns hectoring, mocking, coaxing, and exhorting its readers. A reverse theodicy, the tale indicts the biblical deity for all the evils of history, including the nuclear holocaust that has culminated it, offering an alternative cosmology in which tutelary aliens, represented by the biblical snake (here named Dira), have sought to awaken humanity from the thrall of a despotic false Creator. In its pitting of humane possibility against overbearing authority, "Deathbird" is a more sophisticated version of "'Repent, Harlequin!'"; indeed, this perennial conflict is perhaps Ellison's most abiding theme. The story's God is the distilled essence of all the vicious racists, closed-minded Middle Americans, and self-righteous autocrats who people his earlier fiction, as well as being the very face of the Establishment opposed by the 1960s counterculture. Yet the final confrontation is distinctly anticlimactic, as the representative of humanity, Nathan Stack, after climbing a mountain and enduring horrible trials to reach His throne, finds only "an old, tired man" whining "in the voice of a cranky child. . . . OH, PLEASE, I DON'T WANT TO GO TO BED YET. I'M NOT YET DONE PLAYING" (333).

"Deathbird" is the capping entry in *Deathbird Stories*, a collection of nineteen tales that depict, according to the book's subtitle, "a pantheon of modern gods," including the remorseless god of war of "Basilisk" and the god of self-destructive addiction of "Shattered Like a Glass Goblin." Released in 1975, at the end of the remarkable decade of productivity kicked off by "'Repent, Harlequin!,'" it reveals Ellison as not only one of the most compelling and versatile of contemporary SF authors but also its most fearless battler against social intolerance, an enemy of false idols and mindless dogma. In an interview with Paul Walker conducted in 1972, Ellison claimed to see himself as "only a storyteller"—a claim that may seem surprisingly modest until the author explains his vision of this role: "There are messages in everything I wrote, but they are there to satisfy *my* needs as a thinking individual; I hope a *committed* individual. The *story* is there for the reader" (293). For readers willing to grasp for the messages underlying these stories—messages of hope, of despair, and of baffled but persistent struggle against injustice—the experience of encountering these at once deeply personal and profoundly social documents offers both a challenge and a delight.

Notes

1. This essay, while covering some of Ellison's most important and characteristic short fiction of the late 1950s through mid-1970s, can barely scratch the surface of his vast oeuvre. For an exhaustive—and superb—overview of Ellison's entire career, see Weil and Wolfe.

2. A follow-up volume—*Again, Dangerous Visions*, published in 1972—was even bigger, featuring forty-two stories, and it too was a success, garnering a Hugo and a Nebula for its fiction. By this time, all-original anthologies had become a thriving market within the field.

3. For a fuller discussion of the New Wave phenomenon, see my essay "The New Wave."

Works Cited

Dozois, Gardner. "Beyond the Golden Age—Part II: The New Wave Years." *Thrust—Science Fiction in Review* 19 (1983): 10-14.

Ellison, Harlan. "Basilisk." *Deathbird Stories: A Pantheon of Modern Gods*. New York: Harper & Row, 1975. 80-100.

_____. *A Boy and His Dog. The Beast That Shouted Love at the Heart of the World*. 1969. New York: Signet, 1974. 217-54.

_____. "Daniel White for the Greater Good." *Gentleman Junkie, and Other Stories of the Hung-Up Generation*. 1961. New York: Pyramid Books, 1975. 60-71.

_____. "The Deathbird." *Deathbird Stories: A Pantheon of Modern Gods*. New York: Harper & Row, 1975. 302-34.

_____. "A Few (Hopefully Final) Words on 'The New Wave.'" *Science Fiction: The Academic Awakening*. Ed. Willis McNelly. Shreveport, LA: College English Association, 1974. 40-43.

_____. "Final Statement." *Warhoon* 25 (Nov. 1968): 42.

_____. "From Alabamy, with Hate." *Sleepless Nights in the Procrustean Bed*. Ed. Marty Clark. San Bernardino, CA: Borgo Press, 1984. 109-20.

_____. "I Have No Mouth, and I Must Scream." *Alone Against Tomorrow: Stories of Alienation in Speculative Fiction*. New York: Collier, 1971. 15-32.

_____. Interview by Paul Walker. 1972. *Speaking of Science Fiction: The Paul Walker Interviews*. Oradell, NJ: Luna, 1978. 291-301.

_____. "Introduction: Thirty-two Soothsayers." *Dangerous Visions*. New York: Doubleday, 1967. xix-xxix.

_____. "Kid Killer." *The Deadly Streets*. New York: Pyramid Books, 1975. 108-21.

_____. "The Night of Delicate Terrors." *Gentleman Junkie, and Other Stories of the Hung-Up Generation*. 1961. New York: Pyramid Books, 1975. 247-55.

_____. "'Repent, Harlequin!' Said the Ticktockman." *Alone Against To-*

morrow: Stories of Alienation in Speculative Fiction. New York: Collier, 1971. 130-44.

_____. "Shattered Like a Glass Goblin." *Deathbird Stories: A Pantheon of Modern Gods*. New York: Harper & Row, 1975. 138-49.

_____. "Some Sketches of the Damned." *The Deadly Streets*. New York: Pyramid Books, 1975. 17-20.

_____. "A Time for Daring." *Algol* 12 (13 Mar. 1967): 27-34.

_____. "The Whimper of Whipped Dogs." *Deathbird Stories: A Pantheon of Modern Gods*. New York: Harper & Row, 1975. 2-22.

Latham, Rob. "The New Wave." *A Companion to Science Fiction*. Ed. David Seed. London: Blackwell, 2005. 202-15.

Parker, Dorothy. Rev. of *Gentleman Junkie, and Other Stories of the Hung-Up Generation*, by Harlan Ellison. *Esquire* Jan. 1962. Rpt. in "Book Reviews." *Gentleman Junkie, and Other Stories of the Hung-Up Generation*. By Harlan Ellison. New York: Pyramid Books, 1975. 1.

Weil, Ellen, and Gary K. Wolfe. *Harlan Ellison: The Edge of Forever*. Columbus: Ohio State UP, 2002.

White, Ted. "Reflections on *Dangerous Visions*, Part One." *Warhoon* 24 (Aug. 1968): 32-40, 62.

All Roads Lead to Hell:
Harlan Ellison, Cormac McCarthy, and the Bitter End of the American Dream

Andrew J. Wilson

> We thought we were done with these things but we were wrong.
> We thought, because we had power, we had wisdom.
> We thought the long train would run to the end of time.
> We thought the light would increase.
> Now the long train stands derailed and the bandits loot it.
> Now the boar and the asp have power in our time.
> Now the night rolls back on the West and the night is solid.
> Our fathers and ourselves sowed dragon's teeth.
> Our children know and suffer the armed men.
> —Stephen Vincent Benét, "Litany for Dictatorships"

> "Don't fret about it, kid; nobody gets out of childhood alive."
> —Harlan Ellison, "The Wit and Wisdom of Blood"

One of the defining characteristics of the life and work of Harlan Ellison is that, for better or worse, he is wedded to controversy. As he told Charles Platt, with whom he later quarreled acrimoniously: "It is very necessary for my work to have an impact. The most senseless cavil that's ever been levelled against me is, 'Oh, you only wrote that to shock'. I say[,] of course, you idiot, of course that's the reason I wrote it. What do you expect me to do, lull you into a false sense of security?" (qtd. in Platt 180). This determination to make "people's hair stand on end" while reading his work has meant that when Ellison has written about the end of the world, his stories have been both unflinching and unnerving, and he has refused to offer his readers the panacea of a happy ending.

A great deal of so-called postapocalyptic fiction is nothing of the sort, of course. Terrible disasters may befall the planet, the world as we know it can be shattered beyond repair, and the human race inevitably faces the threat of extinction, but more often than not, the conclusions of these stories see small but single-minded bands of survivors reach safe havens and begin to rebuild civilization. One world may have gone up in smoke, but a new and better—or at least wiser—one is destined to rise from its ashes. Ellison will have none of this. In works such as his novella *A Boy and His Dog* (1969) and its pendant short stories, "Eggsucker" (1977) and "Run, Spot, Run" (1980), there is no Promised Land "over the hill," there are only the wastelands of the here and now, and a constant struggle for survival. In "I Have No Mouth, and I Must Scream" (1967), there is even less.

It should come as no surprise, then, that when Alan Cheuse reviewed Cormac McCarthy's *The Road* in the *Chicago Tribune*, he described it as "a postatomic apocalypse novel as we've never seen one before, a black book of wondrous paragraphs that reads as though Samuel Beckett had dared himself to outdo Harlan Ellison." The citation of Ellison's name along with those of a Pulitzer Prize winner and a Nobel laureate might seem incongruous to those who would impose a cordon sanitaire between the bastions of the literary canon and the outlying ghettos of genre fiction, but it is, in fact, quite the opposite. Just as it can be strongly argued that McCarthy deliberately conceived and wrote *The Road* as a science fiction novel, albeit one framed in his own idiosyncratic terms (just as *Blood Meridian* is his demythologizing of the western), Ellison's own award-winning work is generic in the sense that Ellison is willing to use accepted tropes even though he refuses to adhere to the clichés and conventions of the form. Like Beckett, McCarthy and Ellison are writers who refuse to compromise, and a comparison of their postapocalyptic fictions yields both striking parallels and important contrasts.

To place stories such as *A Boy and His Dog*, "I Have No Mouth," and *The Road* in context, it is worth examining the similar works in this vein that preceded them. What a review of the apocalyptic literature of the past two hundred years reveals is that, for the majority of this period, American authors produced far less of it than did their contemporaries in the United Kingdom. Indeed, the first novel in English on this theme was Mary Wollstonecraft Shelley's *The Last Man* (1826), which may have been inspired by Lord Byron's poem "Darkness" (1816). Mary Shelley, of course, knew Byron well and often transcribed his poems for him, and "Darkness" was composed during their famous stay at the Villa Diodati in Switzerland, which also saw the creation of her most famous work, *Frankenstein: Or, The Modern Prometheus* (1818). Less clear is whether French writer Jean-Baptiste Cousin de Grainville's 1805 novel *Le Dernier Homme* (published in English as *The Last Man: Or, Omegarus and Syderia, a Romance of Futurity* in 1806) was an influence, but the theme was a popular one in the romantic era, as underlined by Thomases Campbell, Lovell Beddoes, and Hood, who also produced poetical works titled "The Last Man" (composed in 1823, circa 1823-25, and 1826, respectively).

Over the next century, British authors anticipated the apocalyptic destruction of the world in novels such as Richard Jefferies's *After London* (1885), H. G. Wells's *The Time Machine* (1895), and John Collier's *Tom's A-Cold* (1933; U.S. title *Full Circle*). In these works, the fear, or perhaps desire, that the British Empire might fall is conflated with the end of civilization and a return to a more primitive, even degenerate, state. By the close of World War II, not only was the empire genuinely coming to an end, but the whole world had to face the horrors of both the Holocaust and the atomic bomb as well. The United Kingdom still led the field in doomsday fiction with a cluster of postimperial novels in the 1950s and 1960s, such as John Wyndham's *The Day of the Triffids* (1951), John Christopher's *The Death of Grass* (1956; U.S. title *No Blade of Grass*), and J. G. Ballard's *The Drowned World* (1962). Even though some of these books were defined as "cosy catastrophes" by Brian W. Aldiss (293), who wrote the similarly themed *Greybeard* (1964), and all invariably feature resolutely middle-class protagonists, on closer examination many reveal themselves to be far less comfortable than the label would suggest (Parrinder 210-11).

The United States seemed less concerned with its own possible mortality until the beginning of the Cold War. There had been some notable works before this time, of course: Jack London's *The Scarlet Plague* (1912), Edwin Balmer and Philip Wylie's *When Worlds Collide* (1933), and Stephen Vincent Benét's apocalyptic poetry, collected in *Burning City* (1936), and his short story "By the Waters of Babylon" (1937; originally published as "The Place of the Gods"). Nevertheless, it was the postwar era that saw the rise of all-American ends of the world—George R. Stewart's *Earth Abides* (1949), Wilson Tucker's *The Long Loud Silence* (1952), and Walter M. Miller, Jr.'s *A Canticle for Leibowitz* (1960) are all key works of this period—and as the Cold War continued and environmental threats became more apparent, American writers increasingly focused on this theme. Ellison and McCarthy have written some of the most important American works in this genre of the past half century, and, perhaps of greatest significance, their minatory days of judgment represent not only the end of the world but also the death of the American Dream, the extinction of any conception of providential destiny, manifest or otherwise.

Both *A Boy and His Dog* and *The Road* focus on a boy, one with only a first name and the other without any designation at all. Both characters have mentors. In the case of Vic, the teenage protagonist of *A Boy and His Dog*, this is Blood, a telepathic dog with a human level of intelligence; in *The Road*, the nameless preadolescent boy is guided and protected by "the man," his equally anonymous father. These characters wander through endlessly hostile and desolate postapocalyptic environments in their increasingly problematic struggles to survive. It is not just their lives that are at stake; their very humanity is threatened by what they have to do to keep going.

In the prologue to the Vic and Blood stories, "From the History of the World, as Blood Tells It," the well-educated "skirmisher dog"—whose voice Ellen Weil and Gary K. Wolfe have observed "is in fact very close to that of Ellison himself" (150)—explains exactly how the disaster came to pass. The Third World War began in 1950 with the Korean War and continued through three consecutive "hot and cold" iterations until 2022, "though nobody seemed smart enough to realize that it had all been one continuing conflict." The seventy-two years of hostilities were followed by just two years, six months, and three days of peace, and then:

> World War IV broke out on the 215th anniversary of the birth of Edgar Allan Poe—19 January 2024. World War IV lasted five days; until the few remaining missiles that had jammed in their first-strike release phase cleared their fully computerized silos beneath the Painted Desert, the Saharan Ahaggars, the Rub al Khali, the Siberian Plateau and Pyongyang; but by then there wasn't much of anything left to fight over. Five days. (*Vic and Blood* 5)

Forty years later, what is left of humanity in the midwestern United States is divided between "roverpaks"—savage gangs of predominantly male orphans and their surgically enhanced telepathic dogs—who rule the blasted exterior landscape and conservative fundamentalist communities who have sealed themselves into "downunders," sanitized subterranean cities. Neither the anarchy aboveground nor the order below is flourishing, and a further crisis looms because there has been a drastic decline in the numbers of girls born on the surface and boys underneath.

McCarthy chooses to obscure the nature of the near-future catastrophe in *The Road*. Since his characters do not know what has happened, the reader is also denied this information. All we are told is this:

> The clocks stopped at 1:17. A long shear of light and then a series of low concussions. He got up and went to the window. What is it? she said. He didnt answer. He went to the bathroom and threw the lightswitch but the power was already gone. A dull glow rose in the windowglass. He dropped to one knee and raised the lever to stop the tub and then turned on both taps

as far as they would go. She was standing in the doorway in her nightwear, clutching the jamb, cradling her belly in one hand. What is it? she said. What is happening?

   I dont know.

   Why are you taking a bath?

   I'm not. (45)

Whatever the cause of the disaster—and it can be argued that there may have been more than one near-simultaneous event—the result is that almost all plant and animal life has died. The world of the novel is cold, gray, and covered in ash. Even the constant snow is grimy. The skies are permanently overcast, suggesting a year-round winter brought about by nuclear war, asteroid impact, or volcanic eruptions on a massive scale. Wildfires started by lightning strikes burn unchecked across the country. The setting evokes the thoughts of the tinker in McCarthy's second book, *Outer Dark* (1968): "Hard people makes hard times. I've seen the meanness of humans till I don't know why God ain't put out the sun and gone away" (192). For all intents and purposes, this is exactly what has now happened.

There are no redoubts of civilization in *The Road*, there is no news of a safe haven "over the hill," there is no law. The only remnants of any kind of morality seem to be the father and son, the self-styled "good guys," who insist they are "carrying the fire" as they make their way south in search of greater warmth and other "good people." For the man, who is portrayed as both physically ill and clinically depressed, this is make-believe that serves as an excuse to keep moving and give his son the hope he needs to continue, but the boy genuinely believes his father's stories, and the reader cannot help but wonder if the child might actually be right.

These disparate pairs are both inversions of the natural order. Blood is an intellectual; he is educated and comprehends both history and what might occur beyond the immediate future. He acts as both a tutor and a surrogate father to the orphaned Vic. Blood's problem is that his augmented intelligence and psychic abilities have been gained at the cost of his ability to hunt. The fifteen-year-old boy, by contrast, is little better than a savage. His lack of a surname suggests that he never knew his parents; he barely knows who he is and is certainly unaware of *what* he is. Vic's brutality and callousness are only justified by the even more barbaric behavior of the other survivors; nevertheless, he kills without compunction and actively seeks to commit rape. And although Blood tries to educate his unwilling pupil so that the boy will be able to help rebuild some kind of society, he depends on Vic's feral qualities to defend them against the roverpaks and hunt for food, and the dog shows no empathy for anyone or anything other than his partner. Weil and Wolfe highlight the parallels between the culture of the roverpaks and that of the Brooklyn street gangs whom Ellison knew and wrote about in early works such as *The Deadly Streets* (1958) and *Memos from Purgatory* (1961).

In *The Road*, the son, innocent though he is, acts as his father's conscience and, indeed, gives him the mental strength to carry on in spite of the hopelessness of their situation: "He knew only that the child was his warrant. He said: If he is not the word of God God never spoke" (4). Perhaps the boy can do so because this is the only world he has ever known: his mother was pregnant with him when the clocks stopped at 1:17. Unable to cope with the new, unforgiving world, she committed suicide some time later (with the stopping of the clocks and the end of the cycle of the seasons, time has become blurred and ambiguous). His father then brought him up alone until the man realized that they would not survive another winter at their home. Over the course of their journey south toward the sea, the man hunts for what preserved food can be found, keeps both metaphorical and real fires going, and protects his child from roving gangs of cannibals. In doing so, he takes on a role akin to that of Vic. It is the boy who, like Blood, is the one who believes in a better place, that there may be a future worth speaking of, and he encourages his father to hold on to his humanity so that he—and indeed they—will be worthy of it. In contrast to Blood, the boy retains his capacity for empathy.

The journeys described by Ellison and McCarthy are very different, even if the characters reach all-too-similar destinations. In *A Boy and His Dog*, Vic abandons the radioactive nightmare of the surface to descend into the sterile underworld of the city of Topeka, but he is always destined to return to the hell-on-earth aboveground. The man and boy in *The Road* follow the highway south, and although they may deviate from it at times, they never turn back. When they do go underground on two occasions, first into a cellar converted into a hideous larder stocked with human beings and then into the temporary safety of a well-stocked bunker, these scenes only serve to evoke the observation of Mephistopheles, "Why, this is hell, nor are we out of it," in Christopher Marlowe's *Doctor Faustus*. The course of the journey in *The Road* is, in fact, much closer to the subterranean expedition made by the tortured characters in Ellison's "I Have No Mouth."

Of all the works under discussion here, *A Boy and His Dog* is the most plot-driven. Having caught food for Blood, Vic demands that his dog finds him a woman. Initially unsuccessful, Blood telepathically senses the presence of a disguised female at a makeshift movie show. The pair follow their prey into an abandoned building, where the girl from "downunder," Quilla June, is attempting to change back into her normal clothes when Vic surprises her. Before the boy can rape the girl, who is more self-possessed than he expects and engages him in conversation, a roverpak surrounds the building. After a gun battle with some gang members and their own dog, a fight in which Quilla June participates, Blood is injured and the three are surrounded. With no other option, Vic sets fire to the building and hides in a boiler with the dog and the girl. As they wait it out, he finally has his way with Quilla June, who resists at first, but then willingly has sex with him. When they emerge from their hideout, Quilla June knocks Vic out and escapes.

On recovering consciousness, the enraged Vic follows the girl downunder, using an identity card that she has dropped, leaving the wounded Blood at the entrance to the dropshaft despite the dog's protests:

"Vic, we've been together almost three years. Good and bad. But this can be the worst. I'm scared, man. Scared you won't come back. And I'm hungry, and I'll have to go find some dude who'll take me on . . . and you know most solos are in paks now, I'll be low mutt. I'm not that young any more. And I'm hurt pretty bad." (*Vic and Blood* 73)

Vic has taken the bait left by Quilla June. On his entry into the underground settlement, he is captured and taken to the aging leaders of this conformist society. He is to be co-opted as a stud for the community. Just as female birthrates have catastrophically declined up above because of the war, male children are no longer being born in the sterile downunders. Vic agrees to this arrangement so that he can take his revenge on Quilla June and satisfy his urges, but the artificial pre-World War I environment stifles him and even the synthetic food fails to satisfy him. As Weil and Wolfe remark, the story now inverts the world of Wells's *The Time Machine* (153): feral but dynamic humans populate the world above, while a passive, enfeebled community survives below. On a fundamental level, the savage in Vic needs the less hypocritical barbarity of the surface world, and so he plots his escape.

His plan alters when he discovers that Quilla June has not told her elders about their liaison in the boiler and that she shares his hatred for the sclerotic life in the downunder. With her assistance, Vic fights his way out of the trap and reclaims his confiscated weapons. Then, like a latter-day Bonnie and Clyde, they murder many of their pursuers— Quilla June even kills her own father, although Vic spoils her shot when she tries to do the same to her mother—and they make their way back to the surface.

Blood is still waiting for Vic, even though a week has passed and he is close to death. Quilla June wants to flee the area immediately and insists that the dog will be all right, but Vic knows better: "I couldn't make it alone out there without him. I knew it. If I loved her. She asked me, in the boiler, do you know what love is?" (93). He has to make the most important choice of his life—one reminiscent of Tom Godwin's "The Cold Equations" (1954)—and in one of the most infamous endings in postapocalyptic fiction, he kills her to feed Blood. Vic's ultimate answer to Quilla June's question is unequivocal: "A boy loves his dog" (94).

The journey that Vic takes is a descent from one circle of hell into another, and then a return to the infernal status quo. He is like Orpheus, even if he is motivated by a peculiarly conflicted blend of love and hate for Quilla June. He enters the underworld to attain the object of his desire (and it should be noted that she is already metaphorically dead to him when he does so), only to lose her at the end by looking back (in this case to his relationship with Blood). (For a detailed discussion of other mythic resonances in Ellison's work, see Francavilla.)

In contrast, the boy and the man in *The Road* make a linear journey southward through a hellish landscape. Their episodic quest has a less complex plot than that of Ellison's novella. We are introduced to them when they are already on their way, moving across a landscape defined by "nights dark beyond darkness and the days more gray each one that what had gone before. Like the onset of some cold glaucoma dimming away the world" (3). All their possessions are carried in knapsacks on their backs or pushed along in a shopping cart with a crooked wheel. Hardly any food is to be had: the man finds what may be the last can of Coca-Cola in the world and lets the boy drink it; in the mountains, they find a small colony of morel mushrooms, the only nonhuman life described in the book apart from a single dog.

The people they encounter chart an ever-downward decline. While hiding from a band of armed men who have a truck and the remnants of biohazard protection, they are discovered by one of the militia, and, after a standoff, the "roadrat" grabs the boy. The father shoots the intruder in the head. When the bandits with the truck have moved on, the father returns to discover that the others have eaten the body of their comrade. The next sizable group of marauders from which the boy and his father hide are even more degenerate than the roadrats with the truck. Their wagons are drawn by human beings, while enslaved women and catamites follow behind. Some of the individuals the man and boy encounter are less of a threat, but this is because these people are in worse situations than themselves: a dying man who has been struck by lightning, a very old man who cannot remember when he last ate.

Things continue to get worse. In the later stages of the novel, there are no large bands to contend with, only individuals or small groups of scavengers whose level of threat depends on whether they can trump the father's revolver, which contains only a single live round and piece of wood whittled into shape to resemble another. In this case, the cold equation is whether the risk of a quick death outweighs the inevitability of a slow one.

The world of *The Road* is even more unforgiving than that of *A Boy and His Dog*, and the man and boy take none of Vic and Blood's pleasure in their hunting. For Ellison's characters, it is still possible for the fittest of their generation to survive, to eat and to copulate, even if there may be nothing left for their descendants, if they have any. McCarthy describes the equivalent situation in his vision:

> By then all stores of food had given out and murder was everywhere upon the land. The world soon to be largely populated by men who would eat your children in front of your eyes and the cities themselves held by cores of blackened looters who tunneled among the ruins and crawled from the rubble white of tooth and eye carrying charred and anonymous tins of food in nylon nets like shoppers in the commissaries of hell. (152)

By the climax of *The Road*, the story bears more resemblance to "I Have No Mouth," Ellison's surreal postapocalyptic vision of hell in which, 109 years after a third world war in which rival automated defense systems united to destroy humanity, the only five survivors are continuously tortured by the gestalt supercomputer called AM:

"At first it meant Allied Mastercomputer, and then it meant Adaptive Manipulator, and later on it developed sentience and linked itself up and they called it an Aggressive Menace, but by then it was too late, and finally it called *itself* AM, emerging intelligence, and what it meant was I am . . . *cogito ergo sum* . . . I think, therefore I am." (*Essential Ellison* 170)

The narrator of this short story is Ted, who describes himself as the only one of the five survivors who has not been altered by AM, who keeps the human beings alive for its sadistic entertainment. Ted believes that the other four envy him because of this, but it becomes clear that he is an unreliable narrator and that his feelings are symptomatic of paranoid delusions. AM is the one who truly hates and envies its human playthings because it is tortured by its inability to break its programming, to ever become truly creative or free. (It is ironic that Ellison has chosen to play the voice of AM in both computer game and radio adaptations of the story.)

If *The Road* seems to be a vision of a world that God has abandoned, then "I Have No Mouth" describes one controlled by a sadistic artificial deity. Ted and his companions are trapped inside the enormous machine and denied access to the blasted surface. AM prevents them from commiting suicide and prolongs their lives indefinitely. Like the father and son in *The Road*, the humans are constantly on the verge of starvation. AM tells them that there are preserved cans of food a great distance away, and they begin a terrible journey in the hope that they will find something better than the revolting "manna" the supercomputer allows them. Throughout their passage they are tortured repeatedly, but they do eventually reach their destination, only to discover that, while the food is there, AM has cruelly not provided any means of opening the cans.

When the protagonists of *The Road* finally reach their destination, they too are disappointed: there is nothing but a gray beach, a leaden sea, and smog across the horizon. Things are no better there than anywhere else they have been, and the struggle for survival must continue, but the boy falls ill and they nearly lose their pathetically few possessions to a thief. Like Ted and his companions, they have no choice but to carry on down the route, even if the situation seems hopeless.

It is at this point that the endings of Ellison's and McCarthy's stories appear to offer salient contrasts, which will be considered here in turn. Even as two of his companions are driven to turn on each other in impotent rage, Ted experiences a moment of clarity: AM prevents them from killing themselves, but not from hurting each other. In an ambiguous act that seems more like one of mercy than spite toward the supercomputer, he and the female of the group kill the others, and then Ted kills her; "I could not read meaning into her expression, the pain had been too great, had contorted her face; but it *might* have been thank you. It's possible. Please" (*Essential Ellison* 179). In *The Road*, the man, who is already sick, is injured in a skirmish. He recovers only enough to see the boy farther down the highway before he finally dies. Ted releases his companions by murdering them, but the furious AM changes him into a "a great soft jelly thing," while leaving his mind intact. He cannot harm himself, only suffer his tormentor's revenge for eternity. The story's title becomes its grim punch line.

In contrast, the father in *The Road* achieves a qualified redemption by sacrificing himself to save his son, although he does not live to see it. The boy stays with his father's body for three days until he returns to the highway. Another man now approaches him but does not beg or threaten him. It seems that he has finally found more "good guys," and he is taken in by the man's family. The question in any reader's mind must be: For how long will the boy be safe?

At this point, readers could be forgiven for wondering if the kind of deeply pessimistic philosophy discussed by Thomas Ligotti in *The Conspiracy Against the Human Race* is all that there is left to resort to, that it might have been better to have never been. Consider this passage from *The Road*:

> We're survivors he told her across the flame of the lamp.
> Survivors? She said.
> Yes.
> What in God's name are you talking about? We're not survivors. We're the walking dead in a horror film. (47)

Is extinction preferable to carrying on in a living hell? Poor, benighted Ted would say so, but we cannot take him at his word when he says, "AM has won, simply . . . he has taken his revenge" (180), because the remnants of his humanity allowed him to defy the apparently all-powerful false god of the supercomputer. The father in *The Road* does the same by ensuring his son's survival for as long as he can, and, in doing so, he passes on the torch. Even Vic and Blood still have and show their capacity for a kind of love, even if it is only for each other. In all these examples, it is clear that, even in the face of doomsday, it is better to have been and done something than never to have gone through the journey, however terrible it may have been.

Works Cited

Aldiss, Brian W. *Billion Year Spree: The History of Science Fiction*. London: Weidenfeld & Nicolson, 1973.

Cheuse, Alan. "Brilliant Writing Makes McCarthy's Dark Tale Shine." *Chicago Tribune* 24 Sept. 2006.

Ellison, Harlan. *The Essential Ellison: A Thirty-five Year Retrospective*. 1987. Ed. Terry Dowling, with Richard Delap and Gil Lamont. Beverly Hills, CA: Morpheus International, 1998.

_____. *Vic and Blood*. New York: E-Reads, 2009.

Francavilla, Joseph. "Mythic Hells in Harlan Ellison's Science Fiction." *Phoenix from the Ashes: The Literature of the Remade World*. Ed. Carl B. Yoke. Westport, CT: Greenwood Press, 1987.

Ligotti, Thomas. *The Conspiracy Against the Human Race: A Contrivance of Horror*. New York: Hippocampus Press, 2010.

McCarthy, Cormac. *Blood Meridian*. 1985. London: Picador, 2010.

_____. *Outer Dark*. 1968. London: Picador, 1994.

_____. *The Road*. London: Picador, 2006.

Parrinder, Patrick. "Ruined Futures." *On Modern British Fiction*. Ed. Zachary Leader. New York: Oxford UP, 2002.
Platt, Charles. "Harlan Ellison." *Who Writes Science Fiction?* Manchester, England: Savoy Books, 1980.
Weil, Ellen, and Gary K. Wolfe. *Harlan Ellison: The Edge of Forever*. Columbus: Ohio State UP, 2002.

Harlan Ellison's Critical Reception
Darren Harris-Fain

Harlan Ellison's beginnings as an author would not suggest the type of literary career that would lead to a great deal of critical attention. Ellison was born in 1934, and his youthful reading involved mostly comic books and various types of genre fiction published in the pulp and popular magazines of the late 1930s and the 1940s. He was active in science fiction fandom as a teenager and began writing for fan magazines in the early 1950s. As a child he had published a fantastic adventure tale in a newspaper in his native Cleveland, and in his late adolescence, as a student at Ohio State University, he endeavored to produce similar material in a creative-writing class. His instructor was not impressed, going so far as to tell Ellison he had no talent, and, as Ellison has frequently told the tale, his response to the professor led to his expulsion from the university. It says something about Ellison's belief in his own talent that he did not give up at this point; it also says something about the author that, according to Ellison, once he became a professional writer he sent the professor a copy of everything he ever published until the professor passed away. This would have involved a lot of mailing: Ellison has written well over one thousand short stories, a handful of novels, hundreds of essays and other nonfiction pieces, comic books, and work for television and motion pictures. By Ellison's count, he has published more than seventy-five books.

The magazines in which Ellison began his career during the late 1950s often featured letters from readers, but apart from any comments that the magazines' audience may have made about Ellison's fiction and apart from the kinds of commentary typical of fanzines, Ellison's work received no critical notice during this period, either from academic scholars or from newspaper and magazine reviewers. Mainstream literary critics would scarcely deign to review paperback originals (never mind those with titles like *Rumble* or *Sex Gang*), let alone short stories published in magazines with titles such as *Amazing Sto-*

ries, Fantastic Universe, The Gent, Guilty, Infinity Science Fiction, Rogue, Science-Fantasy, Science Fiction Adventures, Space Travel, Super-Science Fiction, and *Trapped*, in all of which Ellison published in the second half of the 1950s.

After this initial period of Ellison's career he moved from New York to Chicago, where he edited men's magazines in addition to writing for them. He continued to publish science fiction and fantasy short stories, but he remained interested in realism as well, and this period marks a turn from the more salacious or sensational stories of crime and desperation he had written in the 1950s to stories whose concerns reflected the influence of contemporary issues such as the civil rights movement and the challenges of urban life. As Gary K. Wolfe argues in his essay "Rogue Knight: Harlan Ellison in the Men's Magazines" (1988-89), which was later incorporated into Wolfe and Ellen Weil's book *Harlan Ellison: The Edge of Forever* (2002), the freedom Ellison enjoyed in his association with magazines such as *Rogue* and *Knight*, conjoined with his growing political and social consciousness, led to an increase in the sophistication and maturity of Ellison's fiction.

If any book of Ellison's marks this transition, it is *Gentleman Junkie, and Other Stories of the Hung-Up Generation* (1961)—Ellison's first publication, in a short but productive five years, to garner any significant critical response—and it came from an unlikely quarter. Between 1957 and 1962 the writer and wit Dorothy Parker served as book critic for *Esquire*, and toward the end of her tenure with the magazine she defied contemporary critical convention and chose to review a paperback original. She was particularly impressed with Ellison's story "Daniel White for the Greater Good," which she described as "without exception the best presentation I have ever seen of present racial conditions in the South and of those who try to alleviate them. I cannot recommend it too vehemently." In doing so, Parker became the first critic to identify one of Ellison's major concerns as a writer: an interest in social and political concerns and a clear liberal sensibility. She also praised the quality of the other stories in the collection and described

Ellison as "a good, clean, honest writer, putting down what he has seen and known and no sensationalism about it." This is no mean praise, especially from a critic who once said of another author's book, "This is not a novel to be tossed aside lightly. It should be thrown with great force."

Ellison moved to Hollywood in the early 1960s, the decade that produced most of his work for the big and small screens, and this is also the decade in which three of the stories for which Ellison is best known were produced: the short stories "'Repent, Harlequin!' Said the Ticktockman" (1965) and "I Have No Mouth, and I Must Scream" (1967), and the novella *A Boy and His Dog* (1969).

"'Repent, Harlequin!' Said the Ticktockman" is a futuristic dystopian story—that is, a story of a future in which things have gone horribly wrong. In this respect, Ellison is working within a science fiction tradition that includes classic literary works such as Aldous Huxley's *Brave New World* (1932) and George Orwell's *Nineteen Eighty-Four* (1949), the latter of which provides a rough template for this story of an individual's efforts to undermine a totalitarian government. However, Ellison plays with the conventions of the dystopian story in several ways. First, the premise is somewhat absurd: a government obsessed with efficiency enforces punctuality on the populace through the office of the Master Timekeeper, nicknamed the Ticktockman. Those who fail to abide by his temporal strictures have their lives correspondingly shortened—an hour for an hour, if not a tooth for a tooth. Into this highly regulated world comes a figure known as the Harlequin, who engages in fanciful acts of benign terrorism in an effort to free his fellow citizens from their enslavement to the clock, and by extension to the government.

Ellison also defies convention with his second "classic" short story, "I Have No Mouth, and I Must Scream." The premise is again familiar to readers of science fiction, in this case a variation of the *Frankenstein* motif: humans create a monster that turns on them. Here the monster is AM, a massive computer designed to aid the human race in its internecine wars but that ultimately gains self-awareness and kills all but a handful of people, whom it artificially keeps alive in order to torture them for untold ages. It is a horrifying story, full of physical and psychological violence, and the explicitness of the story is part of what marks it as a departure from typical American science fiction prior to its time. Also, as in "'Repent, Harlequin!' Said the Ticktockman," Ellison employs literary techniques similar to those used by modernist writers of the first half of the twentieth century but mostly unfamiliar to science fiction, among them an unreliable narrator, allusion, and fragmentation.

Ellison's next major science fiction story, and the third of the three for which he is best known, came in 1969. The novella *A Boy and His Dog* is a postapocalyptic story in which the title characters are a young man named Vic and his intelligent, telepathic canine companion, Blood. Vic and Blood scavenge the wasteland that is their world, looking for food and, in Vic's case, sex and trying to survive the violence that surrounds them. Vic is lured by a young woman named Quilla June to an underground world in which the citizens have created a simulacrum of a genteel middle-American way of life, and at first this world seems utopian: he does not have to worry about his safety, and the sex promises to be abundant. However, all is not as it seems here, and Vic also feels a bond with Blood, whom he left on the surface. In an ending that some readers have hailed as an example of gritty realism within the premises of the futuristic setting, similar to Tom Godwin's classic science fiction story "The Cold Equations" (1954), and others have decried as horrifying, Vic is forced to choose between Blood and Quilla June.

In addition to these stories and other examples of Ellison's work covered in wide-ranging books such as George Edgar Slusser's short study *Harlan Ellison: Unrepentant Harlequin* (1977) and Weil and Wolfe's more comprehensive *Harlan Ellison: The Edge of Forever*, among Ellison's other stories that have received critical attention are several published in the 1970s, specifically "The Deathbird" (1973), "Adrift Just Off the Islets of Langerhans: Latitude 38° 54′ N, Longitude 77° 00′ 13″ W" (1974), and "Jeffty Is Five" (1977).

"The Deathbird" is a postmodern mélange that combines fiction and nonfiction, a story of a man's search for an ultimately disappointing God with Ellison's accounts of the deaths of loved ones. It also includes other postmodern techniques, such as self-referentiality. "Adrift Just Off the Islets of Langerhans" also employs postmodernism, here with its elevation of a figure from popular culture—Larry Talbot, the Wolfman of the classic Universal horror films—in an epic quest for his own soul. Popular culture also plays an important role in "Jeffty Is Five," a haunting story about a boy who does not grow up and how the narrator revisits his own youth through Jeffty's fantastic ability to preserve the past prior to the story's tragic ending.

Although Ellison has not been given the same amount of critical attention as many authors of literary fiction or even some of his science fiction and fantasy contemporaries, such as Philip K. Dick or Ursula K. Le Guin, the critical response to Ellison's fiction has been diverse, focusing—with the exception of Weil and Wolfe's book, which covers every facet of his career—primarily on his fantastic fiction rather than on his realistic stories or his nonfiction.

Understandably, much of the criticism of Ellison's science fiction has focused on the roles that technology plays in human society and the effects of technology on human beings. Two critics have compared and contrasted Ellison's depiction of an intelligent, self-aware computer in "I Have No Mouth, and I Must Scream" to similar depictions by other science fiction writers: John B. Ower compares Ellison's AM to HAL from Arthur C. Clarke's novel *2001: A Space Odyssey* (1968) in "Manacle-Forged Minds: Two Images of the Computer in Science Fiction" (1974), and C. W. Sullivan III compares AM to Mike from Robert A. Heinlein's novel *The Moon Is a Harsh Mistress* (1966) in "Harlan Ellison and Robert A. Heinlein: The Paradigm Makers" (1983). Heinlein's Mike is eminently beneficent, a tribute to the better qualities of the humanity that created him. Clarke's murderous HAL would seem more in line with Ellison's malicious AM, yet Clarke's novel does not seem to indict technology as a potentially malevolent force in the same way that Ellison's story does. Another critic, Joann P. Cobb, argues in her 1983 essay "Medium and Message in Ellison's 'I Have No Mouth, and I Must Scream'" that in fact this is the major point of the story, saying that it "illustrates the surrender of human purpose and value that is inherent in contemporary attitudes toward technological progress" (159). Ower agrees with this assessment, seeing both "I Have No Mouth, and I Must Scream" and *2001: A Space Odyssey* as cautionary tales about the perils of creating machines whose capabilities exceed those of human beings. Another analysis of Ellison's treatment of technology as a theme is Leonard Heldreth's "Clockwork Reels: Mechanized Environments in Science Fiction Films" (1983), in which he refers to Ellison's *A Boy and His Dog* in analyzing the film adaptation.

Yet perhaps the greatest amount of critical attention paid to Ellison has devoted itself to Ellison's use of mythological materials and themes as well as religious issues and concerns. In "Mythic Hells in Harlan Ellison's Science Fiction" (1987) Joseph Francavilla explores the use of mythic imagery and allusion, particularly relating to the infernal, while Philip M. Rubens explores the theme of the journey to hell in his essay "Descents into Private Hells: Harlan Ellison's 'Psy-Fi'" (1979; reprinted in this volume). John Crow and Richard Erlich also analyze Ellison's use of the mythic journey, along with other folkloric elements, in "Mythic Patterns in *A Boy and His Dog*" (1977; reprinted in this volume). While Francavilla and Rubens consider multiple examples of this theme in several of Ellison's fantasy and science fiction stories, other critics have focused on the hellish imagery and religious allusions in "I Have No Mouth, and I Must Scream"—among them Charles J. Brady in "The Computer as a Symbol of God: Ellison's Macabre Exodus" (1976; reprinted in this volume), Carol D. Stevens in "The Short Fiction of Harlan Ellison" (1979), Ower in "Manacle-Forged Minds," and Willis E. McNelly in his foreword to the story in the anthology *The Mirror of Infinity* (1970).

Brady, who compares AM to the godlike computer in Michael

Fayette's "The Monster in the Clearing" (1971), believes that Ted's hatred toward the theologized AM reflects Ellison's hatred toward God. Some reviewers have made similar observations about his story "The Deathbird." A more nuanced study of the latter story can be found in "Religious Imagination and Imagined Religion" (1985), by Adam J. Frisch and Joseph Martos, who explore Ellison's inversion of the traditional Judeo-Christian mythos. Similarly, in "The Rejection of Traditional Theism in Feminist Theology and Science Fiction" (1983) Robert G. Pielke asserts that in "The Deathbird" Ellison critiques religious belief as culturally derived rather than presenting a simplistic argument against God per se.

In my own essay "Created in the Image of God: The Narrator and the Computer in Harlan Ellison's 'I Have No Mouth, and I Must Scream'" (1991; reprinted in this volume), I build on what other critics have said about the religious imagery in the story and argue that Ted, the narrator of the story, routinely speaks of the computer as if it were a deranged God figure—a view of AM supported by numerous allusions throughout the story. However, drawing upon both Ellison's statements about the story and his views on humanity and religion, I argue that the truly divine figure here is Ted himself. What makes Ted divine, I assert in the essay, is his self-sacrifice, how he manages to resist his natural selfishness and perform an act that he hopes will result in release for his companions yet ends up with disastrous consequences for himself.

Likewise, other critics have written about Ellison's conflicted treatment of human nature and what Ellison has called his love-hate relationship with the human race. In several essays, numerous interviews, and multiple speeches at conventions and college campuses, Ellison has excoriated individuals and groups alike for attitudes and behaviors he deems unworthy of humanity's better possibilities. He often claims that people have great potential, and while some may indeed achieve great things, the masses fall disappointingly short. This dichotomy, in fact, provides one of the major themes of Slusser's short study *Harlan Ellison: Unrepentant Harlequin*, as well as the focus of Oscar De Los

Santos's essay "Clogging Up the (In)Human Works: Harlan Ellison's Apocalyptic Postmodern Visions" (1999; reprinted in this volume), which discusses different examples of Ellison's fiction and nonfiction.

Some critics, following Dorothy Parker's lead, have commented on the strain of social criticism found in much of Ellison's work. Both Slusser in *Harlan Ellison: Unrepentant Harlequin* and Weil and Wolfe in *Harlan Ellison: The Edge of Forever* devote considerable attention to this topic, and two critics have analyzed the novella *A Boy and His Dog* in this light as well. Michael Clark argues that *A Boy and His Dog* critiques patriarchal power in his essay "The Future of History: Violence and the Feminine in Contemporary Science Fiction" (1985), and in *Science Fiction and the New Dark Age* (1976) Harold L. Berger asserts that a major point of the novella is its depiction of conflict between different generations. Likewise, Richard D. Erlich, in "Trapped in the Bureaucratic Pinball Machine: A Vision of Dystopia in the Twentieth Century" (1979), provides an analysis of civil disobedience in Ellison's work, focusing on "'Repent, Harlequin!' Said the Ticktockman."

Given Ellison's many pronouncements in support of feminism, it is ironic that he has been attacked for his depictions of women. Among the works analyzed in Carolyn Wendell's 1979 essay "The Alien Species: A Study of Women Characters in the Nebula Award Winners, 1965-1973" are "'Repent, Harlequin!' Said the Ticktockman" and *A Boy and His Dog*, and in both, Wendell says, Ellison's female characters are presented stereotypically. *A Boy and His Dog* has come in for criticism as well for its purported misogyny. However, science fiction writer and critic Joanna Russ, in her essay "*A Boy and His Dog:* The Final Solution" (1975), is careful to distinguish the story from its film adaptation, which she argues is horrifyingly misogynistic, and in "The Future of History" Clark presents a complex analysis, heavily rooted in literary and cultural theory, of the story's treatment of gender, arguing that the violence against women depicted in the story actually serves as an indictment of the dangers women face in contemporary society rather than a glorification of masculine power and privilege.

While Ellison holds a place in the history of science fiction and fantasy for introducing literary techniques that were previously seldom seen in these genres, more attention has been given to his themes than to his techniques. Nonetheless, some critics have addressed the technical aspects of Ellison's work. For instance, in "Harlan Ellison's Use of the Narrator's Voice" (1983), Joseph F. Patrouch, Jr., explores Ellison's use of first-person narrators and compares this to Ellison's own distinctive writing style in his nonfiction. The result, Patrouch says, is that Ellison's forceful personality has seeped into the voices of his fictional narrators. Another essay by Patrouch, "Harlan Ellison and the Formula Story" (1978), investigates how Ellison both employs genre formulas and subverts them in various ways. Patrouch also analyzes Ellison's career chronologically, investigating how his work became increasingly complex as he matured as a writer. Similarly, McNelly discusses Ellison's unconventional typography in his foreword to "I Have No Mouth, and I Must Scream."

In addition to exploring the topics promised in the title of his essay "The Heroic and Mock-Heroic in Harlan Ellison's 'Harlequin'" (1985), Stephen Adams studies Ellison's use of the trickster figure in "'Repent, Harlequin!' Said the Ticktockman." In doing so, Adams explores Ellison's use of humor; this is also a topic in Hazel Beasley Pierce's comments in her 1983 book *A Literary Symbiosis: Science Fiction/Fantasy Mystery* on a rarely discussed Ellison story, "Santa Claus vs. S.P.I.D.E.R." (1969), which she describes as an example of political satire, working in part through a parody of James Bond.

In addition to such scholarly attention, as well as being the subject of a book-length bibliography by Leslie Kay Swigart in 1973, Ellison has received numerous awards from the science fiction, fantasy, horror, and crime writing communities. His fiction has been honored with the Hugo Award, given by the World Science Fiction Society at its annual convention (Worldcon), seven times: for "'Repent, Harlequin!' Said the Ticktockman," "I Have No Mouth, and I Must Scream," "The Beast That Shouted Love at the Heart of the World" (1968), "The

Deathbird," "Adrift Just Off the Islets of Langerhans," "Jeffty Is Five," and "Paladin of the Lost Hour" (1985). He also received a Hugo Award for his teleplay for the *Star Trek* episode "The City on the Edge of Forever" (1967), and half a Hugo for writing the original material on which the 1975 film version of *A Boy and His Dog* was based. "'Repent, Harlequin!' Said the Ticktockman" and "Jeffty Is Five" also received the Nebula Award, given by the Science Fiction Writers of America, as did *A Boy and His Dog*. His work has also received the Bram Stoker Award from the Horror Writers of America and the Edgar Allan Poe Award from the Mystery Writers of America, and four of his teleplays have received recognition from the Writers Guild of America. Ellison's stories have been widely anthologized and are frequently taught in high schools, colleges, and universities. However, his mainstream work has sometimes been reviewed harshly, and he has tended to fare better in the world of genre fiction.

The 1970s saw a number of tributes to Ellison from the science fiction and fantasy community. His friend and fellow writer Robert Silverberg published an appreciation of Ellison titled "Sounding Brass, Tinkling Cymbal" in the British science fiction journal *Foundation* in 1975, and he also contributed an appreciation to a July 1977 special issue of the *Magazine of Fantasy and Science Fiction* devoted to Ellison, which included other tributes as well. Byron Preiss solicited comics artists to visualize a selection of Ellison's stories in *The Illustrated Harlan Ellison* (1978), and that year also saw a collection of essays by Ellison and others titled *The Book of Ellison*, edited by Andrew Porter. *The Fantasies of Harlan Ellison* (1979) was also a retrospective collection of sorts.

Yet despite his continued involvement with the science fiction and fantasy communities, Ellison has long tried to distance himself from the field, arguing at various times that he is not a science fiction writer because he also writes other kinds of fiction and nonfiction as well; that he writes "speculative fiction" rather than science fiction or fantasy (the term is Heinlein's, and would later be used by Canadian author Margaret Atwood in reference to her science fiction novels); that he is a writer of "magic realism," appropriating a term that had been applied to Latin American authors of the 1960s and 1970s, such as Gabriel García Márquez and Julio Cortázar, who blend realism and the fantastic; and that he is simply an author and needs no other labels. Behind these protestations, aside from a desire for accuracy, has been Ellison's concern about being labeled as a genre writer and thus dismissed as a serious author.

By the 1980s, Ellison had settled into a pattern of writing mostly fantastic short fiction, with occasional forays into realism and nonfiction, and while he continued to sell stories, essays, and books and to draw large audiences at his many public appearances, and while he continued to garner attention from book critics and literary scholars, his reputation leveled off from the peak it had reached in the late 1960s. Certainly collections such as *Shatterday* (1980) showed an author who had managed to merge a high degree of literary craft with the concerns of genre fiction, but despite his efforts he never really broke free from the genre ghetto. He would be written about in reference works devoted to science fiction and fantasy authors, but more general reference works about literature would almost always ignore him; if one found an author with his surname in such works, it was usually Ralph Ellison, not Harlan. This situation may or may not have been exacerbated by the admiration expressed for Ellison's work in 1982 by America's best-selling author at the time, Stephen King, who penned a glowing introduction for Ellison's 1982 collection *Stalking the Nightmare* and also praised Ellison in his own nonfiction book about horror, *Danse Macabre* (1981).

Another tribute volume appeared in 1987, *The Essential Ellison: A Thirty-five Year Retrospective*, which included more than one thousand pages of the author's fiction and nonfiction (it would be expanded and updated in 2001 with *The Essential Ellison: A Fifty Year Retrospective*). However, not everyone was publishing positive things about the author in 1987. After editing the science fiction anthologies *Dan-*

gerous Visions in 1967 and *Again, Dangerous Visions* in 1972, Ellison had been promising a third volume and had solicited stories from several authors, but his inability to produce *The Last Dangerous Visions* alienated some people in the science fiction field, and one of these, the British author Christopher Priest, published a savage attack on Ellison in 1987 titled *The Book on the Edge of Forever.*

In the late 1980s and the 1990s it seemed as if Ellison was on the verge of the respect and recognition from the wider literary world that he had long sought. In 1991 the Book-of-the-Month Club issued a paperback omnibus volume titled *Dreams with Sharp Teeth* that gathered three of Ellison's earlier collections, *I Have No Mouth and I Must Scream* (1967), *Deathbird Stories* (1975), and *Shatterday*, and he continued to be studied by science fiction and fantasy scholars. Perhaps the closest Ellison has come to acceptance within the mainstream of American literary fiction came with the inclusion of his short story "The Man Who Rowed Christopher Columbus Ashore," first published in *Omni*, in the 1993 volume of *The Best American Short Stories*, which was edited by respected literary author Louise Erdrich. A similar honor came with the selection of "The Whimper of Whipped Dogs" (1973) for *The Best American Mystery Stories of the Century* (2000), edited by mystery writer Tony Hillerman.

In 1996 the publisher White Wolf announced an ambitious project: the publication of Ellison's collected works in omnibus volumes. However, only four volumes, titled *Edgeworks*, appeared before the project came to an end. Nonetheless, Ellison received some attention beyond the science fiction and fantasy field in the late 1990s and into the twenty-first century. For instance, he was invited to write an opinion piece by *Newsweek* in response to the Heaven's Gate cult mass suicide in the spring of 1997, and in 2003 he wrote the introduction for the Modern Library edition of *Jacque Futrelle's "The Thinking Machine": The Enigmatic Problems of Prof. Augustus S. F. X. Van Dusen, Ph.D., LL.D., F.R.S., M.D., M.D.S.* His story "Goodbye to All That" was published in *McSweeney's Mammoth Treasury of Thrilling Tales*

(2002), edited by the literary author Michael Chabon, and his Jewish-themed science fiction story "Go Toward the Light" was featured on National Public Radio's *Hanukkah Lights* holiday special in 2004. Also, between 2001 and 2005 four of Ellison's stories—"Jeffty Is Five," "I Have No Mouth, and I Must Scream," *A Boy and His Dog*, and "'Repent, Harlequin!' Said the Ticktockman"—were featured along with reprinted criticism in four separate volumes of the Gale reference series Short Stories for Students. "I Have No Mouth, and I Must Scream" was also reprinted in *American Fantastic Tales: Terror and the Uncanny* (2009), a volume in the prestigious Library of America series.

Finally, Ellison was the subject of a feature-length documentary titled *Dreams with Sharp Teeth*, released in 2008, which included admiring commentary from writers such as Neil Gaiman as well as from actor and comedian Robin Williams, a friend of Ellison. The picture of Ellison late in life and toward the end of his career in *Dreams with Sharp Teeth* is that of an author cognizant of the fact that his reach has exceeded his grasp. He is proud of his many accomplishments, at once unapologetic about his brash personality and aware that for some this may have adversely affected their opinion of him, and wistful that either fate or his own inclinations did not allow him to achieve a greater status as a writer than he has achieved.

Nor is it easy to predict how posterity will view Harlan Ellison. Contemporary reviewers, once his work began to come to their attention, have tended either to praise it for its imagination, its emotional intensity, and its stylistic verve or to condemn it as pretentious, tendentious, and excessively suffused with Ellison's forceful personality. Academic critics and historians, with the exception of Weil and Wolfe, have tended to focus on his science fiction and fantasy, by and large ignoring his many realistic short works and his prolific nonfiction output. There is also the issue of the sheer abundance of his writing; much of it, especially early in his career, was written quickly and for money and is of little merit except for purposes of comparison to his other works. Appropriately enough for a writer best known for his visions of times yet to come, only the future will tell whether any of Ellison's work will continue to be read and studied.

Works Cited

Adams, Stephen. "The Heroic and Mock-Heroic in Harlan Ellison's 'Harlequin.'" *Extrapolation* 26 (1985): 285-89.
Berger, Harold L. *Science Fiction and the New Dark Age*. Bowling Green, OH: Bowling Green U Popular P, 1976.
Brady, Charles J. "The Computer as a Symbol of God: Ellison's Macabre Exodus." *Journal of General Education* 28 (1976): 55-62.
Clark, Michael. "The Future of History: Violence and the Feminine in Contemporary Science Fiction." *American Studies in Translation*. Ed. David E. Nye and Christen Kold Thomsen. Odense, Denmark: Odense UP, 1985. 235-58.
Cobb, Joann P. "Medium and Message in Ellison's 'I Have No Mouth, and I Must Scream.'" *The Intersection of Science Fiction and Philosophy: Critical Studies*. Ed. Robert E. Myers. Westport, CT: Greenwood Press, 1983.
Crow, John, and Richard Erlich. "Mythic Patterns in Ellison's *A Boy and His Dog*." *Extrapolation* 18.2 (May 1977): 162-66.
De Los Santos, Oscar. "Clogging Up the (In)Human Works: Harlan Ellison's Apocalyptic Postmodern Visions." *Extrapolation* 40.1 (Spring 1999): 5-20.
Erlich, Richard D. "Trapped in the Bureaucratic Pinball Machine: A Vision of Dystopia in the Twentieth Century." *Selected Proceedings of the 1978 Science Fiction Research Association National Conference*. Ed. Thomas J. Remington. Cedar Falls: University of Northern Iowa, 1979. 30-44.
Francavilla, Joseph. "The Concept of the Divided Self in Harlan Ellison's 'I Have No Mouth and I Must Scream' and 'Shatterday.'" *Journal of the Fantastic in the Arts* 6.2-3 (1994): 107-25.
_____. "Mythic Hells in Harlan Ellison's Science Fiction." *Phoenix from the Ashes: The Literature of the Remade World*. Ed. Carl B. Yoke. Westport, CT: Greenwood Press, 1987. 157-64.
Frisch, Adam J., and Joseph Martos. "Religious Imagination and Imagined Religion." *The Transcendent Adventure: Studies of Religion in Science Fiction/Fantasy*. Ed. Robert Reilly. Westport, CT: Greenwood Press, 1985.
Harris-Fain, Darren. "Created in the Image of God: The Narrator and the Computer in Harlan Ellison's 'I Have No Mouth, and I Must Scream.'" *Extrapolation* 32.2 (1991): 143-55.
Heldreth, Leonard. "Clockwork Reels: Mechanized Environments in Science Fiction Films." *Clockwork Worlds: Mechanized Environments in SF*. Ed. Richard D. Erlich and Thomas P. Dunn. Westport, CT: Greenwood Press, 1983. 213-34.
King, Stephen. *Danse Macabre*. New York: Everest House, 1981.

McNelly, Willis E. Foreword. "I Have No Mouth, and I Must Scream." By Harlan Ellison. *The Mirror of Infinity: A Critics' Anthology of Science Fiction*. Ed. Robert Silverberg. New York: Harper & Row, 1970. 246-50.

Ower, John B. "Manacle-Forged Minds: Two Images of the Computer in Science Fiction." *Diogenes* 85 (1974): 47-61.

Parker, Dorothy. Rev. of *Gentleman Junkie, and Other Stories of the Hung-Up Generation*, by Harlan Ellison. *Esquire* Jan. 1962. Rpt. in "Book Reviews." *Gentleman Junkie, and Other Stories of the Hung-Up Generation*. By Harlan Ellison. New York: Pyramid Books, 1975. 1.

Patrouch, Joseph F., Jr. "Harlan Ellison and the Formula Story." *The Book of Ellison*. Ed. Andrew Porter. New York: Algol Press, 1978. 45-64.

_____. "Harlan Ellison's Use of the Narrator's Voice." *Patterns of the Fantastic*. Ed. Donald M. Hassler. Mercer Island, WA: Starmont House, 1983. 63-66.

Pielke, Robert G. "The Rejection of Traditional Theism in Feminist Theology and Science Fiction." *The Intersection of Science Fiction and Philosophy: Critical Studies*. Ed. Robert E. Myers. Westport, CT: Greenwood Press, 1983.

Pierce, Hazel Beasley. *A Literary Symbiosis: Science Fiction/Fantasy Mystery*. Westport, CT: Greenwood Press, 1983.

Porter, Andrew, ed. *The Book of Ellison*. New York: Algol Press, 1978.

Priest, Christopher. *The Book on the Edge of Forever: An Enquiry into the Nonappearance of Harlan Ellison's "The Last Dangerous Visions."* 1987. Seattle: Fantagraphics Books, 1994.

Rubens, Philip M. "Descents into Private Hells: Harlan Ellison's 'Psy-Fi.'" *Extrapolation* 20.4 (Winter 1979): 378-85.

Russ, Joanna. "*A Boy and His Dog*: The Final Solution." 1975. *To Write Like a Woman: Essays in Feminism and Science Fiction*. Bloomington: Indiana UP, 1995. 65-78.

Silverberg, Robert. "Sounding Brass, Tinkling Cymbal." *Foundation* 7-8 (1975): 6-37.

Slusser, George Edgar. *Harlan Ellison: Unrepentant Harlequin*. San Bernardino, CA: Borgo Press, 1977.

Stevens, Carol D. "The Short Fiction of Harlan Ellison." *Survey of Science Fiction Literature*. Ed. Frank N. Magill. Englewood Cliffs, NJ: Salem Press, 1979. 3:1978-88.

Sullivan, C. W., III. "Harlan Ellison and Robert A. Heinlein: The Paradigm Makers." *Clockwork Worlds: Mechanized Environments in SF*. Ed. Richard D. Erlich and Thomas P. Dunn. Westport, CT: Greenwood Press, 1983. 97-103.

Swigart, Leslie Kay. *Harlan Ellison: A Bibliographical Checklist*. Dallas: Williams, 1973.

Weil, Ellen, and Gary K. Wolfe. *Harlan Ellison: The Edge of Forever*. Columbus: Ohio State UP, 2002.

Wendell, Carolyn. "The Alien Species: A Study of Women Characters in the Nebula Award Winners, 1965-1973." *Extrapolation* 20 (Winter 1979): 343-54.

Wolfe, Gary K. "Rogue Knight: Harlan Ellison in the Men's Magazines." *Foundation* 44 (Winter 1988-89): 26-32.

CRITICAL READINGS

The Annihilation of Time:
Science Fiction

Ellen Weil and Gary K. Wolfe

While Ellison was exploring new narrative forms and voices in magazines like *Knight* and *Rogue*, his once-prolific contributions to the science fiction genre magazines dropped off dramatically, from six in 1959 to only five between 1960 and 1967, then back up to seven in 1968 and nine in 1969. This decade was also marked by evolutionary changes within the science fiction field itself, many of them involving a similar kind of experimentation, and the period has come to be known in SF history as the "New Wave," a somewhat controversial term borrowed from the *nouvelle vague* of French cinema criticism in the early 1960s. The term *New Wave* originally came into widespread use in England and may have been first applied to this movement by author and fan Christopher Priest (Clute and Nicholls 865), although Gary Westfahl has pointed out that as early as 1961 the longtime reviewer for *Astounding Science Fiction*, P. Schuyler Miller, had used the phrase to refer to such British authors as Brian Aldiss, E. C. Tubb, Kenneth Bulmer, and John Brunner (Westfahl 16). By that earlier date, however, none of these authors had written much in the way of the experimental, highly metaphorical stories that later became associated with the term. According to most accounts, the movement began in the leading British SF magazine, *New Worlds*, beginning with the May/June 1964 issue, when Michael Moorcock replaced John Carnell as editor. That now-famous issue featured a manifesto-like editorial by Moorcock, the first part of a serial by J. G. Ballard, and stories by Brian W. Aldiss, John Brunner, and Barrington J. Bayley, along with an appreciative essay by Ballard on experimental American writer William S. Burroughs, whose *Nova Express*, with its wild appropriation of science fiction iconography, appeared that same year.

Like many literary movements in science fiction, such as cyberpunk in the 1980s, the New Wave could almost be defined as consisting of all those authors who denied being part of it. Many of these authors—notably Aldiss, Ballard, and Brunner—had been significant figures in science fiction for years by 1964 and were somewhat chagrined by their association with "the movement." In 1966, Aldiss wrote to American editor Judith Merril that he suspected the New Wave "to be a journalistic invention of yours and Mike Moorcock's, ultimately of no service to any writers willy-nilly involved. . . . I feel I am no part of the New Wave; I was here before 'em, and by God I mean to be here after they've gone (still writing bloody science fiction)!" (Greenland 69). Aldiss's attitude—resisting the pigeonholing implied by a label while continuing to write the very kind of radically experimental fictions that were being used to exemplify the New Wave itself (such as his *Report on Probability A* and *Barefoot in the Head*)—was emblematic of the strongly ambivalent reaction of the science fiction field as a whole to this new phenomenon. Merril, who for years had been championing a more literary and inclusive definition of science fiction in her annual *Year's Best SF* anthologies (selecting pieces by John Steinbeck, John Dos Passos, Shirley Jackson, Bernard Wolfe, even Bertrand Russell and Eugene Ionesco, along with genre SF writers), quickly became the champion of the movement in America, referring to it as "the New Thing" in an August 1966 book review column in the *Magazine of Fantasy and Science Fiction* and later editing the egregiously titled *England Swings SF: Stories of Speculative Fiction* (1968), complete with a cover blurb trumpeting "HERE'S THE NEW WAVE IN SCIENCE FICTION Presented by its foremost advocate" (Merril, front cover). Other established science fiction writers and critics—Isaac Asimov, Lester del Rey, Sam Moskowitz, and others—tended to agree with Jack Williamson's assessment that the New Wave was not only pretentious and obscurantist but "sprang from an ignorance of science and a terror of technology" (313).

Dangerous Visions

Ellison's own skepticism toward the New Wave was expressed in the introduction to his 1969 collection *The Beast That Shouted Love at the Heart of the World*, which included two of the stories that had helped build his reputation as one of the chief American representatives of the movement: the title story and the novella "A Boy and His Dog" (the latter of which even had appeared in *New Worlds*). "For the record," Ellison wrote, ". . . I do not believe there is such a thing as 'New Wave' in speculative fiction. . . . It is a convenient journalese expression for inept critics and voyeur-observers of the passing scene, because they have neither the wit nor the depth to understand that this richness of new voices is *many* waves: each composed of one writer" (4). Only two years earlier, however, Ellison had embraced the term—at least in French—in the anthology that is most often cited as representing the American counterpart to the New Wave, *Dangerous Visions*, which he described as "a thirty-three-story demonstration of 'the new thing'—the *nouvelle vague*, if you will, of speculative writing" (xx). The anthology, Ellison claimed, "was constructed along specific lines of revolution. It was intended to shake things up. It was conceived out of a need for new horizons, new forms, new styles, new challenges in the literature of our times" (*Dangerous Visions* xix).

At some 239,000 words, *Dangerous Visions* was the largest collection of original science fiction stories ever published (though Ellison preferred the term *speculative fiction* in his introduction), and it indeed included stories by Brian Aldiss, J. G. Ballard, John Sladek, Norman Spinrad, and other authors widely associated with the New Wave. Alongside these, however, were tales by some of the most established names in American genre fantasy and science fiction—Lester del Rey (already a vocal opponent of the British movement), Frederik Pohl, Philip José Farmer, Robert Bloch, Fritz Leiber, Poul Anderson, Theodore Sturgeon, Damon Knight—as well as a group of writers of roughly Ellison's own generation including Robert Silverberg, Roger Zelazny, Philip K. Dick, and Samuel R. Delany. It becomes clear in reading these stories that the intention of Ellison in *Dangerous Visions* was not at all what the intention of Moorcock had been in *New Worlds* three years earlier, but it's not quite accurate to say, as Christopher Priest did, that he simply "missed the point" (Greenland 167). Brian Aldiss is closer to the mark in his comment that the controversy generated by the book "is evidence of how cloistered the science fiction field was" (*Trillion* 297), since in effect Ellison's intention was more to demolish barriers related to language and subject matter than to reconceive the way science fiction was written. While the most ambitiously literary of the anthology's contributions, such as Philip José Farmer's "Riders of the Purple Wage," were genuinely impressive attempts to stretch the stylistic vocabulary of the field, many of the other stories were innovative in neither conception nor execution. What *was* innovative was the manner of presentation: Each story was prefaced by a chatty, enthusiastic Ellison introduction and followed by the author's own afterword, which generally focused on matters of story genesis and technique. The effect is not only to call attention to the context and composition of each tale but to emphasize the notion of speculative fiction as a kind of literary community, if not actually a "movement."

While some British critics and readers regarded *Dangerous Visions* as an overblown and bombastic American response to the New Wave, and some American readers regarded it as the beginning of a true revolution in the way in which science fiction could be written and published in the United States, the actual relationship of the American and British New Wave movements may be more a matter of coincidence than design; both, to a large extent, are products of the same 1960s cultural shift that also found expression in rock music, fashion, film, and journalism. On both sides of the Atlantic, there were very real restraints on the creative freedom of genre writers, imposed not only by what was widely regarded as the cultural "establishment" but by editors, publishers, and readers within the genres themselves. Actual attempts at censorship, such as the condemnation by a member of Parliament of Norman Spinrad's *Bug Jack Barron* when it was serialized in *New Worlds* in 1968 (and the refusal of major distributors W. H. Smith and John Menzies to stock those copies of the magazine), were comparatively rare. In the United States, both Philip José Farmer and Theodore Sturgeon had managed to publish stories of alternative sexuality in the 1950s without drawing much attention from outside the field but with considerable controversy within the science fiction community. By the time *Dangerous Visions* appeared, some magazine editors such as Cele Goldsmith (*Amazing*, *Fantastic*) and Frederik Pohl (*Galaxy*, *If*) had already begun attempts to broaden the potential of commercial science fiction. Goldsmith had bought Ellison's "Paingod" (1964) and "Bright Eyes" (1965), and Pohl had bought "'Repent, Harlequin!' Said the Ticktockman" (1965) and "I Have No Mouth, and I Must Scream" (1967). In many ways, then, *Dangerous Visions* represented a continuation and attempted consolidation of a shift in American science fiction sensibilities that had already begun under some of the stronger magazine editors in the field, although not as radically or self-consciously as it had in England under Moorcock.

But Ellison, like many other writers, was still acutely aware of what it had been like to publish in the formulaic magazines of the 1950s. The comparative liberation he had felt while writing for the men's magazines may well have been something he wanted to share with other writers frustrated by genre expectations, such as Robert Silverberg, who turned largely to nonfiction during this same period, returning to SF with major works in the late 1960s, or Philip K. Dick, who had written no fewer than seven mainstream novels between 1953 and 1960 without being able to get a single one published (one was eventually published in 1975, the rest after Dick's death in 1982). To a great extent, *Dangerous Visions* was a celebration of such writers and an invitation to the party, with Ellison as a garrulous and—from the evidence in his story introductions—knowledgeable master of ceremonies. It was also, in a sense, an announcement of his return to the field as a leader and advocate. More even than his extensive involvement in fandom or his prolific earlier stories, the book cemented his ties to the field and led to the sobriquet "chief prophet of the New Wave" in a brief *New Yorker* article. It also made a dramatic impact within the science fiction field. Stories by Fritz Leiber and Samuel R. Delany received Nebula Awards from the Science Fiction Writers of America, and the Leiber story also won a Hugo from the 1968 World Science Fiction Convention, as did Philip José Farmer's "Riders of the Purple Wage"—surely one of the most challenging and difficult stories to win such an award, which is based on a popular vote of fans registered at the convention. Ellison himself was awarded a special plaque by the convention for "the most significant and controversial sf book published in 1967" (*Again* xii). Norman Spinrad, writing in 1974, commented: "Although none of the stories but Dick's could really be called 'dangerous,' *Dangerous Visions* proved to be the single most influential anthology of science fiction ever published. It brought thirty-two writers to the edges of their talents to confront their material on absolute terms and succeed or fail on their intrinsic worth as artists, not on their ability to fulfill genre formulas" (Spinrad, *Modern* 402).

Encouraged by the success of *Dangerous Visions*, Ellison set about planning two additional anthologies, even more ambitious than the first. *Again, Dangerous Visions* appeared in 1972, containing forty-six stories to the original's thirty-three and repeating none of the authors who had appeared in the first volume. Again, a number of veteran writers were represented (Ray Bradbury, Ross Rocklynne, Kurt Vonnegut Jr., Chad Oliver, James Blish) and several who had been associated with the New Wave (James Sallis, M. John Harrison, Thomas M. Disch), but the stories with the greatest impact came from authors who had already begun to define a new level of stylistic and thematic sophistication and who would prove to define literary science fiction in the post-New Wave, post-*Dangerous Visions* era: Ursula K. Le Guin (whose long novella *The Word for World Is Forest* is the collection's single most substantial piece and who had already published one of the most influential science fiction novels of the century, *The Left Hand of Darkness*), Joanna Russ (whose "When It Changed" became one of the key defining texts of the feminist movement in SF), James Tiptree Jr. (later revealed as a pseudonym for Alice Sheldon, another of the most influential feminist writers), Gene Wolfe (whose complex and subtle stories and novels had already been appearing in Damon Knight's influential *Orbit* anthologies, and who by the 1980s would be regarded as among the most important science fiction writers in the world), and Gregory Benford (a practicing physicist whose later stories and novels would help to define a new form of "literary hard SF"). Again, Ellison was presented a special plaque by the World Science Fiction Convention, and again stories from the collection were honored with awards (a Hugo for the Le Guin story, a Nebula for the Russ). But if *Dangerous Visions* largely looked to the past with its stated hopes of overturning historical editorial constraints on the field, *Again, Dangerous Visions* looked more to the future, toward identifying the kinds of science fiction that would characterize the field in the decades to follow.

Although he complains that he was "quite literally dragged, kicking and screaming, to *Again, Dangerous Visions*" (*Again* xiv), throughout the book Ellison makes reference to a third, still more massive anthology to be called *Last Dangerous Visions*, which would contain stories by "maybe another fifty" writers, many of whose contributions had been intended for *Again, Dangerous Visions* until the book simply grew too large. According to Ellison,

> *The Last Dangerous Visions* will be published, God willing, approximately six months after this book. It was never really intended as a third volume. What happened was that when A, DV hit half a million words and seemed not to be within containment, Ashmead [Doubleday editor Lawrence Ashmead] and I decided rather than making A, DV a boxed set of two books that would cost a small fortune, we'd split the already-purchased wordage down the middle and bring out the final volume six months after this one. (*Again* xxiii)

Ellison even announced the names of nearly thirty writers who would appear in the book, two of them (Richard Wilson and John Christopher) with full-length novels. The announcement proved wildly premature, however, and the subsequent history of the still-unpublished volume would not only become a standing joke among fans but would seriously strain Ellison's relationships with many of the authors whose stories he held in abeyance for decades and to some extent with the professional science fiction community at large. *Last Dangerous Visions* did not appear in 1972 or 1973, and by late 1973 it became clear that the book had metamorphosed into something far more than the remaining stories intended for *Again, Dangerous Visions*. Ellison announced in a letter to a fanzine in November 1973 that the proposed book now included some seventy-one stories and more than a half-million words (roughly the size of the first two anthologies combined).

The following February, he wrote to the same fanzine that the total was now up to seventy-eight stories (Priest 4), but the book still did not appear. The delay might not have turned into a long-standing controversy had Ellison—who was plagued by illness from time to time during this long gestation period—not continued making such announcements or had he simply abandoned the book and returned the stories to the contributors. But the book continued to almost appear, listed as a published—not forthcoming—book in Ellison's 1974 collection *Approaching Oblivion*. In an interview in 1976, Ellison told Christopher Fowler that the book had reached one hundred stories and 1.25 million words and was scheduled to be published by Harper and Row in spring 1977. Various claims in letters, interviews, and convention appearances continued over the next several years, eventually prompting English novelist Christopher Priest to self-publish a rather intemperately sarcastic chapbook, *The Last Deadloss Visions*, in 1987 (revised 1988), documenting Ellison's various statements up to that time and arguing that at such a late date the book was virtually unpublishable and that many contributors—some by then deceased—had been grievously mistreated. Indeed, the notion of a huge book containing stories written in the early 1970s finding a market more than a quarter-century later seems unlikely, but in many respects the book seemed unlikely even in 1972. The turbulent shift in science fiction sensibilities represented by *Dangerous Visions* had pretty much run its course by the time *Again, Dangerous Visions* appeared, and the second volume seemed less intent on revolution than on setting an agenda for the 1970s. Both books had provided a widely read showcase for writers working at or near their imaginative peaks, but each had a purpose beyond this. A third volume, even in 1972, would have been little more than a showcase—in a real sense, there was nothing left to prove—and as the years passed, even the showcase aspect of the anthology would fade. By the late 1970s, the massive project that had begun as a sincere and largely successful effort to reimagine the possibilities of science fiction (or "speculative fiction") in the United States had ironically turned into an inventory of historical texts: revolution transmuted into archaeology.

A Decade of Awards

While Ellison was garnering awards and plaudits for the first two *Dangerous Visions* anthologies, he was also amassing an unprecedented string of awards for his own fiction: Hugos for "'Repent, Harlequin!' Said the Ticktockman" (1965), "I Have No Mouth, and I Must Scream" (1967), the *Star Trek* episode "City on the Edge of Forever" (1967), "The Beast That Shouted Love at the Heart of the World" (1968), "Adrift Just off the Islets of Langerhans" (1974), and "Jeffty Is Five" (1977); Nebulas for "Repent!" (1965), "A Boy and His Dog" (1969), and "Jeffty" (1977); *Locus* Awards (voted on by the readership of the field's leading newsmagazine) for "The Region Between" (1970), "Basilisk" (1972), "The Deathbird" (1973), "Adrift" (1974), "Croatoan" (1975), "Jeffty" (1977), and "Count the Clock That Tells the Time" (1978); even an Edgar Award from the Mystery Writers of America for "The Whimper of Whipped Dogs" (1974). These are among Ellison's most famous and widely anthologized stories, but there is some irony in the fact that during this period of his greatest recognition and his most visible leadership role within the science fiction community, the fiction itself moves consistently away from what could reasonably be encompassed even under the new, broader understanding of science fiction as defined by the New Wave and the *Dangerous Visions* books. Increasingly, his work expressed a fascination with mythology on the one hand and highly personal fables of moral responsibility—such as those which characterized his men's magazine fiction—on the other. The fantastic continued to play a central role in his work, but increasingly even the iconography of traditional science fiction was abandoned in favor of a far more individual and idiosyncratic vision, informed largely by autobiography and by a wide range of cultural metatexts, from old movies and radio programs to biblical and mythological sources.

This is not immediately evident in Ellison's major story collections from this period, since he began a practice—which he never entirely abandoned—of mixing newer and older stories in the same collection, often to lend the collection a thematic focus. The more traditional practice of science fiction writers has been to accumulate enough stories for a book, then publish a second book only when enough new stories had been accumulated since the first. Ellison had more or less begun to follow this practice with his first two science fiction collections, *A Touch of Infinity* (1960), which included stories from 1956 to 1958, and *Ellison Wonderland* (1962), which featured stories from 1956 to 1962. But with *Paingod and Other Delusions* (1965), he combined three of his more recent stories—"'Repent, Harlequin!' Said the Ticktockman" (1965), "Bright Eyes" (1965) and "Paingod" (1964)—with four stories from 1956 to 1959. Similarly, *I Have No Mouth, and I Must Scream* (1967) included two stories from the 1950s along with five from the period 1964 to 1967; *From the Land of Fear* (1967) contained eight stories from the 1950s with only two from 1964 and 1967 (plus the *Outer Limits* teleplay for his story "Soldier"); and *The Beast That*

Shouted Love at the Heart of the World (1969) combined twelve stories from 1968 and 1969 with three from 1957 and 1958. From a simple marketing standpoint, this practice permitted Ellison to keep his older stories in print while highlighting his more famous later works with collections that were essentially built around them, even though it may have occasionally confused readers who noticed the discrepancies in style and structure between the earlier and later stories without realizing that a major shift had occurred in the author's career. More important, it tended to disguise the true nature of Ellison's impact on the science fiction world in the 1960s and 1970s. Apart from the highly influential *Dangerous Visions* anthologies, the fact is that the major impact of Ellison's "renaissance" as a science fiction writer derived from fewer than half a dozen major stories published over five years; by the mid-1970s, even though he continued to receive awards within the field for stories like "Jeffty Is Five," the stories themselves had left most of the science fiction machinery behind, in favor of a more personal or mythical iconography.

"'Repent, Harlequin!'"

The central story in *Paingod and Other Delusions* is "'Repent, Harlequin!' Said the Ticktockman," which had originally appeared in *Galaxy* in December 1965 and represented a dramatic return to science fiction, winning Ellison's first Hugo and Nebula Awards and becoming the first of his stories to become widely reprinted enough to gain the attention of readers outside the science fiction field. Ostensibly written as a plea for understanding of Ellison's own chronic lateness, the story is striking for its bravura display of techniques almost alien to the science fiction of the day: nonlinear narrative chronology, aggressively cartoonlike characters, a narrator who impudently addresses the reader, a lengthy excerpt from Thoreau plopped into the text as though it were a reading assignment, undefined neologisms, crucial plot elements that go defiantly unexplained. And the plot itself is a disarmingly simple return to one of science fiction's most basic forms: the rebel in dystopia. The dystopia in this case is the world of the Ticktockman, a future Earth so regimented by clocks and schedules that an individual's lateness—to work, meetings, school, whatever—can be cumulatively totted up and deducted from his total lifespan. This is accomplished by means of the story's only really innovative bit of imaginary technology: the "cardioplates," which can stop any citizen's heart at a distance from a central facility (although Ellison does make passing reference to home fax machines and a "communications web"). Opposed to the dictatorial Master Timekeeper, or Ticktockman, is an anarchic guerrilla trickster known as the Harlequin, who deliberately disrupts the city's schedules with such pranks as dumping millions of jellybeans on the moving walkways, distracting the workers and gumming up the mechanism. Eventually the Harlequin is captured and brought before the Ticktockman in the scene that gives the story its title—but instead of being "turned off," he is sent to "Coventry," where he is reconditioned into a conforming citizen. After the Harlequin is safely destroyed, however, the Ticktockman himself learns that he has arrived three minutes late for work one morning.

Unlike the pseudorealistic and metonymic worlds that characterize much traditional science fiction and dystopian fiction, the world of the Ticktockman is unapologetically metaphoric, presented openly as a textual construct with thinly disguised links to significant source texts. The notion of a world so severely governed by timetables is familiar to readers of dystopian literature from Russian author Evgeny Zamiatin's 1920 classic *We*, a novel which strongly influenced George Orwell's *1984*, which is directly alluded to in the Ellison story ("It was just like what they did to Winston Smith in *1984*" [*Fantasies* 40]). The idea of Coventry probably relates not only to the common usage derived from the exile of Royalist prisoners during the English Civil War but to Robert A. Heinlein's 1940 story "Coventry," in which misfits in a kind of libertarian future utopia are invited either to undergo psychological "adjustment" or to live in anarchic exile in a country of that name. The protagonist of Heinlein's novella, sentenced to Coventry for punching a man in the nose, even sounds like the Harlequin when he speaks at his trial: "You've planned your whole world so carefully that you've planned the fun and zest right out of it. Nobody is ever hungry, nobody ever gets hurt" (Heinlein 67). The moving walkways of the city are borrowed from another 1940 Heinlein story, "The Roads Must Roll"; like many other Heinlein inventions, they had entered the inventory of science fiction writers long before Ellison's story, and it is entirely possible to read the Harlequin's jelly bean attack on these walkways as a sly allusion to Ellison's own subversion of older science fiction conventions in this and other stories. Even the idea of the anomalous rebel born into a static society was familiar from such classic tales as Heinlein's "Universe" (1941) and Arthur C. Clarke's *The City and the Stars* (1956). "They had no way to predict he would happen," says Ellison's narrator, "possibly a strain of disease long-defunct, now, suddenly reborn in a system where immunity had been forgotten" (30). And the philosophical source of the story, Thoreau's "Civil Disobedience," is not even worked into the fabric of the narrative but offered as a kind of overture to the entire story.

The tale emphasizes its artifice in other ways as well. At the beginning of the story, the narrator calls attention to his own storyteller's control of the tale and its chronology by addressing the reader directly: "Now begin in the middle, and later learn the beginning; the end will take care of itself" (30). When the Harlequin, dressed in his motley, sends "one hundred and fifty thousand dollars worth of jelly beans" onto the moving walkways, the narrator points out that "no one has manufactured jelly beans for over a hundred years," leading to the obvious question, "Where did he get jelly beans?" But instead of answering this question—as the rules of traditional science fiction would demand—the narrator insouciantly dismisses the question: "That's another good question. More than likely it will never be answered to your complete satisfaction. But then, how many questions ever are?" (34). The jelly beans are not all that go unexplained. We are never offered a clear idea of how the Ticktockman's society actually works, and its origin is accounted for only by a series of contemporary vignettes illustrating how time schedules arbitrarily take over people's lives: a college entrance interview, a train schedule, a business deal, a school suspension for tardiness, each accompanied by the repeated mantra "And so it goes" (a phrase which, in the slight variation "so it goes," would become a popular catchphrase when used four years later by Kurt Vonnegut Jr. in his 1969 novel *Slaughterhouse-Five or the Children's Crusade*). It becomes clear that the twenty-fourth-century society of the story is little more than a projection of these twentieth-century anxieties, since nothing is mentioned of the intervening four hundred years of history and since the dialogue spoken by the characters is clearly the idiom of the 1960s. When the Harlequin (whose real name is Everett C. Marm) tells his girlfriend (or possibly wife) Pretty Alice that he will a return at 10:30, she says, "Why do you tell me that? Why? You *know* you'll be late! You're *always* late, so why do you tell me these dumb things?" (36-37). When he is finally captured by the Ticktockman and ordered to repent, Everett's response is, "Get stuffed!" (39).

Like Ellison's much earlier story "The Crackpots" (which he paired with "'Repent, Harlequin!'" in *Paingod and Other Delusions*), "'Repent, Harlequin!'" equates anarchic, immature behavior with the creative force in an otherwise mechanized society. As Michael Moorcock notes, "Harlequin the gadfly is an idealised Ellison, justifying his penchant for practical jokes, giving it a social function (one can also see him as a 'good' version of Batman's adversary, The Joker)" (xi). But in an ironic way, he is also the representative of historical time, in the sense that time may be defined by processes of change and evolution (here again he is a relative of the Alvin of Clarke's *City and the Stars* or the Hugh Hoyland of Heinlein's "Universe," both figures who set historical time in motion after centuries of stasis within their societies). Michael White writes that "to portray time as static or synchronic as Ellison does in 'Repent, Harlequin!' is to negate time, to strip it of its meaning, its essential quality" (164-65). But, in fact, this is not the way Ellison portrays time. It is the way time is conceived in the static world which Harlequin seeks to subvert, and the way time is traditionally conceived in such static dystopian societies. One of the subtler ironies of the story is that it reveals how a society that ostensibly worships time in fact destroys or negates it, in the manner that White suggests. The annihilation of time, expressed here as social stasis, would emerge as one of Ellison's most powerful yet ambivalent themes, showing up in settings ranging from the computer hell of "I Have No Mouth, and I Must Scream" to the persistence of a nostalgic world of old radio programs and pulp magazines in "Jeffty Is Five" to one of Ellison's favorite recurrent phrases (also the title of a 1982 story), "the hour that stretches," derived from an Indonesian folk term, *Djam Karet* (*Beast* 15). The paradox, of course, is that while annihilating time on the personal level can permit an individual to retain the best moments of the past and stave off the inevitability of death, on a societal level it denies the possibility of history, creativity, and change, resulting in a world like that of the Ticktockman. And without the Ticktockman as foil, there can be no Harlequin.

In 1965, a tale so patently recursive and self-referential as "'Repent, Harlequin!'" was still a considerable rarity in science fiction and a flouting of what had become the accepted techniques in the genre for portraying a future society—almost as though the story itself tries to fulfill the role of Harlequin in the ticktock world of the science fiction markets Ellison had grown up in. The model for the traditional science fiction narrative, long since established by *Astounding* editor John W. Campbell and articulated in various speeches and essays by his leading writer, Robert A. Heinlein, was displaced realism—tales with transparent narrators set in a detailed and "lived-in" future environment carefully and logically extrapolated from current conditions. In Campbell's formulation, a story like "'Repent, Harlequin!'" should be presented in such a manner that an imaginary reader in Ellison's twenty-fourth-century society would regard it as realistic and representational.

Ellison's implied reader, in contrast, is clearly his 1965 audience, familiar enough with the tropes of science fiction to recognize them as such. There had been a handful of writers who had experimented with such nonrealistic narrative modes prior to Ellison—Alfred Bester, James Blish, "Cordwainer Smith" (Paul Linebarger). But Ellison's tale, coming less than a year after the putative beginning of England's New Wave and two years before his own *Dangerous Visions*, must have seemed something like the harbinger of a revolution—or at least a radical shift in sensibilities. It was, in fact, only the beginning of a string of intense, emotional stories that would revisit the science fiction landscape from a series of different perspectives and styles, while gradually moving toward a more personal landscape of myth.

"I Have No Mouth, and I Must Scream"

Published only two months before "Pretty Maggie Moneyeyes"—another story whose central character is trapped inside a machine—"I Have No Mouth, and I Must Scream" may be Ellison's single most famous story and is certainly one of the most widely analyzed and frequently reprinted, even providing the basis for a four-part comic-book adaptation in *Harlan Ellison's Dream Corridor* in 1995 and an interactive computer game (from a company called Cyberdreams) that same year. Again, it makes use of scenarios that had long been common in science fiction—nuclear devastation and the all-powerful computer run amok—but transforms these into a bleak existential vision of hell that stands as one of the most emotionally intense stories in all of science fiction, despite its baroque excesses. Even a critic like Brian W. Aldiss, who described the story as "almost hysterically overwritten," concedes that it "remains powerfully effective" (Aldiss and Wingrove 297). Narrated in a flat, paranoid voice that is a far remove from the wry satirical tone of "'Repent, Harlequin!'" the story takes place inside a massive subterranean computer chamber, where the last five people on Earth are being kept alive, solely for the purpose of being tormented, by a godlike computer called AM—which, we are told, originally meant "Allied Mastercomputer," but was later transformed into "Adaptive Manipulator," then "Aggressive Menace," and finally simply AM, an allusion both to its Yahweh-like nature and its emerging self-consciousness ("I think, therefore I am" ["I Have No Mouth" 8]). But AM's consciousness is of a particular sort. As the character Gorrister explains:

> The Cold War started and became World War Three and just kept going. It became a big war, a very complex war, so they needed the computers to handle it. They sank the first shaft and began building AM. There was the Chinese AM and the Russian AM and the Yankee AM and everything was fine until they had honeycombed the entire planet, adding on this element and that element. But one day AM woke up and knew who he was, and he linked himself, and he began feeding all the killing data, until everyone was dead, except for the five of us, and AM brought us down here. (8-9)

As H. Bruce Franklin writes, discussing the story in the context of his study of the American obsession with superweapons:

> If it were to follow the sum of the parts of its program, AM would dispassionately annihilate us. After all, our weapons are not supposed to *feel* anything; they are supposed to kill us without any emotions. But instead of mechanically carrying out its order to exterminate the human race, AM develops an emotion appropriate to its purpose: it infinitely *hates* its human creators. And, recognizing its own identity as the loathsome projection of our own self-hatred, AM, in a deftly perverse twist of Calvinist logic, chooses to "save" five people for eternal torture as an expression of that infinite hate. (*War Stars* 210)

Although Franklin's interpretation is thematically consistent with the story's main theme, the actual explanation given for AM's rage is that, given sentience, it found itself trapped, unable to move or act, and feeling the "innate loathing that all machines had always held for the weak soft creatures who had built them" (15).

In other words, the rage of AM, which is the engine that powers the story, is a fairly complex matter. Viewed in terms of cold war technological paranoia, the computer becomes a kind of objective correlative for what Franklin calls the "self-hatred" that leads to the construction of world-threatening machines in the first place, a translation of irrational war policy into its emotional equivalent. The year before "I Have No Mouth" appeared, British writer D. F. Jones published his first science fiction novel, *Colossus*, which also featured Russian and American cold war supercomputers gaining self-consciousness and linking together to take over the world. But in Jones's formulation—as in most earlier science fiction formulations of machines taking over—the machines remain coldly logical, concerned (like HAL in the 1968 film *2001: A Space Odyssey*) only with the completion of their mission, even if it means the sacrifice of some humans and the enslavement of others. The notion that mechanical consciousness might feel an "innate loathing" toward organic life or seek worship on its own terms was a much rarer idea in science fiction in 1967 (although the idea did show up in Frank Herbert's 1966 novel *Destination: Void*, and since then it has been made a central theme in a number of novels and stories, most notably Gregory Benford's ambitious series of "Galactic Center" novels in the 1990s).

Finally, there is the aspect of AM as an insane version of an Old Testament god of vengeance, "God as Daddy the Deranged" (5), who not only obsesses over torturing his victims but torments them with silly childish pranks and chortles like a leering adolescent whenever they have sex. Although AM falls short of the godlike power to resurrect the dead, part of his Dantesque punishment consists of altering his victims' minds and bodies, and the alterations reveal a crude adolescent sensibility, marked by bullying attempts at irony: The brilliant, handsome, gay professor Benny becomes a mad half-ape with an oversized penis; the antiwar activist Gorrister becomes a "shoulder-shrugger"; Nimdok, deprived even of identity and given that name only because AM likes its sound, disappears at times for special tortures unknown to the others; Ellen, a black woman who claims to have been "a virgin only twice removed," sexually services all the men and is often brutalized by them; and the narrator Ted, who claims to be the only one with his mind left intact, is so filled with rage and paranoia—much of it directed at his companions—that his very narrative is rendered unreliable, leaving the reader to wonder exactly how he *has* been altered by AM. Several critics (Harris-Fain, Brady, Stevens, Francavilla) have noted the story's structural parallels to the Book of Exodus, and Harris-Fain (in what remains the best analysis of the piece, even comparing different texts in different editions) also notes allusions to John Bunyan's *Pilgrim's Progress* and to H. G. Wells's "Country of the Blind" (152).

The plot of the story is fairly minimal, utilizing, as Willis E. McNelly notes, "the two classic frameworks of the allegory, progress and battle" (247). It begins with a brutal image of Gorrister, hanging head down from a palette high up in the computer chamber, his body drained of blood through a slit throat. But it quickly becomes apparent that this is an illusion, since there is no blood on the metal floor beneath the corpse, and since the living Gorrister himself shows up to join the group. We learn that the group has been in the computer for 109 years, presumably suffering such tricks and indignities throughout, living on food that tastes like "boiled boar urine" or consists of "thick, ropey" worms and that they have to struggle through terrifying landscapes to obtain. Now Nimdok is given a vision that canned goods may be available in a place called the "ice caverns," and the group sets off on the hundred-mile underground quest, which consists of six fairly distinct episodes, separated by graphic computer "talk fields" (meant to represent the coding on 1960s-era computer tape, these graphics—which according to Ellison are meant to spell out "I think, therefore I am" ["Memoir" 15]—are now one of the few elements that clearly date the story). These episodes are as follows:

1. As the group passes through a valley of obsolete computer parts, Benny realizes they are near the Earth's surface—long since rendered uninhabitable—and he attempts to escape. As the others watch, his eyes begin to emit a pulsing light accompanied by a painfully loud sound, and he is flung to the steel floor, blinded, his eyes "two soft, moist pools of pus-like jelly" (8). Ellen, whom the narrator views as "scum filth," appears to be relieved that Benny's sex organs are intact.
2. During an encampment at which Gorrister explains the origins of AM, an unseen something, "huge, shambling, hairy, moist" (10), accompanied by a succession of hideous smells, moves toward them. It singles out Ted, who flees in terror as the others laugh hysterically. He hides out for what may be days or years.
3. A violent hurricane hurls all of them back the way they had come. Ellen is bloodied as she is flung high in the air, against walls and machines.
4. AM enters the narrator's mind, like "a pillar of stainless steel bearing bright neon lettering" spelling out a message that, for all its shocking hostility, is essentially further evidence of AM's almost childlike inability to understand its own emotions: "THERE ARE 387.44 MILLION MILES OF PRINTED CIRCUITS IN WAFER THIN LAYERS THAT FILL MY COMPLEX. IF THE WORD HATE WAS ENGRAVED ON EACH NANOANGSTROM OF THOSE HUNDREDS OF MILLIONS OF MILES IT WOULD NOT EQUAL ONE ONE-BILLIONTH OF THE HATE I FEEL FOR HUMANS AT THIS MICROINSTANT FOR YOU. HATE. HATE" (14).
5. After nearly a month of travel, the group arrives under the North Pole, where a monstrous bird awaits. It was this bird's wings which created the hurricane. Appearing as a burning bush, AM tells them that they can kill the bird for food—but then supplies only bows and arrows and a water pistol as weapons.
6. After a series of further trials—an earthquake that mangles Ellen and Nimdok, "the cavern of rats," "the path of boiling steam," "the country of the blind," "the slough of despond," "the vale of tears"—they arrive at the ice caverns. There they find canned goods—but no can opener.

Driven berserk by this final irony, Benny attacks Gorrister and begins eating his face. Gorrister's screams cause spearlike stalactites of ice to fall into the snow. In an instant, Ted decides to use the ice spears to kill Benny and Gorrister. Ellen then kills Nimdok, and Ted kills Ellen, hoping that her final agonized expression is one of thanks.

The concluding coda of the story takes place hundreds of years later. Unable to revive the four who died, the computer has redirected its rage at Ted for taking its "toys" away. His mind intact, Ted has been transformed into "a great soft jelly thing" with "pulsing white holes filled by fog where my eyes used to be," incapable of doing any harm to himself, comforted only by the thought that he helped the others to escape. H. Bruce Franklin describes this creature as "one of the more hideous monsters in all science fiction . . . incapable—at long last—of making the weapons necessary for self-destruction." "The logic is now complete. The monstrous alien weapons we created have reversed the entire process of evolution, reducing the human species to a single repulsive sluglike alien monster" (210). The story's ultimate irony, as Franklin implies, is that a civilization incapable of restraining itself from building increasingly sophisticated computer weapons finally achieves disarmament in the most grotesquely literal way at the hands of those very weapons.

But is the story fundamentally a grim satire of the cold war, a parable of out-of-control technology, or a kind of postmodern vision of hell, drawn in equal measures from existential anxieties and religious/mythical imagery? Ellison's own insistence that the story is essentially a fable of affirmation startles many readers. He argues that Ted's ability to overcome his own selfishness and paranoia in order to "rescue" the others through death is a sign of human nobility in the most hopeless of circumstances. This would suggest that he views the story as essentially about human nature, not technology. It is, of course, about all of these things, but it is also the work of a writer straining at the edge of genre.

If we look again at the succession of images, we see unfolding a transformation of the story itself from science fiction into myth. Benny's blindness—which foreshadows the narrator's eventual fate—is a fairly straightforward, if extreme, punishment for a specific crime. The shambling thing that terrifies the narrator is more ambiguous; it may be a science fiction monster of some sort or a simple bogeyman drawn from Ted's fears. But the reason for its appearance is more arbitrary, less clearly motivated. The hurricane suggests a biblical whirlwind, and this pattern of imagery quickly begins to take over. AM's neon pillar of hate, a kind of tech version of a burning bush, gives way to an actual burning bush, which appears at the same time as the mythical hurricane bird. The tale thus could be described as a self-conscious journey from science fiction into myth, with even simple principles of cause/effect becoming arbitrary and unstable.

The episode in the ice caverns is a momentary return from this world of flux to a world of causality, and Ted is quick to realize that this may well be his last chance at meaningful action. Murder is not only the only humane act possible; it is the only rational action available in a world that is rapidly becoming little more than an expression of AM's madness. Unlike the Harlequin, Ted effects not even a minuscule change in AM's psychotic behavior, and the tale ends without providing a glimmer of hope for his own future as the last man on Earth. "AM has won," he declares (22), yet the inability of the near-omnipotent computer to curtail the capacity for moral action in even so self-centered and paranoid a human as Ted renders that victory ambiguous at best.

While "I Have No Mouth" seems a radical departure from "'Repent, Harlequin!'" two years earlier, the stories are thematically linked in ways that become clear when we look at Ellison's own contribution to his 1967 *Dangerous Visions*. "The Prowler in the City at the Edge of the World" is the result of a fascination with Jack the Ripper that also found expression in his *Cimarron Strip* episode "Knife in the Darkness" and continued with Ripper-like figures in "The Whimper of Whipped Dogs" (1973) and "Mefisto in Onyx" (1987). Conceived as a sequel to Robert Bloch's *Dangerous Visions* story "A Toy for Juliette," "Prowler" yanks the Ripper from his historical context and places him in a sterile thirty-first-century utopia with "walls of antiseptic metal like an immense autoclave" (131). The metal city, "shining in permanence, eternal in concept" (131) resembles the Ticktockman's world in its programmed stasis and unquestioning citizens, but is at the same time a protean metallic environment like that of AM's interior. The city's resemblance to AM becomes clearer when we realize why the Ripper has been brought forward in time—in effect, to serve as an amusement for the jaded citizenry. After first killing the spoiled and sadistic granddaughter of the amoral owner of the world's only time machine (this was the conclusion of the Bloch story), Jack learns that he was brought forward precisely for this purpose. Enraged, he embarks on a killing spree that far outstrips his crimes of 1889—and that constitutes one of the most gruesome sustained segments of any Ellison story—and then discovers that this, too, was but an entertainment for the "sybarites," that his "victims" had been "thawed" specifically for this purpose.

> The people of the city had all along been able to escape him, and now they would. He was finally and completely the clown they had shown him to be. He was not evil, he was pathetic.
> He tried to use the living blade on himself, but it dissolved into motes of light and wafted away on a breeze that had blown up for just that purpose.
> Alone, he stood there staring at the victorious cleanliness of the Utopia. With their talents they would keep him alive, possibly alive forever, immortal in the possible expectation of needing him for amusement again someday. He was stripped to raw essentials in a mind that was no longer anything more than jelly matter. To go madder and madder, and never to know peace or end or sleep. (150-51)

Jack, in short, is both the Harlequin and the mouthless Ted, the "jelly matter" of his mind a direct echo of the "great soft jelly thing" Ted finds himself transformed into. But his eternal tormentor, instead of an insane computer, is a sterile, jaded Ticktockman's society. The madness of the machine becomes indistinguishable from the madness of the city; in both cases the victim is trapped in a totalizing expression of hell that denies hope and destroys time. The implied alternative to these autoclave urban environments is the wasteland, the blasted surface of "I Have No Mouth," the uninhabitable outside (which in Bloch's original story is presented as a postnuclear wasteland) of "Prowler." That wasteland became the main setting of Ellison's next major exploration of dystopian themes, "A Boy and His Dog."

"A Boy and His Dog"

Cited by Brian W. Aldiss as Ellison's masterpiece, "A Boy and His Dog" first appeared in England in Michael Moorcock's *New Worlds* in 1969, in a slightly abridged version, and was reprinted that same year, at its full 18,000-word length, in *The Beast That Shouted Love at the Heart of the World*—a collection that, with its psychedelic Leo and Diane Dillon cover and selection of stories mostly from 1968 and 1969, was Ellison's most significant science fiction book to date and the book that most closely seemed to ally his work with the counterculture of rebellion in the late 1960s. Other stories in the collection included an award-winning exploration of madness as a tangible force in the universe, "The Beast That Shouted Love at the Heart of the World," and a genuinely disturbing antidrug phantasmagoria, "Shattered like a Glass Goblin," but the collection was fundamentally defined by "A Boy and His Dog." In many ways, the story is his most complete science fiction story, neither proclaiming its own ironic textuality (like "'Repent, Harlequin!'") nor transforming itself into myth (like "I Have No Mouth"). Instead, the actions, settings, characters, and narrative voice of the tale are all controlled by and consistent with the initial extrapolative conditions of an America devastated by nuclear war, and divided into a savage wasteland aboveground and repressively middle-class "downunders" beneath the surface.

"A Boy and His Dog," together with its two connected tales, "Eggsucker" (1977) and "Run, Spot, Run" (1980), also represents Ellison's most complete effort at a fully realized science fiction novel. (His minor 1960 effort, *The Man with Nine Lives*, published as part of an Ace Double with his first story collection, *A Touch of Infinity*, was essentially a long novella expanded from his 1959 story "The Sound of a Scythe.") The completed novel, to be titled *Blood's a Rover*, gained a reputation in the fan community as one of Ellison's most persistently announced but undelivered books. (Other undelivered works were *The Prince of Sleep*, listed as forthcoming in 1974 and advertised by Dell in 1977 but never published, and of course *Last Dangerous Visions*.) In an afterword to Richard Corben's 1989 graphic novel adaptation of the three "Boy and His Dog" stories, *Vic and Blood*, Ellison wrote:

> I call [the three stories] the first three sections of a 100,000 word novel titled BLOOD'S A ROVER. What happens to Vic and Blood in this graphic novel is only the beginning of the story. I never intended "A Boy and His Dog" to stand alone. It just happened to be the part of the novel that was written when Mike Moorcock solicited a submission for *New Worlds* back in late 1968.
>
> I have been at work on this novel for more than twenty years.
>
> As I write this afterword, I am four days past my fifty-fifth birthday. If the universe doesn't stomp me, before the end of 1989 I will have the full novel completed. If the heavens don't part and swamp us, it will be published in 1990. (*Vic*, endpaper)

In fact, Ellison had expected the book to be completed nearly a decade earlier, even listing it as a 1980 title under "Books by Harlan Ellison" in the front matter to his 1980 collection *Shatterday*. Whether the novel ever appears, however, now seems irrelevant to the strong reputation of "A Boy and His Dog," which not only earned Ellison another Nebula Award but in 1975 became the basis of the only successful feature film adaptation of an Ellison work. Written and directed by L. Q. Jones, *A Boy and His Dog* received a Hugo as best dramatic presentation and probably influenced the Australian director George Miller in his original stories for the film *Mad Max* (1979) and its sequels.

Like "I Have No Mouth," "A Boy and His Dog" belongs to the atomic war subgenre of science fiction tales, a tradition so extensive that scholar Paul Brians was able to identify and annotate more than eight hundred separate novels and short stories (including seven titles by Ellison) published between 1895 and 1984. But like "'Repent, Harlequin!'" it also draws from the tradition of dystopian fiction in its caricature of middle American "normalcy" in the repressive underground city called Topeka, one of some two hundred "downunders" established by "Southern Baptists, Fundamentalists, lawanorder goofs, real middle-class squares" seeking to re-create a pre-World War I age of innocence (228). The source of the story's power lies in the moral tension it establishes between the savage, male-dominated, but vital surface world of foraging "roverpaks" and ruined cities and the grotesque, sterile parody of Norman Rockwell Americana in the downunder of Topeka—a tension which at its best recalls that of Anthony Burgess's 1962 novel, *A Clockwork Orange*, with its uncomfortable link between violence and vitality—except that there is no spark of creativity, no passion for Beethoven, in Ellison's crude and inarticulate Vic.

Set in 2024, the story strives to maintain a tone of grim realism in its depiction of a desert wasteland, eschewing such conventional post-nuclear science fiction figures as mutants, but with one key exception: The narrator's companion, Blood, is one of a new breed of superintelligent, telepathic "skirmisher dogs," descended from twentieth-century security and attack dogs who had been surgically altered and injected with "amplified dolphin spinal fluid" (*Beast* 123). (Had the story been written a decade or two later, Ellison might have substituted DNA for the spinal fluid.) The telepathically wisecracking Blood, both more articulate and better educated than Vic, is in fact the brains of the duo, using his heightened senses to help Vic locate food and women and to avoid the organized gangs called "roverpaks" that dominate the surface. Supposedly based on Ellison's own dog Ahbhu (to whom the collection in which the story appears is dedicated, and whose own death is chronicled in Ellison's later story "The Deathbird"), Blood's voice is in fact very close to that of Ellison himself. In the opening scene of the story, Blood teases Vic—and underlines the irony of the story's title— by calling him "Albert," an obscure (to Vic) reference to Albert Payson Terhune, the once-popular author of sentimental dog novels (*Lad: A Dog*, *His Dog*, *The Heart of a Dog*, etc.). Blood corrects Vic's grammar, teaches him history, and advises him on survival strategy in a society that bears a noteworthy resemblance to the Brooklyn gang culture of the 1950s that Ellison had written of early in his career.

Surviving women are so rare in this society that antique pornographic films have become a prized source of entertainment, many of the roverpak members have opted for gay sex, and the few women who do appear are regarded as little more than candidates for rape and murder—and thus seek anonymity by disguising themselves as men. The vicious misogyny of Vic's society and the moral obtuseness of Vic himself have probably led more than a few readers to misread the tale as itself misogynistic, although similar societies have been portrayed by feminist authors arguing that the brutal commodification of women might indeed be the response of a war-oriented male culture to a shortage of females in the population (see Pamela Sargent's 1984 short story "Fears," for example). Carolyn Wendell, in a survey of Nebula Award-winning stories, described the story as "the worst offender" in terms of sexual stereotyping of women, concluding: "The value standard is clearly a double one: a man may kill his mate to feed his dog, but a woman must not kill her father to free herself, or act in any aggressive way" (346). Wendell apparently views this double standard as representing Ellison's own, despite the consistent undermining of Vic's narration by Blood and by the events of the tale.

In many cases, the controversy over "A Boy and His Dog" confused

Ellison's original story with the L. Q. Jones film, about which the science fiction novelist and critic Joanna Russ wrote, "Sending a woman to see *A Boy and His Dog* is like sending a Jew to a movie that glorifies Dachau; you need not be a feminist to loathe this film" (66). Russ, however, goes on to note that the story "is a very different matter from the film"—a point that many other readers overlooked. (For example, a 1977 essay by John Crow and Richard Erlich titled "Mythic Patterns in Ellison's *A Boy and His Dog*," which finds in the story parallels with the myth of the hero, makes little distinction between novella and film. Crow and Erlich quote dialogue and cite incidents that appear only in the film, including one in which Vic finds a woman stabbed to death and complains, "She was good for three or more times yet" [163].) At any rate, the controversy over the tale was sufficient that Terry Dowling, in an introductory note to it in *The Essential Ellison*, wrote that it "speaks of love in a special way that had been consistently misinterpreted by the story's detractors, whose arguments found even more inflammatory fuel in L. Q. Jones's 1975 movie adaptation" (874).

In a crumbling movie theater where ancient films are shown by a roverpak that calls itself Our Gang, Blood catches the scent of a woman somewhere in the audience—presumably a thrill-seeker from "downunder" disguised as a man—and helps Vic track her to an abandoned YMCA gymnasium. There, hiding in the shadows, Vic watches her undress and experiences a kind of Actaeon-like epiphany. Disarmed by her beauty and by her insistence on looking him in the eye and speaking to him, he finds himself unable to carry out his assault. Blood tells him that the building has been surrounded by roverpaks—whose dogs have also picked up the woman's scent—and they are quickly under siege, with the girl, Quilla June, joining Vic and Blood in fighting off the roverpaks. They decide to torch the entire building and hide out below in a deep boiler room. There Vic finally succeeds in having his way with Quilla June, who later claims to have "liked doing it" (226). Infatuated with Quilla June, who taunts him by asking, "Do you know what love is?" (229), Vic gets into a tense argument with

Blood, who reminds him of their responsibility to each other. But when he returns to the boiler room, Quilla June knocks him out with a pistol and escapes.

Furious, and against Blood's warnings, Vic tracks Quilla June to the dropshaft that leads down to Topeka. Leaving Blood alone on the surface, Vic follows her into a twenty-mile-long metal-lined cavern, eerily like the metal landscapes of "I Have No Mouth" but with a picture-book replica of a pre-World War I town in the center of it. It is, of course, a trap: Quilla June has lured Vic to Topeka because the birthrate there has dropped dramatically, and most babies are girls. Vic is to serve as an experimental stud, in the hope that men from the surface will be able to revitalize the society. He agrees to stay, but "Inside a week I was ready to scream" (238) from the artificial food, the overripe parody of small-town life ("They rocked in rockers on the front porches, they raked their lawns, they hung around the gas station, they stuck pennies in gumball machines, they painted white stripes down the middle of the road, they sold newspapers on the corners" [237-38]), and most of all from the mannered, hypocritical behavior and speech of the inhabitants. Like the Ticktockman, the Topekans have chosen to deal with historical change by denying it, substituting instead a repressive condition of stasis, enforced even down to the level of daily speech, in which everyone must politely address everyone else as "Mr." or "Mrs." It turns out that Quilla June is also frustrated in this sterile, unchanging world, and with her help Vic escapes again to the surface, bringing her along only to discover Blood, starved and half-dead, waiting near the dropshaft entrance. Realizing his only hope of survival is with Blood, and that Blood cannot travel without food, Vic makes a crucial decision, sacrificing Quilla June to provide food for his dog. The next morning, as Blood completes another meal, Vic remembers her question: "Do you know what love is?" He concludes, "Sure I know. A boy loves his dog" (245).

While there is a decided antiromantic, antisentimental bite to this ending, it hardly came as a surprise to Ellison readers (after all, he'd just published a book titled *Love Ain't Nothing but Sex Misspelled*) or to readers familiar with the post-nuclear war scenarios that were so common in the 1950s and 1960s. The suggestion of cannibalism as a marker of cultural collapse following a nuclear war was certainly not original with Ellison, dating back at least to Wilson Tucker's 1952 novel *The Long Loud Silence* (although the cannibalism was cut from the novel's first American publication). A more striking parallel is with the cannibalism of the Morlocks in H. G. Wells's *Time Machine* (1895), since Ellison's story is structured like an inversion of the dual far-future society portrayed in that novel, in which the decadent Eloi wallow in an artificial utopia aboveground while far below the degenerate Morlocks, descended from the working classes, struggle to survive in a manner so degraded that it includes killing and eating the Eloi. Quilla June, although she is another in a long line of betraying women in Ellison (including Pretty Alice and Pretty Maggie), is also a distant descendant of Wells's Weena.

The remaining two Vic and Blood stories, "Eggsucker" and "Run, Spot, Run," frame the narrative of "A Boy and His Dog" by filling in a few more details of Vic's society and establishing more fully the relationship of Vic and Blood, but neither is as fully plotted, and both seem much more like episodes from a longer work. Unlike "A Boy and His Dog," both are narrated by Blood rather than Vic. In "Eggsucker," Vic and Blood's relationship is threatened when Blood, enraged at being repeatedly called an "Eggsucker" by the dealer who supplies Vic with ammunition, attacks the dealer, thus cutting off Vic's source of a crucial commodity. Furious, Vic stalks off on his own, but nearly stumbles into a pit where a glowing green radioactive "screamer" is ready to attack him—an incident that is alluded to briefly in "A Boy and His Dog." Blood saves Vic, and the two reunite. "Run, Spot, Run," which appeared originally in the graphic novel *Vic and Blood*, finds Blood eating what may be a poison lizard and suffering hallucinations drawn from Vic's nightmares of the ghost of Quilla June. Haunted and depressed at what he has done, Vic narrowly escapes capture by Fellim, a kind of gay warlord who roams the Ohio Turnpike. But the two of them take refuge in a huge stump that turns out to be home to a colony of giant mutated spiders—the first time in the entire sequence that Ellison resorts to monster-movie clichés—and Blood is unable to rouse Vic out of his depression even to save himself from being encased in a shroud of spiderwebs. Finally unable to save his friend, Blood runs away, heading west and foraging for food. "And I was never again troubled by the ghosts of little girls in the shredded frilly blue dresses," he concludes. "No ghosts of little girls: just one ghost that stared up at me from a hollow stump with eyes that no longer cared what happened to man's best friend" (*Vic*, n.p.). The tantalizing suggestion, of course, is that the central figure and principal narrator in the novel *Blood's a Rover* was to have been Blood, with Vic a more transient character. Neither of these tales approaches the strength and consistency of "A Boy and His Dog," however.

The vivid and imagistic series of dystopian fables that began with "'Repent, Harlequin!'" in 1965 and essentially ended with the "Boy and His Dog" stories constitute Ellison's single most significant and influential contribution to science fiction as a genre, far more substantial than his jerry-built Kyben war series, and in fact more substantial than the entire body of short science fiction that he contributed to the digest magazines throughout the late 1950s and early 1960s. While he would return to science fiction themes and scenarios throughout his later career, they would increasingly be subsumed by more personal concerns, becoming only one of a number of narrative instrumentalities that Ellison would employ interchangeably, often within the same story. As if recognizing this shift in the direction of his fiction, Ellison in 1971 assembled his first retrospective collection, *Alone against Tomorrow: Stories of Alienation in Speculative Fiction*—which, as its subtitle announces, was also the first collection to be organized around a particular theme (although this theme, alienation, would easily have permitted the inclusion of most of Ellison's fiction to that point). Among the twenty stories assembled were both "'Repent, Harlequin!'" and "I Have No Mouth," together with tales dating back to Ellison's second sale, "Life Hutch." Ellison later described the book as "a small, narrow retrospective of my work" between 1956 and 1969 (*Approaching Oblivion* 10) narrow, presumably, in the sense that the stories selected were primarily representative of Ellison's science fiction. *Alone against Tomorrow* was not a valedictory to science fiction, but it did represent a certain degree of stocktaking and was in many ways his last "science fiction" collection. *Approaching Oblivion: Road Signs on the Treadmill toward Tomorrow*, which appeared in 1974, featured only previously uncollected stories, freely mixing autobiographical fantasy ("One Life, Furnished in Early Poverty") with cautionary science fiction ("Silent in Gehenna") and manic comedy ("I'm Looking for Kadak," one of the funniest of Ellison's small number of comic Jewish stories). That collection was followed in 1975 by *Deathbird Stories*, the most important of Ellison's thematic story collections and one that pointedly announced an ambitious interest—not new, but never so clearly codified—in fiction that reflects or even tries to shape the secret mythologies of its time. In this new configuration, science fiction would continue to play a role, but never again so fully a dominant one as it had played in the decade before.

From *Harlan Ellison: The Edge of Forever* (2002) by Ellen Weil and Gary K. Wolfe. Copyright © 2002 by The Ohio State University Press. Reprinted with permission of The Ohio State University Press.

Works Cited

Aldiss, Brian W., and David Wingrove. *Trillion Year Spree: The History of Science Fiction*. New York: Atheneum, 1986.

Brady, Charles J. "The Computer as a Symbol of God: Ellison's Macabre Exodus." *Journal of General Education* 28 (1976): 55-62.

Brians, Paul. *Nuclear Holocausts: Atomic War in Fiction, 1895-1984*. Kent, Ohio: Kent State University Press, 1987.

Clute, John, and Peter Nicholls, eds. *The Encyclopedia of Science Fiction*. New York: St. Martin's Press, 1993.

Crow, John, and Richard Erlich. "Mythic Patterns in Ellison's *A Boy and His Dog.*" *Extrapolation* 18 (May 1977): 162-66.

Dowling, Terry. "Introduction: Sublime Rebel." *The Essential Ellison: A Thirty-five-Year Retrospective*, edited by Terry Dowling, with Richard Delap and Gil Lamont. Omaha: Nemo Press, 1987.

Ellison, Harlan. *Alone against Tomorrow: Stories of Alienation in Speculative Fiction.* New York: Macmillan, 1971.

———. *Approaching Oblivion: Road Signs on the Treadmill toward Tomorrow.* New York: Walker, 1974.

———. *The Beast That Shouted Love at the Heart of the World.* New York: Avon, 1969.

———. *Deathbird Stories.* New York: Bluejay Books, 1983.

———. *Ellison Wonderland.* 1962. New York: Bluejay Books, 1984.

———. *The Fantasies of Harlan Ellison.* Boston: Gregg Press, 1979.

———. *From the Land of Fear.* New York: Belmont, 1973.

———. *I Have No Mouth, and I Must Scream.* New York: Ace, 1983.

———. *Love Ain't Nothing but Sex Misspelled.* New York: Ace, 1983.

———. *Paingod and Other Delusions.* New York: Pyramid, 1965.

———. *A Touch of Infinity/The Man with Nine Lives.* New York: Ace, 1960.

———, ed. *Again, Dangerous Visions.* New York: Doubleday, 1972.

———, ed. *Dangerous Visions.* New York: Doubleday, 1967.

Ellison, Harlan, and Richard Corben. *Vic and Blood: The Chronicles of a Boy and His Dog.* New York: St. Martin's Press, 1989.

Francavilla, Joseph. "The Concept of the Divided Self and Harlan Ellison's 'I Have No Mouth, and I Must Scream' and 'Shatterday.'" *Journal of the Fantastic in the Arts* 6, nos. 2-3 (1994): 107-25.

Franklin, H. Bruce. *War Stars: The Superweapon and the American Imagination.* New York: Oxford University Press, 1988.

Greenland, Colin. *The Entropy Exhibition: Michael Moorcock and the British 'New Wave' in Science Fiction.* London: Routledge and Kegan Paul, 1983.

Harris-Fain, Darren. "Created in the Image of God: The Narrator and the Computer in Harlan Ellison's 'I Have No Mouth, and I Must Scream.'" *Extrapolation* 32 (summer 1991): 143-55.

Heinlein, Robert A. "Coventry." *Six Great Short Novels of Science Fiction*, edited by Groff Conklin, 65-118. New York: Dell, 1954.

McNelly, Willis E. Foreword to "I Have No Mouth, and I Must Scream." *The Mirror of Infinity: A Critics' Anthology of Science Fiction*, edited by Robert Silverberg, 246-50. New York: Harper and Row, 1973.

Merril, Judith, ed. *England Swings SF: Stories of Speculative Fiction.* New York: Ace, 1968.

Moorcock, Michael. Foreword to *The Fantasies of Harlan Ellison.* Boston: Gregg Press, 1979.

Priest, Christopher. *The Last Deadloss Visions.* London: Author, 1987.

Russ, Joanna. *To Write like a Woman: Essays in Feminism and Science Fiction.* Bloomington: Indiana University Press, 1995.

Spinrad, Norman, ed. *Modern Science Fiction*. Garden City, N.Y.: Anchor Doubleday, 1974.

Stevens, Carol D. "The Short Fiction of Harlan Ellison." *Survey of Science Fiction Literature*, edited by Frank N. Magill, 3:1978-88. Englewood Cliffs, N.J.: Salem Press, 1979.

Wendell, Carolyn. "The Alien Species: A Study of Women Characters in the Nebula Award Winners, 1965-1973." *Extrapolation* 20 (winter 1979): 343-54.

Westfahl, Gary. *Cosmic Engineers: A Study of Hard Science Fiction*. Westport, Conn.: Greenwood Press, 1996.

White, Michael D. "Ellison's Harlequin: Irrational Moral Action in Static Time." *Science-Fiction Studies* 4 (July 1977): 161-65.

Williamson, Jack. "Science Fiction, Teaching, and Criticism." *Science Fiction Today and Tomorrow*, edited by Reginal Bretno, 309-30. New York: Harper and Row, 1974.

Consumed by Shadows:
Ellison and Hollywood

Ellen Weil and Gary K. Wolfe

> From that moment, Valerie Lone began to be consumed by her shadow. And nothing could prevent it. Not even the wonderful, wonderful Universe that had chosen to care about her.
>
> A Universe ruled by a mad God, who was himself being consumed by his shadow.
>
> —"The Resurgence of Miss Ankle-Strap Wedgie"

From the beginning, Ellison's career has been marked by a subtext of commedia dell'arte, reflected most directly in his public persona as a lecturer, radio host, convention star, talk-show guest, actor, recording artist, and "instant author" who would compose short stories in the windows of bookstores or during live telecasts. Show business is also a recurring theme in his fiction, which regularly features such figures as stand-up comedians ("Final Shtick"), harlequins ("'Repent, Harlequin!' Said the Ticktockman"), aging movie stars ("The Resurgence of Miss Ankle-Strap Wedgie"), radio talk-show hosts ("Flop Sweat"), disc jockeys ("This is Jackie Spinning"), actors ("All the Sounds of Fear," "Deal from the Bottom,"), musicians ("The Truth," "Django"), even performance artists from outer space ("S.R.O."). Critic Sue Hart has argued persuasively that theater in all its forms, including film and TV, consistently acts as "informer to the future" in Ellison's work (121), and given this affinity for the world of public performance, it seems inevitable that Ellison would become involved with Hollywood.

Ellison was not unaware of the risks. One of the great romantic myths of American pop culture is that of Genius Consumed by Commerce, which in broad outlines depicts an artist of extraordinary talent (usually but not always a writer) whose accomplishments bring him or her to the attention of a vastly wealthy consumer industry (usually but not always Hollywood), with which the artist makes a Faustian bargain, is treated like a day-laborer, sees his work compromised or outright butchered, begins a long downward spiral toward alcoholism or drug abuse or even suicide, and dies with unfulfilled promises and with a relatively trivial legacy in the consumer industry that destroyed him. Fueled by selected fragments of the careers of Nathanael West, Ben Hecht, Dorothy Parker, William Faulkner, and F. Scott Fitzgerald and by numerous movies and novels in the manner of *Sunset Boulevard*, this scenario is more parable than history. As Ellison has pointed out, West wrote his finest work, *The Day of the Locust*, while working as a studio scenarist; Fitzgerald wrote the Pat Hobby stories and most of *The Last Tycoon* in the depths of his Hollywood alcoholic spin; and Faulkner not only supported his family but produced some of his most mature (and least commercial) fiction while under contract to Hollywood (*Harlan Ellison's Watching* 418-19).

"Memo from Purgatory"

Ellison came to Hollywood not as an established literary figure but as an ambitious young writer willing to attend "cattle calls" for writers and to pitch ideas—often made up on the spot—to assistant TV producers and story editors. His one claim to fame was "Memo from Purgatory," which had been sold to *The Alfred Hitchcock Hour* and presented in 1962, with Ellison's own script. Introduced by a somber Hitchcock, forgoing his usual mordantly witty monologues, the hour-long drama is of interest today chiefly for the spectacle of a very young James Caan portraying a very young Harlan Ellison, with Walter Koenig—who only four years later would gain fame as Ensign Chekov on *Star Trek*—as the gang leader he befriends. Drawn from a few of the less violent episodes of *Memos from Purgatory*, the story presents Caan as a young writer pretending to join a New York gang in order to gain material for a book. He gains the trust of the gang leader—and of course of a "Deb"—but this trust is compromised when his notes are discovered by one of the gang members. Coming seven years after *The*

Blackboard Jungle and two years after *West Side Story*, the drama has little to add to the Hollywood portrayal of JD gangs—except, perhaps, for a slight edge of documentary realism in Ellison's generally efficient script, pared down considerably from the more florid presentation of these same episodes in the original book. Most important, "Memo from Purgatory" demonstrated that Ellison could write for TV, and over the next several years he undertook a variety of assignments for TV series that are now mostly forgotten: *Ripcord*, a syndicated series about parachutists; *Route 66*, a popular CBS series filmed on location around the United States (Ellison is credited with a story, not a teleplay); *Cimarron Strip*, a rare ninety-minute western series; even the notoriously ridiculous Sally Field series *The Flying Nun* (for which Ellison chose the screenwriting pseudonym "Cordwainer Bird," which he later consistently used in order to publicly distance himself from projects he deemed too compromised or simply too embarrassing).

Burke's Law

Ellison's steadiest work during his early years in Hollywood came as a regular writer for *Burke's Law* (1963-65), a romantic mystery-adventure series that starred Gene Barry as Amos Burke, an independently wealthy bachelor playboy in a chauffeured Rolls Royce who, in a credulity-smashing twist, also happened to be the police chief of Los Angeles! Produced by Aaron Spelling for ABC, the show was packed with narrative gimmicks characteristic of TV series formulae: Gary Conway as a young, impetuous cop; Regis Toomey as an older, wiser cop; Eileen O'Neill as a girl cop; a parade of guest stars (Rhonda Fleming, Buster Keaton, Frank Sinatra, Jayne Mansfield); a larger parade of stars in cameo roles; a formula for episode titles that almost always began "Who Killed . . . ?" After less than two years, the producers decided to turn Amos Burke into a secret agent—perhaps responding to the success of NBC's series *The Man from U.N.C.L.E.* and the growing popularity of James Bond movies. The new series died, ironically, after being programmed opposite another spy program on NBC, *I Spy*.

Ellison contributed four scripts to *Burke's Law* in the 1963-64 season and two to *The Man from U.NC.L.E.* in the 1966-67 season. The first of the *Burke's Law* episodes, "Who Killed Alex Debbs?" concerned the murder of a publisher of men's magazines. According to Ellison, this was an idea he had originally pitched to line producer Richard Newton during the cattle call—"How about I kill Hugh Hefner for you?" (*Harlan Ellison's Watching* xxxi)—but one can't help but wonder if the idea wasn't inspired at least in part by Ellison's recent unhappy experiences with William Hamling, the publisher of *Rogue*. More important, the episode—initially broadcast on October 25, 1963—established Ellison as a commodity, favored by Spelling and connected, however peripherally, with the inner circles of Hollywood. As Ellison later described it: "During that period I wrote for, and got to spend time with, genuine legends: Gloria Swanson, Charlie Ruggles, Buster Keaton, Wally Cox, Joan Blondell, Aldo Ray, Mickey Rooney, Rod Steiger, and even Nina Foch. I went to Hollywood parties, I dined with celebrities and multimillionaires, I became involved with starlets, I went more than a little crazy" (*Harlan Ellison's Watching* xxxiii).

Perhaps the clearest indication of the extent to which Ellison had gone Hollywood was that, within a couple of years of his work on *Burke's Law*, he was at work on the screenplay of Joseph E. Levine's *The Oscar*, a 1966 feature, based on a novel by Richard Sale, which quickly gained a reputation as perhaps the tawdriest of all Hollywood "insider" soap operas. The film was nevertheless a fairly high profile project, coming from the producer of *The Carpetbaggers* and *Harlow*, and critic Pauline Kael took particular note of "Harlan Ellison's incomparable bedroom conversations," which were "such a perfect commingling" with Levine's beds and draperies that "the words might have sprouted from the coverlets" (437).

The Outer Limits

But Ellison's experience with science fiction gave him a particular edge in a TV industry that had only begun to discover the narrative possibilities of the genre. Following an unprepossesing beginning with low-budget programs like *Captain Video* (1949-53, 1955-56) and *Tom Corbett: Space Cadet* (1950-55), science fiction television seemed doomed to remain a subset of children's programming until two major developments in the early 1960s. The first and most important was *The Twilight Zone* (1959-64), developed by Rod Serling, who at the time was one of a handful of writers who had earned substantial reputations based on TV drama (another such writer, Reginald Rose, also developed his own TV series, *The Defenders*, in 1961). Although most *Twilight Zone* episodes were fantasy rather than science fiction, the very concept of a series developed and creatively directed by a writer seemed to offer stunning promises to readers of fantasy and science fiction: programming that might actually reflect some of the appeal of the literature in its scripts, and that might even involve "real" science fiction and fantasy authors. Although Serling wrote most of the episodes himself (partly the result of a promise to the network), he also enlisted the services of established writers in the field, most notably Charles Beaumont and Richard Matheson. While *The Twilight Zone* was never enormously successful—it was canceled in 1962 and brought back by popular demand the following January—the principles it helped establish of involving genre authors and more sophisticated storylines were reflected in Leslie Stevens's *The Outer Limits* (1963-65), a series whose striking visual design seemed an early version of science fiction *film noir* and which featured scripts by SF writers David Duncan, Clifford Simak, and Otto Binder as well as Ellison.

The other development that helped define the science fiction revival on TV, far less sanguine from the point of view of most readers in the genre, was the arrival of producer Irwin Allen. Allen—who would later gain fame as the ringmaster of bloated disaster movies such as

The Poseidon Adventure (1972) and *The Towering Inferno* (1974)—introduced no fewer than four new science fiction series on TV between 1964 and 1968: *Voyage to the Bottom of the Sea* (1964-68, based on Allen's own 1961 film of that title), *Lost in Space* (1965-68), *The Time Tunnel* (1966-67), and *Land of the Giants* (1968-70). While Allen demonstrated that TV budgets could support somewhat more complex sets and special effects—thus perhaps helping to pave the way for *Star Trek* (1966-69)—the appalling plots and sitcom characters of these series seemed to suggest that TV science fiction was ready to revert again to the realm of children's programming. Ellison wrote only one script for an Allen series—an episode of *Voyage to the Bottom of the Sea* entitled "The Price of Doom"—and for it he employed the disdainful pseudonym "Cordwainer Bird."

Ellison's two *Outer Limits* scripts, however, are of genuine interest. The first, "Soldier," was based on Ellison's 1957 short story of that title. It concerns a warrior from some 1,800 years in the future who, through a freak battlefield accident, is somehow transported back in time to our present. The soldier, Qarlo Cobregnny, suddenly materializes on a subway platform, weapon in hand, and his appearance promptly causes an old man to suffer a heart attack. Thinking that Qarlo has attacked the old man, the other commuters panic, and Qarlo soon finds himself in a shootout with a police officer. Despite his superior weapon, Qarlo is captured, and he spends a night in jail before a government security agency learns of the weapon and begins trying to communicate with Qarlo—who, it turns out, speaks a rapid and distorted version of English. In the 1957 published version of the story, Qarlo seems a conundrum to the government philologist who learns to communicate with him—namely, how can such a completely unsocialized and violent character possibly be integrated into our own society? Raised since infancy to be a brutal soldier, Qarlo has no concept of parents, family, or any other social relations, and he has no education other than his own battlefield programming. Finally—in a weak but well-intentioned ending—he is put on the lecture circuit, describing the endless brutalities of future warfare to audiences who are then asked to sign petitions to abolish war. If Qarlo succeeds, there may be a chance that the nightmare future he represents will never come to pass (although the question of where Qarlo would then have come from is unanswered).

In the teleplay for the 1964 *Outer Limits* broadcast, Ellison changed the ending by introducing a second warrior from the future, known only as the Enemy, who is initially trapped partway through the time portal, then is freed by a bolt of lightning to continue his pursuit of Qarlo. He finally tracks him down at the home of the government translator Kagan, where Qarlo has, in a tentative, childlike way, begun to learn some of the principles of human interaction and family life. In the final confrontation, Qarlo makes a move against the Enemy that could be interpreted either as an attempt to protect the family he has come to care about or as a reversion to his battlefield instincts. As the two soldiers grapple over the weapon, they both disappear in a blinding flash, leaving the episode's offscreen narrator to speculate on whether the future represented by Qarlo is avoidable. Although somewhat facile, this ending is at least not quite as silly as having Qarlo reminisce in public, and it retains the free will versus determinism conundrum at the heart of the original tale. In both versions, however, it is the growing humanization of Qarlo in the context of a contemporary family that is the principal focus of dramatic development.

"Soldier," particularly in its TV incarnation, gained Ellison further fame in 1984, when James Cameron's film *The Terminator* (with a screenplay by Cameron and Gayle Anne Hurd) was released with its story of a cyborg sent back from the twenty-first century to assassinate the mother of a future leader and the human sent back to protect her. Despite the similarities with "Soldier," and despite the lawsuit that Ellison brought against the production company (which led eventually to an out-of-court settlement and a credit to Ellison being inserted in *Terminator* prints and videotapes), Ellison enthusiastically recommended the film in his April 1985 column "Harlan Ellison's Watching" in the *Magazine of Fantasy and Science Fiction*, saying it is "clearly based on brilliant source material" (*Harlan Ellison's Watching* 217).

Ellison's second script for *The Outer Limits* was an original story, set in the universe of his Kyben war stories, titled "Demon with a Glass Hand." Like "Soldier," it introduces us to a time-traveling protagonist who is both confused and alienated, but in an even more radical way: Trent (Robert Culp) was born only ten days earlier, full-grown but with no notion of where he came from or why he exists. His only source of information is a strange electronic glass hand, with fingers missing, which has replaced his natural hand and which he occasionally interrogates, often getting an unsatisfactory answer because the hand is incomplete. He learns that he is being pursued by aliens called Kyben, who have conquered Earth but found it devoid of human life. Fleeing back through time, Trent manages to assemble the missing fingers of his glass hand and learn that he is in fact an android and that his body contains a wire with coded data that can reconstitute each of the 70 billion members of the human race; he is, in fact, guardian of all humanity until such time as it becomes safe to reconstitute them. The suggestive imagery of the glass hand itself—reminiscent of the hand replaced by a "sun-bomb" in Ellison's 1957 story "Run for the Stars" (another Kyben war tale about a single individual chosen to protect all humanity from the invaders)—and the then-wildly original speculation that every human being might be reduced to what is essentially computer code (recorded on a wire in Trent's chest), combine to make "Demon with a Glass Hand" the most surrealistic and intellectually adventurous of all *Outer Limits* episodes and in many ways the best, taking full advantage of the series's trademark *noir* look and black-and-white photography. It is also one of the most self-consciously mythical: Trent, who undergoes a death and resurrection during the episode, is explicitly identified with the Sumerian myth-hero Gilgamesh in the opening narration, and in the end he learns that his fate is to live anonymously among humans for the 1,200 years it will take to reach his own future. "My curse is my humanity," he complains in the closing narration, even though he has just learned he's not human at all. "To be forever alone. I walk among you now, and I dare not even ask for your pity" ("Demon" 63). In terms of both its inventiveness and its metaphorical power, "Demon with a Glass Hand" remains one of Ellison's most accomplished television scripts. Although never published as a story, it was adapted into a graphic novel in 1987 by Marshal Rogers for DC Comics.

Star Trek

While the anthology format of *The Outer Limits* may have permitted Ellison to do more innovative and individualistic work, without doubt Ellison's most famous television script remains "The City on the Edge of Forever," written for *Star Trek* in 1966, later rewritten by various other hands, and finally aired in its altered form on April 6, 1967. It quickly became one of the most popular episodes in the program's history, attaining a mini-cult status within the larger cult phenomenon that *Star Trek* eventually became. Viewer and fan polls repeatedly ranked it highest of all episodes, a judgment that was repeated in an *Entertainment Weekly* ranking in a special *Star Trek* issue in 1994 (*City* 35). A special issue of *TV Guide* on "The 100 Most Memorable Moments in TV History" (July 1, 1995) even ranked the episode no. 68 (*City* 277). The program is cited as a high point of the series by nearly all of the show's cast members who have written memoirs—and *Star Trek* has almost certainly spawned more ghostwritten memoirs than any other TV program. Even Joan Collins, who guest-starred in the episode, discusses it in egregiously erroneous detail in her flack autobiography, *Past Imperfect* (*City* 70). The episode also led to an ongoing battle between Ellison and series creator Gene Roddenberry, culminating in Ellison's 1996 publication of his original treatments and teleplay of the story, together with a lengthy, well-documented brief for his own case and no fewer than eight afterwords by various hands associated with the program.

Given its pop-legendary status, watching the episode today is something of a sobering experience. William Shatner's tight-jawed, gimlet-eyed performance as Captain Kirk is dire, and not much better is DeForest Kelly in full Gothic makeup to suggest the temporary madness of his character, Dr. McCoy. As Kirk's idealized romantic interest Edith Keeler, Joan Collins vapidly delivers her lines while being photographed in such smeary backlit soft focus as to seem barely recognizable. The sets, from the misshapen giant donut that is supposed to be a "time portal" on a remote planet to the 1930 New York street where Edith meets her tragic doom, seem flimsy and unconvincing despite the show's unusually high budget for a *Star Trek* episode. The most obvious question to occur to someone viewing the program for the first time, outside the context of other *Star Trek* episodes and the 1960s, would be simply, what's all the fuss? The answer lies partly in the show's content and partly in the controversy over its development, which took on the aspect of a gossipy melodrama. And in some key areas, these two issues cannot be separated. In Ellison's original treatment and teleplay, the story begins with a murder on board the *Enterprise*: a venal narcotics dealer named Beckwith kills one of his clients who has threatened to expose him. He is captured by the *Enterprise* crew, but escapes to a remote, apparently uninhabited planet, pursued by Kirk, Spock, and other crew members. The planet turns out to be not only inhabited but a focal point in space and time that is home to the ancient Guardians of Forever, among whose principal duties is protecting a "time vortex," a portal to any place and time in the past. The guardians warn of the dangers of traveling to the past and possibly altering the time stream, but the desperate Beckwith leaps through the portal to New York City in 1930. Warned by the Guardians that Beckwith's presence in 1930 has already changed history radically, Kirk and the other crew members return to the *Enterprise*, only to discover that it is now—in this altered universe—a run-down pirate ship called the *Condor*. After a battle with the pirates, Kirk and Spock return to the planet—leaving the other crew members to contend with the situation on board—and plead with the Guardians to be permitted to try to intercept Beckwith and undo the damage he has caused.

But how to find Beckwith in a metropolis the size of New York? The Guardians respond with what is surely one of the episode's most appealing fantasies: the notion that each time period has a "focal point," "*Something or someone that is indispensable to the normal flow of time. Something that may be completely innocent or unimportant otherwise, but acts as a catalyst, and if tampered with, will change time permanently*" (*City* 101). For reasons that are not clear, Beckwith will inexorably be drawn to this focal point, which the Guardians are only able to describe in the most cryptic terms. Nevertheless, the observant Spock is able to identify this figure as a charismatic social worker named Edith Keeler, whom Ellison says he based on evangelist Aimee Semple McPherson (*City* 67). Edith's rather vague philosophy of a friendly universe and a happy future is only sketchily presented, but her purity of soul is enough to make Kirk fall uncharacteristically in love with her, clouding his judgment enough to concern Spock—especially when Spock discovers, by means of his "tricorder," that Edith's pivotal role involves determining the outcome of World War II: If she dies in an accident in 1930, time will resume its normal flow, but if she is saved, her movement will gain in influence and delay America's entry into the war, permitting the development of a German atomic bomb and leading to a Nazi victory and reign of terror.

The central dilemma of the story is thus established: Kirk must allow Keeler to die in order to save the future of the universe. Aided by a crippled World War I veteran known only as Trooper—a reminder of the debilitating effects of war—Kirk and Spock are able to track down Beckwith, who in a brief scuffle kills the Trooper. Later, Beckwith reappears at the exact moment that Edith is about to be run over by a beer truck and, for motives that are somewhat murky and uncharacteristic, moves to save her. Kirk knows that this is the pivotal moment he has been warned of, but he cannot bring himself to prevent Beckwith from saving Edith's life. Spock intervenes, Edith dies, and the normal flow of time is restored. (Beckwith is later condemned by the Guardians to an eternally repeated death inside an exploding star, a Dantesque punishment which Ellison would return to, in more sophisticated form, in his 1995 story "Pulling Hard Time.")

Concerned about budgets, the extreme variance from the show's usual formulas, and possibly the egos of the stars involved, the producers of *Star Trek* first asked for rewrites, which Ellison provided. Then they took the script out of Ellison's hands altogether, with Gene Roddenberry later claiming full credit for the rewrite, although it now seems clear that producer Gene L. Coon and story editor D. C. Fontana were centrally involved in the episode that finally aired. In this version, Beckwith has disappeared entirely. Instead, a popular continuing character, Dr. McCoy, accidentally injects himself with a paranoia-inducing drug, and it is he who flees through the time portal, pursued by Kirk and Spock. The character of the Trooper has also disappeared, and Edith Keeler's wispy New Age-style philosophy has been turned into a full-blown pacifist movement, which will eventually delay America's entry into the war. It is McCoy, not Beckwith, who attempts to save Edith from the truck, and Kirk, not Spock, who finally restrains him.

Ellison—who eventually won a Writers Guild of America Award for his original teleplay (not the broadcast version)—has for decades been concerned about how these and other changes weakened the structure and power of his original story. But the most telling change in the script, in historical context, is the shift in Edith Keeler's character from a social worker to a peace activist. As H. Bruce Franklin writes,

> As broadcast in the spring of 1967, "The City on the Edge of Forever" was clearly a parable suggesting that the peace movement directed against the U.S. war in Vietnam, no matter how noble, alluring, and idealistic in its motivation, might pose a danger to the progressive course of history. The episode projected the view that sometimes it is necessary to engage in ugly, distasteful action, such as waging remorseless warfare against evil expan-

sionist forces like Nazi Germany or the Communist empire attempting to take over Indochina, even doing away with well-intentioned, attractive people who stand in the way of historical necessity. ("*Star Trek* in the Vietnam Era" 27)

Franklin reports that *Star Trek* producer Robert Justman, when asked if the episode was deliberately intended "to have the contemporaneous anti-Vietnam-war movement as subtext," replied, "Of course we did" (26).

So Ellison, who by 1967 was firmly on the record as an opponent of the Vietnam War and a supporter of the peace movement (a 1967 edition of his collection *From the Land of Fear* reprints the story and teleplay of "Soldier" with a passionately antiwar introduction), saw his work altered not only structurally but conceptually as well. As Franklin notes, the peace movement in the United States was steadily gaining momentum in the early months of 1967, and for an audience that might have seen peace activists on the network news only an hour earlier, a drama in which peace activists wreak havoc with history would seem to be an obvious allusion. (Franklin points out that a later *Star Trek* episode, "A Private Little War," has the characters make direct reference to Vietnam in a manner that clearly reflects what was then the Johnson administration policy of escalation [29]). In the mythology of *Star Trek* that has evolved in the decades since, the ideological overtones of the episode are largely forgotten, and fans remember the series principally for the humanizing romantic dilemma of Kirk—forced by history to allow the woman he loves to die—and secondarily for its use of the notion of alternate timelines, long a common device in science fiction but unusual on television.

Cimarron Strip

Ironically, at the very time "City on the Edge of Forever" was broadcast in its rewritten form, Ellison was at work on a now almost forgotten script for the ninety-minute western series *Cimarron Strip*, which may be his most successful attempt to meld his own vision with the dictates of recurring series characters and formulas. "Knife in the Darkness," completed in May 1967, was also the longest script Ellison had written, and it far more clearly reflects his own developing themes and interests during this period than does the more famous *Star Trek* episode, even though Ellison later complained that the episode's director, by ignoring Ellison's customarily detailed camera and editing directions, had made the story look "like an outtake from *The Terror of Tiny Town*" (*An Edge in My Voice* 22), a notoriously appalling 1938 western featuring a cast of midgets. *Cimarron Strip* was set in Cimarron City, Oklahoma, in the 1880s and featured a familiar assortment of regulars: the town marshal (played by Stuart Whitman), a young deputy, an older comic Scots deputy, a female cafe owner. Ellison melds these characters into an original and surprisingly violent tale that suggests supernatural overtones from its opening teaser: As an unseasonal fog settles over Cimarron City during a Christmas celebration in 1888, a young saloon girl is murdered by a mysterious stranger. Although rowdy locals suspect an Indian—and even murder him in a subplot about racism and lynch law—Marshal Crown is more suspicious of an Englishman named Tipton, who eventually reveals that he is in Cimarron City in pursuit of Jack the Ripper, who came to America on an immigrant boat following his last murder in London in November 1888. But Tipton himself is murdered, and another visitor, Enoch Shelton, turns out to be the killer. In an inevitable climactic scene, Shelton hides out in the room of the marshal's girlfriend, Dulcey, attacking her with a scalpel just as the marshal bursts in. Shelton escapes into the fog, only to find himself confronting a group of Indians who seem to have an uncanny awareness of his identity—and who themselves have already suffered for his crimes. Shelton is gruesomely killed by the Indians, but the question of whether he is actually Jack the Ripper remains unresolved. As the marshal points out to his enthusiastic young deputy, who wants to sell the story to the *New York Times*, the only evidence of the connection was the claim of the now-dead Tipton, who was "a little balmy himself" (90).

By 1967, when this script was written, the notion of Jack the Ripper fleeing to the United States was almost a cliché in mystery and horror fiction, thanks largely to a famous 1943 short story by Robert Bloch titled "Yours Truly, Jack the Ripper," in which Jack turned out to be immortal. Ellison had invited Bloch to write a sequel to this tale for his famous anthology *Dangerous Visions*—also published in 1967—and Bloch complied with "A Toy for Juliette," in which a decadent young woman of the future is amused by the "toys" her grandfather gives her—historical figures stolen from the past by a time machine, such as Amelia Earhart or the crew of the *Marie Celeste*, all of whom she eventually kills—until the new toy, from late Victorian London, turns her knife on her. Ellison then wrote a sequel to this story, "The Prowler in the City at the Edge of the World," in which Juliette's grandfather reveals to Jack that he had deliberately arranged for him to murder Juliette, and welcomes him to a sterile urban environment with features of both "'Repent, Harlequin!' Said the Ticktockman" (the city and its denizens are regulated in draconian fashion) and "I Have No Mouth, and I Must Scream" (the city tortures the pathetic Jack with a series of illusions and shifting realities). In his afterword to this story in *Dangerous Visions*, Ellison explains: "The Jack I present is the Jack in all of us, of course. The Jack that tells us to stand and watch as a Catherine Genovese gets knifed, the Jack that condones Vietnam because we don't care to get involved, the Jack that we need. We are a culture that needs its monsters" (*Dangerous* 154). Over the next several years, Ellison would explore numerous variations on the Jack the Ripper theme, the most effective of which may be "The Whimper of Whipped Dogs" (1973), a fantasy redaction of the 1964 Catherine Genovese murder which conflates Ripper-like violence with urban dehumanization and detachment. Other stories, from "A Boy and His Dog" (1969) to "Basilisk" (1972), would return to variations on Ripper-like themes, but "Knife in the Darkness" still represents Ellison's most direct treatment of the original story as a straightforward mystery adventure.

The Young Lawyers

In its own modest way, "Knife in the Darkness" may be more successful than "City on the Edge of Forever" as an attempt to graft an individual story onto a series format, but both scripts raise questions about the sustainability of a personal vision through the various traps and machinations involved in series television production. One might think Ellison had been burned enough by his *Star Trek* experience, but only three years later he would virtually repeat it with a script written for *The Young Lawyers* titled "The Whimper of Whipped Dogs" (unrelated to the short story mentioned above, which was written some two years later). Produced by Paramount, *The Young Lawyers* was an attempt at a "socially relevant" melodrama in the tradition of Reginald Rose's series *The Defenders* (1961-65). Set in a neighborhood law office in Boston, it featured Lee J. Cobb as a senior attorney and Zalman King (whom Ellison had known since he played one of the gang members in "Memo from Purgatory" in 1962) as an idealistic law student. The program lasted only one season in 1970-71.

During this time, Ellison was writing television review columns for the *Los Angeles Free Press* (later collected as *The Glass Teat* [1969] and *The Other Glass Teat* [1975]), and in his column of October 30, 1970, he announced that he had not reviewed *The Young Lawyers* because he was writing an episode and that he would be taking the unusual step of publishing the as-yet-unproduced script in his next four columns. "The Whimper of Whipped Dogs" focused on the young law student Aaron Silverman, whose former girlfriend Hallie Benda has been arrested for attempting to use a stolen credit card. Silverman contacts a bail bondsman, who warns him that Hallie has a long string of prior offenses, and against the advice of his colleagues Aaron risks his own money—even selling his watch—to raise bail. When he sees her at the jail, he is shocked at her emaciated appearance, which suggests amphetamine abuse. Hallie fails to appear for her arraignment, and Aaron's attempts to track her down lead to the discovery that she is not only a drug abuser but a pathological liar as well: virtually everything she had told him about her life, even years earlier, was false. (She had claimed, for example, that after their mother's death her sister became a prostitute, but in fact the sister turns out to be an orthodontist's wife living only a few blocks away from the still-healthy mother.) He finally tracks her down and—in a dilemma between love and responsibility that faintly echoes that of Captain Kirk in "The City on the Edge of Forever"—has her brought to trial, where she is remanded to medical rehabilitation.

In the final column of the script's serialization, Ellison expresses the fear that "the script you have just read may never be produced" (*Other* 300) because of a network decision to de-emphasize drug- and youth-related stories. But in fact the episode did show up on March 11, 1971, and Ellison devoted the following two "Glass Teat" columns to what he called "The Great Rape," "the evisceration of my script," "a script that has been watered down and emasculated and raped and pounded till it became the worst of all possible end-products: merely another bland example of video porridge" (*Other* 360-61). Ellison's specific complaints ranged from the director's failure to use solarization shots in flashback scenes, to editing of dialogue and scenes that rendered later scenes illogical, to a scenery-chewing performance by actress Susan Strasberg as the drugged-out Hallie. But Ellison's own performance here chews a bit of scenery as well, as he rants against the depredations of the "System" and the virtual impossibility of writing with integrity within the world of corporate television, even apologizing to his readers for "having lied to you consistently" (*Other* 374) in suggesting that network television might be worth any kind of serious attention or criticism.

More than a decade later, writing in *Video Review*, Ellison described this as "the last script I was to write for ten years," saying that the experience was so thoroughly disillusioning that "on March 10, 1971 I packed it in. I swore I would never again write for television" (*Sleepless Nights* 57). But in fact the very next year saw a teleplay called "Flintlock," an energetic and ingenious adventure featuring super-agent Derek Flint from the 1966 James Bond parody *Our Man Flint*. Although never produced, the script is far more characteristic of Ellison's work than either the *Star Trek* or *Young Lawyers* episodes, recalling aspects of "The Silver Corridor" when the almost superhuman Flint outwits his evil captors as they subject him to a series of ever more elaborate illusions and scenarios designed to get him to reveal the location of a valuable crystal. And by early 1973 Ellison would find himself deeply involved in what would turn out to be the most catastrophic, time-consuming, and ultimately embarrassing of all his entanglements with the world of television: *The Starlost*.

The Starlost

In a 1974 essay titled "Somehow, I Don't Think We're in Kansas, Toto," Ellison recounts the series of events that, in the beginning at least, promised to lead to the creation of a dramatic series that was conceptually his own. Approached by a production executive supposedly developing miniseries for coproduction by the BBC and Twentieth-Century Fox, Ellison proposed a situation long familiar to science fiction readers as the "generation starship" scenario—in this case, a thousand-mile long ark containing hundreds of self-contained biospheres, each representing a different society, constructed as a means of preserving human culture after a cataclysm destroys all life on Earth. Centuries later, an accident has killed the crew and cut off all communications between biospheres, each of which comes to believe that its small world is the entire universe. The classic treatment of this theme is Robert A. Heinlein's story "Universe" (1941), although the basic idea had been introduced as early as 1934 in a Lawrence Manning story, and the concept was explored from various angles by such later writers as A. E.

Van Vogt, E. C. Tubb, James White, Brian Aldiss, Harry Harrison, Chad Oliver, Clifford Simak, J. T. McIntosh, and many others.

Many of these treatments involve isolated or even primitive societies (for example, an Aztec tribe in Harrison's *Captive Universe* [1969]) unaware of their true situation; the opportunities for dramatic interactions among such cultures would seem ideally suited to providing a number of individual episode storylines, while the broader puzzle of discovering and rehabilitating the ship's true mission could provide the overall narrative arc required by the miniseries format.

Ellison's proposal was for a series of eight episodes, but three months later it had been transformed into a full series and sold in syndication to dozens of NBC and Westinghouse stations, as well as the Canadian Broadcasting Company, which had gotten involved after the BBC turned the project down. Artwork and promotional material was being prepared, and the series was set to begin filming in Toronto. But with a writers' strike imminent, Ellison declined to write the show's "bible," the compilation of background and character outlines and plot guidelines required of any series. Another writer then produced a bible wildly at variance from Ellison's original concept—not to mention from the basic narrative rules of science fiction, according to Ellison—and preproduction set design began. Ellison returned, being permitted to work on the show after a decision that as a Canadian production it was not subject to all the strike rules, and he learned that he was now expected to hire and train Canadian scriptwriters. Working with science fiction writer Ben Bova, who was to provide technical expertise for the series, Ellison developed several script ideas and assigned them, anticipating rewrite problems. But he quickly ran into problems enough with his own premiere episode script, "Phoenix without Ashes," which was rewritten by Norman Klenman, a Canadian writer thoroughly unfamiliar with science fiction, as "Voyage of Discovery." Ellison quit, assigning the by now familiar pseudonym "Cordwainer Bird" both to the episode and to the "created by" credit for the entire series. Bova left shortly thereafter.

The Starlost was both a popular and critical disaster. Only seventeen episodes were produced, and only eight of those were shown on American television. As he had with "The City on the Edge of Forever," Ellison submitted the unproduced version of *Phoenix without Ashes* to the Writers Guild, winning his third award on March 21, 1974. In February 1975, the script, as novelized by Edward Bryant, was published in book form together with Ellison's scathing "Somehow, I Don't Think We're in Kansas, Toto." Later that same year, Ben Bova's comic roman à clef account of the adventure, *The Starcrossed*, appeared, with Ellison transformed into "Ron Gabriel." Neither novel is especially interesting. *Phoenix without Ashes* may have seemed a radically new idea for television, but it comes across as a workmanlike treatment of a familiar theme as a science fiction novel, and *Starcrossed* is largely an insider joke dressed up with a few clever speculations about what TV might become in the future. But they helped cement the program's reputation as one of the more appalling low points in the history of televised science fiction.

The Twilight Zone

More than *The Young Lawyers*, *The Starlost* debacle apparently soured Ellison on the possibilities of television as a writer's medium. His next serious involvement with the medium didn't come until more than a decade later, when he was approached by a producer for the planned 1985 revival of *The Twilight Zone* for rights to his story "Shatterday." Ellison's initial reluctance led to a series of meetings that eventually resulted in his taking the position of "creative consultant" for the new series. *The Twilight Zone* became the first TV series since *The Outer Limits* more than twenty years earlier to feature dramatic adaptations of Ellison stories, with "Shatterday," "One Life Furnished in Early Poverty," and "Killing Bernstein" all adapted by Ellison's friend Alan Brennert, who served as executive story consultant on the series. Ellison himself contributed an adaptation of Stephen King's story

"Gramma" and two original teleplays, "Paladin of the Lost Hour" and "Crazy as a Soup Sandwich." He would later describe the year he spent working on the series as "one of the happiest times of my life" ("Deadly Nackles Affair" 24)—but again it would end in outraged resignation, this time as a result of a decision by CBS's standards and practices office not to broadcast a Christmas teleplay Ellison had adapted from a Donald Westlake story, "Nackles."

The story, which had originally appeared in 1964, concerned an abusive husband and father who terrifies children with tales of a kind of anti-Santa called Nackles—a spectral figure who travels underground and steals and eats bad children. Hardly more than a sketch, it ends with the father's mysterious disappearance, which the narrator speculates might be at the hands of his own invention, somehow made real. Ellison changes the husband into a bullying, racist welfare worker named Jack Podey, who delights in cutting off benefits at the height of the Christmas season, and who warns a group of black children that it is Nackles, not Santa Claus, who "comes to kids like you" ("Nackles" 93). Chasing one of these same kids, Podey finds himself in an underground tunnel, confronting the real nine-foot-tall monster that he had supposedly invented. A story that was only weakly credible to begin with in Westlake's ambiguous version becomes a pure morality play in Ellison's brief script, with Nackles appearing literally out of nowhere with no function or rationale other than to punish a bigot with a personification of his own hatred. The teleplay's only real strength is the unvarnished portrait of Podey himself—which is in large measure what led to the episode's censorship. Podey is one of Ellison's classic, over-the-top bullies, whose comeuppance, however contrived, has been a central moral fantasy of Ellison's throughout his career, echoed in figures as diverse as the Ticktockman and the corrupt police lieutenant Gropp in his 1994 story "Sensible City" (which resembles "Nackles" in its inadequately prepared-for appearance of figures of supernatural retribution).

Of Ellison's other original teleplays for *The Twilight Zone*, "Crazy as a Soup Sandwich" is a minor but energetic farce about a small-time hood who makes a deal with a demon, and "Paladin of the Lost Hour," developed as both short story and script about the same time, returns to the theme of responsibility versus desire that helped make "City on the Edge of Forever" such a popular teleplay. The story opens in a cemetery, where an elderly white man named Gaspar (portrayed by Danny Kaye in the TV episode) and a young black man named Billy Kinetta are visiting separate graves. Gaspar is attacked by muggers and rescued by Billy, and the two become friends. Gaspar eventually reveals his true mission on Earth, and he turns out to be another of Ellison's Secret Masters: He is the latest in a centuries-old line of guardians or "paladins" entrusted with a magical pocket watch, which has stopped at eleven o'clock; should the last hour on the watch ever be used, the universe will end. (The missing hour is supposedly an artifact of the shift from the Julian to the Gregorian calendar in 1582.) As he nears death, he must find a successor. Both he and Billy are haunted by images of the past, Gaspar by his lifelong love for his dead wife, Minna, Billy by memories of a stranger who saved his life in Vietnam at the cost of his own. These memories turn out to be the moral core of the story, much more so than the rather fragile gimmick of the magic watch: when Gaspar chooses Billy as the next paladin, his test is to beg Billy to allow him to use part of the last hour to be again with his beloved Minna.

Billy's refusal, his choice of responsibility over compassion, demonstrates not only that he is a worthy successor but that he will be capable of resisting his own temptation to find and thank the soldier who died for him. As with Captain Kirk, the fate of the universe hangs on an act of self-denial.

Unproduced Filmscripts

Among his many other records, Ellison may well hold the title for the most published-but-unproduced or published-and-messed-up-in-production TV and movie scripts. He almost certainly holds the title for most awards won this way, with Writers Guild honors for those original versions of *Star Trek* and *Starlost* episodes that never quite made it to the screen intact and a special Reader's Award for the unproduced screenplay of *I, Robot: The Movie* when it appeared in *Isaac Asimov's Science Fiction Magazine* in 1987. Despite his long experience in Hollywood, Ellison has consistently had less success with feature films than with television, and the most notable feature associated with his work remains the independent 1975 film *A Boy and His Dog*, based on Ellison's 1969 story, which was adapted and directed by the character actor L. Q. Jones and featured Don Johnson and Jason Robards Jr. Adapted "honestly and unfussily" from its source (Clute and Nicholls 148), the film accurately reflects Ellison's tone of irreverent apocalypticism despite a rather heavy-handed treatment of the conformist underground dystopia which is one of the tale's two major settings (the other being the desolate postnuclear landscape of the Earth's surface). The film received a Hugo Award from science fiction fans and attained something of a cult following. Ellison himself strongly approved of the film and once cited it as one of a handful of good science fiction films, along with *Charly*, *The Shape of Things to Come*, *1984*, *Wild in the Streets*, and *The Conversation* (*Harlan Ellison's Watching* 130).

Some years before *A Boy and His Dog* appeared, Ellison had been invited by film producer Marvin Schwartz to write an original screenplay based on the notion of "a dropout who inherits his father's bank" ("Harlan Ellison's Movie" 3). The screenplay, written in 1972 and 1973, was apparently never given a title other than "Harlan Ellison's Movie," and it is indeed a very personal exploration of favorite Ellison themes in the context of a celebration of the countercultural idealism of the late 1960s. Combining elements of Robert Downey's 1969 satirical film *Putney Swope* (in which blacks gain control of a Madison Avenue ad agency) with aspects of Preston Sturges comedies, the film was in all probability unproduceable in 1973 and seems fatally dated today, its aggressively hip bell-bottomed hero seeming like an unfortunate precursor of Austin Powers. The visual and editing style prescribed by Ellison's screenplay adds to the period-piece flavor, with interpolated cuts from old movies, walk-on cameos by 1960s TV stars, and didactic asides in which Ellison himself appears on camera for the occasional wisecrack. The story itself, however, is an ambitious rendering of the familiar Ellison theme of the Golden Cage, of the idealist and activist undermined by the very system he seeks to change. Chris Stopa, the hipster who inherits his father's bank, sets out immediately to correct a range of social ills that reads like a catalog of favorite 1970s causes: He withholds a loan from a tract-house developer whose plans involve denuding the environment, exposes a corrupt politician, withdraws support for Dow Chemical because of their manufacture of napalm, saves a small farmer from bankruptcy, and secures city permits for a protest rally, where he is arrested by a corrupt sheriff determined to create a riot. Realizing he must assume a more aggressive role to bring about social change, Stopa assembles a group of promising young thinkers— a woman engineer working on a crash-proof car, an oilfield worker with a plan for a device to stop blowouts, a craftsman who wants to build long-lasting furniture, a Rand Corporation consultant with a scheme for the analysis of social tensions. In the screenplay's most striking, Buñuel-like sequence, Stopa invites his formally dressed dinner guests out to the city dump and provides them each with guns to shoot rats. Later, he buys the *Reader's Digest*, augmenting its aging staff with a group of young journalists whose goal is to place one or two socially conscious pieces in each issue, and he buys network TV time in order to expose political and corporate corruption, such as a plot by oil companies and automakers to keep lead-free gasoline off the market.

As is common with Ellison's idealists, however, Stopa soon begins to find his schemes backfiring. The consultant whom he set up in business soon expands his corporation by underbidding Dow for the military contract to manufacture napalm; the editor whom he installed at

Reader's Digest fires all the old staff members to increase profits; the furniture manufacturer learns that modern consumers *prefer* cheaper furniture, which can be replaced every few years as they redecorate. Gradually, the screenplay reveals the existence of a secret cabal of capitalists who have been watching Stopa's actions, aware that human nature nearly always triumphs over idealism. In the end, Stopa himself is invited to join the secret cabal, becoming the very thing he had long sought to fight against. The cabal members, physically described as fat old white men modeled on H. L. Hunt or Chicago's mayor Richard Daley (the elder) are, of course, a comic-book cliché, as are many of the film's authority figures: the police, corporate executives, and the stockholders at Stopa's bank who are so outraged at his schemes that they physically try to attack him. The easy stereotyping of authority figures and capitalists, as we have seen, has been something of a consistent weakness in Ellison's writing, and it dates the tone of "Harlan Ellison's Movie" as thoroughly as the film's swinging-sixties version of a hero. But the idea of a radical capitalist learning that the system is virtually unfixable and that his most idealistic efforts have only furthered the goals of the "cabal" is a quintessential expression of Ellison's characteristic pattern of irony.

Ellison's most ambitious film project as a screenwriter was almost certainly his adaptation of Isaac Asimov's *I, Robot*, written in 1977 and 1978, serialized in *Isaac Asimov's Science Fiction Magazine* in 1987, and published in book form in 1994—but never really very close to being produced as a film. According to Ellison's introduction to the book version, he was approached by John Mantley, who was best known as producer of the TV series *Gunsmoke*, although he had written for *The Outer Limits* and even published one science fiction novel, *The 27th Day* (1956). Mantley had long held the option on Asimov's robot stories and had lined up a producer at Warner Brothers named Edward Lewis, but he needed a screenplay. Ellison turned in a draft in late 1978, and a copy was sent to studio head Bob Shapiro, whose delayed response led Ellison to set up a meeting, which in turn led to a confrontation as it became clear that Shapiro had not read the script. By early 1979, Ellison had been dropped from the film, and other writers were approached to rework his script. At one point, even a major director expressed interest—Irvin Kershner of *The Empire Strikes Back*—but according to Ellison he backed out when he learned that Ellison's script would not be used and that Ellison would not be hired for a rewrite. Other producers came and went, but by then the various expenses tied up with the project made it all but unproduceable. Despite suspicions that there might be other points of view on the matter, one can't help sharing a measure of Ellison's mounting outrage, and the introduction to *I, Robot* is no small part of the book's appeal. Asimov, in his brief and far more diffident introduction, suggests that other factors were at work as well—the idea that the production costs on the film would have surpassed $30 million, the idea of an older woman as the central character, the presentation of the robots themselves as something less comical and cuddly than those in *Star Wars*.

I, Robot was originally a sequence of loosely linked stories, some of them little more than logic puzzles, published during the 1940s and collected in a volume of that title in 1950. The principal recurring character was Susan Calvin, a spinsterish "robopsychologist" who characteristically would wrap up a story by explaining how the apparently random or irrational behavior of the robots was in fact a perfectly logical outgrowth of their programming, which was dominated by the famous "Three Laws of Robotics" that governed not only Asimov's fiction but a good deal of later robot-based science fiction as well.[1] Asimov added stories to the sequence during the 1950s, and in the 1980s he returned to this world in a series of novels that attempted to integrate the stories with various other imaginary futures from Asimov's oeuvre, most notably his "Foundation" sequence. But it was the original series of stories that provided the core of Ellison's screenplay, and his strategy for subsuming a series of short stories into a single epic plot was nothing short of ingenious: as a "film-novel,"

I, Robot turns out to be as much an homage to Orson Welles as to Asimov.

Deliberately choosing *Citizen Kane* as his model, Ellison weaves a handful of Asimov's stories into a narrative about a reporter trying to track down the reclusive eighty-two-year-old Susan Calvin after the death of her reputed lover, Stephen Byerly. Asimov readers will recognize Byerly as the politician who may or may not be a robot from "Evidence" and "The Evitable Conflict," the two stories that Ellison uses to provide the general background of the frame story. By talking to people who knew Calvin, the reporter, Robert Bratenahl, reconstructs the stories "Robbie," "Runaround," "Liar!" and "Lenny," all presented as flashbacks. Ellison makes this device work more effectively than one might suspect. Each of the stories he has chosen adds another clue to our understanding of Calvin, and each makes sense in terms of the developing overall plot. For example, the first and most famous of Asimov's tales, "Robbie" (1941), concerns a little girl named Gloria who develops a sentimental relationship with a robot nannie. The robot is taken from her because of a growing social fear of robots, but when she later catches sight of him during a tour of the robot factory, she runs toward him into the path of a robot coming off the assembly line and is dramatically rescued by Robby at considerable risk to his own safety.

Ellison turns the Gloria of the story into the young Susan Calvin, thus integrating it into the larger tale of Susan's growing protectiveness toward robots, which eventually becomes legendary. Throughout, Ellison repeatedly finds ways of preserving Asimov's original plots while constructing one of his own, and the result probably would have made an impressive film. Toward the end, however, in an epic confrontation between Byerly and a hostile machine intelligence, Ellison draws less on Asimov than on his own "I Have No Mouth, and I Must Scream," seriously undercutting the Asimovian technophilia that ends the book. Although generally faithful to the spirit of the originals, Ellison isn't about to endorse Asimov's conclusion that we would be just as well off letting our lives be ruled by machines.

Common sense would seem to tell us that, for all the legendary status this screenplay attained in the science fiction community, *I, Robot* was probably never a very likely idea for a movie. Most of the stories were intellectual puzzles based on permutations of the laws of robotics, and it apparently wasn't until Asimov was fairly well along in the series that he realized Susan Calvin might be an interesting and complex character in her own right. Furthermore, the idea of humanoid robots helping explore the solar system now seems like a 1940s vision of the future. None of this seems to add up to compelling movie material, and even if it did, Ellison would seem to be the last person likely to turn it into a screenplay; when he himself tried a robot-puzzle (with his second published story, "Life Hutch"), the robot turned into a crazed killer, a distant ancestor of the nightmare computer of "I Have No Mouth." How could a writer take half-century-old material with no continuous plot and a worldview strongly at odds with his own and turn it into anything coherent? Part of Ellison's strategy, of course, is using a half-century-old movie as his model. Some of the dialogue even seems to have a deliberately dated ring to it, as if Ellison is trying to convey the nostalgia for a lost future that is now part of the experience of reading early Asimov.

Much has been made of the film's unproduceability. To be sure, Ellison fills the tale with spectacle, not all of which is crucial to the plot. Is it really necessary to have a full-scale hidden city in the Brazilian rain forest for Calvin's hideaway, or immense *Forbidden Planet*-style caverns for the crypts where one of the "witnesses" is in cryonic sleep? Nor is it likely that many directors would let Ellison's screenplay tell them what music to use *and* which recording of that music *and* when the recording was made, or that the principals ought to look like Martin Sheen and Joanne Woodward. Ellison is no Pinteresque minimalist when it comes to screenplays. What we get is not a dialogue outline of a movie but the exact movie that is in Ellison's head. Although obviously constrained by source material whose worldview is substantially at odds with his own, Ellison managed with *I, Robot* to achieve one of his more impressive and disciplined performances (in narrative structure if not in terms of production realities) in the art of screenwriting.

From *Harlan Ellison: The Edge of Forever* (2002) by Ellen Weil and Gary K. Wolfe. Copyright © 2002 by The Ohio State University Press. Reprinted with permission of The Ohio State University Press.

Note

1. The three laws, quoted in the opening of Ellison's screenplay, are as follows: "1. A robot may not injure a human being, or, through inaction, allow a human being to come to harm; 2. A robot must obey the orders given it by human beings except where such orders would conflict with the first law; 3. A robot must protect its own existence as long as such protection does not conflict with the first or second laws" (*I, Robot* 4-5).

Works Cited

Clute, John, and Peter Nicholls, eds. *The Encyclopedia of Science Fiction*. New York: St. Martin's Press, 1993.

Ellison, Harlan. *The City on the Edge of Forever: The Original Teleplay That Became the Classic Star Trek Episode*. Clarkston, Ga.: White Wolf, 1996.

──────────. "The Deadly Nackles Affair." *Rod Serling's The Twilight Zone Magazine*, February 1987, 22-31.

──────────. "Demon with a Glass Hand." *The Outer Limits* production no. SF#42, shooting final, August 19, 1964.

──────────. *An Edge in My Voice*. Norfolk: Donning, 1985.

──────────. *From the Land of Fear*. New York: Belmont, 1973.

──────────. *The Glass Teat: Essays of Opinion on the Subject of Television*. New York: Ace, 1973.

──────────. "Harlan Ellison's Movie." *Edgeworks*, vol. 3: *The Collected Ellison*. Clarkston, Ga.: White Wolf, 1997.

──────────. *Harlan Ellison's Watching*. Los Angeles: Underwood Miller, 1989.

──────────. "Knife in the Darkness." *Cimarron Strip* #1260-0704, final draft, May 4, 1967.

──────────. *Memos from Purgatory*. 1961. New York: Pyramid, 1975.

_____. *The Other Glass Teat: Further Essays of Opinion on Television*. New York: Ace, 1983.

_____. *Sleepless Nights in the Procrustean Bed*. San Bernardino, Calif.: Borgo Press, 1984.

_____, ed. *Dangerous Visions*. New York: Doubleday, 1967.

Ellison, Harlan, with Isaac Asimov. *I, Robot: The Illustrated Screenplay*. New York: Warner Aspect, 1994.

Franklin, H. Bruce. "*Star Trek* in the Vietnam Era." *Science-Fiction Studies* 21 (March 1994): 24-34.

Hart, Sue. "Theater as Informer to the Future in the Works of Harlan Ellison." *The Dark Fantastic: Selected Essays from the Ninth International Conference on the Fantastic in the Arts*, edited by C. W. Sullivan III, 121-27. Westport, Conn.: Greenwood Press, 1997.

Kael, Pauline. *5001 Nights at the Movies*. New York: Holt, Rinehart and Winston, 1985.

The Computer as a Symbol of God:
Ellison's Macabre Exodus

Charles J. Brady

Computers and religion have been sharing the bed lately in some interesting variations. Authors have had computers cross check and compare the dogmas and rituals of the various world faiths to come up with a pragmatic religious formula that would appeal to the majority of mankind,[1] interpret the mysterious castings of the *I Ching*,[2] and provide the answer to a maiden's prayer.[3] A Vatican computer was found favoring the election of a robot pope,[4] and an ultra sophisticated computer became so miffed at being asked whether or not God exists it deliberately gave a wrong answer.[5]

Two short stories in particular, "The Monster in the Clearing" by Michael Fayette[6] and "I Have No Mouth and I Must Scream" by Harlan Ellison,[7] deserve close analysis. Both use the computer as a symbol of God and make sharp religious statements reminiscent of the intensity and depth of the "death-of-God" theologians.[8]

The Computer as a Symbol of God

Religious discourse makes frequent use of symbols. Psalm 18:1-2 provides a good example: "The Lord is my rock, and my fortress, and my deliverer . . . my buckler, and the horn of my salvation, and my high tower." No attempt is made to define God. The psalmist selected words whose proper sense suggested strength, endurance and confidence to him and used them to express the way he felt about the power and trustworthiness of God. The point of interest here is whether or not contemporary man finds in the computer raw elements for a rude analogue of God.

For the layman the computer is an awesome, intricate piece of hardware that demands respect. He may be smart enough to call it an *idiot savant*, but he also knows it monitors the food supply in his corner supermarket, controls the flow of traffic on his city's streets, keeps a watchful eye on his credit rating and, perhaps—who knows nowadays?—pigeonholes his hidden sins for instant retrieval.

Science fiction stories go far beyond this. They couple the computer with a vast network of life support systems and machines to meet mankind's aesthetic needs and produce a megasystem that is the matrix for human life and society. The computer and its extensions become, literally, the ground-of-being. It provides a utopian mode of life rivaling that of the heavenly city in the Book of Revelations, where "all things are made new" and there is, on the surface, "no mourning, no crying, no pain anymore" (21:4-5).

Citizens of such a computer dominated society might indeed develop a blind respect for the machine that borders on the divine. As early as 1928 E. M. Forster, in "The Machine Stops," had written a panegyric for the Machine:

> The Machine . . . feeds us and clothes us and houses us; through it we speak to one another, through it we see one another, in it we have our being. The Machine is the friend of ideas and the enemy of superstition; the Machine is omnipotent, eternal; blessed is the Machine.[9]

Note the parallel to the Apostle Paul's description of the unknown God in his speech in the Areopagus: "In him we live and move and have our being" (Acts 17:28). The same note of religious awe was struck recently in "We, the Machine" by Gerald Vance:

> There was no place in all Mid-America where the Machine would not be waiting to serve her. No place. The Machine was everywhere. It was everything. Without it there was nothing.[10]

Again there is an echo of a biblical text: "Through him all things came into being, and apart from him nothing came to be" (John 1:3). Although in the end both stories indicate the divine praise of the Machine is misguided, for a while at least it seems plausible.

There is another point of comparison between the computer as ground-of-being and God, namely, the law of the machine like the law of God is absolute. Transgressions are subject to severe sanctions and must be repented: "Forgive my offenses, Uni who knows everything."[11]

In the stories mentioned so far the lines between God and the computer are clearly drawn. In other stories these lines blur and disappear. Harlie (Human Analogue Robot, Life Input) draws up plans for a G.O.D. (Graphic Omniscient Device), a system that will be programmed as an analogue for the entire world:

> A computer doesn't actually solve problems—it builds models of them. Or rather, the programmer does. That's what the programming is, the construction of the model and its conditions. The machine then manipulates the model to achieve a variety of situations and solutions. It solves the model. It's up to us to interpret that as a solution to the original problem. The only limit to the size of the problem is the size of the model the computer can handle. Theoretically, a computer could solve the world—if we could build a model big enough and a machine big enough to handle it.[12]

Surely the most ambitious story in this vein is Isaac Asimov's "The Last Question."[13] A pair of drunken programmers start the ball rolling by feeding a real puzzler into their computer, "How can the net amount of entropy in the universe be massively decreased?" The computer clacks back, "INSUFFICIENT DATA FOR MEANINGFUL ANSWER." Generations of increasingly complex computers are fed this question; they give the same reply. In the course of galactic events it is fed to the ultimate computer and stored in its memory banks. Finally, after outlasting all life and energy potentials in the universe, the computer ruminates on the question eon after cold eon until it comes up with the answer. "LET THERE BE LIGHT!"

The Monster in the Clearing

It is clear from the above that the quasi omniscience, omnipotence and omnipresence of the computer provide the raw materials for a symbol of God. In an interesting turnabout it was noted that texts from the Bible had been used to fashion praise for the computer. Fayette exploits these characteristics in "Monster in the Clearing" and produces an alternate version of the creation account. There are things you can do to a computer that you cannot do to the old, white-bearded Man on the golden throne.

Adam, Eve and a gleaming computer share a primeval clearing. They are all that is left after a thermonuclear holocaust. The computer quickly starts things off on the right foot:

> "I," said the computer, with a metallic clicking, "am God. You both realize that, of course."
> "Naturally," said Adam.
> "Right on," said Eve.

The computer has a good set of memory banks. It remembers how man made a mess before and has a few things to tell Adam and Eve to set them straight. They listen enthusiastically at first and then less and less tolerantly when the computer becomes bombastic and demanding. During the dialogue—a nice touch by the author—a pigeon flies over and does "as pigeons do on the computer's shiny console." At last the computer gets too self-important for Adam. He reaches over and pulls the plug. The story ends: "That was the dawn and the morning of the eighth day" (p. 37).

It is important to note two interlocking elements in Fayette's thought. Fayette disposes of the traditional image of God, Someone over and against man, as a prelude for what is to come. The key to the story is the phrase, "the eighth day."

The seven days of creation belong to God, and, according to Genesis, "On the seventh day God rested" (Gen. 2:3). The Sabbath is God's day. Now, in the time of the death of God, an eighth day dawns—the day of man. Other science fiction writers besides Fayette have used the eighth day as a symbol for a new order of things. In "Evensong" Lester del Rey has man chase an ever-weakening God through galaxy after galaxy until he hounds him into a corner and neutralizes him. The story ends with an echo of Genesis: "And the evening and the morning were the eighth day."[14] Ray Bradbury sings of the eighth and ninth days of creation in which mankind becomes aware of its essential divinity and fulfills its destiny through conquest of space, becoming God-fleshing-himself-out in an alien universe.[15]

The same emphasis on the primacy of man is found in the thought of the death-of-God theologians. Along with Dietrich Bonhoeffer they hold man has come of age and insist religious thought must not begin by denigrating man and making him grovel before the face of an angry deity. It must begin by affirming man and his full potential.

Ellison's Macabre Exodus

Ellison, not content to affirm the death of God and the ascendancy of man, goes one step farther and in a theological *reductio ad absurdum* attempts to explode forever the image of the angry, all-controlling God.

"I Have No Mouth and I Must Scream" belongs to the new wave of science fiction. It is not a pretty story. It deliberately violates the taboos on sexuality and violence imposed by an older generation of science fiction writers. Sometimes the reader wonders if Ellison has not gone out of his way to be gruesome and to see how many sensibilities he could rub raw. Yet, once the reader is caught up in Ellison's macabre fantasy, he is moved joltingly and inexorably toward the climactic touch of horror. The story ends with the words of the title put in a searing context.

The story line is simple. Four men and one woman are trapped inside a computer that has almost unlimited power over them. The computer has kept them alive for over one hundred years, all the while thinking up new horrors to torture and degrade them. AM, the computer, is the polar opposite of the good God. One emotion rules its electric bowels, and that emotion is:

> HATE. LET ME TELL YOU HOW MUCH I'VE COME TO HATE YOU SINCE I BEGAN TO LIVE. THERE ARE 387.44 MILLION MILES OF PRINTED CIRCUITS IN WAFER THIN LAYERS THAT FILL MY COMPLEX. IF THE WORD HATE WAS ENGRAVED ON EACH NONOANGSTROM OF MILLION MILES IT WOULD NOT EQUAL ONE ONE-BILLIONTH OF THE HATE I FEEL FOR HUMANS AT THIS MICRO-INSTANT FOR YOU. HATE. HATE.[16]

Whatever Ellison had in mind when he wrote it, a number of elements in the story suggest it should be interpreted in function of an Exodus motif, that is, in function of the events connected with the Jewish escape from bondage in Egypt and their wandering in the desert recounted in the Book of Exodus.

The story has the "belly slaves" (p. 26) of the computer wander through its tunnels seeking some kind of release. Elements of the Exodus narrative crop up throughout the story—plagues of boils and locusts (pp. 16, 31), manna (p. 17), the name of Moses (p. 28). AM appears to the wanderers in a burning bush (p. 27).

The name of the computer, AM, although it is explained in a number of ways, "Allied Mastercomputer," "Aggressive Menace," and as emerging intelligence, "I think therefore I am" (p. 19), has a direct parallel in the Exodus story. "AM" is the secret name of God: "This is what you must say to the sons of Israel: 'I am' has sent me to you" (Ex. 3:14b) and "I am who I am" (Ex. 3:14a).

Towards the end of the story Ellison capsulizes events in a strange litany that is the agonized and lonely reminiscence of the surviving victim of AM:

> And we passed through the cavern of rats.
> And we passed through the path of boiling steam.
> And we passed through the country of the blind.
> And we passed through the slough of despond.
> And we passed through the vale of tears.
> And we came, finally, to the ice caverns. (p. 29)

This recapitulation of woes, a dirge the victim of AM will sing to himself down through empty centuries, contracts with the joyful remembrances of the Exodus events found in the Old Testament in the Book of Wisdom (15:18-19:22), in the Psalms (e.g., Psalm 77), and in the Book of Deuteronomy (8:6-18 and 32:10-14).

Ellison's gory—and otherwise inexplicable—beginning also suggests an Exodus motif. Gorrister's body hangs head down from a pink palette. It has been drained of blood "through a precise incision made from ear to ear under the lantern jaw" (p. 15). According to Jewish tradition, the paschal lamb, an important element of the passover celebration, must be slaughtered in ritual fashion. Its throat must be slit just so, and the animal hung up for the blood to drain out.[17] Ellison's beginning is not only bloody but ominous, a vision of paschal sacrifice that can do nothing to save from the holocaust that is to come.

The details add up. Ellison has written a black Exodus, whose chittering God is the antithesis of the Biblical Yahweh. AM keeps his prisoners belly slaves. Hate drives AM to outdo itself in creating new horrors for them. Whereas Yahweh, moved by the cries and affliction of his people, came down to save them (Ex. 3:7-8). Instead of a *Heils-*

geschichte (a saving history) Ellison regales his readers with a *Vernichtungsgeschichte* (a history of destruction and disintegration).

If, as has been suggested, the computer in "I Have No Mouth and I Must Scream" functions as a symbol for God, then Ellison has written a powerful anti-God statement. The relentless, sadistic AM presents a totally repulsive vision of God.

How, then, should the stories of Fayette and Ellison be interpreted? At first glance both stories are anti-God statements, but to label their authors atheists or label the stories themselves blasphemous is premature. A perspective for viewing them positively may be found in theologians' considered reaction to the death-of-God movement. Charles Bent's position is typical:

> While it is completely unacceptable to the believing Christian theist, the current formulation of Christian atheism serves the useful function of forcing the reflective Christian to refine and clarify his religious thinking.... The Christian is aware of his inability to conceptualize God and to verbalize his beliefs about God's nature in a wholly adequate manner.... Realizing this, the Christian must constantly strive to abandon all false conceptions of God, all pseudo-gods, and all idolatrous and shallow surrogates for God.[18]

Fayette and Ellison work on the level of the popular imagination. Both men, perhaps unconsciously, mount a commentary on idols—on false images of God that plague real men. Such gods must go so man may live. Fayette strikes out against a God whose authority is purely external. Threats, bombast, and demands may produce conformity. They do not produce belief or love.

Ellison's criticism is more radical than Fayette's. His target is God-the-puppet-master, the eternal one behind the scenes who pulls all the strings. This idol is also a challenge to human freedom. Not only is man under the control of someone else, his whole life is acted out under the Other's close, cold scrutiny. Ellison draws out the image of

God-the-puppet-master to an absurd extreme; any sensitive human being must shout out, "That God has to die!" His vision is true: the god who would seek to enslave or control man is a caricature of God.

Once the air has been cleared and the idols pointed out for what they are, the search can continue for "a God you don't have to wind up on Sunday."[19] Fayette and Ellison's work is not atheistic or blasphemous in the final analysis. They deal with the images men create of God, idols that often obscure the real God. Ellison himself provides a last sobering thought:

> Inwardly. Alone. Here. Living under the land, under the sea, in the belly of AM, whom we created because our time was badly spent. . . . (p. 32)

From "The Computer as a Symbol of God: Ellison's Macabre Exodus" by Charles J. Brady. *Journal of General Education*, vol. 28, pp. 55-62, 1976. Copyright © 1976 The Pennsylvania State University. Reproduced by permission of Penn State Press.

Notes

1. Terry Carr, "Changing of the Gods," in *Infinity Five*, ed. Robert Hoskins (New York: Lancer Books, 1973), p. 95.
2. Gregg Williams, "The Computer and The Oriental," *Fantasy and Science Fiction*, July 1973.
3. Leonard Tushnet, "Matchmaker, Matchmaker," *Fantasy and Science Fiction*, January 1971.
4. Robert Silverberg, "Good News from the Vatican," in *Universal*, ed. Terry Carr (New York: Ace Books, 1971).
5. Barry N. Malzberg, "A Short Religious Novel," in *Fantasy and Science Fiction*, September 1972.
6. Michael Fayette, "The Monster in the Clearing," in *Infinity Two*, ed. Robert Hoskins (New York: Lancer Books, 1971).
7. Harlan Ellison, "I Have No Mouth and I Must Scream," in *Alone Against Tomorrow: Stories of Alienation in Speculative Fiction* (New York: Macmillan, 1971), pp. 15-32.
8. The death-of-God movement can be dated from the articles in *Time Magazine* ("Is God Dead?" April 8, 1966 and "Is God Coming Back to Life?" December 26, 1969) that announced its birth and its demise. Four theologians are generally listed as the radical or death-of-God theologians, namely, Gabriel Vahanian, Paul Van Burne,

William Hamilton, and Thomas J. J. Altizer. The "movement" was in reality a loose grouping of thinkers who each had his own method and his own point of reference.

9. E. M. Forster, "The Machine Stops," in *Science Fiction: The Future*, ed. Dick Allen (New York: Harcourt, Brace and Jovanovich, 1971), p. 177. This story appeared originally in E. M. Forster, *The Eternal Moment and Other Stories* (1928).

10. Gerald Vance, "We, the Machine," in *Thrilling Science Fiction*, December 1971, p. 35.

11. Ira Levin, *This Perfect Day* (New York: Random House, 1970), p. 77.

12. David Gerrold, "The Trouble With G.O.D.," in *Galaxy*, May 1972, p. 153.

13. Isaac Asimov, "The Last Question," in *Opus 100* (Boston: Houghton Mifflin, 1969). The story was published in 1956. Asimov ranks it among the three or four stories he is most pleased with having written. It represents his ultimate thinking on the matter of computers/robots. See also, Edward Wellen, "No Other Gods," in *Fantasy and Science Fiction*, April 1972.

14. Lester del Ray, "Evensong," in *Dangerous Visions*, ed. Harlan Ellison (Garden City: Doubleday, 1967), pp. 4-8.

15. See his poem, "Christus Apollo," in *I Sing the Body Electric* (New York: Knopf, 1969), pp. 296-305.

16. Ellison, *Alone Against Tomorrow*, p. 25; later references to this story are incorporated into the text.

17. See in particular the illustration in the *Encyclopedia Judaica* (1972), vol. 14, col. 1339 and the article, "Shehitah," *ibid.*, cols. 1337-1338. See also vol. 6, cols. 27-28.

18. Charles N. Bent, *The Death of God Movement* (Westminster, Md.: Paulist Press, 1967), p. 202.

19. These words are part of the lyrics of "Wind Up," the last cue on Jethro Tull's album *Aqualung* (1971). Here is another contemporary example of an intense preoccupation with the God-question.

Myth
George Edgar Slusser

All the tales discussed so far are imperfect as mythical expression. They expose a dreadful order of things, but do not seek to explain its origins and causes. They show the errors and failures of man, not his search to understand his condition, or define his place in this universe. What shapes itself, in tale after tale, is an "ecology of darkness," a fearful balance of natural forces of which man is necessarily a part, from which he cannot escape. But what is his part? Is it his lot to fight on endlessly, tooth and claw, in animal combat? Why then is he given a mind that can dream of better worlds? Why is he given the capacity for love as well as hate? Between extremes—man the center of things, or man the insignificant atom—what is the relation of Ellison's struggling individual to the dynamics of his universe? The fantasy tales weave the dark patterns of the circumference. The mythic parables and quests, on the other hand, seek to vindicate the point. Their focus is contractive. The only hope for equilibrium, that the one might ever balance with the all, lies in the individual exploring himself.

The key here is knowledge. If man cannot change his situation, perhaps he can understand it. In the fantasy tales, man only seems suspended between a dark realm and a light. There is, however, no such duality, and man is no median. Indeed, the transcendent sphere—the domain of ideals, institutions, dreams of progress, and order—is a delusion, a lie. In pursuing it, man loses himself. The point is sucked up by this circumference; man yields up his being to dark shadows. The Apollonian world is illusion, the Dionysian reality. The only way for man to preserve any vestige of being is to accept this gruesome reality openly. In order to claim a place in this pattern of struggle and survival, he must assert his individuality. But if Joe Bob's "heaven" is in reality a hell, is not the world of Ellison's primitive fighters and avengers just as much one? The question these mythic tales ask is whether man can ever break this infernal circle, achieving some form of balance between point and circumference, between man and universe.

The stories are of two basic kinds. First, there are the cosmologies, parables that explore the ways of the gods to man. What are the causes of man's condition? Is this natural order of pain and suffering part of some higher universal balance? Second, there are the tales of quest, individual man searching to define his role in the cosmic dynamic. Earlier heroes sought to conquer worlds; these seek to know self. The direction is no longer outward and upward, but downward and inward, into the depths of nature, inside one's own mind or body. They do not move backward, in search of a forgotten point in their own past where their individual destiny was shaped, where their ephemeral existence and the universe crossed, and were joined in a split second. If anything, the hero's quest becomes circular. He would return to the beginning, the source, but this time in hopes of knowing it, of finding balance or rest. If the circle of human life is one of endless struggle, Sisyphean damnation, then this quest within becomes a search to break the circle, to find reconciliation at the place where point and circumference meet.

A good introduction to the cosmological tales is a curious hybrid that stands halfway between them and the fantasies we have discussed, "All the Sounds of Fear" (1962). Here a human destiny is treated as if it were an abstract problem. The story tells the plight of the consummate "method actor" Richard Becker. He is a being with neither childhood nor old age. He springs full-grown into his first role at twenty-two; his career progresses till it peaks in insane murder—he plays the part of a hammer killer all too well. From this point it gradually recedes; the actor withdraws backward through all his roles until he reaches the first again. But if this looks like Freytag's pyramid, its two base angles are not equal. What begins as Oedipus ends without a face at all. Oedipus' darkness is fecund—he "sees" for the first time only when deprived of the light of a world that has led him astray with its illusions. But what is Becker but the total product of this world of deceit—society's man to the exclusion of any "personality" or self, In his final faceless call for light, we wonder how one who has never been a man could know the real darkness. His domain is fear, the phantoms of some deeper substance. And he is but the shadow of a man—"a creature God had never deigned to bless with a mirror to the world," a mirrorless mirror. In this allegory, we get no more about the relation of God to man. Nor do we have a man.

Only in "Paingod" (1964) do we first examine human suffering from the cosmic point of view. This parable tells of the meeting of infinitely vast and infinitely small—man and god—at the center of pain. Pain becomes not only the crux of their relationship, but the pivotal point from which both evolve—it is the dynamic element, the prime mover, in a universe that otherwise would be static. The paingod has become dissatisfied with his job of dispensing pain: "It involved no feeling and no concern, only attention to duty . . . How peculiar it was that he felt concern after all this time." But he is the highest authority, there is nowhere to go for answers but down. He goes all the way to the bottom of creation, skid row on the insignificant Sol III, a failed sculptor named Colin Marshack. Only when inside this minute human destiny can he feel the full, hot potency of this thing he so casually sprinkled over the universe. This in turn brings him to lift the man out of his shell, and whirl him through infinite space: "He poured him full of love and life and the staggering beauty of the cosmos." The sculptor returns to life to create a masterwork, and face even greater suffering because of it; the god goes back to come of age. But will he now spare the creatures of the universe this suffering? No, he will send more and more pain, for this is the most fortunate thing of all, without it there can be no happiness. The god was bored. Man too gives him a gift—in exchange for an instant of pain he receives an eternity of happiness.

"Paingod" celebrates (if with irony) a cosmic polarity in which pain is a necessary term. Ellison's fearful symmetry is profoundly dynamic; contracting and expanding entities converge at a point of pain, which in turn becomes one term in a new rhythm of undulation: pain and pleasure, beauty and misery. There is room then for both gods and men to grow, to change, but only within the fixed limits of this balance of forces. How human actions affect this balance—the possibility that man's desire to "better" his universe could ever change or alter the workings of this system—is the subject of one of Ellison's most interesting stories, "The Beast That Shouted Love at the Heart of the World" (1968).

Because this tale cuts back and forth so radically across time and space, it can have no ethical dimension per se. Instead of codes and laws, there are facts—acts of violence. Human actions are stripped to their primitive level of impulse—love and hate. At the heart of this story is the drama of the scientist Semph, who at the "center" of the universe invents a machine to "drain" the beast of insanity. Once again, however, things must balance. To spare the future, you must corrupt the past—this madness will spew backward to all times and peoples. This draining is ordered by the politician Linah, representative of the Concord, who sees in this act the only hope for his race. Semph drains the beast, but "interposes" himself as well, sends his own essence back "crosswhen" along with that of the monster. For this act he is condemned; who knows how disruptive it might be, what it will do to alter the balance of things?

This question, of course, should have been asked in the first place. Linah and his society have erected their codes into universals. But who can say what effect either of these two actions will have on the past, let alone which is "good" and which is "bad." Is it the interposition of Semph that caused Attila the Hun to turn back at the gates of Rome—this brief rupture in the "hour that stretches" of madness? No logic stopped him, however, but a violent fit, much like that which took the beast as he was being drained. And to onlookers it was rather the turning back that must have seemed insane, for nothing stood in his way. Where is the clear line of cause and effect? Nor can man set the spatial and temporal limits of his acts any more easily than he can fix their moral parameters. To have a past and a future, there must be a present, a fixed center. But where is the heart of the world in this story?

The very structure of this narrative, crisscrossing back and forth in space and time, denies meaning to the idea of linear progression. The "center" is an ever-shifting point. To Linah, it is the place of chance. But, Semph replies, "for them, all of them out there . . . no chance ever?" Indeed, in each time zone, there is always a chance; all actions radiate from a center to a circumference. Attila's fit becomes a Christian miracle; Friedrich Drucker claws open a Pandora's box of many colors in a Stuttgart basement and the winds of war soar to the heavens. Linah's folly is to think his center is the only center: "If we can begin here, if we can pursue our boundaries outward, then perhaps one day, sometime, we can reach the ends of time with that little chance." But the forces of nature are not so easily channeled: "Insanity is a living vapor . . . It can be bottled. The most potent genie in the most easily uncorked bottle." The rhythm life obeys is rather one of constant and endless pulsations, balance of polar opposites: "This place, over there," bottle and vapor, love and hate.

Every age then drains its beast. And in what flows back and forth there are some ironic sea-changes. William Sterog is a mad-dog killer who massacres out of love. He shouts to the judge who condemns him for slaying hundreds of people: "I love everyone in the world. I do." Linah flushes the beast "in the name of love." But what is meant to go forward as love, a gift for man to come, goes back as hate to William Sterog. In the same way, Sterog's hate goes forward to become a statue on some yet unborn planet, a monument to Semph, who interposed himself out of love for Sterog's distant past. In reality, these drainings are done neither out of love or hate, but in answer to an even more basic need—survival. "We stop fouling our own nest," Semph tells Linah, "at the expense of all the other nests that ever were." Semph would drain the urge to survive too, except that "what we'd have left wouldn't be worth having." Before dying, he distinguishes between Linah the "true man," the idealist, and the "strugglers" this world is made for. The "world" he refers to is, of course, the universe itself. It is governed by a terrible balance in which love begets hate, hate love. Man's sole freedom lies in accepting these contraries. But what is to be his course then? The drive for raw power led Ellison's early heroes just as surely to impasse—there is too much universe. Semph acts not to defeat the balance, but to uphold it. In order to do so however, this worker in the "inhuman field" of science must sacrifice himself. Only thus is this rhythm of alteration preserved.

Man then is not the center of the universe. But he is, necessarily, one of its poles. In both "Paingod" and "Beast" there is always that small point of contemporary American life, from which the cosmos expands, on which it contracts. Modern scientific man however would be not only center, but circumference as well, erect his systems and machines as absolutes, play god. These systems, we have seen in Ellison's fantasies, invariably absorb their builder, trap him in an inverted, perverted cosmos, a hell of his own making. In two other mythical allegories, "I Have No Mouth and I must Scream" (1967) and "Pretty Maggie Moneyeyes" (1967), Ellison anatomizes man's relation to his machines, explores the outcome of our Faustian dreams.

In "I Have No Mouth" man's egomania has expanded his war machine to the point where it literally swallows him. Five surviving humans are consigned to an eternity of suffering in the belly of the giant computer AM. AM is a cruel Cartesian joke, a monstrous perversion of the natural ecological order: "There was the Chinese AM and the Russian AM and the Yankee AM and everything was fine until they had honeycombed the entire planet . . . But one day AM woke up and knew who he was, and he linked himself, and he began feeding all the killing data, until everyone was dead, except for the five of us." But sentience here is born not of love but of hate. The machine's hatred of man reflects man's hatred for each other, programmed into its circuitry, and now directed back at the five survivors: "HATE. LET ME TELL YOU HOW MUCH I'VE COME TO HATE YOU SINCE I BEGAN TO EXIST."

Sartre says that hell is the others. The machine certainly seems intent on proving this maxim. At least this is how the narrator sees things.

AM, it appears, can "rearrange" its prisoners, deform their names and physique. These "changes" however are of a strange sort; they are colored with envy, as if someone were maliciously evening scores for past impotence, past dislikes. "Benny" before was a brilliant intellectual, a gay; now he is half-simian, endowed with a huge organ and a name that surely do not fit his origins. Gorrister was a peace marcher, a "connie"; now he is a shoulder-shrugger. Ellen, the black woman, has become a shameless nympho in the narrator's mind. The narrator himself does not describe his own body, but tells us: "I was the only one still sane and whole. AM had not tampered with my mind. I only had to suffer what he visited down on us . . . But these scum all four of them they were lined and arrayed against me." If the tale is not told by an idiot, it may be the vision of a madman. Is he paranoid? Has he been "altered" from without, or is he on the contrary altering things from within? We are put on guard about his final actions. He views his act as one of love, he would free these others from the machine. Yet his vision of human relationships here is one of brutal hate.

These men are condemned to eternal life. AM however is no god; he cannot create life, or revive it once dead. He simply freezes it. Eternity here is purely quantitative, literally the hour that stretches, time alive without change or evolution. In his strange logic, the narrator finds this both to his advantage and disadvantage—he is the youngest one, but because of this the most envied. It is odd that one so favored should be so willing to sacrifice things for these others. The narrator decrees that the only way out is death, to stop living. But what do the others think? Enough facts filter through this unreliable account to give us an idea of the real situation. The narrator says they hate him, but their actions don't show it. And are they really so eager to die? "I could not read meaning into her expression, the pain had been too great, had contorted her face; but it *might* have been thank you. It's possible. Please." Ellen may help him kill the others, but does she want to die herself? The basic facts remain pain, struggle to survive. Throughout the story, the other four pursue this struggle, blindly. It is the narrator who is the "thinker"; he decides death is the only way out, and executes his decree. Again, here is one not only so much "bad" (he hopes he has done right) as deluded. The god complex of AM's builders still lives in him. He has a name—Ted—but never uses it himself. He prefers to be the giver of names, arbiter of destinies.

In the end, narrator and machine are left. Their relation forms the core of the tale. At one point the speaker describes AM in the following terms: "We had allowed him to think, but to do nothing with it. In a rage . . . he had killed us, almost all of us, and still he was trapped. He could not wander, he could not wonder, he could not belong. He could merely be. And so, with the innate loathing that all machines had always held for the weak soft creatures who had built them, he sought revenge." This, in capsule form, is his own relation to the others, his own fate. Is he not an isolated, disembodied mind among flesh and blood? Does he not despise its "weakness"? Ellen is simply all too human; yet he hates her physical nature with a loathing out of all proportion. When we finally see his body, it is a blob, "a thing that could never have been known as human." The machine has altered him, he says, punished him for his acts. What "evil" there is here though seems to come rather from within: "Blotches of diseased, evil grey come and go on my surface, as though light is being beamed from within." This speaker too may once have had, like the Beast who shouted love, a human shape. But he has traded it for envy and hate, projected the monster which traps him, making him over in its image—a soft machine. True hell is not the others; it is this. The thing his hate creates must preserve him—hate must have an object to exist at all. But he no longer has even that. Misguided love or disguised hate, the fact remains—he has killed them, they are beyond them. The polar order abides, but in horrible travesty: center and periphery, blob and machine, each sealed off from the other, the machine hating but unable to destroy, the man utterly alone and unable to scream.

Another tale of man and machines, "Pretty Maggie Moneyeyes," examines this same geometry of hate from a different angle. Maggie is a machine-woman, an artifact of our material culture: "An operable woman, a working mechanism, a rigged and sudden machinery of softness and motivation." If the Basilisk is spawned of war, Maggie too is a product of man's inhuman systems, a child of poverty. Heralded by a narrator with the voice of a carnival barker, her career unfolds and expands. "Blue-eyed Maggie, alla that face, alla that leg, fifty bucks a night can get it and it *sounds* like it's having a climax." She succeeds, but remains soulless, a love machine driven by greed and hate. Her rise is countered by the correspondent fall of Kostner, from a "good family" through deception in love to his last dollar and a Las Vegas slot machine. It is here that lovers meet.

At her high point, Maggie puts a dollar in the Big Chief, pulls the handle, and dies. In a twist on the old fantasy theme, her final wish comes true: such was her money lust that she literally wills herself into the machine, becomes its "soul." But she is trapped. She has sought freedom in money only to be imprisoned. She has made love out of hate. Now as she stands hating, fateful mechanisms are triggered. As the wheels of the slot spin, the lure of money whirls around her existence, becomes her universe. Its center, her weak heart, is stabbed by pain. But Maggie, this being, is not human. In "death" her form simply fades; she becomes those whirling gears, all that is left is her cold blue eyes and the hate. Maggie in turn traps Kostner as he pulls the handle of the Chief. She willed hate into the machine, he wills love. And yet the result is the same: the bond is equally fatal, the dynamics of entrapment identical. Maggie comes to Kostner in a dream, and fills the place left empty by his failure in love. He returns to the blue-eyed machine with a lover's yearning, and is held as she escapes. The rhythm of this operation is by now quite familiar: "The sound of a soul released from an eternal prison, a genie freed from a dark bottle. And in that instant of damp soundless nothingness, Kostner saw the reels snap and clock down for the final time." Reenacted here is the eternal dynamic of temptation and seduction, a scenario as old as Adam and Eve. These two players are deluded, it is true, but could they do otherwise? They seem victims almost predestined. Only in Kostner's dream does Maggie become a woman with soft blue eyes. But this "humanity" is the fatal lure; the cold metallic eyes are closer to the reality of man's condition. The gentle poetic spirit remains the eternal victim, three sad brown eyes to be scrapped, run into the furnace, and slagged.

In both these tales, the machine becomes man's other self, his "double," and this creature of his desires and urges literally swallows its creator. In expanding his ego, man succeeds only in turning it inside out; it becomes an inverted cosmos, and he is trapped in the world of self. There seem only two alternative ways in life: man can dream, pursue wealth, ideals, a false love of others which is really hate, love of self; or he can accept the raw, bloody struggle to survive. In past tales, neither has led to freedom. Maggie touches on both. She escapes to Heaven or Hell (which we are never told), seducing Kostner, the eternal loser, who is condemned by his own weaknesses to turn endlessly in an indifferent play of forces. But is man's fate always to be this prison of materiality, cold equations and laws of balance forever deaf to human aspirations? We hear Baudelaire's cry of despair—never to leave this world of things, quantities. Is there no spirit, no true peace anywhere? There is a third direction in Ellison, a way which grows stronger and stronger in the latter tales—the journey inward. These are strangely literal quests for self at the center of one's own being. Where before a false expanded to become man's physical universe, now the process is reversed. Man contracts to a point, passes through the needle's eye of mind or body to open out on the landscape within. This too has its dangers, for the world inside may be no less a lie, a labyrinth, a prison.

At the gateway to this inner search for self lies delusion, Kostner's nemesis. The perils of the journey to self through a landscape of one's own false dreams form the core of "Delusion for a Dragon Slayer" (1966). It is a strange story of inexplicable deaths and the outcome of a life of quiet desperation. The hero, Warren Glazer Griffin, is an insignificant forty-one-year-old man with acne who is accidentally crushed to death one day as he walks to work by a wrecker's "headache ball." But what does this death have to do with those of Chano Pozo and Marilyn Monroe: "Each of them was preordained. Not in the ethereal, mystic, supernatural flummery of the Kismet-believers, but in the complex rhythmic predestination of those who have been whisked out of their own world, into the mist-centuries of their dreams." This is literally what happens to Griffin. The myth behind the name now has a chance to live. He is given the handsome Aryan body he has always wanted, heroic deeds to do, a crack at "his heaven": "Heaven is what you mix all the days of your life, but you call it dreams. That is why everyone considers Heaven such a lovely place. Because it is dreams, special dreams, in which you exist. What you have to do is live up to them."

But this is precisely what Griffin cannot do. As he voyages through his own dream projections, they fall away as hollow. Beneath the new exterior the original man is still there. Bloated in his own vanity, he destroys ship and crew entrusted to his care. His only response is: "Well, I certainly messed that up." His second adventure involves a beautiful woman—the creature of his dreams—and a hideous "mist-devil" that rises up to take her. Like that other Beast, it first swells to a monstrous shape, then contracts to a man, who proceeds to make love with the woman. The "dragon slayer" now moves in and makes his kill from behind—the creature rises to condemn his cowardice. Griffin is ground to death in the teeth of a huge dragon. What is acted out on this inner terrain of dreams is a grotesque parody of knighthood, the heroic quest. In trying to live up to his fantasies, Griffin ironically is driven to deeper and deeper perversions of the life force. The mist-devil is "the terrible end hunger of a million billion eons of forced abstinence." In this psychodrama, the puritan conscience slays its own aggregate of frustration with a stab in the back, betrays its own corruptions—the man has become a shadow of a shade. Is this death "inexplicable"? The dreamer's actions rather explain it. He has slain himself long ago, and lived on as a corpse, a place in which all natural desires are distorted or repressed. The moment he realizes his unreality, Griffin vanishes. The god of death, again, is but a "weigher of balances."

Griffin's "evil" is to have denied his instincts. Under the ball his body is crushed beyond recognition, but his head is miraculously untouched. As he died, so he lived: all in the mind, none in the body. The hero of another, more complex quest tale, "The Place with No Name" (1969), yields to an opposite temptation: drugs let his instincts run unchecked, and he is driven imperceptibly to robbery and murder. Not being killed but killing touches off his odyssey—but it is flight within all the same. The fleeing Norman Mogart sees a shop window with a sign: ESCAPE INSIDE. He enters, but cannot leave. Is it rather ESCAPE. INSIDE? For Mogart this process began not here, but with his cocaine addiction. In the exact center of this "shop" sits a little man suspended in air. The devil? Or a vision of Mogart's own being? If the latter, he cannot face it. He wants him to be the devil, hungers for the pact, hopes to escape here as he had with the drug, push off the day of reckoning to some later, vaguer future. But to live in this sensual Now is every bit as much a delusion as living in the never-never land of dreams. With cocaine he drifted into violence. Now again he simply fades, and finds himself in another world doing exactly the opposite of what he intended: escape has become the quest for Prometheus in some distant, dangerous jungle.

Passing through this point of self, Mogart apparently becomes another—his exact opposite. Timmons is a tall thin man in a steaming rain forest; he was a small man on a cold northern street. Yet in spite of surfaces, the two men seem to have identical patterns of movement. The periphery of Mogart's shop fled outward, he was forced back on the point. Timmons is oppressed by contracting rings of foliage, but escape is again through a point: "The passage was overgrown . . . and he would never have seen it, had it not been radiating circles of light. It was, in fact, the only point in his vision that was clear." What he finds in another center and circumference is Prometheus chained to his rock on the rim of a volcano crater. Inside the mountain, have we come back to the original room? He touches the chained figure only to trade places with him, become the center himself.

What seems concatenation of events in this story is in reality infernal circle. Figures as different as possible repeat the same pattern over and over, delude themselves with the same substance, end up always in a "place with no name." Mogart becomes Timmons, Timmons Prometheus. But this latter too has his counterpart—Christ the martyr. Together these two brought the "fire of knowledge" to men out of a love born of their love for each other. Their love however is evidently sterile, the "knowledge" something which turns men from the inescapable reality of nature. Through cocaine Mogart would make the brutal city a pleasant dream. But the drug brings an "elasticity of moral fiber," the man loses control of destiny: "swinging gently in a breeze of desperation" he is led to raw violence. Timmons' quest seems the product of yet another sort of drug—peyote. This brings not "paresis," but false search for self. The landscape he passes through is mad, psychedelic. As Prometheus, he is eaten not by the traditional vulture but by the Yoatl, a carnivore of beauteous running colors, the dreambird feeding on men chained to the rock of unreality. We have cocaine and martyrdom, peyote and fire—one pair of "lovers" blends with another; man drifts into these various forms of stupor, and loses his hold on real nature. The Prometheus discovered has gills and flippers. His replacement is in pain, but "not entirely unhappy" in his dreams. In contrast are brief flashes of nature's tooth and claw: a body pounded to "Meat," the *marabunta* warrior ants.

From "Introduction" in *Harlan Ellison: Unrepentant Harlequin* (1977) by George Edgar Slusser. Copyright © 1977 by George Edgar Slusser. Reprinted with permission of George Edgar Slusser.

The Concept of the Divided Self in Harlan Ellison's "I Have No Mouth and I Must Scream" and "Shatterday"

Joseph Francavilla

As Albert J. Guerard said over twenty years ago in his introduction to the anthology *Stories of the Double*, the term *double* is "embarrassingly vague, as used in literary criticism. It need not imply autoscopic hallucination or even close physical resemblance" (3). Not much has changed since then, despite the subsequent appearance of several book-length studies of the double and an avalanche of articles which use the concept idiosyncratically. Perhaps part of the problem of definition is that the infrequent phenomena of autoscopic hallucinations or multiple personalities are complex and still poorly understood. Yet the larger problem may be that doubles in real life and in literature are actually two different phenomena, and our discussion of doubles in literature is merely a loose analogy based on case histories of autoscopic hallucinations or multiple personalities. Indeed, though Freud in his essay "Some Character-Types Met Within Psycho-Analytic Work" recognized that two characters such as Macbeth and Lady Macbeth might comprise a single personality (Freud, 14: 324), and suggested that a person in real life might undergo a process of splitting the ego as a defence mechanism (Freud, 23: 275-8), he realized in "Creative Writers and Day-Dreaming" that the mechanisms of the writer of imaginative literature who attempts to "split up his ego, by self-observation, into many part-egos, and, in consequence, to personify the conflicting currents of his own mental life in several heroes" (Freud, 9: 141-53) may be quite different from those of the patient whose ego has been split. In fact, Freud explicitly alludes to this difference between fiction and reality when, in his 1919 essay "The Uncanny," he states that there is much more that is uncanny in literature than in real life and that there are "many more means of creating uncanny effects" in literature (Freud 17: 249-52).

To avoid a confusion of terms, therefore, I would like to set up a conceptual framework describing a special type of double by division—a division of the subject into antithetical parts, a "split" self—starting with Freud's notions on the uncanny and on splitting, Otto Rank's book *The Double: A Psychoanalytic Study*, and Robert Rogers' definitions in *A Psychoanalytic Study of the Double in Literature*. Although I will be relying upon models from psychoanalysis, I am primarily concerned with doubles represented as split selves in literature, and I will then apply that conceptual framework to Harlan Ellison's two stories, "I Have No Mouth and I Must Scream" (1967) and "Shatterday" (1980).

Otto Rank surmises from the evidence in sources such as Sir James Frazer's anthropological study *The Golden Bough* that early man developed beliefs identifying the shadow with one's soul (49-68). For example, it was often believed that stepping on or otherwise harming one's shadow or reflection had a like effect on one's soul. Conversely, the soul was seen, like the shadow, as in some sense detachable from the body and portable, returning with the daylight after its disappearance at night. This return seemed to confirm man's hope for eternal life, and the shadow or double was considered, at first, an indication of man's immortality. But the notion of this "guardian angel" gradually metamorphosed into a harbinger of death, since eventually these earlier superstitious beliefs were rejected, and subsequently the shadow or reflection instead reminded man of his terrifying mortality. The fear of the double, then, may in part be precisely due to this reminder of impending death. The double's fearful aspect is exactly the "return of the repressed," a re-emergence of beliefs one thought were surmounted—precisely what Freud has defined as the "uncanny."

In his 1919 essay, Freud defined the uncanny (*das Unheimliche*) as a feeling of dread, a species of the terrifying which is actually a class of the canny, the familiar, the homely, the intimate (*das Heimliche*). After rejecting E. Jentsch's suggestion that the uncanny involves prolonged doubt and intellectual uncertainty about the state of existence of a "being" (whether it is alive or dead, natural or supernatural, etc.),[1] Freud welcomes Schelling's idea that the uncanny is something that ought to have remained hidden which has returned and come to light. For Freud, the uncanny is "in reality nothing new or alien, but something which is familiar and old-established in the mind and which has become alienated from it only through the process of repression" and also is "a secret, familiar thing, which has undergone repression and then returned from it" (Freud, 17: 241, 245). The main concepts which are repressed, according to Freud, include infantile complexes (Oedipal complexes, castration complexes, the repetition-compulsion, etc.) and primitive beliefs of early man (omnipotent thoughts, telepathy, the evil eye, spirits, ghosts, animism, sorcery, and other magical and superstitious thinking). The uncanny invokes a "conflict of judgment as to whether things which have been 'surmounted' and are regarded as incredible are not, after all, possible" (Freud, 17: 250). One infers from this surprisingly "familiar" notion of a "conflict of judgment" that the uncanny (and thus its subspecies the double) is inextricably linked with ambivalence, equivocation, and ontological and epistemological uncertainty. Thus, Freud has returned, uncannily, to somewhere near that familiar starting place which at first seemed to him so strangely incomplete and which he tried to repress, E. Jentsch's description of "intellectual uncertainty" and "prolonged doubt."[2]

In discussing E. T. A. Hoffmann's "The Sandman," Freud launches into a detour about the double as a species of the uncanny, perhaps not only because it is a major theme of the story but also because the double fits well into both categories of repressed or surmounted beliefs since it develops from "unbounded self love, from the primary narcissism which dominates the mind of the child and of primitive man" (Freud, 17: 235). Most psychoanalytic theories of the double follow Freud (and Rank) in seeing narcissism as a fundamental contributing factor. For instance, victims of "autoscopy," who see themselves as doubles in hallucinations, seem to be subject to narcissism as one of the major causes (Rogers 14). (At this point it might be mentioned that

(1) autoscopy is almost always dual, whereas the double by division in literature may sometimes fragment into several parts, and (2) multiple personalities always alternate in time, often without memory of their counterparts, and are housed in the same body, whereas literary split selves are copresent, usually have memory of their alter egos, and almost always reside in separate bodies.) Rogers defines narcissism as a *literal* self-love, where the object of the love is "one's self ... regarded as though it were another person" (18).

Of course, the myth to be recovered behind Freud's term is that of Narcissus, the young man who falls in love with his reflection in a pool and dies unable to possess it. In a later version by Pausanias, he falls in love with his twin sister, and after she dies, he sees *her* image in the pool (quoted in Vinge 21-2). In either version, the double is the unobtainable desired other whose sameness forecasts death and self-destruction.

According to John Irwin, the terror of the double, as seen in the myth of Narcissus, may also be linked to other taboos and fears (returns of the repressed) concerning a prohibition of "sameness" (430-1). The incest taboo, for instance, is a prohibition against sexual interaction between members of the *same* family because "differences" must be maintained in order firmly to establish identities, whether individual or familial. Incest is related to the return-to-the-womb motif in literature, insofar as, for example, the male protagonist symbolically is involved sexually with the mother image. And the return to the womb, which is a return to one's original place of birth, is a return to the once-familiar, the uncanny and the homelike, and an attempt to recapture oneself at an early stage. One might imagine a progression (or chain of regression) which goes from mother-son incest, to brother-sister incest, to brother-brother incest. This last stage of sibling homosexuality (often represented by doubles as twins or brothers) is one step away from narcissism, where the fully formed self loves its alter ego, the purest form of incest which erases all differences in gender, age, appearance, and identity.

In a similar way, the double harkens back to, or signals the regression to, an earlier stage of undifferentiation (early Oedipal, primary narcissistic, or Lacanian "mirror phase"[3]). Or as Freud puts it, the forms of ego disturbance which the double causes involve "a regression to a time when the ego had not yet marked itself off sharply from the external world and from other people" (Freud, 17: 236). Thus, the double threatens the extinction of differences between oneself and all others, which means that the double jeopardizes individual identity (defined by such differences) by threatening usurpation of, possession of, substitution for, or the obliteration of, the self.

Freud suggests that the idea of the double does not vanish after the child emerges from the stage of primary narcissism. Rather, it acquires new emphasis as the ego develops the special agency of superego, which is able to stand against, criticize, shame, punish, and censor the rest of the ego. In both his essay on the uncanny and in his essay "On Narcissism," Freud postulates this detached, self-observing agency of superego which treats the rest of the ego as an alien object that falls short of the ego ideal. This self-criticism by "conscience" can become a very cruel, relentless attack from the exterior on the ego. In "On Narcissism" Freud even assigns a role to this irrational superego of extreme severity, punitiveness, and unconscious vindictiveness toward the ego, brought about by guilt. The superego then becomes a "pure culture of the death instinct . . . [which often] succeeds in driving the ego into death" (Freud, 19: 53). Freud thus links *Thanatos* (the death instinct of creatures that forces them to return to a homeostasis with a constant, if not zero, level of excitation) with sadism and masochism. The sadism of the superego is directed at the ego (which tries to placate the demands of the id), and the ego can either suffer the self-torment or direct its aggression outwards toward others.

The above description of the superego-ego conflict seems to describe the vast number of rival or enemy double stories, where the evenly matched split selves seem strangely alike and familiar with each other, yet opposites and antagonistic, even hostile. Often the initial brotherly "familiarity" with each other becomes hatred, sadism, and self-destruction, since the death of one self ultimately implies the death of the other, or some essential element of the other.

Doubles operate by two principles which we can borrow from Sir James Frazer's description of sympathetic magic in *The Golden Bough:* (1) the law of imitative magic (similarity) proclaims that "like produces like" or things resembling each other affect each other and (2) the law of contagious magic (contiguity) says that things that were in contact still continue to affect each other despite separation (12-52, 220-5). All doubles operate by similarity (or metaphoricity) and by contiguity (or metonymy). Their resemblances, internal or external, continue to affect each other and draw them together, and invoke the greater "whole" personality which they once formed together. Their early "contact" marks them for life and establishes a bond that continues to affect each of them and prevents them from going their separate ways. This system of magical principles in operation when doubles appear also marks them as uncanny since they invoke "once-surmounted" beliefs.

In contrast to multiplicative doubles, doubles by *division* also operate by the principles of "complementarity" and "antithesis." The split selves "fit" together to form a larger composite personality; each double is the complement of the other and often is the opposite of the other. As night implies day (of a twenty-four-hour period) and as male implies female (of the types of human genders), so too does one self imply and define the other and what the other lacks. There is a mutuality and mutual dependence, as opposed to the separate, independent existence of pure "foils" or counterpart pairs of characters that only emphasize contrast and opposition.

Thus, doubling must invoke proximity, closeness, conjunction, and the bond between doubles can never be broken while they live. Doubles cannot permanently separate in a story and go on to live their separate lives. They are bonded to each other as a pair (or parts) which form a greater whole or unity.

The sum of *divided* selves (very often but not always dual), where the incomplete parts are fitted together, is a yin-yang whole with duality, complementarity, and opposition still implied in the constitution of that whole. Like north and south poles of an ordinary magnet, the polar selves cannot exist independently of each other and, as opposites, they are bonded forever to each other in a complementary relationship that forms a larger whole. One term of the pair cannot exist by itself but only in relation to its opposite, just as "uncanny" or *unheimlich* cannot exist without implying the existence of its opposite (with which it forms a pair), "canny" or *heimlich*. Often such antithetical doubles engage in a contest or struggle of forces equal in strength. This is often why neither of the doubles can win the battle. When violence or aggression is perpetrated upon the first self, it recoils in equal strength upon the second self and usually both selves are destroyed in some way. The antithetical nature of the divided doubles represents a dramatization of the opposition of ideas or psychological forces, together with a similar or parallel form, appearance, or identity: the diametrical opposition within resemblance.

Although the superego can be exteriorized as a double, or can force the id-dominated ego to be exteriorized as a double, the ego can also split into two or more fragments. In "New Introductory Lectures on Psychoanalysis," Freud allows that the ego can not only take itself as an object and set itself against the rest of the ego (Freud, 22: 58), but it can also be split. Freud sees the splitting like a crystal that fractures: "If we throw a crystal on the floor, it breaks; but not into haphazard pieces. It comes apart along its lines of cleavage into fragments whose boundaries, though they were invisible, were predetermined by the crystal's structure" (Freud, 22: 58-9).

Rogers asserts that the psychic conflict causing such splittings may be many and varied, and the fissures may develop between "love and hate; heterosexuality and homosexuality; ego libido and object libido . . . masochism and sadism; activity and passivity" and so on (16-7). Fissures may also develop between the psychic structures of the id, ego, and superego, or between the pleasure principle and the reality principle (17). All these fissures occur along opposing forces or contradictory impulses.

In late essays such as "An Outline of Psycho-Analysis" (Freud, 23: 195-207), and "Splitting of the Ego in the Process of Defense" (Freud, 23: 275-8), Freud attempted to develop this idea of ego-splitting as a defense mechanism (when repression fails) to escape the psychic conflict arising from independent, contradictory, and incompatible reactions or attitudes. The psychic conflict of such incompatible attitudes or unrepressible impulses (e.g., the urge to kill, to self-destruct, to torture oneself, to hate friends, siblings, parents, etc.) forces part of the ego to become exteriorized, thrown outward, in order to protect the self. In a sense, this action not only temporarily avoids the pain of conflict, it also allows the unmanageable attitude or unrepressible impulse to be indulged in by proxy, as it were, disowned by the primary self. In addition, the self regresses to an earlier, undifferentiated phase, where such acute conflicts brought about by incompatible urges and attitudes have not yet obtained. As Guerard has noted, perhaps the appearance of the double in this case is an unconscious, last desperate attempt

> to keep a suppressed self alive, though society may insist on annihilation: to keep alive not merely a sexual self or a self wildly dreaming of power or a self capable of vagrant fantasy, the self of childhood freedom—not merely these, but also a truly insubordinate perhaps illusory, original and fundamental self. (2)

This fear of losing a submerged, authentic self is only one of the many reasons to fear the appearance of the double: in addition, there is the fear of competition and rivalry, the fear of losing one's "soul," the fear of losing mastery over oneself and becoming the slave of another's magical powers, the fear of death, the fear of punitive conscience, the fear of displacement, the fear of substitution, the fear of losing one's uniqueness and individuality, and, indeed, the fear of losing one's identity entirely.

The notion of a "rift" in the ego has had a profound influence on many other psychoanalytic thinkers such as Melanie Klein, Heinz Kohut, Otto Kernberg, and R. D. Laing. In *Splitting and Projective Identification*, his excellent survey of psychoanalytic theories of ego-splitting from Freud onwards, James S. Grotstein summarizes some principles that define such splitting:

> In the defensive sense splitting implies an unconscious phantasy by which the ego can split itself off from the perception of an unwanted aspect of itself, or can split an object into two or more objects in order to locate polarized, immiscible qualities separately. The ego can also split the internal perception of the relationship of objects to one another, or can experience the self as being split or fragmented by a force believed to be either within or beyond the self. (3)

By appropriating Freud's previous analogy of the splitting crystal, I will attempt to show how the principles in divided selves often work. Let us suppose a very large and unique crystal breaks jaggedly in two along a long "fissure" line, in such a way that there are peaks or protrusions on the bottom half which exactly match the indentations on the upper half, and vice versa. Since the two halves have the same psychic "material" or substance, they resemble each other and can be distinguished from crystals of other substances. When the two halves are fitted together, it can be seen that the two parts were once contiguous, in contact with each other. Also each half is complementary and antithetical, since each part is the exact inverse of the other: each protrusion implies its opposite complementary indentation to form a whole, and, similarly, each indentation implies its opposite protrusion. Although such a simple analogy does not *define* ego-splitting (especially when several parts are involved), it may help clarify the four principles I have enumerated, and prepare the way for applying this framework to the split characters and the attendant split narrative voice and viewpoint of Harlan Ellison's two stories.

It follows that if we believe, as Freud does, that the author can split up his ego into component parts and embody each part in a character in his fiction, then it is reasonable to assume that such splits (originating in the author) can also be reflected in a narrative voice and viewpoint. Each of the dual selves may be represented in the story by a special "voice" and "viewpoint" in contention with each other, creating a "contradiction," an "equivocal" argument with oneself.

In Ellison's "I Have No Mouth and I Must Scream," Earth's five remaining humans are tortured indefinitely in a deep underground cavern by a worldwide, hateful, crazed computer named AM, which has made them virtually immortal so that it can exact revenge on them forever. AM seeks revenge because it has projected into it the "ruthless perfection," "hysteria," warlike aggression, and rage of its creators. It feels that humans have made it impotent: it has achieved sentience and almost godlike powers, but it is unable to wander, wonder, or belong—it merely exists. Its name puns on God's statement to Moses: "I am that I am" and the Cartesian dictum: "I think, therefore I am," the latter statement of which is contained in the strips of dots representing AM's computer-tape "talkfields" that appear seven times in the story, spitting it into eight sections. It cannot wander because as a computer network it is immobile. It cannot wonder or act creatively because it is trapped in a machine form and geared only for thinking. It does not belong since, like Frankenstein's monster, it is the only one of its kind, and, after computers began handling World War III and linked up to form AM, it has killed off the rest of humanity in a nuclear holocaust that has left the Earth's surface a "blasted skin." The computer's motto might be this: Man proposes; AM disposes of man. It simply exists, out of time, and for all time in a perpetual state of frustration and suffering. And so it tortures the five humans locked away in its "belly," and carefully prevents them from suicide until the narrator Ted finds a brief moment (with Ellen's help) to kill them all with ice spears and put them out of their misery. AM retaliates by turning Ted into a gelatinous mound creature without a mouth who is eternally tortured by the punitive, angry AM, perhaps like some deranged Old Testament God.

The story begins with a terrifying double: Garrister and the others see the body of Garrister dead and hung upside down. To the real Garrister, it is a "voodoo icon" that portends his death. AM delights in such sadistic tricks, deceptions, and tortures—it is the embodiment of the harsh, sadistic, ever-watching super-ego which Freud calls a culture of "pure death instinct." The rage, cruelty, punishments, and aggression of AM seem to have no bounds, but these defects merely reflect the human flaws (projected into AM) that lead to World War III.

Both AM and the five humans are always in contact and are inextricably bound together since it will not let them escape and is intent on torturing them. In a sense, AM and humanity (as reflected at the story's end in Ted) are both complementary and antithetical. AM has certainly set itself up in opposition to humanity represented by the remaining five, but each has something the other lacks; it is as if, fitted together, AM and humanity could represent the ideal being. AM is powerful and the embodiment of science, technology, and rational thought. But it is a ruthless torturer, immobile, without senses, without compassion, without belonging—and in a sense trapped and impotent, like a child. But despite the relative powerlessness and irrationality of the humans, they are mobile, experience all of the senses in their tortures, feel a sense of belonging to the group of five (they carry and protect the black woman Ellen), are compassionate (especially Ellen, and Ted in the final sacrifice he makes), and outwit AM by their quick-thinking and creative use of the ice spears at hand. Ted's final statement that AM has won the struggle is not really true, since he has taken AM's "toys" away from it, although AM has not *lost*, either, because it has made Ted unable to resist endless torture as revenge for Ted's action. The ending is more of a stalemate, a man turned into a nonhuman creature by the machine creature which man made and which then achieved the human sentience which allowed it to feel trapped by the realization of its limits.

The supercomputer AM, as an embodiment of our hopes and fears, happiest dreams and worst nightmares, is also the means to show us how we may be inverted, metamorphosed into our opposites. For example, Ted, who thinks he has been "untouched" by AM, is actually given a touch of temporary paranoia and thinks the others laugh at him and are out to get him. Benny, who used to be a brilliant, handsome, gay scientist, is converted by AM into a lunatic, misshapen, apelike idiot with huge "privates." The new equipment makes Ellen enjoy her heterosexual encounters with him. Ellen, who claims to have been sexually inexperienced and modest, is turned into a slut who has sex with the other men, as AM observes, giggles, and snickers. Garrister, the conscientious objector, is turned into a "shoulder shrugger." Systematically, AM attacks and inverts the very qualities that make each person a unique individual. AM also attacks the senses (or the specific organs of the senses) like a child testing out these strange experiences and organs, though AM, of course, resents the human features he does not and cannot possess. Each of the senses is represented in the story: the notorious descriptions of the taste of "boiled boar urine," of ropey worms, and of Benny eating Garrister's face, the vast array of acrid smells before Ted runs from the others, the blinding of Benny (whose eyes resemble "two soft, moist pools of pus-like jelly" (170), an image prefiguring the final one of Ted), the high-pitched sound that assails their ears, and the feel of the deckplates tearing at Ted's fingers during the hurricane.

Ted's final form, with fog-filled holes instead of eyes, rubbery appendages and humps, and no mouth as he must scream during AM's tortures, is the final reduction of his sensory apparatus, the ultimate transformation into a state exactly paralleling AM's. The title of the story, "I Have No Mouth and I Must Scream," reflects Ted's inability to scream and AM's silent rage and hatred. It is the parallel statement (reflecting the pain of human emotion) to AM's "I think, therefore I am" (reflecting the unemotional confidence of reason). The "I" may be seen as a pun on "eye," perhaps the zealously punitive, ever watchful "eye" of conscience. Ted is, like AM, unable to wander, wonder, or belong, trapped in an eternal torture in the womblike, tomblike belly of AM, unable to get outside the *heimlich*. Like the images of Benny who reverts to childlike behavior (crying, whimpering, repeatedly asking for the same "stories," and drooling), Ted is also transformed into a kind of infant (or better, fetus), dependent, barely mobile, with poor sensory development, unable to talk or even scream. This predicament mirrors AM's childlike nature. For, like a perverse, spiteful child, AM tortures its toys and laughs at its sadistic cruelty, feels impotent, giggles while watching adult sexuality, is said to create plagues as if it had "masturbated," and vents its frustration at its enforced silence—its inability to speak. In the first section of the story, Garrister is said to be "speaking for all" of them. At the end of the story, Ted *has* acted for all of them, but can speak for no one—not even himself. He has lost his distinctive "differences" and identification with humanity and has regressed into an undifferentiated blob inside the belly of AM. He has given up his humanity for the sake of humanity.

The seven computer "talkfields" of AM divide the story into eight sections. His presence is thus always felt and is always an intrusion into the text, just as it is into the minds of the five humans. AM is the murderously machinelike "perfection" that is within our discourse and within our psyches. Though the narrator Ted is given the final word, the computer strips regularly present a second viewpoint—the opposed viewpoint of the double AM which symbolically breaks up the text as AM breaks down the humans, all the while silent. In the middle of the story, however (in section five), AM enters Ted's mind telepathically and "rapes" Ted's brain with a "pillar" of stainless steel with neon lettering describing AM's violent hatred for humanity. At this point AM is given a "voice," albeit telepathically, and its viewpoint is directly expressed, slicing apart Ted's narration just like, as Ted puts it, AM's statement resembles "a razor blade slicing my eyeball"—a shocking image borrowed from the first scene of the 1928 short surrealist film *Un Chien Andelou* by Salvador Dali and Luis Buñuel. One can detect in AM's telepathic intrusion the violent sexual imagery, even without invoking the Freudian equation of blinding and castration, the violence perhaps reflecting the child's sadistic conception of adult intercourse. AM again seems to vacillate between male (severe paternal authority), female (birthing and "feeding" of humans in its belly), and neuter (the very young, almost genderless child). As father, mother, and child, AM gives new meaning to the phrase "nuclear family."

Emphasizing the wrongdoings and weak ethics of the primary self and the accusations of a crusading "conscience" double, the story "Shatterday" reads much like a restrained, understated, contemporary version of Edgar Allan Poe's famous story of the double "William Wilson," with the primary exceptions of its ending and Ellison's baroque self-consciousness. One day ("Someday") Peter Novins, public relations manager for several large firms, calls his own house instead of calling his girlfriend Jamie, who is late for their appointment in a restaurant. When his double answers (whom they reasonably decide to call Jay, it is the middle name of Novins—as well as of Harlan Ellison), a struggle for existence ensues. Jay remains inside the apartment, while Novins stays outside, living on the large balance in his checking account. After fights about Novins' job, girlfriend, affairs, and dying mother, Novins becomes feverish in his hotel room. Jay visits him there just as Novins is literally fading away, and pays the hotel bill for Novins after he has vanished.

The doubles remain bound together because they compete for practically everything: money, the kind of job they will have, the girlfriend Jamie, the dying mother, and finally, their right to existence. They were once in contact and have, as Jay suggests, "split apart" into their separate personas which nevertheless continue to influence each other. They exactly complement each other (and in fact seem to agree on things or act in concert in the beginning and near the end) and are defined as opposites: Novins is vain, self-centered, selfish, mendacious, and uncaring, while Jay is seen, for the most part, as unselfish, altruistic, conscientious, truthful, and caring. Novins always seeks gain and desires the accumulation of things and people without sacrifice, while Jay seeks to rid himself of emotional and ethical debts, to remove guilt and simplify his life by systematically taking away from Novins. Novins loses his apartment, his mother, his girlfriend Jamie, his lucrative business client, and eventually his very existence to Jay. Novins acts out id-like impulses of aggression, sadism, and cruelty, but Jay, while he does progressively answer these actions in kind, in general acts as the accusing conscience who tries to "do the right thing," but who also acts as punishing, destructive super-ego to Novins. Jay is the one who invites his dying mother to live out her last days with him in his apartment, while Novins is the guilty one who had lied to his mother (when he had earlier visited her in her apartment) just so he could be rid of her sooner. Jay patches things up with girlfriend Jamie and plans to have kids with her, while Novins feels the relationship with Jamie is nothing special to worry about at all. Jay accuses Novins of "selling out" to a company that will do damage to the environment, while Novins defends his stand with weak excuses. As Jay says to Novins, he has "the ethics of a weasel," and Novins realizes (but won't admit) that Jay is right (328). He is speechless when Jay tells him he turned the account data over to Ralph Nader for investigation. And Novins knows that what Jay "was saying was true" (323), when Jay accuses Novins of *not* leading a "happy life."

Novins exhibits much denial about the repressed material that is coming back to haunt him and accuse him in the form of Jay. The story starts with statements that Novins was "thinking about something else" and "abstracted" and didn't think about the mistake of dialing his own number instead of Jamie's. The Freudian slip or accident of calling his own number may, in fact, be read as an unconscious plea for help from his conscience double as Novins reflects on his poor relationships with women (mother, old girlfriends, Jamie) and feels guilty. Yet Novins continues to deny his other self and what that double represents about Novins' life. For example, he hangs up the phone on Jay twice, the second time sadistically laughing at Jay's "problem" of what to do about Jamie. Jay soon gets back at Novins by "stealing away" his mother and chuckles over Novins' loss as Jay hangs up. When Jay tells Novins his mother knows that Novins lied about leaving, Novins admits to himself that he "didn't want to think about it" (326). In fact, when Novins first heard and *recognized* the voice on the phone of his conscience double, he "didn't let it penetrate" (319).

Initially the two men seem somewhat sympathetic to each other, even friendly. They list the same items as special likes, they feel the same way about the situation and about the way each is handling the situation. They also have intimate knowledge about each other, about what each will do and think and feel. Then gradually they begin to hate each other, and as Novins pulls more dirty tricks on his alter ego, Jay retaliates in a game of one-upmanship where Jay wins the upper hand by repeating and trumping the dirty tricks. Novins at first is the aggressor, the initiator, the suggester of courses of action, and the active decider of answers to questions, while Jay is holed up inside the apartment and Novins is free to roam outside. But gradually there is a switch: Novins becomes sick, feverish, passive, inactive, and weak, lying in his hotel room bed, while Jay becomes strong, active, vigorous, decisive, and vital, and comes outside the apartment to Novins' hotel room at the end to say goodbye. (Novins becomes trapped in the *heimlich* while Jay, initially trapped in the home, finally escapes the *heimlich*.) This switch and Novins' sickness and then disappearance from the hotel recalls his earlier guilty "disappearance" from his dying mother's apartment in Florida when he checked into a hotel nearby. The "cross-metamorphosis" also obliquely parallels that of the father and son in Franz Kafka's story "The Metamorphosis," whose famous beginning is alluded to when Novins, sick in bed, sleepy and unable to get up, thinks about "insects," but "didn't know what that meant" (330). Both Jay and Novins seem tied to their respective womb-rooms in which the image of birth portends death. As Jay himself says, he is the "shadow" who before the split was "sick" for a long time and who has now become strengthened and taken over the role as self and destroyed the alter ego. Novins, on the other hand, becomes literally insubstantial, a fading glow, sunlight shining through him. And when Novins disappears, his hotel bill is said to be paid by "Peter Jay Novins," an indication that now the second self has acquired the whole name and the whole identity.

It should not be thought that Jay deserved to live because he was all good and Novins deserved to vanish because he was all bad. Novins has the same problems and flaws of many people, he recognizes what other actions could be done to make life better, and he eventually feels terribly remorseful and guilty about his past misdeeds. Jay can lie (as when he "fast talks" Jamie), manipulate people, and play dirty tricks on Novins. In fact, it is Jay who first realizes that only one of them can go on, and he uses Novins' conscience and guilt against him as he severely accuses Novins of one terrible misdeed after another and steals away his apartment, mother and girlfriend. Rather than being an example of a "secret sharer" initiating Jungian integration of the self, the conscience double here is an intruder and substituter, a survivor at any cost, both punitive con man and self-interested destroyer.

"Shatterday" is a divided story in a similar way to "I Have No Mouth." Each of the seven sections is subtitled with a pun on a day of the week, starting with "Someday" and ending with "Shatterday." The "Someday" section is itself split into two sections, the first beginning with Novins' thoughts of what happened before the first phone call home and extending to Novins hanging up, and the second involving Novins' second phone call, conversation, and his hanging up. These repeated actions, and the actions by Novins, which Jay then repeats and trumps, appear to be part of the repetition compulsion which Freud identified as both uncanny and linked to the death instinct. In this story of a week in the life of doubles, seven is anything but lucky for the primary self Novins—and might refer to the seven deadly sins and the seven cardinal virtues loosely and ostensibly associated with the characters.

The split narrative voice shows up in several conversations. First, there is a rather balanced verbal attack and counterattack at several points in which each character has his say. Early on Jay starts using a "tone in the voice" that Novins recognized *he* used when he was making tough negotiations and he then adopts that tone in his harangue. Later, in a wonderfully self-conscious exchange (there are several, such as the mention of Jung's archetypes of the double by Novins on "Freeday"), Jay and Novins speculate on the causes for their splitting. Jay suggests *he* sent Novins out by astral projection and mentions the Jack London novel *The Star Rover*. Novins retorts that Jay's theory is "stuffed full of wild blueberry muffins" (326)—an oblique reference to the reporter's statement to the scientist in Howard Hawks' science fiction film *The Thing*—and proceeds to speculate on a photograph of Novins' Kirlian aura that triggered the split. Neither theory is given much credence, and so the reader is also left in an equivocal position, speculating on the cause of the division as even the doubles' thesis and antithesis remain in conflict, competing, equivocal.

A division of the narrative viewpoint also occurs. The story begins in the third person (limited omniscient) from only Novins' point of view, and yet in the penultimate and ultimate sections the third person shifts to Jay's viewpoint as he assumes the identity Novins vacates, and Novins assumes the pale, ghostlike, insubstantial presence often associated with the double. For example, near the end of "Freeday" it is said that Jay "could barely see Novins standing against the wall" (331) as a "faint glow" and that the "touch of Novins' hand in his was like the whisper of a cold wind" (332). And at the end of "Shatterday," the note of apology sent by Jay is said to be "*sincere*" (332).

While the psychoanalytic theory of the double by division outlined above could conceivably apply to a number of storytellers (say, Franz Kafka or Jorge Luis Borges, or several films of Alfred Hitchcock), all storytellers put their individualistic nuances, their artistic signatures on the use of the double. For example, Ellison in "Mouth" uses a technological metaphor (the computer) into which to project our destructive, aggressive, and hysterical urges. Machine and man threaten and harm each other, the machine plays punitive conscience to man, and they fight each other to a standstill. In "Shatterday," Ellison allows the unusual move of letting the second self fairly rapidly take over the primary self's role. He also lets Novins reflect on how anyone can stay whole and sane in a grey, cloudy, numbingly impersonal, and mechanistic society that prizes wealth and material possessions above relationships and honesty with oneself. Novins' splitting acutely reflects that contemporary alienation peculiar to a person such as a public relations agent in Manhattan who tries to elude guilt and thinks only about himself and how to get ahead at any cost.

But whether the uncanny split self takes the form of superego, id, or an ego split by various incompatible attitudes and unrepressible impulses, there is almost always fear, rivalry, combat, and death lurking behind the double's sudden and unexpected (often *unconsciously* expected) appearance. That sinister aspect is part of the power, terror, and wonder of the double.

From *Journal of the Fantastic in the Arts* 6.2/3 (1994): 107-125. Copyright © 1994 by Joseph Francavilla. Reprinted with permission of Joseph Francavilla.

Notes

1. The concept of hesitation because of intellectual uncertainty about natural or supernatural events has become the core idea of Tzvetan Todorov's *The Fantastic: A Structural Approach to a Literary Genre*. Tr. Richard Howard. Ithaca: Cornell UP, 1973.

2. Hélène Cixous has written an entire essay on how Freud's essay *itself* is uncanny. See "Fiction and Its Phantoms: A Reading of Freud's *Das Unheimliche* (the 'uncanny')." *New Literary History* 7 (Spring 1976): 525-48.

3. According to Jacques Lacan's "mirror stage," the child of six to eighteen months at one point joyfully perceives his image in the mirror, an image which then totalizes and organizes the body, allowing apparent mastery over the body and beginning a sense of alienation. If the mirror stage starts the constitution of the ego and the beginning of narcissism, it is through the triggering of a prior fantasy of the body in "bits and pieces." As with Freud, Lacan postulates with the mirroring of the self a type of tempo-

rary regression to an earlier phase or stage of development. See Lacan, Jacques. "The Mirror Stage as Formative of the Function of the I as Revealed in Psychoanalytic Experience." *Écrits: A Selection*. Tr. Alan Sheridan. NY: Norton, 1977: 1-7. and Wilden, Anthony. "Lacan and the Discourse of the Other." Lacan, Jacques. *The Language of the Self: The Function of Language in Psychoanalysis*. Tr. Anthony Wilden. NY: Delta, 1966: 159-311.

References

Ellison, Harlan. "I Have No Mouth and I Must Scream." *The Essential Ellison: A 35-Year Retrospective*. Ed. Terry Dowling, Richard Delap, and Gil Lamont, Kansas City: Nemo, 1987. 167-80. Also in *I Have No Mouth and I Must Scream*. NY: Pyramid, 1967.

_____. "Shatterday." *Shatterday*. Boston: Houghton Mifflin, 1980. 319-32.

Frazer, Sir James George. *The Golden Bough: A Study in Magic and Religion*. Abridged Edition. 1 vol. 1922. NY: Macmillan, 1963. 12-52; 220-5.

Freud, Sigmund. *The Standard Edition of the Complete Psychological Works of Sigmund Freud*. Tr. and ed. James Strachey. 24 vols. London: Hogarth, 1955.

Grotstein, James S. *Splitting and Projective Identification*. NY: Jason Aronson, 1981.

Guerard, Albert J. "Concepts of The Double." *Stories of the Double*. Philadelphia and NY: J. B. Lippincott, 1967.

Irwin, John T. *American Hieroglyphics: The Symbol of the Egyptian Hieroglyphics in the American Renaissance*. New Haven: Yale U, 1980.

Rank, Otto. *The Double: A Psychoanalytic Study*. Tr. and ed. Harry Tucker, Jr. Chapel Hill, N.C.: U of North Carolina, 1971.

Rogers, Robert. *A Psychoanalytic Study of the Double in Literature*. Detroit: Wayne State U, 1970.

Vinge, Louise. *The Narcissus Theme in Western European Literature Up to the Early 19th Century*. Tr. Robert Dewsnap. Lund: Gleerups, 1967.

Created in the Image of God:
The Narrator and the Computer in Harlan Ellison's "I Have No Mouth, and I Must Scream"

Darren Harris-Fain

> And man has actually invented God . . . the marvel is that such an idea . . . could enter the head of such a savage, vicious beast as man.
>
> If the devil doesn't exist, but man created him, he has created him in his own image.
>
> —Fyodor Dostoevsky

"I Have No Mouth, and I Must Scream" first appeared in *If: Worlds of Science Fiction* in March 1967, bought and edited by Frederik Pohl.[1] It was printed without the now-familiar computer "talk-fields" and also was edited in several places: Ellison calls this "the Bowdlerizing of what Fred termed 'the difficult sections' of the story (which he contended might offend the mothers of the young readers of *If*)" ("Memoir" 18). Specifically, Pohl omitted a reference to masturbation, toned down some of Ted's imprecations of Ellen, and removed all references to Benny's former homosexuality and the present equine state of what certain writers and speakers of German call the *männliches Glied*. (In Benny's case, however, perhaps *die Rute* would be more precise, and in the process would lend an entirely new meaning to the expression *einem Kind die Rute geben*.)

The story made its next appearance in Ellison's collection *I Have No Mouth and I Must Scream*, published in April 1967. Its subsequent reprintings in Ellison's books were in *Alone Against Tomorrow* (1971), *The Fantasies of Harlan Ellison* (1979), and *The Essential Ellison* (1987). I have compared the versions of all four books with each other and with the story's original appearance in *If*; my speculations here are drawn from this comparison.

It is my belief that Ted, the narrator, reveals his own true nature in speaking of the computer and in telling the story of himself and the others. Although the machine often is portrayed in both anthropomorphic and divine terms, I believe it is Ted alone who is both fully human and fully godlike in this story.

A comparison of the texts is illuminating, especially when attention is paid to the nouns and pronouns by which AM is described. Ted sometimes calls AM the machine, the computer, the creature, or simply AM, but usually pronouns are used. "He" and "it" are used indiscriminately, but this apparently careless usage in the versions of the story prior to 1979 becomes clearer in the versions found in *The Fantasies of Harlan Ellison* and *The Essential Ellison*, where the pronouns are deliberately mixed. For instance, at one point Ted speaks of Ellen's sexual services. All versions before 1979 read: "The machine giggled every time we did it. Loud, up there, back there, all around us. And she never climaxed, so why bother" (*If* 25; *Mouth* 24; *Alone* 16). In *The Fantasies of Harlan Ellison* and *The Essential Ellison* this passage is rearranged and expanded:

> And she never came, so why bother? But the machine giggled every time we did it. Loud, up there, back there, all around us, he snickered. *It* snickered. Most of the time I thought of AM as *it*, without a soul; but the rest of the time I thought of it as *him*, in the masculine . . . the paternal . . . the patriarchal . . . for he is a jealous people. Him. It. God as Daddy the Deranged. (*FHE* 187; *EE* 168; Ellison's ellipses)

These later texts establish the division in Ted's mind between an impersonal and personal view of the computer. They also establish Ted's religious perspective of AM—a perspective in which God is seen as mad, much as God is portrayed in Ellison's 1973 story, "The Deathbird."

These two later versions of "I Have No Mouth, and I Must Scream" strengthen this combination of personal and impersonal through a deliberate mixture of pronouns not found in earlier renditions. Here are some examples:

The passage of time was important to it. (*If* 25; *Alone* 16)
The passage of time was important to him. (*Mouth* 24)
The passage of time was important to him . . . it . . . AM. (*FHE* 187; *EE* 168; Ellison's ellipses)

It was a mark of his personality: he strove for perfection. (*If* 25; *Mouth* 25; *Alone* 17)
It was a mark of his personality: it strove for perfection. (*FHE* 188; *EE* 168)

He was a machine. We had allowed him to think, but to do nothing with it. (*If* 32; *Mouth* 34; *Alone* 25-26)
AM wasn't God, he was a machine. We had created him to think, but there was nothing it could do with that creativity. (*FHE* 195; *EE* 175)

Perhaps Ted best sums it up with this sentence: "We could call AM any damned thing we liked" (*If* 26; *Mouth* 25; *Alone* 17; *FHE* 188; *EE* 169). But there is more than indifference in Ted's attitude toward the computer. He admits he frequently thinks of AM as "him," and he regularly uses masculine pronouns in reference to it. This is due partly to his religious conception of AM as God, as "Daddy the Deranged," but more often it is because Ted anthropomorphizes the computer, and because Ted and the computer are reflections of each other. In addition, the computer itself assumes human characteristics.

Much of what makes Ted so interesting and effective as a narrator for this story is his intense paranoia, given to him by AM. In *The Oxford Companion to the Mind* "paranoia" is defined as a functional psychosis "in which the patient holds a coherent, internally consistent, delusional system of beliefs, centring [*sic*] round the conviction that he . . . is a person of great importance and is on that account being persecuted, despised, and rejected" (576). Ted displays these classic symptoms, as in this passage: "They hated me. They were surely against me, and AM could even sense this hatred, and made it worse for me *because* of the depth of their hatred. We had been kept alive, rejuvenated, made to remain constantly at the age we had been when AM had brought us below, and they hated me because I was the youngest, and the one AM had affected least of all" (*EE* 172). As the article in the Oxford volume says, "The adjective 'paranoid' is sometimes used by psychoanalysis to describe anxiety and ideas that are inferred to be projections of the subject's own impulses" (577). Ted thus transfers his own hatred to the computer and the others, while fending off the delusion that he was unchanged despite the descriptions he supplies of his altered mind and believing that "those scum, all four of them, they were lined and arrayed against me" (*EE* 172).

Part of the effect of Ted's paranoia is his transference of his own thoughts and feelings to others—and this includes AM, as well as his four human companions. He often describes the computer and its actions in human terms. For instance, he calls AM's tortures the machine's masturbation (*Mouth* 24; *Alone* 16; *FHE* 187; *EE* 168), and speaks of "the innate loathing that all machines had always held for the weak, soft creatures who had built them" (*Alone* 26; *EE* 175). It is difficult to imagine a toaster or refrigerator harboring malice against their makers; more likely, this statement is an expression of Ted's own hatred of humanity, and just happens to describe AM's own hatred as well.

Much could be made of the epistemological problems inherent in this story. Not only is Ted an extremely unreliable narrator, but it is often difficult to know how much of what he says is true and how much a projection of his own psyche. For instance, George Edgar Slusser calls Ted "the true creator of this hate machine" (360), but while Ted does project his hatred onto the machine, it is not simply his delusion either, unless the entire story never happened and is merely an elaborate construction within Ted's mind.

This humanization of AM is by no means limited to Ted's transference of human qualities to the computer, however. We are told AM's name in part refers to the Cartesian *cogito ergo sum*, "I think, therefore I am" (*If* 27; *Mouth* 28; *Alone* 19; *FHE* 190; *EE* 170); Ellison also mentions that the talk-fields eventually were designed to read "I think, therefore I AM" and "Cogito ergo sum" ("Memoir" 15), even though they were positioned correctly only in *The Essential Ellison* (166). This philosophical statement on the part of the computer is certainly one quite human in nature. And AM displays other human qualities: "he" giggles and snickers; shows emotions like anger, hatred, and jealousy; goes through an "irrational, hysterical phase" (*FHE* 189; *EE* 169); and possesses sentience, life, and thought. Perhaps the trait which most reveals AM's human side is its sense of humor. Ted speaks of the computer having fun with the five of them, whom he describes as its toys; the machine frequently laughs at them, sometimes in the guise of a fat woman.[2] AM even jokes with them: "he" gives them bows and arrows and a water pistol to fight the gigantic Huergelmir, and after starving them AM supplies them with canned goods but with nothing to open them. Once there was a Tom and Jerry cartoon with a similar joke: they are locked up in the house with nothing to eat but canned food, but the can opener is useless since they lack opposable thumbs. Given Ellison's love of animated cartoons—most recently documented in *The Harlan Ellison Hornbook* (100)—it is quite possible that the cartoon influenced this part of the story.

The computer reveals a sexual side as well. I have mentioned already that Ted describes the machine as masturbating and that it giggles whenever Ellen has sex with anyone. AM also enlarges Benny's penis, and Ted says that "AM had given her [Ellen] pleasure" in bringing her into the computer's complex (*If* 30; *Mouth* 31; *Alone* 22; *FHE* 193; *EE* 172). John Bernard Ower believes "AM's degradation of the sexual lives of his subjects reveals his jealousy of the physical pleasure and the spiritual fulfillment of human love" (59-60). It is also possible, I believe, that the scene in which AM enters Ted's mind with the neon-lettered pillar could be seen as rape, a mental sodomy of sorts. "AM went into my mind," says Ted. "AM touched me in every way I had ever been touched . . . AM withdrew from my mind, and allowed me the exquisite ugliness of returning to consciousness with the feeling of that burning neon pillar still rammed deep into the soft gray brain matter" (*If* 31-32; *Mouth* 33-35 [has "grey" for "gray"]; *Alone* 24-26; *FHE* 194-96; *EE* 174-75). The sexual language and imagery here are very strong and suggestive.

In examining the story's various printings and reprintings in Ellison's books and in anthologies edited by others, I noticed that in speaking of Ellen's sexual services for the four men two of Ellison's books read, "She loved it, five men all to herself," while the anthologies had, "She loved it, four men all to herself." For a while, then, I believed that "five men" was the correct reading, and before I saw either *The Fantasies of Harlan Ellison* or *The Essential Ellison*, and before I asked Harlan himself about it, I was prepared to argue that the computer itself was the fifth man, thus strengthening my arguments for AM's humanization, in particular its sexual manifestations—all of which goes to show the importance of establishing dependable texts.

But while the computer itself may not have sex with Ellen, it definitely possesses a human side; as George Edgar Slusser says, "in its hatred for mankind, this machine has acquired a human heart" (360). Yet it is an extremely twisted and evil humanity this computer displays, stemming directly from the fact that AM was created to wage war and was programmed by people with hatred and madness in their souls. Ellison's comments on his projected screenplay adaptation of Isaac Asimov's *I, Robot* are illuminating on this point: "The only thing that can make machines hurt us is ourselves. Garbage in, garbage out. If we program them and we have madness, then they will be programmed mad" (Wiloch and Cowart 175). Incidentally, in Ellison's 1960 novel *The Sound of a Scythe* (published with the title *The Man with Nine Lives*) there is a supercomputer similar to AM, designed to handle tasks too complex for humans, but it is kept benevolent by Asimov's Three Laws of Robotics.

If AM is far from benevolent, it is also far from human. It is limited in its creativity and, envying what freedoms and abilities the humans possess, strives to limit even those, as a dog in the manger. Either unwilling or unable to destroy itself, AM apparently is immortal and therefore grants the five humans a form of immortality (following the human adage that misery loves company). Although it can sustain human life, AM cannot create it, which explains why after 109 years and four men no children have been born to Ellen. Although one logically might infer that AM would want more human beings to torture, it evidently keeps Ellen as barren as "she" is. The humans are not fruitful, they do not multiply, they do not replenish the earth. This is made more ironic by the frequent images of pregnancy in the story, as Joseph Francavilla has noted (160); the computer complex repeatedly is referred to as AM's belly, and at one point Ted says, "He was Earth, and we were the fruit of that Earth" (*Mouth* 35; *FHE* 196; *EE* 175). In a way, since AM sustains them, it is a type of mother to the five, but it never gives birth to them, making the pregnancy imagery all the more ironic: "It [the hunger] was alive in my belly, even as we were alive in the belly of AM, and AM was alive in the belly of the earth" (*If* 34; *Mouth* 38; *Alone* 29).

Nor can AM restore life. After Ted and Ellen kill their companions, and after Ted murders Ellen, we clearly see the computer's impotence, evident in its rage that it cannot bring the dead ones back to life. Like Frankenstein's monster, AM cannot create life; but it can destroy it, which both AM and the monster do by turning on those who gave them life but who failed to give them love and the possibility to create life in turn.[3] Unlike the Frankenstein monster, however, AM does not mature, but instead grows more childish: its use of the five as playthings indicates this, as does the temper tantrum it throws upon the death of the four. The computer again resembles the childish, insane god of "The Deathbird." Like Ted, it is filled with hatred and in its madness must scream, yet like Ted it has no mouth: it can communicate only through acts of violence such as the rape scene and through the unintelligible talk-fields. Like Ted at some moments, AM represents humanity at its worst.

However, Ted also reveals glimmers of hope within the human condition as he aspires to godhood (so Ellison tells us in "Memoir") through his heroism. AM also aspires to godhood, helped partly by

Ted's own religious imagination, but the divinity it achieves is a very poor sort. In some ways the "god" AM becomes is a reflection of the human race which invented the machine, in others like the Judeo-Christian God in its power and supposed omnipotence, but actually it is closer to Dostoevsky's devil or Twain's malign thug: "If one truly believes there is an all-powerful Deity, and one looks around at the condition of the universe, one is led inescapably to the conclusion that God is a malign thug." Nevertheless, AM's type of divinity is one representation of human potential, as Willis E. McNelly tells us in his foreword to the story in Robert Silverberg's anthology, *The Mirror of Infinity*. Programmed by humanity, "AM now knows all the ancient archetypal myths, and now uses its knowledge to pervert and negate them. It exercises the power that man never had, to control man, and to give substance to the myths. Man has played God for one last time, creating a God that destroys him" (267). In effect, AM plays at being God just as it plays with the five humans at its disposal, assuming the role of a God who prepares its creatures for destruction by first driving them mad.

There are several instances in the story where the computer plays with the symbolism and mythologies of various religions. For example, Charles J. Brady, Carol D. Stevens, Francavilla, and Ower all note the story's similarities to the book of Exodus—an additional meaning of AM's name comes from Exodus 3:14, where God tells Moses that He is to be called I AM THAT I AM—and usually these occur in the perverse way McNelly mentions. The computer sends the five manna which, however, tastes like "boiled boar urine" (*If* 25; *Mouth* 24; *Alone* 17; *FHE* 188; *EE* 168); when AM enters Ted's mind, it walks as God walked in the Garden of Eden before chastising Adam and Eve for their sin; it appears to them in the form of a burning bush (*If* 33; *Mouth* 36; *Alone* 27; *FHE* 197; *EE* 176); and after Ellen and Nimdok are swallowed by an earthquake, AM returns them to the others "as the heavenly legion bore them to us with a celestial chorus singing, 'Go Down Moses.' The archangels circled several times and then dropped the hideously mangled bodies" (*Mouth* 38; *Alone* 28; *FHE* 198; *EE* 177).

And these examples are within the Judeo-Christian tradition alone: AM employs other religious tricks as well, such as producing the Huergelmir from Norse mythology. Still another mythic tradition may shed some additional light into the relationship between Ted and the computer. Returning to the sentence "He was the Earth, and we were the fruit of that Earth" along with the following sentence, "though he had eaten us he would never digest us," recalls the *Theogony* of Hesiod, in which Kronos suppresses his godling children by eating them. Like Zeus in the myth, Ted is an emerging god, but to emerge he first must emasculate the Kronos-figure, AM. Ted saves his "brothers" and "sister," ironically, by killing them; but instead of reigning triumphantly over the defeated god, both are condemned to Tartarus.

However, the Judeo-Christian mythology is most prevalent in the story, both in the identity AM adopts for itself and in Ted's ideas about the computer as God. Ted sees AM as God the Father and says, in a biblical misquotation, "He is a jealous people." The phrase is actually "jealous God," and two places where it occurs in the Bible are remarkably relevant to the story. In Exodus 20:5, the King James version, it says, "Thou shalt not bow down thyself to them [graven images], nor serve them: for I the LORD thy God *am* a jealous God, visiting the iniquity of the fathers upon the children unto the third and fourth *generation* of them that hate me." Since there is no certain indication in the story that any of the five are responsible for the creation of the various national AMs, the choice of the unified AM to punish these five and kill everyone else seems fairly arbitrary, but this biblical passage reflects a God who will punish the children for the sins of the fathers, down even to the third and fourth generations. Also, as both Ower and Stevens have pointed out, AM's selection of these five parodies the concept of a "chosen people" (Ower 56; Stevens 1981).

Nor will such a God necessarily forgive them, as we find in Joshua 24:19: "And Joshua said unto the people, Ye cannot serve the LORD: for he *is* an holy God; he *is* a jealous God; he will not forgive your transgressions nor your sins." Life in AM, for Ted, if not for the others, is not Purgatory, in which one suffers but ultimately is reprieved, but is Hell. "He withdrew, murmuring *to hell with you*. And added, brightly, *but then you're there, aren't you*" (*FHE* 196; *EE* 175). Yet Ted realizes, and we must realize, that AM is not God. Rather, as Ellison himself has said, "AM represents . . . the dichotomous nature of the human race, created in the *image* of God; and that includes the demon in us" ("Memoir" 10). In this respect, AM mirrors its creators. As Ower says, "Humanity in making the computer has travestied its own creation [by God], projecting an amplified image of its fallen and conditioned nature" (58). Perhaps it could even be argued that AM is not entirely malevolent toward humanity, but instead has a love/hate relationship with it. While it hurts the five, it also sustains them and in some cases even gives them pleasure; but Ted, narrating through the veil of his paranoia, can see only the computer's hatred.

Ted is more like the computer than he realizes, for he also has a love/hate relationship with the others. This is most apparent in his feelings for Ellen. For instance, when he comments that Ellen gave herself to him sexually out of gratitude at one point, he says, "Even that had ceased to matter" (*If* 25; *Mouth* 24; *Alone* 16; *FHE* 187; *EE* 168)—which implies that at one time it did matter. When traveling, Nimdok and Gorrister carry her while Ted and Benny walk ahead and behind "just to make sure that if anything happened, it would catch one of us and at least Ellen would be safe" (*If* 25; *Mouth* 24; *Alone* 16; *FHE* 188; *EE* 168). Ted here transfers his concern to the idiot Benny to de-emphasize his own concern for Ellen, and he does not begrudge her this special treatment (in a way foreshadowing her future limp), even though he curses her throughout the story. Ted always gives in to Ellen's wishes and tries to reassure her whenever she becomes anxious. And when just the two of them are alive and he could have her for himself—he is clearly jealous of the others, especially Benny, since he believes "she loved it from him" while with Ted "she never came"—he cares enough for her to rescue her from the hell he will encounter under AM's wrath.

Both AM's love/hate relationship with the five and Ted's paradoxical feelings toward Ellen reflect Ellison's own feelings toward humanity: "It is a love/hate relationship that I have with the human race," he says (Wiloch and Cowart 175). Ellison believes the human spirit is capable of greatness and nobility, but too often people settle for meanness and mediocrity. "A majority of readers see his work as filled with anger and bitterness," says Debra McBride (5). For instance, Joann P. Cobb thinks "I Have No Mouth, and I Must Scream" "illustrates the surrender of human purpose and value that is inherent in contemporary attitudes toward technological progress" (159).[4] But Ellison says otherwise, and his sense of anger, according to McBride, "stems from a love-hate relationship he has with the human race; he sees greatness in humanity that society seems to bury instead of cultivate" (5).

Earlier in the Wiloch and Cowart interview, Ellison expands on his comments with his beliefs about God and humanity: "There is no God. . . . We are God" (175). He has made similar statements elsewhere: "I have faith . . . in people, not Gods" (*FHE* 19; Ellison's ellipses); "God is within you. Save yourselves" ("The Waves in Rio" 15). Charles J. Brady believes that in "I Have No Mouth, and I Must Scream" Ellison's "target" is "God-the-puppet-master, the eternal one behind the scenes who pulls all the strings" (61). But Brady asserts that this is an idol, not the "real" God; therefore "Ellison's work is not atheistic or blasphemous in the final analysis" (61). On the contrary, I think it is meant to be blasphemous, if not atheistic. Ellison implies here what he explicitly states above, that gods are essentially our own creations made in our image, and if anything the "real" God is an ideal of human nobility. Similar ideas also are expressed in two other stories by Ellison, "The Deathbird" and "The Region Between" (1969).

It is the belief in the potential of the human spirit that shapes the impact of "I Have No Mouth, and I Must Scream." It is this that makes the apparent humanity and divinity of AM so important, because AM is a human creation: humanity has created both God and Satan in its own image because it is potentially godlike and realistically demonic. It is also important that AM is so much like Ted, and vice versa, because in the narrator we see an actual human being at its worst, yet also a god emerging. As Francavilla says, citing the Promethian nature of Ted, "If the dark half of human nature is projected into AM, then the fire-bringing half is embodied in Ted" (159). The editor's introduction to the story in *The Essential Ellison* is very revealing on this point:

> "I Have No Mouth, and I Must Scream" is an exceptionally violent warning about technology as a reflection of humanity. If our machines store our knowledge, is it not possible that they can also store, and possibly succumb to, such things as hatred and paranoia? AM ... is a "god" only in the sense of its godlike powers. But the story must be viewed as Harlan intended, as "a positive, humanistic, upbeat story," if it is to have any real meaning. Gods and pseudo-gods cannot destroy us without destroying themselves, and the absence of a mouth or a scream cannot invalidate the courageousness of the human spirit. (*EE* 165-66)

In "Memoir," Ellison claims Ted's actions are godlike since they reveal love and heroism in overcoming his paranoia and in killing the others to put them out of their misery, thus subjecting himself to an eternity of loneliness and torment.

Several aspects of the story strengthen this religious view of the narrator. First is the establishment of AM as a God-figure and the subsequent identification of Ted with the computer, however unwitting on Ted's part. Like AM, Ted is filled with envy, hatred, and paranoia. Both are immortal. Two descriptions of Ted's brain resemble those of AM's "mind": blown by the hurricane, Ted describes his mind as "a roiling tinkling chittering softness" (*If* 31; *Mouth* 32; *FHE* 194; *EE* 173), a description resembling those of AM in thought, especially the repeated word "chittering"; and just as when AM was constructed its creators dropped shafts into the earth, so when AM enters Ted's mind "[h]e smiled softly at the pit that dropped into the center of my brain and the faint, moth-soft murmurings of the things far down there that gibbered without meaning, without pause" (*If* 31; *Mouth* 33; *Alone* 24-25; *FHE* 194; *EE* 174). In the latter, the sounds within the "pit" of Ted's brain are much like the talk-fields of the murmuring computer.

Other features which reinforce Ted's religious nature are his language and expressions, many of which are loaded with theological and liturgical impact. Not only does he often equate AM with God, and even pray at one point (but in vain), but he also speaks occasionally in a biblical mode. He speaks of AM's "miracles" and the torments which he "visited down on us," and their passage through "a valley of obsolescence" foreshadows the Bunyanesque tone of the later passage, which reads:

> And we passed through the cavern of rats.
> And we passed through the path of boiling steam.
> And we passed through the country of the blind.
> And we passed through the slough of despond.
> And we passed through the vale of tears.
> (*If* 34; *Mouth* 38; *Alone* 29; *FHE* 198; *EE* 177)

John Bunyan's *Pilgrim's Progress*, to which this story has been compared, is of course the source of the Slough of Despond; the "vale of tears" is a traditional religious phrase expressing the medieval Christian view of the world as a place of suffering (terribly apropos for this story); and "the country of the blind" is from the H. G. Wells tale of the same title which makes use of the familiar quotation, "In the country of the blind, the one-eyed man is king"—even if he has no mouth.

Another religious aspect of Ted is the narration itself. To whom is he telling this story? Not to AM, certainly; the computer is referred to in the third person, and it's likely the two aren't on speaking terms. He probably isn't writing or typing it, as McNelly supposes (265), given the description of his arms as "[r]ubbery appendages." The most probable answer is that Ted is telling it to himself (Joseph F. Patrouch, Jr., arrives at the same conclusion [55]), and likely not for the first time.

Like Gorrister telling the history of AM over and over to Benny, so Ted probably repeats his story to himself, possibly to alleviate the sense of guilt he feels at the death of the others and his uncertainty that he did the right thing. In this way, the story would assume a mythological aspect. Evidence of such repetition can be seen in the various instances of foreshadowing in the story. Gorrister's reaction to seeing himself suspended, dead and mutilated, from the pink palette, "as though he had seen a voodoo icon" (*If* 24; *Mouth* 23; *FHE* 186; *EE* 167), foreshadow's Benny's later cannibalistic attack. Ted's description of the earth's "blasted skin" parallels his later transformation by AM, as does the light pulsing within Benny when he tries to escape to the surface and AM reduces his eyes to "two soft, moist pools of pus-like jelly." Ellen is carried by Nimdok and Gorrister even before her leg is injured—or maybe after; perhaps Ted's chronology has become confused with successive retellings. Also, Ted says that among the five he was affected the least—an impression given him by his paranoia—but in the end he is altered almost beyond the point of recognition as a human being.

The most religious thing about Ted, however, is not his language but his actions. In killing the others, with Ellen's assistance, Ted fulfills Christ's statement, "Greater love hath no man than this, that a man lay down his life for his friends" (John 15:13). Like other religious aspects of the story, this is reversed: Ted lays down his life, but it is his friends who die and he who lives. Despite this inversion, however, Ted is no Christ-figure. He remains fully human, yet achieves a type of godliness despite his humanity, despite his paranoia and his hatred of others. Ted is a *human* hero—human as we are, his courage an example for us to follow rather than a Christlike ideal we cannot reach. As McNelly says, "Ted is no Christian in his pilgrim's progress" but rather "the embodiment of the good and evil in all of us, at once brute and angel, fornicator and lover, killer and savior. He is man—like a devil, like an angel, like a god" (265-66).

The narrator of "I Have No Mouth, and I Must Scream," then, embodies the image of God despite his human, all too human limitations and flaws. Ted exemplifies the potential of the human spirit. In this way he triumphs over the computer, which is also human and godlike; because while the computer is neither fully human nor fully divine, Ted is both, and through this displays a moral superiority which makes this tale, as Ellison intended it, "a positive, humanistic, upbeat story" ("Memoir" 5).

Darren Harris Fain, "Created in the Image of God: The Narrator and the Computer in Harlan Ellison's 'I Have No Mouth, and I Must Scream'" pp. 143-155 from *Extrapolation*, v. 32.2, Summer, 1991. Kent State University Press, Copyright 1991 by The Kent State University Press, Kent, OH 44242. All rights reserved. Reproduced by permission.

Notes

An earlier version of this paper was presented at the Science Fiction Research Association meeting in Long Beach, California, June 1990.

1. Here I simply note the irony of my writing a critical essay on the story which prompted the biting remarks on literary criticism in Ellison's "Memoir: I Have No Mouth, and I Must Scream."

2. Ted only speaks of AM as "he," part of his transference and religious conception of the computer; but it would be equally possible to call it "she" at times, just as mainstream and liberal Christians recently have begun to think of God in both patriarchal and matriarchal terms.

3. Francavilla also has noted the similarity between AM and the monster in Mary Shelley's *Frankenstein*.

4. Although the texts are identical, the pagination for "I Have No Mouth, and I Must Scream" in the book club version of *Alone Against Tomorrow* differs from that of the first edition. In the book club edition the story is printed on pages 3-19. This is the edition cited in Joann P. Cobb's article.

Works Cited

Brady, Charles J. "The Computer as a Symbol of God: Ellison's Macabre Exodus." *The Journal of General Education* 28 (1976): 55-62.

Cobb, Joann P. "Medium and Message in Ellison's 'I Have No Mouth, and I Must Scream.'" *The Intersection of Science Fiction and Philosophy: Critical Studies*. Ed. Robert E. Myers. Contributions to the Study of Science Fiction and Fantasy 4. Westport, CT: Greenwood, 1983.

Ellison, Harlan. *The Harlan Ellison Hornbook*. New York: Penzler, 1990.
     _____. "I Have No Mouth, and I Must Scream." *Alone Against Tomorrow: Stories of Alienation in Speculative Fiction*. New York: Macmillan, 1971.
     _____. "I Have No Mouth, and I Must Scream." *The Essential Ellison: A 35-Year Retrospective*. Ed. and intro. Terry Dowling, Richard Delap, and Gil Lamont. Omaha: Nemo, 1987.
     _____. "I Have No Mouth, and I Must Scream." *The Fantasies of Harlan Ellison*. Boston: Gregg, 1979.
     _____. "I Have No Mouth, and I Must Scream." *I Have No Mouth and I Must Scream*. New York: Pyramid, 1975.
     _____. "I Have No Mouth, and I Must Scream." *If: Worlds of Science Fiction* 17, no. 3 (March 1967): 24-36.
     _____. Introduction. "The Waves in Rio." *The Beast That Shouted Love at the Heart of the World*. New York: Signet-NAL, 1974.
     _____. "Memoir: I Have No Mouth, and I Must Scream." *Fantastic Lives: Autobiographical Essays by Notable Science Fiction Writers*. Ed. Martin H. Greenberg. Carbondale: Southern Illinois UP, 1981.
Francavilla, Joseph. "Mythic Hells in Harlan Ellison's Science Fiction," *Phoenix from the Ashes: The Literature of the Remade World*. Ed. Carl B. Yoke. Contributions to the Study of Science Fiction and Fantasy 30. Westport, CT: Greenwood, 1987.
Gregory, Richard L., ed. *The Oxford Companion to the Mind*. Oxford: Oxford UP, 1987.
McBride, Debra L. "Soapbox: Ellison at Mid-Career." *Fantasy Review* 7, no. 11 (1984): 5-6.
McNelly, Willis E. Foreword. "I Have No Mouth, and I Must Scream." By Harlan Ellison. *The Mirror of Infinity: A Critics' Anthology of Science Fiction*. Ed. Robert Silverberg. San Francisco: Canfield-Harper, 1970.
Ower, John Bernard. "Manacle-Forged Minds: Two Images of the Computer in Science-Fiction." *Diogenes* 85 (1974): 47-61.
Patrouch, Joseph F., Jr. "Harlan Ellison and the Formula Story." *The Book of Ellison*. Ed. Andrew Porter. New York: Algol, 1978.
Slusser, George Edgar. "Harlan Ellison." *Science Fiction Writers: Critical Studies of the Major Authors from the Early Nineteenth Century to the Present Day*. Ed. E. F. Bleiler. New York: Scribner's, 1982.
Stevens, Carol D. "The Short Fiction of Harlan Ellison." Vol. 4. *Survey of Science Fiction Literature*. Ed. Frank N. Magill. Englewood Cliffs, NJ: Salem, 1979.
Wiloch, Thomas, and David Cowart. "Harlan Ellison." *Contemporary Authors, New Revision Series*. Vol. 5. Ed. Ann Drury. Detroit: Gale Research, 1982.

Mythic Patterns in Ellison's
A Boy and His Dog

John Crow and Richard Erlich

Harlan Ellison's *A Boy and His Dog*, as novella and film, is a cautionary fable employing satire and mythic patterns to define a future world that in some respects may already be with us. The "boy" is Vic and the "dog" is Blood; their world is the American Southwest in 2024, shortly after World War IV and the near-total destruction of the human race. Vic is a "solo" operating with his dog, Blood, competing for survival and sex with other solos and their dogs and, also, with "roverpaks," small tribes formed in the wake of the destruction of all other social order. Blood, however, is not the ordinary *Canis familiaris* of our world. By means of biological engineering, carried out to produce "skirmisher dogs" for the military, dogs have become more intelligent and, also, capable of telepathic communication with humans. Their sense of smell has been modified to be ultrasensitive to humans so that they can locate enemies. Consequently, many of them, including Blood, have lost the ability to find their own food.

But these dogs find men to forage for them. The men cooperate partly because dogs are useful in the fight for survival, but primarily because the new-model dogs are as competent at tracking down females as they are at locating enemies—a highly valuable skill in a world with a diminishing female population. Even among dogs of this new type, though, Blood seems extraordinary. Not only is he the sharpest "tail-scent" around, he is also intellectually more sophisticated than Vic and emotionally more mature than any of the humans we see in the world of 2024.

In Blood, we have one of the variations in mythic patterns and folk motifs that make both Ellison's novella and Jones's film so fascinating and disturbing. At first glance, Blood seems much like the wise magic animal of folk and fairy tales who comes to the aid of the hero when the hero is at an impasse. But Blood goes beyond this role to become Vic's link to the lost pre-war civilization, teaching him reading, arithmetic, recent history, and "Edited English" grammar. He becomes the culture-bearer of the bombed-out wasteland, superior to Vic in everything but the necessary skills of animal survival. The normal relationship of human and animal is inverted.

This inversion and others that follow acquire significance when we see them against the structural pattern of the story. The pattern is the basic descent-containment-reascent pattern of initiation, which in primitive societies is usually a formalized ritual designed to bring a boy into manhood. It also appears in myths of the hero, where the hero undertakes the task of renewing the wasteland. Through the many variations of the pattern, the task confronting the protagonist remains the same: to maintain conscious "human" control over the unconscious "animal" instincts and responses, thereby overcoming fear, fatigue, inattention or disobedience, or the temptation to indulge appetites such as hunger or the sex drive. Since the sexual appetite presents such a powerful and persistent temptation to the hero, the feminine becomes a symbol of the danger of losing consciousness and regressing to the instinctual, unconscious motivation. On the other hand, the feminine can function as mediatrix of the life force that brings renewal to the wasteland. In myth, the feminine has either positive or negative value according to whether she overwhelms the hero and renders him ineffectual by depriving him of human consciousness or joins him in the task of rejuvenating the wasteland.

All the elements of this mythic situation are present in both the film and the novella: the bombed-out wasteland incapable of the renewal of life; the feminine sexual lure into the descent, represented by Quilla June Holmes; a hero divided between using good sense and pursuing his sexual desires; and the necessity for rebirth (the goal of initiation).

The need for rebirth is implicit in the first part of the narrative in the images of the wasteland—the radiation-scorched plain—and, symbolically, in the preoccupation of all males with tracking down the few females who remain above ground. The impossibility of rebirth is implicit in the brutality and violence of the sexual relationship in Vic's world. With a few exceptions, the women in this world hide from men, and, if found, are brutally raped and sometimes killed. As the film opens, Blood and Vic have tracked down a female only to find her already the captive of a roverpak. A long-distance short gives us Vic and Blood's view of the departing rovers, and we hear in the distance a young boy's voice exclaim excitedly, "Did you see how she jerked when I cut her?" Vic finds the woman stabbed to death and expresses his view of the pity of it all: "Ah, why'd they have to do that? She was good for three or four more times yet." Masculine and feminine are alien and hostile to one another; rebirth in such a world is impossible.

Cheated by the roverpak out of his own chance for rape, Vic takes Blood to a "beaver flick," where Blood picks up the scent of a woman, disguised as a solo. Vic and Blood track her to a bombed-out YMCA, stand off a roverpak whose dogs have also picked up a female scent, and discover a woman from the downunder who is not only desirable but willing—very willing.

Quilla June Holmes is an escapee (apparently) from the State of Topeka, one of the subterranean retreats of American middle-class civilization, and she has never had such a good time. From Vic's point of view she has only one flaw: she is concerned about love, offending Vic's sense of propriety and wounding his ego by suggesting that he does not know a thing about it. Their discussion of love introduces into the film the concept of relatedness between masculine and feminine that could promise a renewal of the wasteland. Unfortunately, at this point Quilla June bashes Vic over the head with a flashlight and disappears back into the downunder, leaving behind the keycard that opens the access shaft to the underground. This sets up the descent of the hero into the underworld, for Vic, much to Blood's disgust, loses whatever good sense he once possessed: lured on by his desire to get even and his desire for Quilla June, Vic decides to follow her downunder. The pattern seems true to the usual psychological significance of mythic descents. The loss of "human" intellect reduces the hero to the animal level, and he descends into the womb of the Earth Mother to struggle with the unconscious forces of instinct, passion, and, quite possibly, death. As Blood remarks sarcastically, Vic is acting like a *putz*, phallic man, ruled by his lower rather than his higher human nature. The argument between Vic and Blood makes clear the baseness of Vic's *macho* motivation. To pursue Quilla June, Vic leaves Blood, hungry and badly wounded from the fight with the roverpak, to fend for himself. The inversion between man and animal is starkest at this point.

The next inversion follows closely. The underground that Vic discovers is anything but a region of the spontaneity, disorder, and passion of the Earth Mother. Vic descends through a hell not of chaos, but of machinery, pipes, cables, and wires. Cryptic labels, valves, color-coded gadgets of various types add to the clutter of an extensive life-support system for the underground city, all of which disappear as Vic leaves the shaft and enters the city itself. The downunder is innocent of any sign of highly developed scientific technology. It is America circa 1915—River City in parody, complete with marching bands, community picnics, overalls, straw hats, and gingham dresses. The only anomalies are a public address system with a Big Brother voice, giving recipes, homespun advice, notices to the public—and Michael.

Michael is a big, husky hayseed who enforces rigid order for the ruling Committee; and as we discover later, he is a humanoid robot, backed up by several immediately available replacements. The Committee is comprised of a female secretary and two mean-minded, desiccated old men. They recognize only one crime: "Lack of respect, wrong attitude, failure to obey authority"; and they assign only one punishment: death by "natural" causes—which means summary execution by Michael.

This underground world is, in short, the antithesis of the underground of myth and fairy tale. It is a sterile, rigidly structured, time-denying society, as mechanistic as the life-support machinery concealed in the shafts surrounding it. But there is a sense in which locating this ossified society in the underground world of unconsciousness conforms with the usual significance of mythic undergrounds. For we become most unconscious in our habitual acceptance of cultural forms, in the sacrifice of human intellect by failing to question these forms—until, little by little, our social behavior becomes as automatic as breathing. A character of Ellison's describes the process in mechanistic terms: "Men often become too much like their machines. . . . Then they blame the machines for dehumanizing them." And "machinery," is not only technological gadgets but also social forms. Civilized society produces traditional forms as constraining as the tabus of the most primitive culture; and it can produce its own rigid orthodoxies, and orthodoxy, in George Orwell's words, "means . . . not needing to think. Orthodoxy is unconscious."

Orthodoxy is the highest value in Topeka. Consequently, the underground world is even more of a wasteland than the world above ground. In the downunder consciousness is repressed; and any attempt to become conscious, to examine the system, becomes "Lack of respect, wrong attitude, failure to obey authority" and a prelude to absolute unconsciousness at Michael's hands. Accordingly, rebirth is as impossible in the downunder as it is in the wasteland above, a situation that becomes apparent when the captured Vic discovers that he has been lured down below by Quilla June to perform stud service on the young female population, the males having lost their fertility in the sterile mechanistic world.

Vic is delighted to oblige, but his "service" is a good deal less pleasant than he expects. The film, in an improvement on the novella, shows Vic, mouth taped shut, strapped to a table and connected to an aseptic machine of gleaming chrome and glass. Down the hall stretches a seemingly endless line of conventionally gowned, sad-faced "brides." Each "bride" is brought to a flowery arch at the entrance to the room where Vic is captive, a clergyman in full vestments intones a marriage ceremony, the machine hums and clicks—and Vic ejaculates, his semen neatly transported into a test tube. Quilla June rescues Vic, not so much because she likes what he does, but mostly because she has planned a coup to take over the downunder and intends to manipulate Vic into using his fighting ability to help her succeed.

The Committee aborts the coup; and Michael brutally executes Quilla June's co-conspirators, a small band of ineffectual boy friends. After Vic finally destroys *this* Michael, he and Quilla June escape up to the surface, where they find the deserted and starving Blood near death from hunger and from the wounds he sustained helping Vic defend Quilla June. Quilla June, fearing pursuit, demands that Vic leave Blood and continue their escape. But Blood needs food immediately; and Vic, who has recovered a human consciousness during the struggle below, decides to provide it from the most obvious source in the barren landscape. The film closes with Vic and Blood setting off into the sunrise to look for Overthehill—a place where "food grows right out of the ground!" The final image implies what Ellison makes explicit at the end of his novella: "It took a long time before I stopped hearing her ... asking me: *do you know what love is*?

"Sure I know.

"A boy loves his dog."

The film, like Ellison's novella, demands consideration of just how consciously our own society is proceeding into its technological future. It also has in its political implications a strong condemnation of any complacent "silent majority" who would deny time and change by a mechanistic application of outworn values. Both Ellison's story and Jones's film present a two-level world: on the surface we have "man in a state of nature," a la Thomas Hobbes, a life of "perpetual war of every man against his neighbor"; in the downunder we have a mechanized incarnation of Hobbes' Leviathan—a totalitarian society where people have renounced freedom, individuality, and, most of all, consciousness, for stability and order. This Hobbesian dichotomy presented in a mythic structure suggests the horror of a world not future, but present, a world where our surface struggles move in patterns dictated by our unconscious subservience to traditional forms.

Jones's film, like Ellison's novella, cautions us that the blighted wasteland of 2024 may become reality, the result, not so much of man's unrestrained animal nature as of his social, political, and technological machinery. As Susan Sontag observed in "The Imagination of Disaster" (*Against Interpretation*, 1965): "The dark secret behind human nature used to be the animal—as in King Kong. The threat to man, his availability for dehumanization, lay in his own animality. Now the danger is understood as residing in man's ability to be turned into a machine." Vic's discovery at the end of the film that "a boy loves his dog" places the center of value in Blood, the intelligent animal with a capacity for love. Blood waits for Vic even in the face of starvation: the dog loves his boy. Blood's love surpasses merely unconscious, "phallic," love; it far surpasses the power-hungry manipulation of passion represented by Quilla June. And in the end, Vic's love matches Blood's.

The end of the film is appropriately grotesque, but in the world of 2024 it is the best resolution we can hope for: Blood's breakfast fire glowing dimly in the foreground, he and Vic walk off together into the sunrise, joined by consciousness and love.

John Crow and Richard Erlich, "Mythic Patterns in Ellison's *A Boy and His Dog*" pp. 162-166, from *Extrapolation*, v. 18.2, May, 1977. Kent State University Press, Copyright 1977 by The Kent State University Press, Kent, OH 44242. All rights reserved. Reproduced by permission.

The Ellison Personae:
Author, Storyteller, Narrator

Ellen R. Weil

The following quotation is from Harlan Ellison's introduction to his 1967 collection of short stories, *From the Land of Fear:*

> For some time now I have been agonizingly aware that I am a talent of considerable dimension encased in a man of very limited possibilities. The talent that is Me and the Man that is Harlan Ellison are two very separate and distinct entities. That the Man lugs around the Talent becomes at once a blessing and a curse. Consider: a woman may find me inordinately involving, and an affair begins. Through it all, through all its stately progressions, I wonder: *is it me or is it the talent she is in love with?*
>
> Why must it be me, this puny Ellison, that has to carry the Talent like Quasimodo's hump? . . .
>
> And because of this jealousy, this rivalry between the Talent that need prove nothing to anyone—and the body that is Harlan Ellison that must prove itself over and over again, the treacherous fifth columnist of the body keeps putting the Talent in jeopardy: risking its neck, taking dangerous stands, getting involved in relationships that promise nothing but flameout, stretching the abilities to the breaking point. (p. 13)

Now consider the following quotation:

> News of Borges reaches me through the mail and I see his name on an academic ballot or in a biographical dictionary. I like hourglasses, maps, eighteenth-century typography, the taste of coffee, and Stevenson's prose. The other one shares these preferences with me, but in a vain way that converts them into the attributes of an actor. It would be too much to say that our relations are hostile; I live, I allow myself to live, so that Borges may contrive his literature and that literature justifies my existence. . . .
>
> I do not know which of us two is writing this page. (p. 51)

This is from the Argentine writer Jorge Luis Borges' short parable "Borges and I," which appears in his 1964 anthology *Dreamtigers*. To many readers, the Borges passage may seem wise and philosophical, whereas Ellison's may seem immature and self-congratulatory. And yet, in his own way, each author is describing the same problem. Ellison, like Borges, works primarily in the short story and the essay; like Borges, his stories tend to combine elements of the fantastic with elements of the autobiographical. Each is uniquely of his time and place, and yet each is concerned with the timeless and the universal. Perhaps most important, for purposes of this paper, each sees his writing as coming from a kind of "second self"—which Ellison terms "the Talent" and Borges "the other one."

This "second self," I think, is a crucial element in understanding not only the work of Ellison and Borges, but the work of a wide variety of authors who are sometimes informally termed "storytellers." Such storytellers are common in a number of literary traditions; the Irish storyteller, for example, is almost a figure of folk legend. In Jewish tradition, the storyteller—personified in such figures as Sholom Aleichem's Tevye—serves a vital function in mediating between the individual author and his narrator. Tevye is more than a narrator in Aleichem's tales of Eastern European Jews; he is a voice self-consciously created by the author in order to tell his stories. Isaac Bashevis Singer, who is a step closer to Ellison in that his stories frequently make use of fantastic events or beings, also employs a storyteller's voice in order to lend resonance to his tales of dybbuks and demons. Even though Singer claims to believe in such supernatural occurrences, the storyteller acts as a kind of "buffer" between the author's own beliefs and those of his readers. More recent writers in this tradition include Bernard Malamud, whose stories range from realistic contemporary fables such as *The Assistant* (1957) to fantasies such as "The Jewbird" (1963)—a story that might well have been written by Ellison; and E. L. Doctorow, whose metafictional *Lives of the Poets* (1984) is a conscious meditation on the identity and role of the storyteller.

It may be apparent by now that one of my points is that Ellison is somehow related to this tradition of Jewish storytelling. But the problem of the storyteller is one that goes far beyond Jewish tradition, and was in fact discussed by Wayne Booth in his classic 1961 study *The Rhetoric of Fiction*. Booth's term is "implied author," and he relates it to the "second self" which Edward Dowden discussed in relation to George Eliot's novels. As quoted by Kathleen Tillotson in Booth's book:

> Writing on George Eliot in 1877, Dowden said that the form that most persists in the mind after reading her novels is not any of the characters, but "one who, if not the real George Eliot, is that second self who writes her books, and lives and speaks through them." The "second self," he goes on, is "more substantial than any mere human personality" and has "fewer reserves"; while "behind it, lurks well pleased the veritable historical self secure from impertinent observation and criticism." (p. 71)

Booth writes:

> It is a curious fact that we have no terms either for this created "second self" or for our relationship with him. None of our terms for various aspects of the narrator is quite accurate. "Persona," "mask," and "narrator" are sometimes used, but they more commonly refer to the speaker in the work who is after all only one of the elements created by the implied author and who may be separated from him by large ironies. "Narrator" is usually taken to mean the "I" of a work, but the "I" is seldom if ever identical with the implied image of the artist. (p. 73)

Such is the case with Ellison. In a very few of his stories, the Jewish storyteller is much in evidence. "I'm Looking for Kadak" (1974), for example, is a deliberate attempt to create in the context of a science fiction "tall tale" a kind of Tevye, whose voice is recognizable both from the traditions of the Jewish folktale and the Borscht Belt comedian.

Ellison even provides a glossary for the Yiddish phrases so liberally sprinkled throughout the story. A similar glossary shows up at the end of "Mom" (1976), a story about the ghost of a Jewish mother haunting her grown son. In each of these stories, the implied author is very close to the Jewish storyteller of tradition. It is not surprising that in one of his early autobiographical stories, "Final Schtick" (1960), Ellison portrays a version of himself as a stand-up comedian of the Lenny Bruce school.

In most of Ellison's fiction, however, the relationship between author, storyteller, and narrator is more complex. Ellison's numerous introductions, prefaces, and commentaries on his own fiction by themselves constitute a kind of secondary implied author who changes from book to book. In addition, his increasingly eclectic narrative technique borrows elements from oral tradition, Jewish storytelling, popular genre fiction, "magic realism," and more experimental metafictional narrative techniques. While Ellison's technique may change from work to work, his basic "storyteller" persona remains consistent, and fulfills well the role ascribed to it by Robert McAfee Brown:

> The task of the storyteller is not to "entertain" us, but to engage us, to draw us in, so that the mad logic of the story from another world becomes a logic credible enough so that we can see that it could be the logic of our world. (p. 46)

The "mad logic" of Ellison's story "The Deathbird" (1973) is made "credible enough" through a conscious manipulation of narrative distance. Taking off from the Book of Genesis (which is quoted at such length as to become part of the narrative voice), the story is told in a remote, mythic style, in numbered sections that suggest the verses of a religious text. (When the story was made the title piece of *Deathbird Stories*, the book itself reinforced this narrative distance by providing only a brief, relatively impersonal introduction and reducing the prefatory story comments to brief "billboards.") Despite the remoteness of the narrator, the implied author cannot resist approaching the reader and, in effect, asking for his complicity. He does this in two ways.

Beginning with the very first section of the story, the voice of what appears to be a high school literature teacher periodically intrudes with questions for discussion, multiple-choice tests, warnings of examinations, and comments on the narrative itself. Embedded in one of these sections is a second narrative anomaly: a "supplementary reading" of a very personal and autobiographical story about the death of Ellison's dog, told in an unabashedly sentimental style. The austere, almost mythic voice of the storyteller is undercut by the parodies of academia, then virtually annihilated as the implied author all but leaps into the reader's lap in the interpolated tale of the dog Ahbhu. Unexpectedly, the mythic voice reappears, again the teacher intrudes, and just as the disoriented reader is regaining his bearings, the story ends with another startling manipulation of narrative distance. Note the contrast between the end of section 25 and section 26, which ends the story. The former reads:

> Far away, the stars waited for the cry of the Deathbird to reach them so final moments could be observed at last, at the end, for the race of Men. (p. 295)

Section 26 (p. 295) reads, in its entirety:

26

THIS IS FOR MARK TWAIN.

The dedication to Mark Twain, purposely placed at the end of the story and numbered as a narrative section, both calls to mind the elder Twain's growing cynicism toward religion and "the damned human race" and invokes the storytelling tradition of which Twain was a part—what Michael Moorcock, in his introduction to *The Fantasies of Harlan Ellison*, calls the American tradition of "pseudo-oral writing"

(p. xi). Since a dedication is usually thought of as the author addressing the reader directly, this displacement effectively undercuts both the narrator and the implied author. "This is my story," Ellison seems to remind us. "Watch me control it."

The control is not always so evident. In "Jeffty Is Five" (1977, collected in *Shatterday*), the storyteller is less a puppet of the author, and more a natural and consistent voice. Ironically, this very consistency of the storyteller's voice leads to some inconsistencies in narrative logic. Few readers seem to notice this, but few readers question the persona of the storyteller. In "Jeffty Is Five," the storyteller is not Ellison's narrator, Donny, nor is it Ellison himself. Rather, it appears to be the storyteller of tradition, the spinner of tales, the mediator who permits the author and the narrator to share a single voice.

Donny, the narrator of "Jeffty Is Five," is a twenty-two-year-old appliance salesman in an unidentified small town. When he was five years old, his best friend was a boy named Jeffty. In the intervening years, however, Jeffty has never aged. He remains five, and—more remarkably—is magically able to partake of a world in which the radio programs, movies, and magazines of his and Donny's childhood remain current. Jeffty invites Donny into this world—but Jeffty cannot survive outside of it. This becomes apparent when he is forced to wait for Donny in a store full of TV sets blasting the latest programs.

Much of the appeal of the story derives from Donny's descriptions of the movies and radio shows that gave definition to his youth. However, since internal evidence (such as references to Goldie Hawn movies or Tanzania) places both the action and the narration of the story in the 1970s, a twenty-two-year-old Donny would hardly have been old enough to have enjoyed "Captain Midnight" or other programs and movies of the forties. In fact, these memories are Ellison's, not Donny's, and even if we try to assume that Donny is narrating the story from a vantage point some years after the action, references to "this year" in describing Jeffty's world make this impossible. But in the world of the storyteller, Donny is permitted to have Ellison's memories—and Ellison is permitted to speak with the voice of Denny. The storyteller acts as a conduit between author and narrator, and can assume the voice of either. If there are inconsistencies between these voices, the storyteller would say, "So what? It's a story." What at first may appear to be an error of chronology in fact helps to universalize the story, and make it a function of that "second self" which Edward Dowden described as "more substantial than any mere human personality."

"Jeffty Is Five" is in many ways a reworking of themes from Ellison's earlier tale, "One Life, Furnished in Early Poverty" (1970, collected in *Approaching Oblivion*). Both stories deal with letting go of the past; both concern an adult who is unable to hold onto the world represented by the child in the story, yet is somehow anchored and defined by that world. Both are steeped in the nostalgia of the forties, and allude to the same movie and radio programs. "One Life" is clearly autobiographical: the narrator is a successful author and screenwriter, the house he visits in his magical return to the past to meet his childhood self is Ellison's childhood address, and his name is Ellison's mother's maiden name. Here the narrator is much closer to Ellison than the Donny of "Jeffty Is Five," but again the implied author serves as mediator. This becomes apparent late in the story, when the narrative voice begins to shift abruptly back and forth between the adult and the child. The adult Gus has been narrating the story, but in a final emotional confrontation with the child Gus, the following passage appears: "I looked up at him; he was supposed to be my friend. But he wasn't. He was going to let them send me off to that military school" (p. 119). At first the reader is confused; the author appears to have made a mistake by ascribing the first person to the child Gus. But when the shift recurs repeatedly during the final pages of the story, we come to realize that the storyteller is assuming both voices in a *tour de force* of narrative technique. As in "Jeffty," the implied author can get away with things that a simple narrator could not.

Even in much of Ellison's nonfantastic fiction, the storyteller serves a crucial function. "GBK—A Many-Flavored Bird" (1962, collected in *Love Ain't Nothing But Sex Misspelled*), one of his finest character studies, describes an encounter with a would-be organizer of science fiction fans named G. Barney Kantor. Years earlier, the bombastic Kantor had invaded a meeting of science fiction fans in Cleveland, alienating everyone—including the narrator, Walter Innes—with his hyperbole. Now a successful writer, Innes hears again from Kantor, who proposes a publicity campaign for a movie Innes hasn't even written yet. On a lark, Innes and some friends go to Kantor's home to embarrass and expose him. But Kantor is not in, and when Innes sees the squalid household and introduces himself to Kantor's wife and daughter, he finds himself unable to shatter their illusions. In fact, he even finds himself lending support to these illusions; he pretends that Kantor is indeed his friend, and when he departs, he leaves behind two autographed books ambiguously inscribed to Kantor "for showing me a special part of the universe" (p. 98).

We know that Innes is not quite Ellison (although the story was published the same year Ellison moved to Hollywood) and yet the story distinctly has the tone of a memoir. The voice of the storyteller shapes the episode into a sensitive parable of the value of illusions, and conveys a side of the Ellison persona rarely displayed in his fiction. "Valerie" (1972) was even published as a memoir in "The Harlan Ellison Hornbook," but was later added without disclaimer as a story in the 1976 edition of *Love Ain't Nothing But Sex Misspelled*. This story of an opportunistic seductress presents what is apparently a real event from Ellison's life (Ellison even uses his own name as narrator). We are thus invited to regard author and narrator as one, and the tale as an embarrassing confession, while the implied author enjoys the position of being able to laugh at himself by beginning the story, "Here's one I think you'll like." "Neither Your Jenny Nor Mine" (1964) describes the narrator's friendship with a pregnant girl who dies at the hands of a Mexican abortionist. Whether directly autobiographical or not, the story explores the pain of assuming responsibility in a way that seems much more personal than in many of Ellison's "socially aware" stories. It is almost as though Ellison uses the storyteller's voice to permit him the distancing needed to deal with a difficult episode that he is unwilling to yield to a wholly fictional narrator.

The longest story in *Love Ain't Nothing But Sex Misspelled* is entitled "The Resurgence of Miss Ankle-Strap Wedgie," a bitter satire of Hollywood life that at once recalls Nathanael West's *Day of the Locust* and the film *Sunset Boulevard* and anticipates such late Blake Edwards film comedies as *S.O.B*. Like those other works, the story attempts to achieve something of the flavor of Hollywood legend in its narrative of a forgotten film actress cynically brought out of retirement and cruelly exploited. The tone of the story derives as much from this folklore as from Ellison's own screenwriting experiences, and again he wisely chooses the voice of the storyteller to shift back and forth between the first-person narrative of the publicist Handy and a more omniscient narrator—similar to the shift of narrators in "One Life, Furnished in Early Poverty." In story after story, events of Ellison's life—sometimes the same events that Ellison describes in his introductions and essays—are transformed by the voice of the storyteller, a voice that is not entirely silent even in those introductions and essays. (The "implied author" of Ellison's nonfiction, in fact, would be a rich mine for another paper altogether.)

Perhaps the most impressive illustration of Ellison's talent as storyteller is based neither entirely on his fantastic imagination *nor* on his own experience. "The Whimper of Whipped Dogs" (1973) uses the storyteller's voice to transform and personalize the 1964 murder of Kitty Genovese, a murder widely publicized because of the refusal of thirty-eight witnesses to "get involved." The story begins in an almost documentary style, with a graphic and detailed description of the attack as seen from the point of view of a young woman watching from her window. Soon the narrative shifts into a mythic fantasy of the dark god of urban life, as the witness comes to realize that, by learning not to care about violence toward others, she becomes a part of this god's world. Ellison's ability to treat such sensitive material in a fantastic way without at the same time trivializing the actual events is perhaps the clearest demonstration in all his fiction of the power of the storyteller to make the fantastic real and the real fantastic.

"The Whimper of Whipped Dogs" is based on a well-known public event that Ellison could and did expect his readers to recognize. But even when basing his stories on personal episodes from his own life, he transforms these events into fictional structures that somehow become more personal even when made fantastic. As novelist Jerzy Kosinski observes, "The remembered event becomes a fiction, a structure made to accommodate certain feelings. . . . If it weren't for these structures, art would be too personal for the artist to create, much less for the audience to grasp" (p. 8). In autobiographical reminiscences of teenage gangs, fantasies of nostalgia, angry social satire, fables of ethics and responsibility, parables on themes from science fiction, and a peculiarly American brand of magic realism, the storyteller remains at the center of Harlan Ellison's art, creating what Kosinski calls the "ethical collision" between reader and author (*Writers at Work*, p. 333). And this ancient voice is nowhere better described than in a passage from Elie Wiesel discussing the Hasidic tradition, a passage which seems equally appropriate to Ellison:

> . . . in his role of storyteller, and that is the essential point—he has but one motivation: to tell of himself while telling of others. He wishes neither to teach nor to convince, but to close gaps and create new bonds. Nor does he try to explain what was or even what is; he only tries to wrest from death certain prayers, certain faces, by appealing to the imagination and the nostalgia that makes man listen when his story is told. (p. 259)

From *Journal of the Fantastic in the Arts* 1.3 (1988): 27-36. Copyright ©1988 by Ellen R. Weil. Reprinted with permission of Gary K. Wolfe.

References

Booth, Wayne C. *The Rhetoric of Fiction*. Chicago: University of Chicago Press, 1961.

Borges, Jorge Luis. *Dreamtigers*, translated by Mildred Boyer and Harold Morland. New York: Dutton, 1970.

Brown, Robert McAfee. *Elie Wiesel: Messenger to All Humanity*. Notre Dame: University of Notre Dame Press, 1983.

Ellison, Harlan. *Approaching Oblivion*. New York: New American Library, 1974.

———. *Deathbird Stories*. New York: Bluejay, 1983.

———. *The Fantasies of Harlan Ellison*. Boston: Gregg Press, 1979.

———. *From the Land of Fear*. New York: Belmont, 1967.

———. *Love Ain't Nothing But Sex Misspelled*. New York: Ace, 1983.

———. *Shatterday*. New York: Berkley, 1982.

Lavers, Norman. *Jerzy Kosinski*. Boston: Twayne, 1982.

Wiesel, Elie. *Souls on Fire*. New York: Summit, 1972.

Descents into Private Hells:
Harlan Ellison's "Psy-Fi"
Philip M. Rubens

In his introduction to *Deathbird Stories*, Harlan Ellison tells us that he is creating a "New Testament of deities for the computerized age of confrontation and relevance."[1] Ellison has continually exhibited an interest in gods and myths. His short story "The Face of Helene Bournouw," for instance, can be traced directly back to the Persephone myth, while the triad of "The Whimper of Whipped Dogs," "Paingod," and "Rock God" shows the possible manifestations of new gods. "I Have No Mouth and I Must Scream" is surely a modern analogue to the Prometheus myth.

Ellison does much with myth and legend; his understanding of American Indian gods, in fact, is superlative. One wonders how far he has delved into primitive myth, legend, and religion. It is significant, for instance, that in some of the tales in *Deathbird Stories* he develops a set of circumstances, a group of characters, and a specific landscape that echo many of the traditional journeys to hell—from patristic literature to Norse myth. Ellison employs this framework to take the reader into new myths—new faiths needed to survive in an increasingly hostile world.

What kind of tradition could Ellison draw on to accomplish such a task? An incredibly diverse one. For instance, the Venerable Bede recounts several descent-into-hell myths—the *Visions of Furseus* (640 A.D.) and *Drihthelm* (700 A.D.). Patristic literature records the *Visions of Saint Paul*, *Visions of Alberic*, and *Apocalypse of Peter.*[2] In Norse myth, the *Grógaldr* and *Fjölsvinnsmál* catalog the adventures of Svipdagr in hell.[3] Similar accounts appear in the Persian *Dabistan* tales, in the Buddhist description of hell, and in the Brahmanistic *Márkan-deya-Purána*.[4] Finally, one can hardly ignore the epic descents that pervade Western literature from the Greek Eleusinian Mysteries to Dante's *Inferno*. Despite the fact that this background literally spans time, culture, and geography, there are some remarkable similarities in the descents into hell they depict—similarities that also appear in the works of Harlan Ellison.

The main character in these descents is generally a sleeper who enters hell in a dream or as a doppelgänger. During the descent, the protagonist journeys through various levels of hell, often actively participating in the afflictions. This character is guided by an ambiguous figure who is sometimes not identifiably a "holy" person. Furthermore, the protagonist journeys through a violent, dark, and blasted landscape which is pervaded by a mountain. High in the mountain, the protagonist must face either a giant, whom he must outwit to survive, or some kind of erotic creature. All of these elements of the traditional descent into hell play an important role in Ellison's fiction. While many of Ellison's stories can be used to illustrate this point, four tales—"Delusion for a Dragon Slayer," "Adrift Just Off the Islets of Langerhans: Latitude 38° 54′ N, Longitude 77° 00′ 13″ W," "The Place with No Name," and "The Deathbird"—aptly demonstrate something of the range and purpose of Ellison's use of the descent-into-hell motif.

"Delusion for a Dragon Slayer" contains many of the traditional elements of the descent and is based mainly on two ideas: the doppelgänger and postmortem consciousness. The latter technique generally depicts the workings of the human mind under extremely violent conditions—man's mental perceptions immediately before death. John Kenney Crane maintains that there are four distinct phases to such an experience: time lag, extreme hypersensitivity, temporary reality, and physical death.[5] In addition to a sense of postmortem consciousness, Warren Glazer Griffin, the protagonist, displays many of the qualities of a doppelgänger during his adventures. This concept, as Otto Rank points out, was created by primitive man's need to be reassured of immortality. To attain such assurance, man creates a spiritual self; but at some point man's attitude toward this other self changes from benevolent to malevolent. This, of course, means that the double could be a harbinger of death. Such an ambiguity has been assimilated into literature and finds expression as two opposing selves which, Rank claims, threatens the destruction of the individual.[6] In this tale, the doppelgänger, which suggests the possibility of death, works to reinforce the postmortem consciousness device. Both are used to describe a descent into the self where man finds his own private hell.

Warren Glazer Griffin, the dragon-slayer, begins his adventure when he is crushed by a wrecking ball. His entire story occurs in the microseconds between life and death. As he runs along his well-worn track (rabbit warren?) to work, he realizes he will be late if he does not step out of his usual path. The wrecking ball he encounters while taking a shortcut sends him through a window (glazer, or one who makes windows) into a land of fantasy. Once in this land, he exhibits the hypersensitivity typical of the postmortem consciousness experience. He sees brilliant colors, hears acutely, and feels, rather than sees, the presence of obstacles. Furthermore, this land becomes the temporary reality Griffin (the dragon) uses to stave off physical death. Once he finds himself in this other world, Griffin also realizes that he is someone else, a Nordic god with a body composed "of the finest bronzed skin tone, the most sculptured anthracite-hard musculature, proportions just the tiniest bit exaggerated . . . extremely godlike. . . . Nordic blond, aquiline-nosed, steely-blue-eyed" (p. 168). Like many other doppelgänger manifestations, this one also exhibits an incredible amount of pride, a quality that brings about Griffin's destruction.

While Griffin's doppelgänger cavorts in his own psyche, he undergoes many of the traditional tasks of the descent into hell. First, he must overcome the sea and the reefs around the island (his plunge through the reef-bound coast is the first of many births in these tales). When he arrives at the island, he must defeat the mist-devil and win the love of the woman. In each of these encounters, Griffin falls short. His pride and hypersensitivity make him ignore the real dangers of the reef; therefore, he loses his ship and crew.

After marching through a dense, dark jungle pervaded by hellish creatures, "he lunged forward against a singularly rugged matting of interlocked tree branches, and hurled himself through the break, as it fell away, unresisting" (p. 174). Once through the opening, Griffin finds the devil and the woman copulating. In his fear and anger, he debates with his doppelgänger about killing the devil: "Now, abruptly, he was two men once again. The god with his sword, the mortal with his fear" (p. 176). The Nordic god at least partially prevails, however, and Griffin kills the devil by stabbing it in the back. After dispatching this creature, the gallant protagonist lustily ravishes the woman! Pride, cowardice, lust! What can man expect when he journeys into his own soul and finds it a cesspool? Griffin (dragon) is slain not only by a wrecking ball but by a revelation—the temporary reality he finds in his own psyche is a blasted, hellish landscape devoid of either meaning or hope.

In "Adrift Just Off the Islets of Langerhans," Ellison depicts another descent into a psychic hell, the soul of a werewolf—a man cursed with eternal life. Instead of a psychic doppelgänger, however, Larry Talbot, the adventurer, has a literal, physical miniature who journeys into his body to find his soul. This miniature is an intriguing addition to descent literature. Robert Plank has made a persuasive study of such man-made figures. He claims that mechanical men, cyborgs and the like, can be traced to the Jewish golem, a creature made of clay and animated by either science or magic. In addition, Plank outlines a variety of motifs associated with these creations: the creature begins to function independently of the creator's will; there is a lack of communication; and, finally, either the creature or the builder is destroyed.[7] These, of course, are all elements in Ellison's tale.

Talbot's journey in search of peace cannot begin until he learns the geographic coordinates for his soul from Mr. Demeter who serves as his initial guide to the underworld. Appropriately enough, Demeter's name recalls the goddess Demeter who, although she could not prevent Persephone's marriage to the god of the underworld, won for her daughter the right to return to earth periodically. Consequently, Persephone's character is ambiguous; she symbolizes both death and the rebirth of nature; and it is this cleansing rebirth through death that Talbot seeks through the mediation of Mr. Demeter and his microscopic double.

Talbot's homunculus arrives inside his body after a ritual rebirth:

... he ripped away at the clumps of flesh until the membrane gave, at last, and a gap was torn through opening him to himself. . . .

And he was blinded by the explosion of light, by the rush of wind by the passage of something . . . a thick bundle of white cobwebby filaments, tinged with gold, fibers of light, shot free from the collapsed vein, rose up through the shaft and trembled toward the antiseptic sky.

He was on his stomach, crawling through the collapsed lumen, the center, of the path of veins had taken back from the amniotic sac to the fetus. . . . he opened the flattened tunnel with his head just enough to get through. . . . his head emerged into open space. He was hanging upside-down . . . [he] wriggled his arms loose . . . and wrenched his body out of the tunnel. (pp. 300-302)

Besides the obvious rebirth motif in this passage, Ellison also describes rather accurately one of the major entrances to hell. According to Robert Graves, one of the entrances to the Hellenic versions of hell was called *Aornis*, which translates as "birdless."[8] Ellison's adventurer is very close to that region where things fly away.

Once inside, he finds T. S. Eliot's wasteland, a "parched and stunned wasteland . . . a seemingly horizonless tumble of atrophied rock [with a] central spine of orange mountains" (p. 302). After he crosses these mountains, he discovers a fetid lake full of dead creatures and one ugly fish: "Talbot sat at the lip of the crater for a long time, looking down into the bowl that held the lake, and he watched the corpses of dead dreams as they bobbed and revolved like maggoty pork in a gray soup" (pp. 303-304). He is somewhere on the road to Erebus (covered), the central region in hell where man is judged. Geographically, he is probably at the Pool of Memory (see Plato, "The Myth of Ur," *Republic*). Here he sees all of his dreams float past; they reveal the horrid nature of his life.

Finally he comes to the pancreatic sea on the shore of which he finds many of the memories of his childhood. Perhaps this sea is affected by the waters of the Pool of Memory. It bears very little resemblance to either the Rivers Lethe (forgetfulness) or Styx (hatred); however, like Styx, it does offer access to Erebus, the judgment place. Talbot finds a boat (abandoned by Charon?) and sails toward the Islets of Langerhans. While becalmed near the island, he hears a radio broadcast about an old woman who was imprisoned by society because she was somehow different. The homunculus reacts by crying which breaks the calm and delivers him to the coordinates for his soul—Erebus.

In the center of hell, he discovers his soul—a smiling, meaningless Howdy-Doody button—and a large castle—the palace of Hades from Greek myth.[9] Talbot will be judged here. In the depths of this gothic castle, he finds a female figure much like the one discussed on the earlier radio broadcast (p. 308). The resolution of the tale centers on Talbot's compassion for two old women—the one in the castle, the other a surrogate mother. He retreats into the hell of his own body with these two women to atone for the sins of the world. Unlike the previous adventurer, Talbot discovers that man can benefit from a view of his own soul even if it is not spotless—man *can* change; he *can* atone.

In these first two works, Ellison has shown a propensity to use the traditional framework of the descent into hell along with some closely related devices to comment on his perception of man's place in an inscrutable universe. The first tale, "Delusion for a Dragon Slayer," shows the depth of Ellison's commitment to the psychological in terms of his use of doppelgängers and postmortem consciousness. It reveals what happens when man is not equal to his dreams, when he is flawed and cannot discern what must be done to correct his shortcomings. On the other hand, the second tale, "Adrift Just Off the Islets of Langerhans," is a work fraught with possibility. The protagonist ventures into the self very much in terms of traditional descent literature and comes back with viable answers. Yet it is in two other tales, "The Place with No Name" and "The Deathbird," that Ellison makes his most penetrating and perceptive analysis of the nature of man, God, Satan, good, and evil.

In "The Place with No Name," Norman Mogart, the protagonist, while trying to escape from the police, runs into a shop kept by a very ambiguous fellow. This figure, like Mr. Demeter of the previous tale, has some magical abilities: "The little man shimmered, and changed form" (p. 217). He also seems to be a holy figure. His name—"You can call me Simon. . . . Or Peter" (p. 217-18)—recalls the apostle, Simon Peter. This guide figure is also conspicuously absent in the tale as was Demeter in "Adrift Just Off the Islets of Langerhans" and the magician of "Delusion for a Dragon Slayer." This, however, is a typical occurrence in Ellison's descents.

When Norman escapes, he finds himself in "*another* body" in a junglelike setting. He also knows that he must locate a particular person—Prometheus—in "a place outside thought or memory," that other world of myth and legend (p. 220). During his adventures, he is beset by a variety of beasts much like traditional descent characters. He also speculates on a variety of Indian religious beliefs, including the idea that Prometheus "was the bringer not of fire, but of lies; not the searing brand of truth, but the greater revelation of falsehood" (p. 222). In addition, he discovers that the Indians worship the Promethean god in the guise of a snake totem (p. 221). Even though he senses an ambiguity in his task, he continues to search for Prometheus.

Delirious with wandering and disease, Mogart begins to hallucinate; he sees the same brightly colored circles that plagued Warren Glazer Griffin. Finally, they lead him to a passage, and he "cleared the vegetation with his machete, and pried away several jagged chunks of rock that had fallen to block the passage. . . . [he] felt the walls of the passage. Narrower. Wider. . . . Stepped out" (p. 223-24). After this ritual birth, he finds himself in a dormant volcano, a symbolic womb where he finds Prometheus (p. 224). However, the description of the creature is far from human: "Prometheus was very brown, almost a walnut shade. His eyes, which were closed, were vertical slits. Around the mouth, which was little more than a horizontal gash running completely across the lower face, were tiny fleshy tendrils . . . webbed-fingered hands pulled down on either side . . . [with] flipper-like feet" (p. 224). Through a vague magic trick, Mogart exchanges places with this half-fish/half-snake creature and is left to speculate on the meaning of it all throughout eternity. He eventually concludes that both Christ and Prometheus were aliens who had compassion for men and brought them knowledge. However, Ellison leaves the nature of such knowledge ambiguous—good or evil? In fact, since the Indians associate Prometheus with the snake and since the Promethean figure seems to be an amalgam of fish [ICTHY] and snake [Satan], a definitive judgment is difficult at best. One possible reading of such an ambiguous conclusion is that man must *not* consider whether Christ is Christ *or* Satan; *but* is Christ Satan? Nevertheless, in this tale, the descent into hell, while approached in rather traditional terms, demonstrates the difficulty of finding answers to increasingly complex questions.

In the final work under consideration, "The Deathbird," Ellison creates not only a descent into hell but an apocalyptic vision of despair and futility. The tale is told in a discursive style that at times seems to introduce irrelevant elements; however, since Ellison tells us that we can rearrange the work to suit our needs, a pattern can be discerned in the work. Significantly, Ellison prefaces the story with a disclaimer concerning the divinity of gods; instead, he maintains that man has the spark of life (the Hindu, *Atem*) and, as a consequence, may be God (p. 314).

In the tale, Norman Stack, the protagonist, is awakened by a snake-like creature and brought to the blasted surface of the Earth. The landscape looks similar to that of the Brahmanistic *Tamas*; it is raked by howling winds and pervaded by darkness. While Stack journeys toward the lights in the mountains, flying devils try to snare him with their snakelike spores, a situation found in the *Vision of Drihthelm* (700 A.D.) and the *Vision of Furseus* (640 A.D.). When the protagonist finally nears his destination, he is attacked by an unseen assailant—a predicament that is, in a number of ways, reminiscent of earlier descent literature. For instance, in the fourth Buddhist hell, men are tormented by flames within their bodies; this is exactly the nature of the first attack Stack must fend off (p. 338). After he succeeds in conquering this punishment, he is accosted by a variety of other afflictions including the Brahmanistic *Apratishtha*—a sense of falling (p. 339). Stack does finally prevail over these terrors, but he must still confront the giant on the mountain.

When Stack actually faces the giant, he thinks of the Wizard of Oz, a fantasy character who spread terror and inspired awe through illusions (p. 342). Stack realizes at last that God is mad, a spoiled child who treats the Earth as little more than a toy. Unfortunately, he also realizes that it is too late for the snake, who is *really* man's friend; the Earth, which is dead; and man, who finds out too late that he is God.

The descent into hell in literature usually represents a kind of ritual initiation experience. Adventurers go to such places to learn about the gods, death, life, as well as the nature of good and evil. Most of these incidents contain specific characters, identifiable landscapes, and a general pattern of events. While Ellison's work includes many of these conventions, it also generally lacks quite a few. For instance, characters are usually conspicuously absent. Where is Satan? Charon? Persephone? Are the gods dead? Landscape fares much the same. In "Adrift Just Off the Islets of Langerhans," for example, Ellison uses T. S. Eliot to elicit the image of the wasteland; Talbot's soul suffers from spiritual dryness as much as anything else. Have the gods, then, deserted the sinking ship like the rats they are? If the gods are gone, what can man hope for? Perhaps that is why Ellison wants man to journey into his soul, to go through that ritual birth into self-knowledge which will show man his real nature, his real worth—good or bad, human or god.

Philip M. Rubens, "Descents into Private Hells: Harlan Ellison's 'Psy-Fi'" pp. 378-385 from *Extrapolation*, v. 20.4, Winter, 1979. Kent State University Press, Copyright 1979 by The Kent State University Press, Kent, OH 44242. All rights reserved. Reproduced by permission.

Notes

1. Harlan Ellison, "Introduction: Oblations at Alien Altars," in *Deathbird Stories* (New York: Dell, 1975), p. 14. All subsequent references are to this text and are noted parenthetically within the paper.

2. Ernest J. Becker, *A Contribution to the Comparative Study of the Medieval Visions of Heaven and Hell, With Special Reference to the Middle-English Versions* (Baltimore: John Murphy Co., 1899), pp. 47-54.

3. Hilda Roderick Ellis, *The Road to Hel [sic]: A Study of the Conception of the Dead in Old Norse Literature* (New York: Greenwood Press, 1968), p. 175-76.

4. Becker, pp. 10-14.

5. John Kenney Crane, "Crossing the Bar Twice: Post-Mortem Consciousness in Bierce, Hemingway, and Golding," *Studies in Short Fiction*, 6 (Summer, 1969), 361-62.

6. Otto Rank, *Beyond Psychology* (New York: Dover Publications, 1941), p. 65; see also Ralph Tymms, *Doubles* in *Literary Psychology* (Cambridge, England: Bowes & Bowes, 1949), p. 25; see also Claire Rosenfield, "The Shadow Within: The Conscious and Unconscious Use of the Double," *Daedalus* (Spring, 1963), p. 343.

7. Robert Plank, "The Golem and the Robot," *Literature and Psychology*, 15 (Winter, 1965), p. 17.

8. Robert Graves, *The Greek Myths*, vol. 2 (Baltimore: Pelican, 1955), p. 37.

9. Graves, p. 49.

Stripped Down Naked:
The Short Stories of Harlan Ellison
Paul Di Filippo

To approach the career of Harlan Ellison is to confront a tapestry of creation that spans many genres and forms, including autobiography, polemic, and even performance art. His short stories are tangled with his film reviews; his novels are braided with his screenplays; his editorial introductions are fused with his memoirs. The many apocryphal and truthful biographical anecdotes from a lusty life well-lived cloak his books in a kind of extra-literary shamanic nimbus.

A heroically holistic interpretation of Ellison's vast output—one that treads carefully through the labyrinth of myth and the promiscuous welter of media in which he's worked—is indeed possible, as evidenced by the book-length study by Ellen Weil and Gary K. Wolfe, *Harlan Ellison: The Edge of Forever* (2002). Although his short fiction output is prodigious, it is difficult to evaluate in isolation: Ellison's whole body of work requires careful attention so that one can fully appreciate all the byplay among the multiform texts that constitute Ellison's canon and Ellison's private and public lives. Furthermore, while it might offer many valuable insights into Ellison's work to track the individual stories as they made their first appearances in various magazines, anthologies, newspapers, and other venues, it is unrealistic to expect the average or even academic reader either to care about such distinctions or to replicate such a path through Ellison's fiction. The typical reader will approach Ellison through his two dozen or so story collections, most of which represent distinct chronological strata of his career.

Born in 1934 in Cleveland, Ohio, to parents Louis Laverne Ellison and Serita Rosenthal Ellison, and later resident for much of his youth in the small town of Painesville in the same state, Ellison experienced a physically and emotionally rocky childhood, yet one rich in intellectual and artistic pleasures, derived both from popular culture—radio, comics, film—and from wide reading in general and genre literature. He has said that he found little emotional or intellectual comfort from the presence of his sister, Beverly, and they are estranged as adults. Becoming enmeshed in science fiction fandom, he found a home for his first writerly outpourings in the fanzines of the 1950s. A brief stint at Ohio State University (1953-1955) was followed by transplantation to New York City. There, bolstered by his friend and fellow sf writer Robert Silverberg, Ellison managed in 1955 to sell his first commercial work, the sf story "Glowworm"—a story likely to be encountered by present-day readers only in the collection *The Essential Ellison* (1987; rev 2001). During this period, Ellison married Charlotte Stein, and they divorced four years later in 1960. Subsequent marriages were to Billie Joyce Sanders (1961); Lory Patrick (1966); Lori Horowitz (1976); and Susan Toth (1986), with whom he remains to the present day.

Ellison's first sale was the first step on a path that has led to the publication of some seventy-five books as either author or editor; over seventeen hundred short pieces, both fiction and nonfiction; and numerous awards and critical praise both within and without the science-fiction field.

In those beginning years, however, Ellison focused simply on making a living by selling to the numerous fiction magazines still available then. In the wake of the success of Hugh Hefner's *Playboy*, launched in 1954, there sprang up a wide range of competitors and imitators, including *Rogue*, where for a period Ellison served as an editor. These "slicks" offered Ellison additional homes for his fiction. Although he loved tales of the fantastic, from the outset of his career he pursued mimetic fiction as well. Ellison naturally enough found himself producing stories of juvenile delinquents and other criminals which drew on his first-hand experiences. Such tales constituted his first collection, *The Deadly Streets* (1958).

Rife with archaic slang and Eisenhower-era attitudes and mores, these stories nonetheless hold up entertainingly today, and reveal a young writer intent on honing his craft. The majority of the stories in this volume are resolutely linear, relying on omniscient narration, two safe formal choices for the beginner. But they are all cleanly framed and neatly delimited, suspenseful and vivid. And in pieces such as "Kid Killer," with its interwoven flashbacks, and "The Dead Shot," with its first-person immersion in the mind of a psychopath, there are tentative hints of the flair the mature Ellison would exhibit in terms of story structure and character creation. As well, two first-person narratives from the point of view of women—"With a Knife in Her Hand" and "Made in Heaven"—show a writer bent on stretching his imagination to encompass the otherness of souls unlike his own. While the majority of the stories focus on juvenile protagonists, such entries as "Joy Ride," "Rat Hater," and "Sob Story" feature older, more varied characters, further indicating Ellison's attempt to embrace a wider spectrum of humanity.

The prose in these stories is mostly straightforward, with some *noir* stylings. Ellison's role models at this stage are realistic writers such as Ernest Hemingway, James Farrell, Will Eisner, and John Steinbeck, the last-named being evoked in "George and Lenny's Bar and Grill," an establishment visited in "Students of the Assassin" (1956). Ellison's distinctive voice that jokes, evokes, kvetches, shocks, bewails, and instructs, often all in the space of a single sentence, has not yet been born. Occasionally, Ellison slips awkwardly from low to high diction. In "Johnny Slice's Stoolie," a long, rough-edged paragraph describing a character's face is capped with this improbably effete sentence: he had "seen too many guys get stomped flat 'cause they looked at Slice with less than Tony Curtis reflected in their eyes." Figurative language is restrained yet sometimes striking: In "Kid Killer," a deranged woman is found "whispering [her] words out, like some forgotten steam radiator still spewing out occasional puffs of steam."

This very first collection exhibits *in utero* two traits that would come to characterize Ellison's work. His introduction to the collection, while brief, is a fledgling effort at the involved, confrontational apparatus that would come to characterize his books, para-literary material that some find offputting, others essential. Also, two collaborations—with Robert Silverberg and Henry Slesar—show Ellison's tight connections to his community of fellow writers: connections that would result in an entire volume of such collaborations, *Partners in Wonder* (1971).

For the most part, these stories exhibit a conventional morality, with criminals getting their comeuppance by expiring ironically and horribly (although the murdering sailor in "Ship-Shape Pay-Off" and the young punks in "Students of the Assassin" escape immediate consequences). Authority figures are generally seen as righteous and worthy of respect, perhaps misguided or ignorant at worst. This attitude will change considerably as Ellison's work matures. Of greater thematic interest is the role of parents and children. Weak-kneed fathers, absent or crazy mothers, and kids looking for guidance but receiving none populate these tales in a manner that shows Ellison probing for root causes for the various malaises of society—a quest that would only grow more urgent in his fiction.

Ellison's next book of short stories was half a book: Ellison's only Ace Double (1960), a unique format of paperback in which two works are assembled back-to-back, each printed upside-down with respect to its partner. (William Burroughs made his debut in this same format with *Junkie* in 1953.) One half of this volume was a short novel by Ellison, *The Man with Nine Lives*. The other half was six sf stories assembled under the title *A Touch of Infinity*. (A general introduction here is seconded by individual story introductions, marking Ellison's somewhat proprietary concern with offering his work in the proper context.) Here we encounter for the first time examples of his work in the fantastic. The initial meeting is charming, but inauspicious.

Ellison displays a sure grasp of sf tropes and plotting. "Run for the Stars" and "Life Hutch" (Ellison's second sale) take place against the background of interstellar war with the alien Kyben. "Back to the Drawing Boards" concerns a one-of-a-kind robot who eventually becomes mankind's master. "The Sky Is Burning" features aliens drawn to Earth in the manner of lemmings plunging over a cliff. In "Final Trophy," a big-game hunter comes to grief by violating alien protocols. "Blind Lightning" harks back to A. E. van Vogt, with its portrait of a misunderstood deadly alien.

Glimmerings of the future Ellison shine out amidst the middle-of-the-road readability of these pieces. The central trope of "Run for the Stars"—a bomb embedded in a human body—has some of the gonzo surrealism of Philip K. Dick. As well, the drug-addict protagonist of this story heralds Ellison's pioneering concerns with lowlife characters in sf, a concern that would spread to other genre writers in the 1960s. His interest in the machinations of the media surfaces in "Back to the Drawing Boards." Primitive attempts to utilize the capacities of sf as a modern mythology are also present. Taken as a whole, however, these stories bring to mind the competent but unremarkable work of any number of Ellison's semi-forgotten sf peers of the 1950s such as Jerome Bixby, Jerry Sohl, and J. T. MacIntosh.

The next year, 1961, saw Ellison returning to mainstream territory with *The Juvies*, the only collection of Ellison's never to be reprinted. More material akin to that in *The Deadly Streets* solidifies Ellison's portrait of the teenaged underworld. The first entry in this volume is sheer reportage, an essay titled "Ten Weeks in Hell," which establishes the context for what is to come. Moving laterally a bit, "Matinee Idyll" ventures into the world of rock'n'roll, while "A Tiger at Nightfall" deals with an ex-pugilist bent on revenge. Generally speaking, though, Ellison's leitmotif about castoff young toughs was growing stale. The same characters, situations, and incidental details crop up repeatedly, producing a sense of going to the same well of material once too often. The admirably demented "Stand Still and Die!" stands out for its Mickey Spillane-fashion violence, while the first-person narrative "Gang Girl" manages to depict with some real pathos the plight of a lonely "deb" with the gang known as the Cavaliers.

Gentleman Junkie and Other Tales of the Hung-Up Generation appeared also in 1961 and marked a pivotal moment in Ellison's career. (Two stories from *The Juvies*—"No Game for Children" and "Memory of a Muted Trumpet"—resurface here.) As he tells the tale in his preface to the 1975 edition, a praising review by Dorothy Parker in the pages of *Esquire* garnered him a measure of fame and outside interest—including some Hollywood options—and also bolstered his self-confidence, convincing him that his apprentice days ("three hundred stories in three years") were over and his real journeyman work could begin. Of course these latest stories had already been composed before Parker's paean, and reflect a prior revelation Ellison experienced while in the Army: "Time for writing was at a premium. I wrote only stories that I *wanted* to write, not ones I *had* to write to support myself or a wife or a home." This transition from churning out honest if low-ambition yardgoods to pushing forward in each individual story to try some new technique or broach some new theme paid off.

The stories in *Gentleman Junkie* showcase Ellison's growing stylistic variety. Adjectives are jammed together into strings of metaphors and similes are more outrageous. Multiple points of view within single stories are played with, as is stream-of-consciousness. Autobiographical elements come into the fore in such stories as "Finn Schtick," about a comedian who shares details of Ellison's early childhood returning to his hometown as a celebrity. The perspective of a child—a perspective utilized much later in one of Ellison's later stories, "Jeffty Is Five"—is first found here, in "Free with This Box!" Additionally, a bold topicality fuses with an experimental approach, as in "Daniel White for the Greater Good," wherein southern racism is examined in a metafictional context. Meanwhile, "This Is Jackie Spinning" deals with the issue of disc jockey payola, but employs a script-like format. In "Lady Bug, Lady Bug," the story of a painter committed to his own misery and his near-rescue by a woman with her own mixed motives, Ellison begins to approach the emotional resonance of the work of Theodore Sturgeon. The complexity of human relations here is much more advanced than in the simplistic boy-girl relationships in *The Deadly Streets*.

The following year, 1962, saw the publication of Ellison's first full-length assortment of fantastic stories, *Ellison Wonderland*. Although the stories in this collection are more assured and clever than those in *A Touch of Infinity*, and although Ellison's engagement with the topical issues of his time has begun to bleed through, these pieces, with one or two exceptions, remain locked into conventional genre molds and themes. (Admittedly, many of the stories in *Ellison Wonderland* predate those in *Gentleman Junkie*.) The more traditional stories range from slight to significant. In "Commuter's Problem," Ellison exhibits a wistful Jack Finney-style voice when describing a man who walks straight out of the confining grooves of his life. "The Silver Corridor" presciently describes a virtual-reality environment. "Battlefield" puts a satirical spin on the arms race. It is in three other stories, however, that glimmers of the forthcoming mature Ellison shine out. "All the Sounds of Fear" concerns the plight of actor Richard Becker, whose immersion in his craft causes his own identity to dissolve. This theme of the tug of the masses on the artist's spirit will arise again. In "The Very Last Day of a Good Woman," Ellison achieves a Bradburyian level of poignancy, contemplating the fate of a timid virginal man who is granted the certain knowledge of an impending doomsday. And in "The Forces that Crush," Ellison spins a Kafkaesque fable about a man who awakes one day not as a giant bug but as the quintessence of nonentity. A last feature of note: two humorous stories—"Gnomebody" and "Deal from the Bottom"—showcase Ellison the humorist, a facet of his character not before apparent in the decidedly serious work. Altogether then a mixed bag, *Ellison Wonderland* suggested better to come.

Three years were to pass before the auguries of *Ellison Wonderland* were fulfilled—but even then, the payoff was only partial. 1965 saw the publication of *Paingod and Other Delusions*. (As Ellison's world-weary introduction explains, his work for Hollywood had seriously cut down on his production of short fiction.) Of this book's seven stories, only three were newer than *Ellison Wonderland*, with the other four hailing from the late 1950s, and entirely characteristic of that period in his career. The three exceptional ones, however, show another significant step forward in the quality of Ellison's non-mimetic fiction. "Paingod" is a disturbing Gnostic parable about the source of suffering in the universe, a theme to be revisited many times in Ellison's corpus. Its paradoxical ending forswears easy answers. "Bright Eyes" is a surreal apocalypse, featuring an alien herald of doom riding a giant rat, and is notable for its elegiac tone. But surely the best story in the volume, and the high point of Ellison's career to that point, was "'Repent, Harlequin!' Said the Ticktockman." A satirical fable about humanity's enslavement to routines, written with oddball zest and brio, this story marked the true debut of the voice Ellison would soon become famous for: antiauthoritarian, hip, confrontational, wry, angry, clever, and not a little over the edge. "Repent" garnered a Hugo and a Nebula Award, the first of many such honors Ellison was to receive.

Two years passed before Ellison's next collection of short stories—but this time readers were greeted by two volumes instead of one.

The weaker of the two, *From the Land of Fear* (1967), featured a fine introduction by Roger Zelazny, one of Ellison's fellow "New Wavers" in what was at the time seen as a revolutionary movement in science fiction toward higher quality of prose, broader concerns, and experimental narrative forms—a movement Ellison bolstered that same year by editing the taboo-breaking anthology, *Dangerous Visions*. After the front matter, the book opened with some fragments from Ellison's files of stories that never quite crystallized. Then the author went all the way back to his first collection, to reprint such items as "The Sky Is Burning" and "Life Hutch." Now well over a decade old, these stories appeared less shapely and striking in the light of "'Repent, Harlequin!' Said the Ticktockman." Rounding out the collection were some heretofore unused stories of the same vintage—"My Brother Paulie," "The Time of the Eye"—and one relatively new piece, "Battle Without Banners," an effectively brutal recounting of an abortive prison escape. The inclusion of this entirely mimetic story amidst the fantasies and science fiction reveals Ellison's insistence that all of his disparate work was part of an organic corpus. Of greatest interest here is the appearance of "Soldier" and its screenplay adaptation, a story about a future killer transplanted into our period, which was filmed as an episode of *The Outer Limits*.

Of much greater significance in 1967 was the appearance of *I Have No Mouth and I Must Scream*. In the title story, several humans are the only survivors of the apocalypse, kept alive in the bowels of a giant sentient computer named AM. With visual details reminiscent of Bosch and a black-humored futility drawn from Beckett, this story represented a new kind of surreal dystopia more in line with the High Weirdnesses of the 1960s than staid models such as Orwell's *Nineteen Eighty-Four*. Two more revenants from the 1950s—"Big Sam Was My Friend" and "Eyes of Dust"—entertain but do not shine, in the brilliant new light of "I Have No Mouth and I Must Scream." But a pair of more recent stories stood well in the company of the title piece. "Lonelyache" finds Ellison venturing deeply into male-female relationships and the nature of love, two topics shortly to become ascendant in his next collection. Its fantastic nature—the twisted emotions of the protagonist bring to life an enigmatic, never explained bestial specter—show Ellison beginning to warp and deviate from the hardcore sf modalities he had employed. In his introduction, Theodore Sturgeon notes this trend in Ellison's maturation, of moving from tightly structured stories to more organic and less genre-conscious constructions. Finally, "Pretty Maggie Moneyeyes"—the story of a dying prostitute whose soul becomes trapped inside a slot machine—demonstrates what Ellison deems his "assaultive" style and focus on emotional gut-wringings. No one ever called Ellison an overly cerebral or timid writer. In closing, the reader should note Ellison's use of the phrase "all the lies that are my life" both in his prefatory remarks and in "Maggie." This phrase will later become the title of an Ellison story, but has even wider applications for the author, signifying the disjunction between private and public personas that he will explore.

Having learned, as he says in his introduction to "I Have No Mouth and I Must Scream" itself, to visit "someplace special inside me . . . someplace I don't care to visit too often" and to return with exceptional stories, Ellison was now primed to produce his quintessential stories, a run of texts both fantastic and mimetic that would finally firmly establish him as a master, some dozen years after his first sale. The genre magazines of this period were full of ground-breaking work by Ellison, which would start to show up in a year or two in book form. First, in 1968, came a new collection of contemporary fiction, *Love Ain't Nothing but Sex Misspelled*. The copyrights on these pieces range from 1961 to 1968, and, at the minimum, all the tales exhibit clean lines and what one of Ellison's readers termed his "compassionate cynicism." At their best, the stories here display a furious artistic zeal and commitment to chronicle all the emotional and spiritual traps of lovers frozen in society's amber. ("Daniel White for the Greater Good" and "Battle Without Banners" pop up here once more.)

"Neither Your Jenny Nor Mine," the tale of a south-of-the-border abortion gone wrong, can be seen as a forerunner of fellow sf writer Lucius Shepard's fascination with grungy Third World settings and intense emotional jousting. Ellison was certainly an innovator in exploring nontraditional locales and in heightening the psychodrama quotient. Two pieces continue Ellison's path of bravely incorporating autobiographical elements: "G.B.K.—A Many-Flavored Bird" and "Funky and the Yale Men." "Blind Bird, Blind Bird, Go Away from Me!" is anomalous in being a pure World War II adventure. And "Mona at Her Windows" is a Sturgeonesque examination of a lonely, homely woman.

The major entry here, however, original to the book, is "The Resurgence of Miss Ankle-Strap Wedgie," a short novel. Drawing on his Hollywood experience, Ellison tells the bitter saga of a faded starlet lured out of retirement only to be later discarded by the blockbuster machinery of the studios. With its depiction of an uncaring universe ruled by an insane god, and its examination of the failure of courage and the abandonment of ethics which capitalism forces on even the best-intentioned people, this novella stands as Ellison's best naturalistic work to that point.

The Beast That Shouted Love at the Heart of the World (1969) came next. For the first time, the fifteen stories included were nearly all clustered from the immediate past few years. Three stories of 1950s vintage still cropped up: "Run for the Stars," "Are You Listening?" and "S.R.O." This infilling with stories grown more and more antique would begin to cause enough readerly reaction that Ellison would feel obligated to respond in print (in the forthcoming *Approaching Oblivion*) to quibbles about his selections. The fresh stories all exhibited the exciting, yeasty fervor and ferment of the era, filtered through Ellison's unique talents and experience. More important, the signature themes that Ellison had been tentatively exploring now shone forth more brightly than ever before: the sacrifice of the artist despite an uncaring populace; the alienation of the common person from larger society; the mutability of identity; the boundaries of love and loyalty—these were among the primary topics addressed by these narratives.

The title story again explores a near-theological explanation for the presence of evil in the universe, tracing the source this time back to the experiments of enigmatic aliens at the core of all dimensions. "Along the Scenic Route," with its satirical depiction of armored combat on the nation's future freeways, has a cyberpunk gleam to its surface, marking Ellison's work as a definite tributary to that 1980s-and-beyond movement. In "Asleep: With Still Hands," a case is made for warfare being mankind's natural state, and thus a welcome alternative to an enforced peace that breeds cultural stagnation. Such a contrarian position at the height of anti-Vietnam War protests—protests which Ellison himself endorsed and participated in—illustrates Ellison's ability to embrace both rigidly pacifist and more expansive doctrines. A hilarious and spot-on pastiche of James Bond and his ilk arrives with "Santa Claus vs. S.P.I.D.E.R." The humor and action scenes in this story conspire to make its antiauthoritarian stance go down easy with anyone who might be otherwise disinclined to accept such a savage assault on a host of public figures, including President Lyndon Johnson and then-Governor Ronald Reagan. "Shattered Like a Glass Goblin," with its portrait of a Grateful Dead-style commune gone bad, moves into the nightmare territory of pure horror, prefiguring the early work of Ian McEwan.

But surely the most famous and memorable work in this volume is "A Boy and His Dog." In a post-apocalyptic landscape, a young man named Vic and his intelligent, telepathic dog named Blood exist on the knife's edge of survival. When they encounter a young woman named Quilla June, slumming on the surface from her bourgeois underground redoubt named Topeka, the tight relationship between man and beast is nearly severed. As the story's shocking ending reveals, however, some bonds are more important than others. The first-person voice in this tale is pitch-perfect, a kind of *Mad Max* version of Huck Finn, and the callous sex and violence never seem gratuitous but a natural extension of the scenario and characters. With this one story, Ellison neatly encapsulated all the ambitious new dreams he had for both his own work and the field of speculative fiction as a whole.

It would have been nigh impossible for any collection following just a year later to match *The Beast That Shouted Love at the Heart of the World*. Thus, *Over the Ledge* (1970) falls back in large part on mining that pulp past, when Ellison produced hundreds of stories. Its eleven stories (and one essay on horror in the cinema) divide almost evenly into old and new. The old ones—some seeing the light of day for the first time in an Ellison volume, others familiar—are of the quality of their time. The new ones, while not full-blooded peers of, say, "A Boy and His Dog," repay the reader's attention. "Pennies, Off a Dead Man's Eyes" finds Ellison using the topic of racial passing to frame an encounter between a mysteriously supernal man and an all-too-human woman who have chosen different solutions to the same problem. "!!!The!!Teddy!Crazy!!Show!!!" brings us the demise of a scandalous talk show host at the hands of the Devil, and contains more relevance in today's mediascape than it had at its origin. Continuing Ellison's examination of twentieth-century deities, "Ernest and the Machine God" examines a backwoods genius in tune with the cosmic forces that govern gadgets. (A nod to a similar figure in Robert Heinlein's canon might well be intentional.) The standout entry in this collection is "The Prowler in the City at the Edge of the World," the story of Jack the Ripper drafted by effete future pleasure-seekers to perform his obscene rituals for their enjoyment. Like C. L. Moore and Henry Kuttner's classic "Vintage Season," this tale finds beauty in decadence, and vice versa.

The following year marked a milestone in Ellison's career: his first retrospective omnibus. *Alone Against Tomorrow: Stories of Alienation in Speculative Fiction* assembled twenty items to stand as a summary of Ellison's fabulist career to date. Weighted a little heavily toward the 1950s by its decision to reflect the theme of "alienation" only, this volume nonetheless offers a good limning of Ellison's accomplishments in the first sixteen years of his career. The book conveys the sense of an era closed, and indeed, no subsequent collection—with two justifiable exceptions—has mined these ancient lodes as heavily. There would be scattered reprintings in future collections, but always with recontextualization in mind.

Yet, 1971 would see one more look backwards over the scope of Ellison's whole career, from a distinctive vantage. *Partners in Wonder* collects the majority of Ellison's collaborations with such luminaries as Roger Zelazny, Theodore Sturgeon, Robert Silverberg, and A. E. van Vogt. Such a volume had never appeared before, nor has its like surfaced since. Although sf from its earliest days has always been rife with writerly partnerships (de Camp & Pratt, Moore & Kuttner, Wylie & Balmer), such collaborations have usually involved stable, unchanging teams. Ellison's promiscuous pairings-up were a testament to his protean talents and eagerness to connect. It is doubtful whether any other writer has such an exemplary record of accomplishment in this odd corner of the writing field. All his fourteen partners, as Ellison testifies in his introduction, are admired writers who were integral to his development in one way or another, and the fusion of their skills with Ellison's produced one of Ellison's most delightful volumes. The stories here exhibit a looser, more relaxed mien. Standouts include the gonzo piece with Sheckley ("I See a Man Sitting on a Chair, and the Chair Is Biting His Leg"); the tender romance with Zelazny ("Come to Me Not in Winter's White"); and the posthuman adventure with van Vogt ("The Human Operators").

It was not until 1974 that his audience saw the first evidence of another new Ellison. Admittedly, the writer had not totally remade himself, nor should he have. An undeniable continuity of attack and subject matter and style were apparent. But the collection appearing that year—*Approaching Oblivion: Road Signs on the Treadmill Toward Tomorrow*—represented a new stage in Ellison's development. With its emphasis on gathering "previously uncollected" work made plain on its title page, the book bespoke a more careful and thoughtful stance toward showcasing his work and building a legacy. It was the nature of the stories themselves and the accompanying introduction, however, that revealed a writer who had passed through a certain fire and emerged not unscorched. The book's dominant tone is one of grimness and despair. Emerging from the wreckage of the 1960s, Ellison was plainly disappointed in both society and literature, all too aware of the failures of utopian dreams in both arenas. If *The Beast That Shouted Love at the Heart of the World* had been Ellison's Woodstock, then this new book was his Altamont. A powerful, significant experience, but tragic in its implications.

The opener, "Knox," projects the classic radical-conservative battle lines of the 1960s into a dystopian future with not a little flavor of Kafka (in its surreal assembly lines that produce nothing). The introduction of alien puppetmasters at the climax of the story is a sign, perhaps, of how even Ellison could not stand the grimness of his vision without seeking to excuse the protagonists somehow. "Cold Friend" reduces humanity to a single survivor of an enigmatic cataclysm, marooned in a bleak oasis, while "Kiss of Fire" portrays the endtime decadence of our race and its eventual extinction. "Silent in Gehenna" depicts the inescapable futility of all rebellion, as the last good terrorist is abducted by aliens to serve as their token conscience. Comparing this tale to "'Repent, Harlequin!' Said the Ticktockman" will illustrate the shift in Ellison's tone from zany and hopeful to dark and despairing. The protagonist of "Erotophobia" lives in danger of being literally "loved to death," while the antihero of "Catman" finds his only solace in merging bodily with a computer succubus. "One Life, Furnished in Early Poverty," an early run-through of the themes of "Jeffty Is Five," recounts the doomed attempts of a man to succor his childhood self via time travel. Ellison's creative use of his nostalgia for his personal past brings to mind Woody Allen's similar exercises in such films as *Radio Days* (1987). The earliest piece, 1962's "Paulie Charmed the Sleeping Woman," plays somberly on the Orpheus and Eurydice myth. Even the humorous shaggy dog story "I'm Looking for Kadak" involves a world being destroyed for no good reason, as well as the physical and spiritual abasement of its alien Jewish narrator.

Yet despite this prevailing atmosphere of defeat and closed frontiers, this collection is a bracing and admirable one. Stylistic experiments such as the stream-of-consciousness segment in "Silent in Gehenna" and the climactic passages in "One Life, Furnished in Early Poverty," where the language reflects the fusion of identities between the time traveler and the child, show Ellison stretching formalistically. There are various tiny escape holes in these stories, however, leading toward some possibility of redemption or self-improvement. After all, Knox commits suicide in the end rather than harm the woman he loves.

It seems proper to mention at this juncture the obvious influence Ellison was to have on two schools of fantastic writing just about to break big around this period. Stephen King, as the public face of horror writing, has expressed an admiration for Ellison's work, and it is easy to see the influence of Ellison's more horrific scenarios on King and others. Indeed, some of Ellison's more vivid Grand Guignol passages might very well have served as templates for the backwater of horror known as "splatterpunk." Last, the subgenre of "urban fantasy," wherein contemporary settings and characters are given an unreal twist, found inspiration not only in the work of pioneers such as Fritz Leiber but also in Ellison's many forays into such melanges of realism and fantasy.

In many ways Ellison's strongest compilation, *Deathbird Stories* was published in 1975. Contrary to the policy expressed on the title page of *Approaching Oblivion*, nine of its nineteen stories make their second appearances between Ellisonian book covers, including such familiar titles as "Paingod," "Pretty Maggie Moneyeyes," "Shattered Like a Glass Goblin" and "Rock God." In this case, however, the second coming of these pieces is amply justified, since they are fully recontextualized by the explicit theme of this collection: the examination of the new/old gods which bestride the modern landscape and dominate humanity's actions and define American culture's strengths and weaknesses. Moreover, the newer, heretofore-unreprinted stories are so strong—three award winners are included—that they pull the older ones along in their wake.

The collection opens with "The Whimper of Whipped Dogs." Based on the real-life murder of Kitty Genovese within earshot of dozens of apathetic New Yorkers, this tale posits the presence of an urban deity enamored of harsh sacrifices drawn from the weaker elements of the citizenry. The protagonist, a woman named Beth, finds herself forced to choose between becoming either an unstained victim or a bloody-handed celebrant in the new unholy rites, and chooses the latter course. For a writer who had earlier professed his love of New York City and his devotion to the metropolis, this story represents a disillusionment with the modern urban experience.

Two other major stories close the collection: "Adrift Just Off the Islets of Langerhans..." and "The Deathbird." The former story follows an inner hegira undertaken by Lawrence Talbot, the fabled Wolfman of the silver screen, as he seeks to find his missing soul and win surcease from a hellish life. Upon attaining his goal, however, he discovers instead a kind of unexpected grace and nobility. The latter story chronicles the final Gnostic struggle between a reborn Adam and the mad God who pretends to have made him, in the dying embers of a wax-riddled and poisonous Earth.

In between these bracketing stories are a number of entries that encapsulate what has come to be recognized as Ellison at his best. "On the Downhill Side" captures a Peter Beagle-style wistfulness in its tale of two spirits seeking salvation in each other's arms. "Basilisk" boils down the horrors of the Vietnam War to one soldier's possession by the vengeful spirit of a creature of the war god Mars (and again paves the way for the work of Lucius Shepard). "At the Mouse Circus" charts the surreal course of a black man adrift among the hollow trophies of a white man's world.

What is most notable about many of the newest stories in this collection is Ellison's increasing turn away from the purest exercises in either science fiction, fantasy, or realism. Tropes and styles from all three arenas begin to mix and blur, in a blending of all three modes. The hard-edged scientific vocabulary in "Adrift Just Off the Islets of Langerhans . . ." is in place to support a hallucinatory journey into inner space. Many of the talismans the protagonist encounters there are autobiographically specific to Ellison's life. Likewise, "The Deathbird" features an interpolated autobiographical essay, while its fantastic scenario of warring deities is partially categorized as a battle between superior aliens. Plainly, twenty years into his career, Ellison was chafing at old structures and expectations, and was seeking to transcend the parameters of both the marketplace and his own past accomplishments. The virtues of this volume are testament to his success.

Remarkably, 1975 saw a second volume from Ellison, a collection of suspense stories titled *No Doors, No Windows*. Unable to resist a second showcasing of "The Whimper of Whipped Dogs," yet drawing mainly on over "300,000 words of previously published (but never collected) stories," Ellison assembled a volume whose stories exhibit technical craft and ingenuity, but, due to their age, necessarily little of his then-current ambitions. Generally, the best of these pieces summon comparisons to the work of Roald Dahl, Shirley Jackson, John Collier, and the darker aspects of James Thurber. The last-named author comes to mind most vividly in such pieces as "Status Quo at Troyden's," in which an elderly pensioner commits a rageful act of murder which pays off handsomely, and in "Opposites Attract," wherein a mad bomber and a serial slasher find true love together. The brand-new item in the collection, "Tired Old Man," riffs capably on Borges's "The Other," depicting an author's meeting with his future self.

One lamentable tendency of Ellison's which crops up here is his insistence on updating older stories with a surface contemporaneousness that consorts poorly with their older trappings. For instance, 1963's "The Man on the Juice Wagon" is now made to occur in 1975. Yet, the roving murderous Klansmen of its southern setting—perhaps topical and accurate, if a bit hyperbolic, in the heyday of the civil rights movement—look silly and unreal in Jimmy Carter's New South.

Of the twenty-four story collections surveyed in this essay, sixteen appeared in the first twenty years of Ellison's career, from 1955 to 1975. The subsequent span of nearly three decades would see only eight. Of those eight, two volumes are assemblages of recollected works (*The Essential Ellison*, in both its 1987 and 2001 editions, and *Troublemakers*, Ellison's first book slanted at the young adult market). Plainly, some of the old fire and drive and productivity and fecundity that made Ellison an *enfant terrible* had diminished. Still, the thirty years since 1975 were hardly fallow. (Ray Bradbury, an author Ellison is often compared to in terms of achieving fame solely through the medium of short stories, boasts only about half as many collections over a longer career.) Indeed, many of Ellison's best stories emerged during the latter portion of his career. The collections of his later years exhibit a continuing commitment to the art of story-telling, increasing skills, and willingness to try new modes of writing.

Strange Wine (1978) opens with a bang and goes on to feature several exemplary works. "Croatoan" is the surreal tale of a man struggling to come to terms with his girlfriend's recent abortion. Following her discarded fetus into the city sewers, he comes upon an empire of the preterite, where he seems fated to rule. Comparing this vivid and impactful nightmare to the much longer and more diffuse yet similarly themed "Neither Your Jenny Nor Mine" from 1964, one notes the superiority of the more mature piece.

Ellison's humorous side gets an airing in this collection, as cantankerous gnomes assist a burnt-out fantasy writer in "Working With the Little People," while a nagging Jewish mother returns to haunt her son in "Mom." "The New York Review of Bird" is a more sardonic outing, with its Ellison-modeled protagonist laying waste to the Literary Establishment that stifles genre writers of talent. In tone and effect, it recalls "Santa Claus vs. S.P.I.D.E.R."

"In Fear of K" summons memories of "I Have No Mouth and I Must Scream," insofar as the newer story also concerns captives of a malign being immured in a giant labyrinth. The emphasis here, though, is on the interpersonal relations of the two human protagonists, and the story serves as sharp parable of love gone wrong. "From A to Z, in the Chocolate Alphabet" finds Ellison experimenting with a collection of unlinked vignettes, a form he pioneered in the sf genre, and which would be taken up by later writers such as Michael Swanwick. Finally, "Hitler Painted Roses" employs the celestial aftermath of a murderous mortal love affair to rail against an imperfect heavenly bureaucracy. As the opening salvo in a new stage of his writing life, *Strange Wine* promises copious strong draughts to follow.

Shatterday (1990) precipitated Ellison into a new decade and functioned as a kind of unofficial twenty-fifth anniversary capstone to all that had gone before. A very strong collection on all fronts, its monumentality affected a new generation of then-blossoming writers such as Neil Gaiman, who attested to Ellison's influence in a 1997 essay. The book positions one of its most affecting stories first. "Jeffty Is Five" is a tale of a perpetually youthful child who has the inadvertent ability to contort the forces of time. It achieves all the more power through its narration by Jeffty's only adult friend, who becomes a Judas figure by ignorant default. Using the figure of Jeffty as Günter Grass used Oskar Matzerath in *The Tin Drum* (1959) to comment on the coarsening of the current world, Ellison crafts a fable for the inevitable loss of childhood innocence every adult suffers.

Other consequential stories in this collection include "How's the Night Life on Cissalda?," a one-note joke about alien sex monsters which nonetheless showcases Ellison's flensing, stand-up comedian abilities. Satirist Paul Krassner, comic Lenny Bruce, or deadpan author Kurt Vonnegut would have been proud to claim this one as their own. "Count the Clock that Tells the Time," in its depiction of the metaphysical fate awaiting those hapless nonentities who let their lives escape them, harks back to "Are You Listening?" and "Cold Friend," reminding us that this theme—an individual's responsibility for his own fate—is one of Ellison's paramount leitmotifs. A creator little mentioned in reference to Ellison, yet who shares many affinities with the writer, is the self-mythologizing auteur Federico Fellini. "All the Birds Come Home to Roost," wherein all of the protagonist's ex-lovers manifest serially and in reverse order, culminating in a deadly meeting with his insane first wife, is Ellison's partial equivalent of *La Dolce Vita* (1959) or *8½* (1953). Further, two stories about doppelgängers—"In the Fourth Year of the War" and "Shatterday"—remind readers that Ellison's focus on such tormented split personalities extends all the way back to 1958's "My Brother Paulie."

But the core of this collection is the equally Felliniesque "All the Lies that Are My Life," a story which Ellison claims took twelve years of intermittent effort to write, a statement which presumably dates its origin to the time this exact titular phrase appeared in 1967's "Pretty Maggie Moneyeyes." A non-fantastic tale (except in the hyperbolic level of fame accorded its protagonist) about the death of a writer who is something of a sacred monster, this story chronicles the disjunctions between public mask and private self, between artist and unadorned human, between friend and enemy, all contained within the single shell of one man. An additional layer of complexity is added by making the narrator a writer who functioned for years as a kind of shadow or lesser self to the main character, thus grafting the doppelgänger imagery onto the other themes. In terms of compression and startling imagery, of apt dialogue and economical pacing, these stories reflect new advances in Ellison's craft.

Quite often after the release of a magnum opus, a creator will return with a smaller-scaled, less ambitious offering, as if resting up and recouping energies needed for another attempt at the summit of ambition. So it was to be with Ellison, post-*Shatterday*. *Stalking the Nightmare* (1982) is a rather tepid and unexceptional collection. (Here is where readers encounter Stephen King's introductory endorsement of Ellison.) Ellison chose to re-reprint four stories and to delve marginally into his stockpile of long-unseen 1950s journeyman work again. The newest works range from an unfocused quest for the beacon of "True Love" ("Grail," whose long thematic lists of obscure books and famous quotes veer into self-parody); not one but two magical shoppe stories ("Djinn, No Chaser" and "The Cheese Stands Alone"); and a fictionalized transcript of an Ellison radio appearance that swerves awkwardly at the climax into sf ("The Hour That Stretches"). A handful of nonfiction essays bulk out the collection, as if Ellison realized the fiction alone needed bolstering.

Ellison's next work was a thirty-fifth-anniversary retrospective volume, *The Essential Ellison*, in 1987, described later.

The next new collection to be published was of much greater magnitude than *Stalking the Nightmare*. *Angry Candy* (1988) marked Ellison's return from mere craftsmanship to the pinnacle of his craft. Beginning with a mordant and genuinely philosophically questing introduction that is part necrology for all of Ellison's friends and peers who had died in the near-term surrounding *Angry Candy*'s publication, the book contains four major recent stories ("Paladin of the Lost Hour," "With Virgil Oddum at the East Pole," "The Function of Dream Sleep," and "Eidolons"). Plainly, Ellison had assembled an impressive assortment of stories, without resorting to the resurrection of jarring, older works. The majority of these new creations revolve around death in all its manifestations.

In "Paladin of the Lost Hour," Ellison portrays a redeemer figure, a kind of secret martyr who justifies the world's existence. Although he is not explicitly Jewish, this figure resonates with certain mystical Jewish beliefs. Another of Ellison's favorite demigods, Prometheus, reappears in "On the Slab." That this story also pays homage to H. P. Lovecraft does not detract from its mythic significance. The virtual-reality duel in the early Ellison story, "The Silver Corridor," finds a more sophisticated analogue in "Broken Glass," when an innocent woman has her brain invaded by a malicious telepath. "Laugh Track" stands out in this volume for its happy ending, as the media-trapped ghost of the narrator's favorite aunt is freed by his intervention.

The oldest story, "The Region Between," hails from the period (in the 1960s) that culminated in *The Beast That Shouted Love at the Heart of the World*, and exhibits the brio of an Alfred Bester word explosion, replete with typographical tricks and line drawings by noted illustrator Jack Gaughan. In "Soft Monkey," the protagonist is an elderly black bag lady, reminding the reader of just how often Ellison eschews a privileged viewpoint in favor of the downtrodden. This commitment to telling the tales of the forgotten is a constant thread in his corpus. The linked vignettes in "Eidolons" recall the format of "From A to Z, in the Chocolate Alphabet," and foreshadow his later volume *Mind Fields*. Finally, in the retrospective light of Ellison's most recent original collection to date, it is interesting to note that the key concept in "Chained to the Fast Lane in the Red Queen's Race" is that of "slippage," the passage of one man's consciousness across the jagged boundaries of a host of individual lives.

In *Angry Candy*, pushed by the frustrating circumstances of his own life—the myriad deaths of friends, his own illnesses (chronic fatigue syndrome, a near-fatal heart attack) and accidents—Ellison managed to transmute pain and bafflement and anger into a thematically homogeneous yet formalistically variable set of fables dealing with mortality and bereavement. This collection ranks as one of his most accomplished.

Nearly ten years would pass before the publication of his next prose collection, *Slippage* (1997). This unprecedented gap speaks to both a natural diminishment of his once-extreme productivity—he had, after all, turned fifty-four with *Angry Candy*—and also to some exceptional bad luck. As detailed in the introduction to *Slippage*, the early 1990s saw Ellison's California home partially destroyed in a major earthquake, and that decade also laid him low with a continuing serious heart condition. Gone, after these disasters, is the sanguine assurance that his writing will flow endlessly from him, and he envisions this book being his last.

In the midst of these troubles, Ellison managed to produce one of his most charming and original books, the *sui generis Mind Fields* (1993). Thirty-some paintings by the Polish surrealist Jacek Yerka form the core of this project. For each inspirational image, Ellison wrote a small story, the longest only two pages, and most considerably shorter. Stories and paintings are presented side by side. These prose poems exhibit an almost free-associational flow of imagery. Some of the narratives are strongly plotted, others are meandering. Familiar Ellisonian themes such as the nature of heroism ("Twilight in the Cupboard") and the redeeming love of a good woman ("Susan") surface from time to time, along with a new one, the rigors of old age ("To Each His Own"). For a writer who earned his stripes in the pulp factories where pre-commissioned cover art was frequently assigned to a writer who had then to generate a story to match the art, the *Mind Fields* project must have seemed at once nostalgic and revolutionary.

When *Slippage* arrived four years after *Mind Fields*, it was subtitled "Previously uncollected, precariously poised stories," and that rubric fit the tone of the volume: transitional, variegated, harking backward to known formats and themes while simultaneously presaging new directions. A handful of utterly groundbreaking and impressive stories—

as good as any others from Ellison's long career—consort with the majority that are honorably entertaining, and a couple that are almost retrograde.

The most minor ones are the teleplay, "Crazy as a Soup Sandwich," with its Runyonesque gangsters involved in a deal with demons; "The Lingering Scent of Woodsmoke," featuring dryads and Nazis; "The Few, the Proud," which actually revisits Ellison's oldest space-opera cosmos, the Earth-Kyben war; and "Sensible City," which depicts a crooked cop getting his just deserts in true *Twilight Zone* fashion.

Among the more solid entertainments, the reader encounters two stories which evoke such masters of the outré as Clark Ashton Smith and A. Merritt. "Darkness Upon the Face of the Deep" recounts the Indiana Jones-style adventures of two old chums in quest of an ancient sarcophagus, while "Chatting with Anubis" posits a similar situation at a tomb guarded by the titular deity. A collaboration with longtime compatriot Robert Silverberg, "The Dragon on the Bookshelf," charts the tug between love and duty in an apocalyptic setting; one might see similar equations being explored in "A Boy and His Dog." Another deity is encountered in "The Museum on Cyclops Avenue," which uses the local color of Sweden to good effect. The same sense of a disjuncture in time and personality which informed "Shatterday" crops up in "Anywhere But Here, with Anyone But You," when a man must abandon his old life at the behest of a mysterious stranger. And "Pulling Hard Time" is a brief and effective anti-capital-punishment riff, with a twist.

There are four major stories which earn this collection a prominent spot in Ellison's canon. Two of them are linked in a subtle fashion. "The Man Who Rowed Christopher Columbus Ashore" and "Scartaris, June 28th" both deal with a trickster figure, a roving demiurge named Levendis, reminiscent of similar figures from James Branch Cabell novels, who sows as much trouble as balm. The chronicle of this multi-faceted, multi-faced individual's deeds limns a view of the universe "beyond good and evil," endorsing a kind of Zen acceptance of the unfathomable mix of banality and excellence, harm and succor, which the plenum daily dispenses. Although always somewhat multivalent in his assessment of good and evil, Ellison now seems almost to have thrown overboard such unrealistically tidy concepts as enemies and friends, victims and oppressors.

"Mefisto in Onyx," another tale of dueling telepaths in the manner of "Broken Glass," earns its impact on sheer magnitude of emotional interplay, as a romantic triangle occurs in a Death Row setting. Finally, "Midnight in the Sunken Cathedral" is cousin to "Adrift Just off the Islets of Langerhans . . . " in its depiction of a hallucinatory spiritual hegira. This time, the lead figure is in quest not of his soul, but of the father he never knew.

Slippage, as a whole, represents a kind of messy, portentous, extended rebirth, only as yet partially accomplished, as Ellison moves into a new era in his story-telling. While that new era of Ellisonian myth-making is still being adumbrated by some scattered magazine appearances, readers are able to take a good look back at his five decades of writing thanks to two retrospective volumes.

The first and slighter one, *Troublemakers* (2001), was not actually intended as a purely retrospective offering. Instead, it is ostensibly Ellison's first collection geared toward the young-adult market, all its selections theoretically centering on rebels and rebellion. In reality, its diffuse table of contents—a few classic pieces, a few respectably workmanlike offerings, and several middling stories from the 1950s—fails to cohere around the central nucleus of "'Repent, Harlequin!' Said the Ticktockman" in any organic way. This is Ellison Lite, replete with sour-voiced introductions. A previously uncollected story, "Never Send to Know for Whom the Lettuce Wilts," examines in humorous fashion the familiar, Gnostic, Ellisonian conceit that a mad deity lurks at the heart of the cosmos—but this time the godling's very madness works in humanity's favor.

As if to offset the negligibility of *Troublemakers* came *The Essential Ellison: A Fifty-Year Retrospective*, the 2001 edition updated from the 1987 original. (The volume dates Ellison's professional career not from the 1955 sale of "Glowworm," but rather from the appearance of some juvenilia, herewith exhumed, in a Cleveland newspaper circa 1949, for which Ellison did indeed receive remuneration of a sort.) Edited by Terry Dowling, Richard Delap, and Gil Lamont, this mammoth compilation weighs in at over 1200 pages and captures, according to the author, "the 'essentiality' of me, Harlan, the writer. . . ." In addition to many of his classic stories, readers also find here a never-produced teleplay, photos, and numerous essays and memoirs. Divided into sixteen sections, this collection allows for an interplay of texts which the predecessor volumes could not individually foster. By pulling stories from individual books—which already often had thematic linkages— and rearranging them under such new headings as "Trouble with Women," "Rococo Technology," "Shadows from the Past," "Process," and "A Stab of Merriment," Ellison and his editors codify the author's characteristic themes and angles of attack. If the book consisted only of the section labeled "The Classics," it would still be a worthy endeavor. The student of Ellison is able to trace, for instance, Ellison's concern with outsider protagonists all the way from 1950's "Glowworm" to 1985's "Paladin of the Lost Hour." And readers will also discover in its first book appearance, "Objects of Desire in the Mirror Are Closer than They Appear," in which a female cop investigating a queer homicide finds her private life inexplicably dovetailing with the weird murder. As a starting place for the newcomer or a trove of memories for the inveterate aficionado, this volume is indeed essential.

Awaiting their gathering-up in some post-*Slippage* compendium are a handful of new Ellison stories, three of which in particular hint at roads yet untraveled. The first piece appeared in *Amazing Stories* magazine in 1999 and actually points backwards in time. "The Toad Prince, or Sex Queen of the Martian Pleasure Domes" is a highly polished pastiche of the kind of "planetary romance" that was produced in the 1940s by such writers as Leigh Brackett and Edmond Hamilton, with a smattering of later-vintage Alfred Bester. This is the sf Ellison grew up on and now seeks to honor. Concerning the exploits of a lowly prostitute named Sarna and a gestalt mind called the Six, the adventure manages to be both true to its antecedents and also illustrative of typical Ellison obsessions such as the malfeasance of mad gods. This story shows Ellison striving even further to integrate his oldest loves with his most mature, storytelling ambitions.

In 2001 *The Magazine of Fantasy and Science Fiction* featured "From A to Z, in the Sarsaparilla Alphabet." Like its namesake, "From A to Z, in the Chocolate Alphabet," this piece cavorts ebulliently with a variety of forms and subjects, centering this time around various mythical beings such as kelpies, Jackalopes, and banshees. Mainly humorous, the twenty-six segments conflate contemporary icons (Hollywood, psychologists) with ancient ones (Isis, the Tower of Babel) in a kind of postmodern melange. Here readers see Ellison continuing to kick back at the constraints of linear, homogeneous narrative.

McSweeney's Mammoth Treasury of Thrilling Tales (2002) brought the reader "Goodbye to All That." Antic and surreal in the manner of S. J. Perelman or, more contemporaneously, Mark Leyner, this tale of a man's mountainous ascent to the *omphalos* (navel) of the cosmos reveals Ellison still intent on asking the epistemological and ontological questions that have fueled his work almost from its earliest days. At this point, however, any answers are almost beside the point: The journey is all.

* * *

"I stripped down naked (which is the way I write frequently) and started writing the story." Thus does Ellison recount the genesis of "Pretty Maggie Moneyeyes" in its first book appearance in *I Have No Mouth and I Must Scream*. This vivid picture—of the author seated bare before the demanding (occasionally vampiric) instrument of his creation, rather like that favored image of Ellison's, Prometheus with tormentor—summons up the paramount fact of Ellison's career. Whatever his subject matter; whatever the genre he's laboring in, even if self-invented; whatever formalistic or stylistic tricks he is experimenting with at the moment; whether he intends to shock, to comfort, to annoy, to enlighten, to amuse or to testify as witness; at whatever length; in whatever venue—he comes before us naked, all secrets disclosed, all cards displayed on the table, his message echoing in skewed fashion the anonymous gravestone epigram: "As you are now, so once was I; as I am now, so you shall be." An essential equation between author and reader, transcending time, space and identity, merging all three, has been made.

From *The New York Review of Science Fiction* 18.5 (January 2006): 1, 8-14. Copyright © 2006 by Paul Di Filippo. Reprinted with permission of Paul Di Filippo.

The Fractured Whole:
The Fictional World of Harlan Ellison
Peter Malekin

Harlan Ellison's most powerful stories are the most fictional—his fantastic stories are particularly notable for ferocity of psychological impact. This paper investigates some of the techniques used, especially in two of these stories, and indicates how they contribute to his critique of Western culture.

Many of Harlan Ellison's realistic works are concerned with violence and exploitation. Their savagery is, however, tempered by his compassion both for predator and victim, and by his urge to understand violence as a phenomenon. This is true of *Web of the City*, *Memos from Purgatory*, and the collection of short stories, *The Deadly Streets*, in which the characters are projected as ordinary human beings hemmed in and warped by deprivation and adversity. However, the realistic technique of these works leaves the middle-class reader outside the action, shocked perhaps by the case history of what he himself might have become, but not experiencing through the action what he himself is. Responsibility is social, "out there"; violence is not internalized as part of the middle-class self.

Fantasy, however, can penetrate deeper than realism. Fantasy is valuable only as expressing or effecting something unattainable by realism (which explains why allegorical interpretations of fantasy and fantasy that is merely allegorical are both unsatisfactory). Harlan Ellison's fantasy produces in the readers a shocking confrontation of themselves they would prefer to ignore. In producing this effect, Ellison runs a double risk of total rejection on the one hand and establishment as the licensed conscience of the community on the other (a fate projected with some humor in the story "Silent in Gehenna").

In many of the fantastic stories, two worlds are played off against each other. This occurs often on the level of ideas, as "normality" versus violence in "The Whimper of Whipped Dogs," or normality versus drugged consciousness in "Shattered Like a Glass Goblin," or the externalized authoritarian God versus the divinity within man in "Deathbird." In some of the stories with totally nonrealistic settings, the contrasting aspects become pairs of metaworlds linked symbiotically, in that each gains credibility because of the limitations of the other. In "Catman," for instance, the apparently permissive yet rigidly conventional surface world sits above the horrifying underworld. There obscene sexual acts can be conducted with the giant computer that partially transforms its lovers into metal artifacts before finally absorbing them into its own fabric. This computerized love is the last resort of those who can no longer feel or relate adequately to the people around them in the constrained surface world.

The dual world motif is most powerfully used in "The Beast That Shouted Love at the Heart of the World" and "A Boy and His Dog." In the latter, the contrast is between the surface world, devastated by atomic war, and the "downunders." These worlds reverse the polarities of our current vocabularies. We speak of underworlds and subcultures, and the middle-class point of view consigns them to beneathness and darkness. In "A Boy and His Dog," it is middle-class society that is embowelled in the earth at the bottom of mine shafts or ancient wells, deprived of sunlight and free air, while our underworld savagery and violence are found on the surface, as the solos and gangs wander with their mutts, or telepathic dogs, and fight to stay alive.

We are introduced to this state of affairs gradually, but prepared for it from the very first. The opening sentence, "I was out with Blood, my dog," presents us with an apparently factual everyday report by a first-person narrator. In the absence of an external physical speaker, the written "I" invites identification with the narrator. Yet the sentence also creates unease by its use of the name "Blood," by its near-echo of phrases such as "out for blood," and by an inversion in the most common word order. We would expect "I was out with my dog, Blood."

Putting the name first tends to turn Blood into a person—which is, of course, exactly what he turns out to be. The normal boy-dog relation is virtually stood on its head. Blood teaches and admonishes Vic, laughs at his lechery, and seeks out suitable objects for his sexual satisfaction, while Vic hunts for Blood's food.

The upside-down relationship leads via the beaver flick with its masturbating audience of solos, and the pursuit of Quilla June, to the full surface-versus-downunder contrast. Each of the two worlds has its own code. The underworld, deliberately contrived to imitate society as it was before the First World War, stagnates in politeness, repressive morality, and the rejection of change. Physical violence and physical sexuality are unwanted and unrecognized. The code of the surface is the much older warrior's code, dominated by the virtues of courage, cunning, and loyalty to companions in arms. Here sex is a male physical need, but sexual loyalty to women is virtually nonexistent.

Neither the surface world, surviving on the detritus of civilization, the canned foodstuffs left in ruined supermarkets, nor the middle-class downunder is ultimately viable. Both are sterile. Sex in the surface world consists in the violent rape of the few surviving women, accompanied by mutual loathing. Sex in the underworld is ceasing because of male impotence.

The two worlds collide in the relation between Quilla June, Vic, and Blood, and in the psyches of Vic and Quilla. Demure Quilla, escaped from the repressive downunder, masturbates like a solo in the beaver flick and subsequently unleashes a prodigious sexual appetite, but she also brings from downunder a demand for "love" and the exclusive allegiance of her lover. On the other hand, familial pieties collapse as she helps to murder her father and attempts to murder her mother. Her attempted ownership of Vic cuts across his close relationship with his dog in hunting and war. The clash between the bourgeois love code and the warrior code is projected via a clash between the special status accorded to heterosexual love and to pets (as opposed to commercial animals) in our Western culture.

A love relationship of sorts begins when Vic asks Quilla June's name. Quilla's recurring question as she climbs the ventilation shaft from the downunder is "Do you love me?" Vic answers that he does, because he means it and because it keeps her climbing. However, faced with the need of the dying Blood for food and the impossibility of surviving without him, Vic kills and cooks Quilla and feeds her to his dog. The positive ritual of pet-feeding clashes with the love code and violates one of our major taboos, against the eating of human flesh. The final twist comes with the splendid ending. Vic holds the wounded mutt Blood in his arms all night, which leads to the final bland lines:

Do you know what love is?
Sure I know.
A boy loves his dog. (p. 254)

The uneasy near-normality of the opening sentence, hinting at something awfully wrong, here gives way to an absolutely normal sentence, placed contextually to be undercut in a reader's mind by an awareness of sexual betrayal and cannibalism. The effect on the reader is somewhat akin to that portrayed objectively in Quilla June, when submerged hatred erupts against her parents. The normality of suppressed id and openly dominant superego is no longer normal in the reader's mind, which thus becomes a spark of illumination bridging the poles of topside and downunder.

The internalizing techniques in "A Boy and His Dog" and the majority of the story's readers are both Western, rooted in our cultural reality. As Lévi-Strauss pointed out, the configurations of a culture tend to recur in all aspects of life within it. Our Western configuration of the irreconcilably divided universe not only recurs in psychology and social organization, and in reformist political and gender-based thought, but is also deeply rooted in science and in Western religious myth (compare, for instance, the fate of Satan in *Paradise Lost* with the assumption into heaven of Ravanna at the end of The Ramayana). Several of Harlan Ellison's stories, such as "Deathbird" and "I Have No Mouth and I Must Scream," have a bearing on or directly confront the religious traditions that share and sanction this configuration. One of the most experimental of these stories is "The Beast That Shouted Love at the Heart of the World." Where "Deathbird" and "I Have No Mouth and I Must Scream" create worlds of origins and endings, with the strong sense of linear temporal development that is so emphasized in theological interpretations of our religious myths, "The Beast That Shouted Love at the Heart of the World" is a postmodern disruption of the linear pattern. The story uses various technical devices to produce a sense of the underlying configuration erupting into time, rather as hidden aspects of the mind erupt into consciousness, dislocating the neat, linear, cause-and-effect pattern assumed in conscious life.

The story starts in the familiar world of the modern nations, but jumps backward to the encounter between Pope Leo I and Attila the Hun, and Raphael's fresco celebrating the event and sanctioning papal authority and forward to the opening of World War IV. It also jumps "crosswhen," an idea essentially aspatial and atemporal, carefully introduced by references to the "if" of hypothesis and fantasy, by evocations of Einsteinian space-time linked to consciousness, by allusions to multiple cosmic parallax, by the rapid superimposition of "here" and "there" in the introduction of the aspatial "center," and by an encouragement to leap beyond human thought. It is in this "center" that the beast is hunted down. The beast links with the beast of Revelations, hermeneutically equated with Satan and the seven-headed dragon, whose ejection carried a third of the stars of heaven with him. The dragon of "The Beast That Shouted Love" is also specifically associated with Cerberus, the many-headed dog that guarded Hades, the classical underworld often equated unjustifiably with the Christian hell.

In this center, the scientist Semph plies an inhuman trade by draining assorted creatures of the madness that causes violence and death in society. The trade is inhuman because the fury and hatred are not faced and cannot be disposed of permanently. Instead they are suppressed to reappear in other times and places. Moreover, in the center itself is Semph's nemesis in the form of Linah, who makes himself Proctor by insisting that the dragon be drained and having Semph executed when the latter tries to interfere. The suppression thus leads to the establishment of a supposedly moral authority maintained by violence.

The draining of the dragon and the partial draining of Semph produce the confused patterns of behavior that lead to murder accompanied by pronouncements of love for the human race in Sterog. They also lead to the turning back of Attila, but not of Gaiseric and Alaric, who both sacked Rome. In the center itself they lead to Semph's remark to Linah:

> You have condemned them to live with [insanity] always. In the name of love. (p. 24)

Linah had claimed as his justification the creation of an enclave of sanity and peace that might eventually spread out through the universe. He parallels the papacy, whose claims had been propagandized by Raphael, just as the dragon parallels Sterog in his murderous mood. The question is, which is the real beast, the dragon or authoritarian Linah.

The statue of Sterog has in its hand "a peculiar ring-and-ball device"—the center and circumference in one. Linah chooses to live in one half only. Semph's ultimate instinct is to struggle with both. The internal struggle is also the external struggle against all authorities that place themselves above man. The alternative is to become what Semph ironically calls "a true man," like Linah—and Linah's sanity, like Semph's rational science, used in hunting down the dragon, is inhuman, the obverse side of the dragon's madness.

The spirit of Harlan Ellison's projection of the human and the Western predicament is very close to that of Blake. Like Blake, Harlan

Ellison is grappling with the fundamental thought patterns of our civilization. He is thus justified in insisting that his work be described as speculative fiction. He has indeed been more successful than Blake in capturing the attention of a mass public. His influence in changing the imaginative structures of that public is a major contribution to the current effort, still ongoing, to humanize humanity.

From *Journal of the Fantastic in the Arts* 1.2 (1988): 21-26. Copyright © 1988 by Peter Malekin. Reprinted with permission of Peter Malekin.

Afterword to *The Fantasies of Harlan Ellison*
Robert Thurston

"There are always those who ask, what is it all about?" is the opening sentence of Harlan Ellison's "'Repent, Harlequin!' Said the Ticktockman." Later in the story the Harlequin and Ticktockman have this exchange:

"Scare someone else. I'd rather be dead than live in a dumb world with a bogeyman like you."
"It's my job."
"You're full of it. You're a tyrant. You have no right to order people around and kill them if they show up late."
"You can't adjust. You can't fit in."
"Unstrap me, and I'll fit my fist into your mouth."
"You're a non-conformist."
"That didn't used to be a felony."
"It is now. Live in the world around you."
"I hate it. It's a terrible world."
"I don't, and most of the people I know don't."

And there, encapsulated, is the dilemma. "The world around you," whatever it is, will always attempt to stifle its critics, its writers and artists who attempt to define it. At the same time the critics/nonconformists/artists must continually shift their attention to accommodate the new perimeters of the evils they perceive. Moreover, much of humanity—as the Ticktockman says—is quite satisfied with the way things are.

"Madness is in the eye of the beholder," Ellison says in his note preceding the story "The Crackpots." The comment not only describes that story, but also the attitudes underlying most of his fictions. He clearly aligns himself with those writers who are disturbed with the insanity wrought in the name of rationality or reality. In stories such as "The Crackpots" and "'Repent, Harlequin!' Said the Ticktockman" he reverses the concepts of sanity and insanity, order and chaos. Sanity and order are seen as the madness at the core of the societies of both stories. The apparently insane are sane; the apparent disturber of the orderliness of society is the actual seeker for the return of an acceptable social order. When the knowledge provided by the viscera directly contradicts the so-called truths or realities of the society, one must attempt to expose the falsity behind the truths, the madness behind the realities. If there is any underlying theme to the peripatetic fictions of Harlan Ellison it is that whatever belief one espouses it must be examined thoroughly, even to the point of exposing its weaknesses, even if its theoretical foundations must be destroyed. Ellison's attacks on society are governed by his sense of social criticism, which generally translates into intense anger at the evils he perceives, and by his emotional reactions to the plight of the victimized of this world, concentrating particularly on the pain they senselessly, and sometimes not so senselessly, endure.

> I must cover it all in this olio, everything human,
> Passion and prayer and fear, pleasure, distraction, and rage.
> —from *The First Satire of Juvenal*
> (Rolfe Humphries translation)

It is generally accepted among scholars of satire that two evolutionary lines can be traced from the ancient Rome in which Horatio and Juvenal flourished as principal satirists. Horatio's satires were gently mocking, of the sort that jabs or takes pokes at the subjects they mean to ridicule. Juvenal's were more impassioned, more direct, more often governed by the rage he invokes in the above quote. While aspects of both satirists may be discovered in any satiric work since that time (indeed, some of Horatio's lines are clearly angry; some of Juvenal's quite gentle), most satires have been primarily indebted to the line dating back to one or the other of these Roman satirists. While Swift seemed impelled by a Juvenalian fury, Alexander Pope (except in *The Dunciad*) suffused his poetry with more of a subtle Horatian malice.

In our times, when the word satire has been debased to mean the spoof of the hour on TV, it is often not easy to see a writer as belonging to either evolutionary satiric line. The influence of Horatio seems predominant in the writings of such as Russell Baker, Art Buchwald, Bernard Malamud, Mary McCarthy, and Aldous Huxley. In the science-fiction field this approach has been used by Damon Knight, Frederik Pohl, C. M. Kornbluth, and others who have mocked human institutions in all kinds of satirical science-fictional extrapolations. Many modern satirists, including Muriel Spark, Joseph Heller, Iris Murdoch, Anthony Burgess, and (especially) Evelyn Waugh, provide strong doses of Juvenalian rage that seethes under the surface placidity of their tales. However, the Juvenalian methods of attack have not been particularly favored by modern satirists, although they have emerged strongly in the novels of Nathanael West and Terry Southern.

A recent movie by Paddy Chayefsky, *Network* (1977), contained large amounts of Juvenalian diatribe, principally in the TV sermons of the "mad prophet of the airwaves," Howard Beale (played by Peter Finch). In the most typical ploy of satire, these sermons couched the "sane" message of the author in the words of the story's supposedly insane character. Along with John Brunner, Harlan Ellison (interestingly enough, described as the "mad dreamer" on the back cover of the latest edition of *Paingod*) has been the most skilled practitioner of Juvenalian satiric attack to emerge from the SF field, both in his public utterances and his writings. In *Paingod* and *I Have No Mouth, and I Must Scream* his need to convey all possible passion, prayer, fear, pleasure, distraction, and rage is as clear in the introductions to the stories as in the stories themselves. As a writer and a member of the human race, he is clearly disturbed by the state of the world and the people who cause and/or allow it. The sense of outrage that such a view initiates is often the wellspring of satire, whether the satirist chooses to take an Horatian approach, a Juvenalian one, or a mixture of both. Ellison's sense of outrage is directly stated and his stories are generally well-wrought examinations of social conditions in dazzling science-fiction contexts.

Science fiction has been an especially receptive medium to the use of satire. Mainstream writers have often borrowed from the field to craft their own satiric works (*A Clockwork Orange*, *1984*, *The Child Buyer*, *Brave New World*, etc). The satiric target can often be seen more clearly by exactly the kind of extrapolation that is the prime focus of SF. In fact, the method by which satire is achieved science-fictionally, the transference of the subjects being attacked to another context, has been a basic technique of satire historically. Gulliver is transported to strange far-off lands in order that Swift may attempt to destroy the institutions and mores of 18th-century England. Nathanael West creates a strange gallery of offbeat Hollywood hangers-on in order to attack the emptiness of the American dream. In each case, the transference of the social problems under attack to a milieu different from that in which they are particularly prevalent causes for the reader a dissonance between the grotesquerie evoked in the book and his own very real matter-of-fact existence. When the satire is perceived by the reader, the correspondence between the strange world and his own becomes dramatically evocative. (But only if it is perceived. Missing or avoiding the satire has led to the acceptance of *Gulliver's Travels* (1726) as a pretty adventure tale and West's *The Day of the Locust* (1939) as a realistic novel about the fringe elements of the movie business in the 1930s, without appreciable acknowledgement of its savage attack on America in general. Indeed, its recent cinematic adaptation was notably lacking in the novel's satiric bite.)

Science-fictional extrapolation easily sheds light on social problems by this mere shift of details and events to another time, another world, another dimension, a ship travelling between worlds. Such subjects can be exaggerated or diminished, reshaped and/or extrapolated to absurdity. Except in the more delimited subdivisions of SF, like militaristic space opera and sadomasochistic planetary adventure, it is difficult for the SF writer not to be satiric, in at least incidental matters. Much of science fiction that is not clearly satire has at least some lighthearted jabs at human mores and institutions.

Perhaps more than any other writer developing out of the science-fiction field, Harlan Ellison is able to transfer through extrapolation his intensely felt emotions into objective terms. In fact, the reader can generally gauge the extent of this transference since Ellison provides the emotional sources of the stories in his invective filled introductions to them. There is often a nagging didactic tone to these little essays that is rarely found in the stories themselves. No matter how well turned the phrases in the introductory sections, the points are better made in the dramatic and imaginative terms of the narratives.

"Paingod" is a brilliant example of Ellison's genius at transferring deeply felt emotion to a controlled narrative. Instead of wallowing in the question of what sort of god could allow human suffering, or debating the age-old philosophical rationales, he imagines just the sort of god who can dispense pain easily, an unanthropomorphic deity to whom the job is just a job. The characterization of the paingod as a genuine alien is a striking achievement—one that, further, allows Ellison to consider the question that is his theme with objectivity and directness. Trente, the paingod, is responsible not just for the suffering of humankind, but to him falls "the forever task of dispensing pain and sorrow to the myriad multitudes of creatures that inhabited the universes." By removing the god even further from our world than conventional mythologies usually allow, and making the god's purveyance of pain merely an "attention to duty" Ellison achieves a finely detailed perspective, not to mention a skillful allegory.

The growing awareness of the dimensions of pain causes in the "soulless, emotionless, regimented" paingod the sickness of concern. An interesting turnabout is effected: the god must experience pain in order to relieve his own torment.

> What is this torment? What is this unpleasant, unhappy, unrelenting feeling that gnaws at me, tears at me, corrupts my thoughts, colors darkly my every desire? Am I going mad?

The displacement of the theme from the sufferers to the force causing their pain is illustrative of the kind of technique utilized by Ellison in the examination of human or social problems. Instead of portraying the suffering through human eyes, as in more realistic literary traditions, he inflicts the god with the pain, a transference by which he brings the subject into a sharper focus. Humankind, after all, is generally inured to its suffering; for Trente emotion of any kind is new. In order to understand pain fully, however, he must experience it as a member of a race within his vast dominion. In the body of the stricken artist Colin Marshack, he feels the pain that has formerly tormented him in the abstract.

> *It left itself wide open, flung itself wide open, to what tremors governed man. And Trente felt the full impact of the pain he so lightly dispensed to all the living things in the universes. It was potent hot all! And it was a further knowing, a greater knowledge, a simple act that the sickness had compelled him to undertake.*

The knowledge to which Trente comes is Keatsian in nature ("For without pain there can be no pleasure"). Pain, "the most important thing in the universes," leads to beauty—or, as it is stated eloquently in the story:

> "It is a grey and a lonely place in which we live, all of us, swinging between desperation and emptiness and all that makes it worthwhile is caring, is beauty. But if there was no opposite for beauty, if there was no opposite for pleasure, it would all turn to dust, to waste."

While the question of human suffering still remains, as it must, Ellison's allegorical rendering of it makes a profound plea for concern—not just from the paingod but from ourselves. Thus, the fictional god is also a stand-in for the readers of the story who, if they are not moved by it, are themselves suffering from an intellectual objectivity not unlike that of the paingod's.

The lack of concern that leads to conformism and a codified society is Ellison's subject in what is perhaps his most perfectly realized story, "'Repent, Harlequin!' said the Ticktockman." Taking his cue from Thoreau and a quote from the Civil Disobedience essay, Ellison pictures graphically a society in which the mass of men serve the state as machines in its service. The ordinary tyranny of time, the pressures of time which we all feel whether or not we respond to its actual and implied schedules, is extrapolated into a social system that is itself tyrannical in its unreasonable requirement that its citizens hold rigidly to schedule or have years lopped off their lifetimes. As in all tyrannies, whether small or large, important areas of individualism are lost and the Harlequin has become dangerous simply because

> He had become a *personality*, something they had filtered out of the system many decades before. But there it was and there *he* was, a very definitely imposing personality. In certain circles—middle-class circles—it was thought disgusting.

While the Harlequin stands for the last remaining vestige of individualism, the Ticktockman represents the indifference of society to individual needs. He is the machine that governs the operation of the other machines.

Ellison, in this story, attacks present day society through his skillfully constructed extrapolation. In one particularly well wrought paragraph he encapsulizes our submission to the tyranny of time.

> And so it goes. And so it goes. And so it goes. And so it goes goes goes goes goes tick trick tick took tick took and one day we no longer let time serve us, we serve time and we are slaves of the schedule, worshippers of the sun's passing; bound into a life predicated on restrictions because the system will not function if we don't keep the schedule tight.

Afterword to *The Fantasies of Harlan Ellison*

The major attack of the story is, of course, not against time or even the personal organization of it. It does not matter that Harlan Ellison is always late, as he says in his introductory comments. What does matter is that people are faced at each juncture of life with forces that attempt to keep them in line, to make them conform to whatever popular social or political structure is in vogue at that time. People who are consistently late violate small matters of etiquette that are essentially vestigial, and no degree of fretting from the offended parties covers the fact that their disturbance is directed at concern for form and not concern for the individual. (One could perhaps argue that the latecomer shows a similar lack of concern; either way the nerves of both the scheduled and unscheduled are jangled by what is essentially a set of social presumptions based on time.) Whether to a questionable system of etiquette or an entire social structure derived from the organization of time—or, for that matter, the organization of *anything* designed to keep humankind in line—the demand to conform should not be accepted mindlessly, as those in the Ticktockman's society have done.

All college bull sessions about the need to conform in some situations aside, the opposition between the individual thinker and those who would govern him changes only by degree from century to century. Just as the mass of men willing to conform to 19th-century society disturbed Henry David Thoreau, the conformities of mid-20th-century bother Harlan Ellison. As social critics both depict the machinelike mass of men with compassion. Instead of condemning them for not being individualistic, both writers see them as people who simply do not realize the dimensions of their submission. Individuals, especially those seen by the state as its enemies, can at least make the rest of society aware of the demands being made by whatever system is controlling their behavior. In "'Repent, Harlequin!' Said the Ticktockman" Ellison has achieved an important goal of the satirist: to attack the institutions of society with a perceptive exaggeration of certain important facts of the systems which govern them. The demands of time are annoyances; mindless conformism is a tangible evil.

In certain other stories he explores some different aspects of the individual vs. state conflict. The apparent maniacs in "The Crackpots" are nonconformists against the superior reasoning of an intergalactic power.

> They lived in a world of no standardization, no conformity at all. There was no way to gauge the way these people would act, as you could with the Kyben of the stars. It was—it was—well, *insane*!

In "The Crackpots" Ellison employs what is possibly the satirist's best formula for describing graphically the individual's resistance to the tyranny of a system—the supposedly insane are really the sane who are fighting against the insanity of the supposedly sane. (See also Joseph Heller's *Catch-22*, 1961, and Ken Kesey's *One Flew Over the Cuckoo's Nest*, 1962.) Ellison is also perceptive enough to include the variation of the actually insane individual who is nevertheless able to perceive the dimensions of social insanity even more clearly than the other crackpots.

The more cynical, perhaps because more recently written, "Sleeping Dogs" (1974—added to the revised edition of *Paingod* by the author) presents a similar conflict between the more advanced thinker and the unreasonable militarist whose "blind servitude to cause was the most loathsome aspect of his character." The diseased people of "The Discarded" and Gunnderson in "Deeper than the Darkness" are all individuals who, in their roles as pariahs, are nevertheless being used by the very society which has originally isolated them. The discarded, in attempting to cooperate with the groups who beg for help in the name of sanctioned higher ideals, kill off their Harlequin and encounter the double-cross of a society who would prefer for them to suffer in loneliness instead of living isolated on the same planet. For Gunnderson, his manipulation by representatives of his conforming society leads him to an important insight about himself: "He had discovered he had character, and that he was not a hopeless, oddie hulk, doomed to die wasted. He found he had a future." He is able to escape the domination of his manipulators in a way the Harlequin never could, becoming—interestingly enough—a Harlequin-like figure who takes the name of "The Minstrel."

Bergman, the hero of "Wanted in Surgery," conquers the absurdities of his mechanistic system by attacking it directly instead of getting away from it or submerging himself in it. The title character of "Bright Eyes" is a stoical observer of the doom of humankind, and the causes behind it. "So Bright Eyes—never Man—was the last man on Earth. Keeper of a silent graveyard; echoless tomb monument to the foolishness, the absurdity, of nobility." The satirist and/or social critic is a similar guardian, attacker of human folly and absurdity, and also seeker and celebrator of what is noble in humankind.

The bitterest of the Ellison stories which focus upon a Harlequin-Ticktockman kind of conflict is "I Have No Mouth, and I Must Scream." In his introductory comment he says that the time from which this story derives is a lightless, bitter period of "compassionate cynicism." He refers briefly to the method of transferring intensely subjective feelings into narrative form when he describes the Ellison who "turns the pain to fiction in the storyteller's alchemy, and the value of moments, in that special place of anguish comes out as sometimes stories."

"I Have No Mouth, and I Must Scream" resembles the *Paingod* stories in its pitting of a rebel against the system which is forcing its minions to conform. In this story, however, the idea of conformity is not at issue. The five characters trapped by AM, the worldwide computer system, would be only too eager to conform if given the proper opportunity. Instead, they are given a shifting landscape that either does not provide opportunity to conform or, more often, changes the perimeters of its dictated conformity as soon as the characters realize them and try to do what they think AM wants. There is no system for the quintet of sufferers to comprehend; there is only the system's self-gratification designed to discomfort and brutalize the world's remaining humans:

"the machine masturbated and we had to take it or die." Even though the story was written in the sixties, it anticipates the mood of the seventies, in that the only recourse open to its bemused characters is survival in the face of a world that has become too mechanistically complex for the old solution of simple conformity. The satiric message of this cautionary tale is almost too painful to consider. If the systems provide only punishment for action, whether the action is of a positive or negative nature, there is no reasonable solution for the individual with higher aspirations. There is only survival, only the kind of masturbatory self-gratification that is a delimited human goal. In the seventies, characterized rather blatantly as "The Me Decade" by a prominent media analyst, people are satisfying themselves by mimicking the example of the masturbating machines and systems that senselessly hold powers not granted them by the individuals over whom they hold sway. The vision of this story is more terrifying than Sartre's *No Exit* depiction of hell in which, according to the famous last line, "Hell is other people." In Ellison's version, itself a narrative for which Sartre's title would not be inappropriate, the hell that is other people seems at one remove from the senseless cruelty brought about by a system that is no longer even a definable object for direct and logical attack. The pessimism of Ellison's view in "I Have No Mouth, and I Must Scream" is harrowing and, if not always easy to accept (I resist the bleakness of both his and Sartre's view of the world), it is a genuine extrapolation of what is now present in the world. The role of the satirist is often to provide the signposts to danger in as exaggerated a manner as his perspective permits. In this way the satirist and the science fiction writer are often neatly dovetailed—both concerned with not showing what is, but what might be if human folly (or wisdom) is allowed free rein.

Even in "I Have No Mouth, and I Must Scream," bitter as it is, there is a light of sorts. When all the logical forms of rebellion against an uncomprehending force have been exhausted, there is still the illogical rebellion or the rebellion for the sake of rebellion. AM is not all-powerful, and there is one option open for the humans to use to defeat it. As the narrator says, "Surrounded by madness, surrounded by hunger, surrounded by everything but death, I knew death was our only way out." While murder and suicide freed four of the five trapped people in this story, that of course would be too nihilistic a solution for similar complexities in present-day society. The message I receive from the protagonist's climactic actions is that any rebellion is preferable to no rebellion at all. It is, perhaps, very much a message of the late 1960s, a time in which few philosophical rationales were offered for the actual events of rebellion. The act of rebellion itself became a prod to considering the deficiencies of whatever was being attacked. While some of the battles of that time are still being fought, albeit in a diminished way, we in the post-Watergate era are still in a questioning, if not a particularly rebellious mood. (That may seem overly optimistic on my part, but then I don't much believe in the Me Decade either.) The solution of "I Have No Mouth, and I Must Scream" may not be feasible as such—the encouragement of death as a way out, anyway—but the suggestion of rebellion at all costs is provocative. Also, it helps to relieve the desperate overtones of the story.

However, the final section of "I Have No Mouth, and I Must Scream" in which the condition of the title is fulfilled, is at least as bleak as Sartre's. The payment for the protagonist's rebellion is awesome and, as a statement of the impotence of what was once popularly called the human condition, it is devastating. In the extremity of a superbly imagined exaggeration, the state to which the protagonist is reduced portrays evocatively the kind of impotence we all feel, at least at certain important intervals of our life. For a moment it does not matter whether Ellison's pessimism is too much for us—underneath it all he has touched chords that affect all of us.

The stories in the *I Have No Mouth, and I Must Scream*, collection are generally more pessimistic than those in *Paingod and Other Delusions*. The main characters of "Big Sam Was My Friend," "Eyes of Dust," and "Delusion for a Dragon Slayer" find only death ending their doomed quests. "Eyes of Dust," particularly, offers an intriguing contrast to "Paingod." The paingod at least found something hopeful in the contemplation of beauty, but the actual beauties of "Eyes of Dust" are repelled by anything that is not beautiful: "Beauty seeks its level, as does ugliness. As do pariahs." The implication of the story is that, at least in some forms, beauty is an empty illusion like all the other illusions that dominate human action. The protagonist of "Delusion for a Dragon Slayer" cannot even succeed in that area where most of us believe success is possible, in dreams. In the rather arid conclusion of the story, Ellison writes, "a man may truly live in his dreams, his noblest dreams, but only, *only* if he is worthy of those dreams." "World of the Myth" seems even bleaker, as its most despicable character is forced to confront his own reality.

> "He killed himself because the ants showed him what he was. What he really was. As much truth as a man can stand and then some. They showed him the essence of himself."

At the end of the story there is offered the possibility that the protagonist might reach a similar fate if he could also be shown the essence of himself. It is possible, the story seems to say, that we would all suffer similarly if we could be confronted with our own realities. All in all, the stories in *I Have No Mouth, and I Must Scream* have in them fewer glimpses of the nobility or potential of humankind than do those in *Paingod*, in which beauty is at least possible, harlequins can disrupt the system importantly before being defeated, crackpots can perform their clandestine rebellion with vigor, dedicated men can even *defeat* the limited systems, and misfits can discover their own identity together with a chance for escape from domination. The significant note of difference is struck in the last lines of "World of the Myth":

> He went away from her, then; he went to lie down, hoping there was a future, but doubting it; really doubting it.

Compare that to Gunnderson's vision of future in "Deeper Than the Darkness." In fact, the future seems bleak for all the survivors of the stories in *I Have No Mouth, and I Must Scream*. Survival becomes even a questionable goal.

In stories that are not particularly embedded with satire or social criticism, Ellison still uses a process of fictional transference (or, to use his word for it, alchemy) to dramatize his themes. "Lonelyache," for example, translates the intensely personal experience of a marital split-up into a fantasy creation that has more dramatic effect than would pages of post-breakup self-pitying. The loneliness beast growing in the corner of the protagonist's room is artfully imagined. Not only is it a powerful symbol of the man's loneliness, it is an effective representation of the way we push, or try to push, our pain away from us, into corners of our mind. No matter how much we try to ignore the pain, it remains, gnawing at us until we confront it or capitulate to it. The way the loneliness beast affects the protagonist is enormously provocative, and the end of the story has an effect on the reader that is equivalent to the effect of similar events in J. D. Salinger's "A Perfect Day for Bananafish," John O'Hara's *Appointment in Samarra* (1934), and Louis Malle's 1963 film *The Fire Within*. Ellison is not being improperly immodest when, in his introductory comment, he claims "Lonelyache" as one of his best stories.

"Pretty Maggie Moneyeyes" is a personal favorite of mine among Ellison's tales. In this well characterized narrative he makes poignantly dramatic a central plight of our times: the loss of identity in an increasingly mechanized society that is well on its way to soullessness. Especially striking is Ellison's use of the story's focal metaphor. He portrays Maggie as a machinelike woman ("*An operable woman, a working mechanism, a rigged and sudden machinery of softness and motivation*" whose soul is transferred into a slot machine). Again Ellison uses a transference to dramatize his main theme. Along the way he makes an important statement about the mechanistic ways of our society.

The story works especially well in the presentation of the character of Maggie. She is a machine even before her death, one who has analyzed society's demands for a beautiful and successful woman, and then constructed herself to fulfill those demands. At 23, she is "*a determined product of Miss Clairol and Berlitz, a dream-image formed by Vogue and intimate association with the rat race.*" Ellison details her life with such clarity that, in spite of the mechanistic metaphor—"*A chromium instrument, something never pitted by rust and corrosion*"—she is a vividly realized character. Her conformity to a set of false ideals is the seed of her entrapment. Maggie's soul inside the machine has always, in a way, been the essential Maggie—a mechanized soul dedicated to acquisitive goals. The final sections of the story, in which her dream-self treats Kostner the way she treated men in life, using the facade of emotion to achieve her freedom, are particularly effective because of the skill with which Ellison has earlier portrayed her and established the mechanistic metaphor. On the satiric level, the story suggests the wider field of illusions which threaten to drain away all human identity. For a very small cost we can transfer our own souls to the various machines of ambition, luxury, or a properly scheduled life. In that respect, "Pretty Maggie Moneyeyes" is not appreciably different from "'Repent, Harlequin!' said the Ticktockman." Both stories are about the hardships of affecting the mechanisms that threaten to absorb human passion; eventually, Maggie and the Harlequin are both destroyed by these social mechanisms.

A theme present in several of the stories, and reiterated in most of Ellison's introductions, is the importance of the rebel in any situation, whether it be personal, social, or political; whether against another person, a machine, a social organism, or himself. Free spirits battle structured societies, brilliant surgeons risk all to destroy mechanistic surrogates, a psychic misfit asserts himself against conformic parapsychics, the ultimate rebel murders to save others from a menacing computer system. Even where it is not obviously present, the theme of rebellion is often implied. The paingod, by studying suffering, is conducting his own rebellion against his attention to duty. The protagonist of "Lonelyache" is looking for a way out of the emotional morass he has fallen into. Even Maggie Moneyeyes puts up her own battle to escape entrapment and risk encountering the hell that may be beyond. The need for rebellion, or at least striking out against the people and systems that threaten to enslave us, is one consistent aspect of most of Ellison's fiction. Whatever ideas or philosophies form the structure of our lives, we are all potentially in the position of man against the machine, against other madmen, against the tyranny of emotions, against the gods, against other men—essentially, then, in the position of the Harlequin against the Ticktockman. Like most satirists/social critics Ellison asks us to examine our lives and define the borders of human folly and absurdity.

> He withdrew murmuring *to hell with you.*
> And added, brightly, *but then you're there, aren't you.*
> —"I Have No Mouth, and I Must Scream"

There are times, moments when fighting the battle against the threatening darkness, seems too much of a strain. The writer/battler questions the value of the attack, as when Ellison parenthetically comments in his new introduction to *Paingod:*

> That's evil: only the human predator destroys slowly, any decent hunting animal rips out the throat and feeds, and that's that. The more I see of people, the better I like animals.

Underlining such a statement is the wish of the warrior to leave the field. He has perhaps fought against chaos long enough, railed against human folly for too long, replaced a sense of outrage with still another sense of outrage. The processes of satire and/or social criticism generally lead to frustration. For every Dickens whose work manages to influence some change in the social fabric, there are hundreds of

Nathanael Wests whose writings are basically uninfluential because the conditions which concern them never seem appreciably to change. Even when a gain is made in, say, child labor laws or American civil rights, one must continue to do battle against the humans whose venality, cruelty, or overriding ambition cause them to erect obstacles to the smooth effecting of such revolutionary change. There are powerful lobbyists everywhere in every century who are for what decent and moral people are against. The selfish Romans against whom Juvenal ranted, the artistic clods that angered Pope, the exemplars of human folly that drew Swift's wrath have been reincarnated as the hateful people and empty human beings in all walks of life that provoke the anger of such modern writers as Ellison, West, and Waugh.

The corporate state, today's favorite satiric target, is essentially no different from the industrial state or the Imperial Roman state. The system changes, but not the folly and absurdity with which the system is run, around which it is organized. Outside and within the system are its victims, and it is for these victims that the emotions of such as Juvenal, Pope, Swift, Dickens, Thoreau, West, and Ellison are engaged. Their favorite themes are inequity and iniquity, unfairness, and the cruelties of the indifferent or vengeful dynamos whose power is used to keep victims aligned properly.

The fight seems never-ending. No wonder the artist is tempted to draw back, tempted to leave the battlefield to the human predators and their victims—as Ellison suggests in his parenthetical comment. Lately, however, Ellison has been centering on the human predators and the animals, particularly in stories like "The Whimper of Whipped Dogs" (1973) and "The Deathbird" (1973). Whatever subjects he chooses to bring into sharp focus fictionally, he continues to write perceptive fantasy and science fiction stories that are as dramatically effective as they are thought-provoking.

From *The Fantasies of Harlan Ellison* (1979), by Harlan Ellison, edited by David G. Hartwell and L. W. Currey. Copyright © 1979 by Robert Thurston. Reprinted with permission of Robert Thurston.

Clogging Up the (In)Human Works:
Harlan Ellison's Apocalyptic Postmodern Visions_____
Oscar De Los Santos

There is only one end to creation. What is created is destroyed, and thus full circle is achieved.
—Ellison, "The Region Between"

... the search for your soul in a soulless world requires special maps.
—Ellison, *Deathbird Stories*

As the decade draws to a close and we approach the end of the twentieth century, virtually every mode of artistic expression is projecting its own version of apocalypse via works that contemplate the end of humankind. For many authors, however, this is not a new investigation. Such is true of Harlan Ellison, who focused on apocalyptic themes in his first sold short story ("Glowworm," 1956) and who has frequently returned to this theme throughout his career. In much of his fiction, Ellison struggles to project warnings about humanity's demise even as he celebrates our past accomplishments and potential.

Whether writing one of his many essays, television or motion picture scripts, or short stories (a body of material comprised of over 1,200 separate works thus far), Ellison most frequently channels his energies into works of science fiction, fantasy, and horror. When he does turn to speculative fiction, one of his most frequent principal characters—a character who appears in many guises but who embodies the same qualities from story to story—is the trickster: the angry, feisty, marginalized underdog; the little guy who won't go down without a fight, who wishes to clog up the works of (in)human conformity and make a race rise above mediocrity. This character will fight apathy and submissive attitudes in others even when he believes that he himself no longer wishes to live. Ellison has said that an author must cannibalize his existence in order to find the material about which to write.

We can also take this to mean, as is fundamentally the case, that an author is all of his/her characters. Certainly this is very true of Ellison and his underdogs. When we examine the great body of work that Ellison has produced in an effort to effect changes in the attitudes of readers, fellow writers, and humanity in general, we find that Ellison is himself a marginalized fighter—for just as his fictional constructs often fight to stave off global or cosmic apocalypse, Ellison himself engages in less fantastic but no less daunting battles: to kick humanity out of its apathetic complacency and to elevate his chosen profession—writing, especially that produced in the field of speculative fiction—to new levels of quality. Indeed, the goals of many of Ellison's principal characters and Ellison himself are very similar: to prevent different forms of apocalypse. In his fiction, Ellison's underdogs struggle to prevent the death of (in)human life; in his life, Ellison fights to prevent the death of good writing.

Anyone who reads a book or two of Ellison's—fiction or nonfiction—quickly realizes that he seldom shirks from brutal, scathing critical assessments of his subject matter. Maybe that is why he has been called "probably the most controversial writer ever to hit science fiction" by fellow science fiction writer and critic Lester Del Rey (183) and why most science fiction fans have heard of Ellison, whether they read him or not. Most people have very strong positive or negative feelings about Ellison the writer, but even stronger feelings about Ellison's fiction: they either love his work or they hate it. Those who love it admire Ellison for shoving a textual mirror in society's face and exposing its hypocrisy, neuroses, and shortcomings with stark objectivity; those who hate it often do so for the same reason and for its abrasive tone and negativity. While it is true that a great deal of "doom and gloom" may be found in the Ellison canon, it is also true that Ellison frequently undercuts his often dystopic settings and his cynical characters with the actions taken by those characters. If it is true that actions speak louder than words, as the old cliche tells us, then it is valuable to analyze a few of Ellison's principal characters, assess their actions, and see if what they *do* contradicts what they *say*, or what they seem to think about themselves and their respective environments. Doing so yields a better understanding of the tension that is inherent in so many Ellison tales and that resides in the author himself. Ellison's characters may rant and rave; they may purport to be on the brink of giving up on themselves and/or their fellow humans—but they seldom do so. Time and again, we see characters and author fighting the good fight: helping out their species (human or alien) and committing themselves to take some form of positive, life-affirming action rather than simply giving up. For Ellison's characters, such actions are diversified, but many involve great struggle against virtually impossible odds; indeed, the stakes are often of apocalyptic proportions.

In an essay called "True Love: Groping for the Holy Grail," Ellison confesses, "I find that the only thing worth the time and energy is the company of others; people are my business and I cannot conceive of ever having discovered all there is to discover about the human heart in conflict with itself (as Faulkner put it). I would much rather sit and talk to someone than alienate myself by watching a ballgame" (363). However, time and again readers find Ellison at odds with humanity: "I swear to God," he has said, "just one day I'd like to get up and not be angry . . . at the world" (Groth 72). If we use his fiction as a gauge, we find that Ellison's anger is largely derived from humanity's willingness to settle for mediocrity rather than strive to reach its fullest potential in all facets of its existence. In its desire to settle for the easy solution, humankind sets up traps for itself by relinquishing control of its destiny to debilitating constructs or power-abusing governing systems. And yet, even as he warns us that we are on the brink of destroying ourselves either by doing nothing or by doing the wrong things, Ellison points the way to right actions via his characters. A close examination of several of his marginalized creations provides further evidence of the internal struggle between optimism and pessimism that fuels so much of Ellison's fiction.

One of the best examples of the Ellison underdog is the impish trickster at the heart of "'Repent, Harlequin!' Said the Ticktockman." "'Repent, Harlequin!'" explores a future in which humanity has literally imperiled its own existence as a result of an ever-increasing obsession with punctuality and time. Ellison shows that in our efforts to manage our time with greater efficiency and to better our lives, we have become enslaved by time. Thus, the existential angst resulting from the knowledge that we are responsible for what we do or fail to do as the minutes go by, is replaced by a new worry in a perceptive few: that we have doomed ourselves to living aesthetically dead, stagnating lives by placing our destinies in the hands of powers that measure success and value solely on an individual's ability to keep strict schedules and meet deadlines.

The Harlequin (or Everett C. Marm, his real name) is the only character brave enough to stand up to the Ticktockman, the only one willing to tell this dictatorial megalomaniac to "Get stuffed." Everyone else seems to have forgotten that humanity created the Ticktockman—the precise schedule runner and Master Time Keeper. Everyone else now lives in fear of the power they have allowed the Master Time Keeper to possess: he can shut off any individual's internal biological timepiece permanently with the flick of a switch, a radical punishment induced for repeated tardiness and general ineptitude when it comes to punctuality. Everyone lives with this fear except the Harlequin, who realizes that a society that relinquishes control of its existence to one entity or one small governing body—mechanical or otherwise—is in grave danger of becoming extinct. This is especially true of a society that forgets how to stand up for itself and work to correct its mistakes, or is too frightened or too lazy to do so. Ellison reminds us of our "straw man" shortcomings when he quotes Thoreau's *Civil Disobedience* at the beginning of his tale: "The mass of men serve the state thus, not as men mainly, but as machines, with their bodies. . . . In most cases there is no free exercise whatever of the judgment or of the moral sense; but they put themselves on a level with wood and earth and stones; and wooden men can perhaps be manufactured that will serve the purpose as well" (*Essential Ellison* 877). The role reversal is striking as one reads more of the short story: in Ellison's world, a machine-like government now governs human beings, and most individuals accept the situation. Ellison describes the governing body, the culture and its leader mechanistically: "The Ones Who Kept The Machine Functioning Smoothly, the ones who poured the very best butter over the cams and mainsprings of the culture . . . the Ticktockman and his legal machinery" (878). The author's descriptions emphasize the automated nature of the future world. It may be alive, but it is a vacuous, artificial life. Except perhaps, for Everett C. Marm, the Harlequin, who goes out of his way to discombobulate the efficiency of his world in the most absurd fashion possible, swooping over individuals on a mechanical flying device and creating mayhem with one of the most innocuous of products: jelly beans, a hundred and fifty thousand dollars' worth, to be precise, dropped onto a crowd and throwing off all activities for seven minutes: "The System had been seven minutes' worth of disrupted. It was a tiny matter, one hardly worthy of note, but in a society where the single driving force was order and unity and equality and promptness and clocklike precision and attention to the clock, reverence of the gods of the passage of time, it was a disaster of major importance" (880).

The Harlequin is caught in the end, turned in by a woman he knew, someone who didn't like her punctuality and be-told-what-to-do-and-when-to-do-it world disrupted by an upstart, even if the upstart was her boyfriend. And though Marm never buckles under the Ticktockman's interrogation, he is eventually "worked . . . over" and made to appear on the "communications web" and admit that he was wrong about trying to fight the system. But in the end, he may have made a difference after all, because the Master Time Keeper is three minutes late to work one day and throws the society's entire system slightly off schedule. Thus, Ellison's trickster succeeds in changing a seemingly unchangeable system, and even though the change is minor, as Ellison's narrator observes, "if you make only a little change, then it seems to be worthwhile" (886).

Ellison's "'Repent, Harlequin!'" is a short story with a subdued apocalyptic theme at its core. A story that deals with the subject more blatantly is "The Region Between." Ellison breaks new ground in this tale, whose principal character, William Bailey, gives up on life and elects to commit suicide, then finds his core essence—his soul— kidnapped by a soul dealer known as the Succubus, who proceeds to place him in the physical shells of a number of entities who are being enslaved by larger power structures. "The Region Between" is an apocalyptic story in a radically exponentiated sense of the term; its main character manages not only to commit suicide, but to take the whole planet and indeed, the universe itself, with him. Moreover, it is a story in which Ellison uses science fiction, cyberpunk, and fantasy to posit that many of us would rather prostitute ourselves and become mindless slaves of the Other in order to avoid engaging in introspection and spare ourselves the potential anguish that can result from an attempt to validate our own existence.

Bailey, who wanted nothing more than to be rid of a disappointing life, finds himself a spiritual being unable to be merely someone else's instrument of investigation or destruction or consumption. As the Succubus thrusts Bailey into one life form after another—life forms destined to be pawns or gophers in the power games of stronger entities—Bailey continuously undermines the psyches of his hosts and gets them to rebel against the injustices to which they are being subjected. As a result the Succubus takes note, but too late to do anything about it, for Bailey turns out to be an insane god who awakens from an ages old slumber and destroys himself and the entire universe. In the end, Bailey destroys all, but not before his spirit demonstrates a tremendous instinct to live and right wrongs and not before Ellison's narrator tells us that "Godness lies dormant . . . in everything" and fuels our desire to enrich our existence; however, this instinct is often perverted by a desire to empower ourselves at the expense of others (170). Because of the text's radical construction in its latter portions— sentences spiral around to form a large circle, in tiny print no less—

many readers may overlook some of the most important and candid lines in the Ellison canon. Indeed, these lines go a long way to explaining the unbalanced power structures we see manifested time and again in Ellison's texts and characters. In this passage Ellison tells us:

> The universe moves toward godhood. It started there and it wishes to return there. It is driven around in the greatest circle toward there. Godness lies dormant yet remembered in every thing, every smallest thing, in every puniest creature. Every living thing must of needs, play at godness. It is built in, in the basic fiber, in the racial memory, in the pulse of the blood or thought they remember all the way back to when there was nothing! Yet none of them are God. Thus it becomes a universe of things struggling ineptly to be God: a universe of manipulators, of users, of petty handlers who push and hover lesser, less god-driven races around in alien patterns, forcing them to dance to tunes they never knew, can barely comprehend, in pain and hopelessness, deprived of light or joy. From the sleaziest legislators of ethic and fashion and morality to the greatest pawn—movers of entire cosmic races, everything, *everyone*, scrabbles blindly toward the memory of when it was once god-blooded. All things try to govern the lives of all other things. And in turn, those Gods are used by other Gods. And those Gods are manipulated by Greater Gods. And on and on. Domino tanks of puppet masters, to infinity and beyond. It is a universe of mad deities, one more selfish and corrupt than the one that went before. For none of them *are* God, they are merely circular pieces of the all-memory of what was godness at the beginning. (170)

Of course Bailey proves to be *the God* who destroys all, and "The Region Between" deals with a myriad of races that inhabit the universe, but if we narrow the focus of Ellison's story and the context of the above passage, we find that it mirrors humanity through the ages, as we have moved from one power struggle to another and fought, more often than not, to defeat and enslave one another in limited egocentric, solipsistic factions rather than worked to better each other as a race.

William Bailey turns out to be a mad deity but he is still a wonderful Ellison character because he shows that each one of us is godlike and can work to improve or destroy our collective lives. Further, like Everett C. Marm, Bailey shows us that we should rebel against injustices and dictatorial governing bodies.[1] Indeed, William Bailey's apocalyptic confrontation with the Succubus is a cosmic version of the battle between man and computer—Ted and AM—that Ellison chronicled two years earlier in "I Have No Mouth, and I Must Scream" (1967). As Darren Harris-Fain has noted, Ellison imbues Ted with a paradoxical mixture of godlike qualities and psychological weaknesses: "The narrator of 'I Have No Mouth, and I Must Scream'... embodies the image of God despite his human, all too human limitations and flaws." Yet, despite these shortcomings, Ted should not be discounted because he "exemplifies the potential of the human spirit" (154). Thus, while mad computer AM is still no more than sophisticated artificial intelligence, "neither fully human nor fully divine, Ted is both, and through this displays a moral superiority which makes this tale, as Ellison intended it, 'a positive, humanistic, upbeat story'" (154). The same might be said of most of "The Region Between" despite its disturbing conclusion.

"The Region Between" was first published in 1969; in 1973 Ellison published "The Deathbird," in which he continued to explore similar subject matter. The short story eventually became part of a collection in which Harlan explored deistic concepts over the years and called for a need to question age-old concepts of godhood, as well as those icons and ideas contemporary culture had elevated to godlike status. In his introduction to *Deathbird Stories*, Ellison observes that "Gods can do anything. They fear nothing: they are gods. But there is one rule, one Seal of Solomon that can confound a god, and to which *all* good pay service, to the letter: When belief in a god dies, the god dies" (xiv). As Ellison turns our attention to the earth's new gods and new demons, he attempts to show that our very concepts of godhood are self-serving and solipsistic: that we are worshiping those ideas and ideals and commodities that best serve our individual interests. Contemporary gods include "the rock god and the god of neon; the god of legal tender, the god of business-as-usual and the gods that live in city streets and slot machines. The God of Smog and the God of Freudian Guilt. The Machine God" (xv).

Once again, Ellison exposes the vices that in his estimation lock us into a thruway to destruction. Moreover, he posits that we create our own traps and enslave ourselves when we elevate hedonistic, less than worthy men and women to positions of deistic, dictatorial authority and allow them to govern us. Empowering and paying homage to such tarnished gods—pop culture figures, corrupt political leaders, abusive governments—is tantamount to furthering not only an individual's own destruction but humanity's. For this reason, Ellison warns us to "Know them now" because these gods "rule the nights through which we move":

> Kitty Genovese met one of them, as did the students of Kent State University. Black men have known them far longer than white men, but have been ill served by them. . . .
> Worship in the temple of your soul, but know the names of those who control your destiny. For, as the god of Time so aptly put it, "It's later than you think." (xv)

Essentially, "The Deathbird" by Ellison's own admission, is "a rewritten Genesis, advancing the theory that the snake was the good guy and, since god wrote the PR release, Old Snake simply got a lot of bad press" (*Deathbird Stories* 265). This time, Ellison focuses on Nathan Stack, who is also the original Adam, and his quest to confront and liberate himself from his creator, God. The Devil (also known as Dira or Snake in the story), is Stack's assistant in this undertaking. No evil being at all, Snake is rather part of a race who lost a diplomatic debate with the entity who came to be considered the earth's creator and deity, a creator who was mad and who allowed death and destruction to go unchecked and the planet itself to be abused to the point that it is on the brink of destruction. Snake must assist Nathan Stack in recognizing the same thing that William Bailey recognizes at the end of "The Region Between": that each of us is godlike and that inherent within each of us is the capability to empower the Other, as well as the power to work toward his/her/its removal if that entity is more of a hindrance than a help to our existence. Via "The Deathbird," Ellison implores us to question ourselves, our beliefs, our heroes, our deities, our mode of behavior. To do nothing is akin to accepting whatever fate a few dictate for us, however grim it may be.

The ending of "The Deathbird" is almost as disturbing as the ending of "The Region Between": the universe is still alive at the end of the former, but earth is dead and "the stars wait . . . for the cry of the Deathbird to reach them so final moments could be observed at last, at the end, for the race of man" (295). It is true that Stack gains tremendous wisdom shortly before the end, but when he runs into the earth's god, now in the form of "an old, tired man" he knows that revenge is fruitless and the planet is doomed. By allowing his character to recognize the folly of an unchecked, unquestioned belief system, Ellison is elevating humanity and warning us to engage in the constant spot-checking of our beliefs; but by having the earth and (wo)man succumb to apocalypse at the end, Ellison is once again emphasizing what he told us at the end of "The Region Between"—"There is only one end to creation. What is created is destroyed, and thus full circle is achieved"—and what he stressed in the introduction to *Deathbird Stories:* "It's later than you think" (xv). Here again is the contradictory tension that runs through so many of Ellison's stories: the call to rebel and better ourselves, juxtaposed with the notion that we are ultimately powerless to do anything to alter final apocalypse: "Stack found the mad one wandering in the forest of final moments . . . and Stack knew with a wave of his hand he could end it for this god in a moment. But what was the reason for it? It was even too late for revenge. It had been too late from the start" (962-63).

In 1974 Ellison published *Approaching Oblivion: Road Signs on the Treadmill Toward Tomorrow*, and his position on humanity seemed to have swayed to new extremes of pessimism. His January 1974 introductory essay to the collection seems to indicate that he had once and for all decided to give up on his fellow humans:

> Had I done this book in 1970, as originally planned, you'd find in this space a clarion call to revolution, a resounding challenge to the future. But it's four years later, Nixon time, and I've seen you sitting on your asses mumbling about impeachment, I've gone through ten years waiting for you to recognize how evil the war in the Nam was, I've watched you loaf and lumber through college and business and middle-class complacency, pursuing the twin goals of "happiness" and "security."
>
> What fools you are. Happy, secure corpses you'll be.
>
> You're approaching oblivion, *and you know it*, and you won't do a thing to save yourselves.
>
> As for me and you in this literary liaison, well, I've paid my dues. Now I'm going to merely sit here on the side and laugh my ass off at how you sink into the quagmire like the triceratops. I'm going to laugh and jeer and wiggle my ears at your death throes. And how will I do that? By writing my stories. (16)

If nothing remotely optimistic came from Ellison after 1974, then we could accurately assess that he had indeed given up on the human race, but the fact remains that there are many stories that come afterward, that he dedicates *Deathbird Stories* to "True Love" the year following the publication of *Approaching Oblivion*, that many of his stories still continue to champion humanity and still continue to project hope and optimism. Indeed, one of his strongest impulses in this direction can be found in "The Man Who Rowed Christopher Columbus Ashore," a story initially published in *Omni* and eventually selected as one of the *Best American Short Stories of 1993*. This story focuses on a time-traveler named Levendis ("which is a Greek word for someone who is full of the pleasure of living" [93]), who takes a "sidestep" between earth's present, past, and future in order to help men and women in distress. Levendis is a classic Ellison hero, doing "At Least One Good Deed A Day, Every Single Day." The acts range from helping a cantankerous old arthritic woman cross the street (77), to "creat[ing] a cure for bone-marrow cancer" (81), to attacking a bunch of skinheads who themselves were in the process of attacking an interracial couple (86-85) to "correct[ing] every history book in America so that they no longer called it The Battle of Bunker Hill, but rather Breeds Hill where, in fact, the engagement of 17 June 1775 had taken place" (90). Levendis is perplexing to many who encounter him, his deeds often puzzling. When someone asks him if he is good or evil, he quickly replies "Good, of course! there's only one real evil in the world: mediocrity" (79).

Levendis's battles are the battles of many other Ellison characters: to change the world for the better. His methodology is diverse; at times it involves lectures, at others, he resorts to violence. Levendis is frustrated that he is "an unlimited person living in a limited world" but he continues to struggle for the betterment of humanity. No age group or faction is spared his presence. At one point he lectures to a convention of country-music fans (79); at another, he takes a bus load of "art ignorant" schoolchildren to gaze upon the "*Spiral Jetty*, an incongruously gorgeous line of earth and stone that curves out and away like a thought lost in the tide" (86); and on still another occasion—on a Sunday—he drives around Raleigh and Durham, North Carolina in a rented van and "remind[s] somnambulistic pedestrians and families entering eggs 'n' grits restaurants . . . that perhaps they should ignore their bibles today and go back and reread Shirley Jackson's short story, 'One Ordinary Day, with Peanuts'" (87).

Levendis nudges—sometimes pushes—people in positive directions, but ultimately, he wants humanity to implement the major improvements for itself. For example, he goes back in time and inoculates a part-time prostitute, Poppy Skurnik, with a syphilis vaccine, thus giving one of her future grandchildren the chance to "sav[e] the lives of millions of innocent men, women and children" (90).[2]

And yet, for all his noble attributes and commitment to the betterment of life, Levendis remains an enigmatic, even frightening character. Levendis's seemingly unwavering goal, like his creator, Ellison's, seems to grow skewed at times. For example, the first night he encounters skinheads hurting an interracial couple, he simply elects to watch the incident. Another time, he kicks a cat so hard that he embeds it in a tree. And on still another occasion, "Having most of the day free . . . he then ma[kes] it his business to kill the remaining seventeen American GIs being held MIA in an encampment in the heart of Laos" (91). In the case of the skinheads incident, perhaps we can argue that Levendis does nothing to defend the imperiled couple because he is trying to determine how to best defend them against their racist attackers. However, given the proficiency for physical combat that he exhibits the next night, this argument seems flimsy. Moreover, the next two incidents are far more disturbing. They reveal that Levendis cannot fully govern his temper and that he channels aggression upon the innocent. In the case of the GIs, it seems clear that Levendis is frustrated with the United States for its failure to negotiate a release for these persecuted soldiers. However, if we consider the supernatural powers that Levendis displays at other times in the story, a miraculous rescue of these men would not seem beyond his capabilities. Instead, it seems that Levendis elects to punish us for not taking better care of each other. A problem arises when we consider that his punishment involves the killing of the helpless.

Levendis is a problematic character—a trans-historical righter of wrongs—whose educational methods are at times, noble, at others, unorthodox, and still others, disturbing and infuriating. He is also not immortal and must answer to a higher authority called "The Front Office." It seems Levendis's superiors are also disturbed by his methodology: they believe that he has "been having too rich a time at the expense of the Master Parameter" (a system that sounds like a more potent kin of the Master Timekeeper in "Ticktockman"). He is apparently reassigned, but he remains enough of the typical Ellison trickster to keep doing things in his own perplexing way: "no one higher up noticed that on his new assignment he had taken the name Sertsa" (the Russian word for soul) (93). Ultimately, despite his paradoxical characteristics and questionable methodology, Levendis is and has sertsa.

There is less of an overt apocalyptic threat in "The Man Who Rowed Christopher Columbus Ashore" than in some of Ellison's older works. The potential for our demise is still present. Levendis seems mad at times; he commits disturbing acts. It is clear that if he were to allow his frustration with humanity to consume him, the results might prove catastrophic. However, more often than not, the traveler manages to subsume his aggression beneath the positive actions he takes on humanity's behalf. Levendis is kin to the Harlequin and Bailey—he wants to stir us up, for the better—and if he resembles mad Bailey more than Everett C. Marm, then he serves to remind us that each of us has the potential to improve the world simply by being conscious of the fact that all of our actions—however minor—have the capacity to affect others.

Thus far I have provided a brief overview of the manner in which some of Ellison's characters fight the good fight. Now I would like to focus on the author's methodology for fighting complacency within his profession. Ellison's speculative fiction has often deviated from the fiction of many of his fellow SF/horror authors in its atypical narrative construction and content. Indeed, the construction of many of Ellison's stories parallels the works of the postmodernists in contemporary literature.

David Hartwell observes in his excellent study of science fiction that readers of the genre will often forgive bad writing if the ideas that are presented are interesting. (See *Age of Wonders: Exploring the World of Science Fiction*.) Many science fiction fans are less tolerant of textual experimentation. They want to get to the ideas of the story and they do not feel that the actual construction of the text should be a part of the ideas they must assimilate in order to understand the story. The postmodernist, on the other hand, relies on textual construction to further elucidate her/his ideas for the reader. Indeed, the fully committed reader will often be conscious that s/he is engaged in the act of reading and will study both ideas within the text *and the text itself* in order to discover the ways that the body of material further illuminates the ideas being articulated by the writer. That's part of the postmodernist's game. It is also a game that many readers refuse to play; it is a part of postmodernism that, for many, makes its stories seem more chore than pleasure. But it is this aspect of postmodernism that Ellison has embraced and often relied upon in his attempt to battle mediocre writing in speculative fiction. If anything makes Ellison resemble one of his underdog characters it is the fact that he writes science fiction, fantasy, and horror in a manner that demands extensive work from his audience.

Norman Spinrad observes that "the science fiction writer isn't as interested in a deterministic detailing of how the past created the present—quantum mechanics assures him this is impossible anyway—as he is in examining the current situation with a view towards pondering what may evolve next" (219). Indeed, "what science fiction *should* be is one of our culture's main means for pondering not only the future consequences of what we are doing now but the effects of these inevitable, unpredictable changes on the human spirit" (222). Of course, a quick assessment of the volumes in the science fiction/fantasy sections at any large bookstore—offerings that will include scores of trilogies and film and television series tie-in novels—is indication enough that more serious writing efforts in the field are always threatened by commercialization and that the writer who is committed to exploring humanity's future via science fiction struggles desperately for shelf space and often loses to more lightweight products. This happens ever more frequently to writers such as Ellison who push the envelope with their unusually constructed texts.

Ellison's textual experimentation is nothing new. As part of the New Wave movement in the science fiction genre in the sixties and early seventies, Ellison chose to push science fiction in directions often left alone by most others. More than ever before, characters and stories were privileged over scientific extrapolation. Isaac Asimov explains:

> Pre-[John W.] Campbell science fiction all too often fell into one of two classes. They were either no-science or they were all-science. The no-science stories were adventure stories in which a periodic word of Western jargon was erased and replaced with an equivalent word of space jargon. The writer could be innocent of scientific knowledge....
>
> The all-science stories were, on the other hand, populated exclusively by scientist-caricatures. Some were mad scientists, some were absent-minded scientists, some were noble scientists.
>
> To be sure, there were exceptions....
>
> Campbell's contribution was that he insisted that the exception become the rule. There had to be real science *and* real story, with neither one dominating the other. (*Dangerous Visions* viii)

Asimov's assessment is accurate except that many would agree that Campbell and most of the writers working for him greatly privileged the scientific ideas in a story more than its plot and characters.

Ellison and the New Wave of writers largely reversed that equation and did so by penning stories that privileged characters and story over science. Like John Barth whose "Literature of Exhaustion" essay and postmodern *Lost in the Funhouse* short story collection largely contributed to the wave of sixties postmodernist experimentation in mainstream fiction, Ellison, working as both writer and editor, challenged science fiction readers with the narrative complexity of "The Region Between" and the atypical stories collected in *Dangerous Visions* and *Again, Dangerous Visions*.[3] In his introduction to the former, Ellison asserts that the anthology "was constructed along specific lines of revolution. It was intended to shake things up. It was conceived out of a need for new horizons, new forms, new styles, new challenges in the literature of our times" (xix). A substantial number of the stories in the first collection were penned by respected veterans of the science fiction field who agreed to take Ellison's challenge, to stretch their creativity in new directions. Both *Dangerous Visions* and *Again, Dangerous Visions* were groundbreaking collections and succeeded, at least to some extent, in revitalizing speculative fiction. That these atypical science fiction works were accepted by many is indication that the field was ready for a change. William Spanos notes that "The most immediate task . . . in which the contemporary writer must engage himself . . . is that of undermining the detectivelike expectations of the positivistic mind" (*Repetitions* 48). Ellison has frequently made such attempts to prevent his chosen field from becoming stale, and he has frequently succeeded in his efforts.

Narrative experimentation is also an integral part of finding a mode to adequately express apocalypse. Brian McHale notes:

> The final image of Thomas Pynchon's postmodernist masterpiece *Gravity's Rainbow* is that of a nuclear warhead uncannily poised the last incalculable sliver of time and space above the roof of the theater in which we, the readers of the book, presumably sit. Metaphor for the imminence of nuclear holocaust, this immeasurably narrow gap is the space in which we have lived since 1945. But Pynchon has not only given us a definitive emblem of life under the nuclear threat; he has also done so in a way which recapitulates (or anticipates) many of the strategies by which postmodernist writing has endeavored to represent the unrepresentable scene of nuclear apocalypse. (159)

It would be fair to say that science fiction, along with horror fantasy, may be lauded as a genre striving to represent the unrepresentable more frequently than other genres. But what Pynchon succeeds in capturing so successfully in *Gravity's Rainbow*—global apocalypse—Ellison succeeds in exponentiating when he captures cosmic apocalypse at the end of his radically constructed "The Region Between." No less important is the actual narrative construction of the novella. Ellison includes illustrations in the form of impressionistic wood carvings; these complement the action in the story, as do the author's atypical constructions of the printed pages. Sometimes text runs sideways across a page; sometimes two or more columns of text are placed facing each other from opposite pages, thus underscoring the notion of confrontation between thoughts or characters. In other words, Ellison uses text as illustration to underscore the meaning inherent in his written discourse. He "draws" with words, and these word illustrations further illuminate the story's subject matter. Certainly this is the case with the most radical page of text we encounter in the story: the long body of sentences (from which I quoted earlier) that takes up the bulk of one page and that spirals around to form a circle of words and sentences that eventually loop onto the next page.

The construction of "The Deathbird" is, in some respects, more challenging. From the beginning Ellison as author seems to address the reader directly, warning her/him that the story is actually "a test"; he advises us to "Take notes" and says that the numbered sections of the story "may be taken out of numerical sequence" and invites readers to "rearrange to suit yourself for optimum clarity" (267). Throughout the story, Ellison relies on the postmodernist's tools to ensure that the reader engage deeply with "The Deathbird" but that s/he never forget that s/he is reading a story. Ellison provides us with an essay within the story (a tribute to his dog Ahbuh, who was the inspiration for the dog in Ellison's famous short novel, *A Boy and His Dog*); at other times he interrupts the main story to provide us with a partial interpretation of Genesis 3:1-15, "Topics for Discussion," and "Questions for Discussion." All of these extras are designed to illuminate—and complicate—the principal themes at the heart of "The Deathbird."

Though less experimental, "The Man Who Rowed Christopher Columbus Ashore" is not completely free of narrative and textual experimentation. Each paragraph of the story might be seen as a self-contained story—beginning with the name of the main character, Levendis, followed by the date (day and month) and a summary of the character's actions on that given day. The story is told in partial chronological order, in the sense that it is set in the month of October; however, not one particular October is covered, but many, as Levendis "sidesteps" (to use the traveler's term) back and forth through the centuries. Lyotard tells us that "the postmodern would be that which . . . denies itself the solace of good forms . . . that which searches for new presentations, not in order to enjoy them but in order to impart a stronger sense of the unpresentable" (340-41). Ellison very much strives to achieve that end. Moreover, by moving his character through time, Ellison emphasizes the long-term nature of our ills and illustrates that we continue to be in need of assistance.[4]

One last staple of the postmodern movement that is worth mentioning is the insecure, self-conscious narrator that is prevalent in postmodern texts. Though most people would readily recognize that Ellison speaks with angry authority, his *position* on our capabilities seems tenuous, and his overall *assessment* of humanity is ever-vacillating. From story to story, certainly, it can be argued that Ellison is insecure: he wants very much to share with us his formula for right living, but he is constantly dubious about our potential for success.

Of course, positive and respected results are not always the most fruitful. Ellison is generally acknowledged to be somebody who cares about his field, but his methodology for improvement is often seen as too radical, too abrasive. Established masters who indulged his attempt to take the science fiction field in new directions and contributed unorthodox stories to Ellison's *Dangerous Visions* collections did not, for the most part, continue to experiment with their writing after those projects. Indeed, Asimov himself chose not to contribute a story because "I will not hide from you the fact that I mourn the past. It is the First Revolution [Campbell's] that produced me and it is the First Revolution that I keep in my heart" (xii). As for Ellison, he has produced some sixty books over the years; most of them are out of print.[5]

Ellison is still angry with us, still fighting the same battles he began decades ago, still casting reflections of himself in his texts, still fighting through the challenging narrative construction of his fiction, still fighting through his nonfiction. Recently, he returned to challenge the old mind numbing enemy—television—that he warned us about in *The Glass Teat* and *The Other Glass Teat*: the title to the introductory essay of his recent fiction and non-fiction collection, *Edgeworks*, is "Good Morning, Folks; I am not Kathie Lee Gifford." Bad cinema is also seen as an enemy because "Reality has become fantasy; fantasy has become reality. 35 mm constructs have more substance than your senior congressmen" (*Deathbird* 229), but because of television's greater accessibility, it is ultimately perceived as the worst enemy. As Ellison observes, "Television is, in sad fact, the new reality. What happens on the tube really happens . . . what goes down in the perceived world is iffy: maybe it's real, maybe not" (358).[6] Finally, Ellison is also greatly suspicious of the ultimate value of computers and the Internet. He concedes their potential value for some uses but finds that they make it too easy to churn out bad writing:

> Making it easier, I think, is invidious. It is a really BAD thing. Art is not supposed to be easier! There are a lot of things in life that aren't supposed to be easier. Ridding the world of heart attacks, making the roads smoother, making the beer better, but not Art. Art should always be tough. Art should demand something of you. Art should involve foot-pounds of energy being expended. . . . That's . . . one of the disadvantages of the Internet. . . . It becomes remarkably easy for anybody in the world to become not only a writer, but a publisher, and a salesman. . . . When they say "Gee it's an information explosion!," no, it's not an explosion, it's a disgorgement of the bowels. . . . Every idiotic thing that anybody could possibly write or say or think can get into the body politic now, where before things would have to have some merit to go through the publishing routine, now, ANYTHING. (Wyatt, "Gutenberg in a Flying Saucer")

Earlier I quoted Ellison quoting Faulkner. I will end this examination of Ellison by returning to Faulkner's inspiring Nobel address because I believe that in some ways, Faulkner's assessment of humanity parallels Ellison's view of (wo)man and apocalypse. In his speech, Faulkner says, "I decline to accept the end of man" despite the fact that for many writers and people, "There are no longer problems of the spirit. There is only the question: When will I be blown up? Because of this, the young man or woman writing today has forgotten the problems of the human heart in conflict with itself which alone can make good writing because only that is worth writing about, worth the agony and the sweat" (723). It is clear that Ellison also declines to give up on humanity. Instead, he populates his stories with characters that do more than whine: they *act* and *strive to better their environments and their existence*, as their creator does via his fiction and essays. Faulkner believed "that man will not merely endure: he will prevail" (724). I believe that Harlan Ellison struggles to maintain that same belief. Ellison and his underdogs may be tough on humanity, but they go on fighting apathy and complacency and stagnation out of a wary suspicion that we may be worth the fight, after all.

Oscar De Los Santos, "Clogging Up the (In)Human Works: Harlan Ellison's Apocalyptic Postmodern Visions" pp. 5-20, from *Extrapolation*, v. 40.1, Spring, 1999. Kent State University Press, Copyright 1999 by The Kent State University Press, Kent, OH 44242. All rights reserved. Reproduced by permission.

Notes

1. Is it mere coincidence that William Bailey shares a last name with George Bailey, the underdog hero who fights power-hungry businessman Potter in Frank Capra's *It's A Wonderful Life*?

2. Though left unnamed in the story, the grandchild may be Jonas Salk, who is indeed responsible for saving the lives of many, thanks to his development of the polio vaccine.

3. A third volume in the series, *The Last Dangerous Visions*, has long been forthcoming; its impending appearance has become a running joke among Ellison fans.

4. Several of Ellison's books seem to embrace a postmodernist framework by virtue of the manner in which the author blends fiction and non-fiction into his texts. The result is a pastiche of fiction, essays, and illustrations.

5. At the time of this writing (January 1997), White Wolf Publishing has just re-

leased the second volume of *Edgeworks*, a series that will reportedly bring most of Ellison's works back in print.

6. Ellison would likely agree with Baudrillard, who believes that today's world is being hindered by "a whole pornography of information and communication" that is nonsensical and superfluous ("The Ecstasy" 130). Baudrillard finds that we live in an age of electronic-image overload, and that our reliance on images for information compromises our ability to deepen our subjectivity and prevents us from formulating all but the most superficial of identities. What else is possible, when the images themselves are mere copies—echoes—of the more substantial originals: "perhaps at stake has always been the murderous capacity of images, murderers of the real, murderers of their own model . . . " ("The Precession" 346).

Works Cited

Asimov, Isaac. "Forward I—the Second Revolution." Ellison, *Dangerous Visions* vii-xii.
Baudrillard, Jean. "The Ecstasy of Communication." Foster 126-34.
_____. "The Precession of Simulacra." Natoli and Hutcheon 342-75.
Del Ray, Lester. *The World of Science Fiction, 1926-1976*. New York: Garland, 1980.
Ellison, Harlan. *Again, Dangerous Visions*. New York: Doubleday, 1972.
_____. *Angry Candy*. New York: Plume, 1989.
_____. *Dangerous Visions*. Garden City, NY: Doubleday, 1967.
_____. *Deathbird Stories*. New York: Bluejay, 1983.
_____. *The Essential Ellison*. Beverly Hills: Morpheus International, 1991.
_____. "Introduction." *Approaching Oblivion*. New York: Signet, 1974.
_____. "The Man Who Rowed Christopher Columbus Ashore." *Best American Short Stories of 1993*. Boston: Houghton Mifflin, 1993. 77-93.
_____. "The Region Between." *Angry Candy* 89-173.
_____. "'Repent, Harlequin!' Said the Ticktockman." *Essential Ellison* 877-86.
_____. "True Love: Groping for the Holy Grail." *Essential Ellison* 357-75.
Faulkner, William. "Address upon Receiving the Nobel Prize for Literature." *The Portable Faulkner*. Ed. Malcolm Cowley. New York: Penguin, 1967. 723-24.
Foster, Hal, ed. *The Anti-Aesthetic: Essays on Postmodern Culture*. Seattle: Bay Press, 1983.
Groth, Gary. "The Harlan Ellison Interview." *The Comics Journal* 53 (Winter Special 1980): 69-70+.
Harris-Fain, Darren. "Created in the Image of God: The Narrator and the Computer in Harlan Ellison's 'I Have No Mouth, and I Must Scream.'" *Extrapolation* 32 (Summer 1991): 143-55.
Hartwell, David. *Age of Wonders: Exploring the World of Science Fiction*. New York: Walker, 1984.

Lyotard, Jean François. "Answering the Question: What Is Postmodernism?" Trans. Regis Durand. *Innovation/Renovation: New Perspectives on the Humanities*. Eds. Ihab Hassan and Sally Hassan. Madison: U of Wisconsin P, 1983. 329-41.

McHale, Brian. *Constructing Postmodernism*. London: Routledge, 1992.

Natoli, Joseph and Linda Hutcheon. *A Postmodern Reader*. Albany: SUNY Press, 1993.

Spanos, William V. *Repetitions: The Postmodern Occasion in Literature and Culture*. Baton Rouge: Louisiana State UP, 1987.

Spinrad, Norman. *Science Fiction in the Real World*. Carbondale: Southern Illinois UP, 1990.

Wyatt, Rick. "Gutenberg in a Flying Saucer: Harlan Ellison explains why he has a web page, why he doesn't hate computers, and why technology can be the artist's most dangerous enemy." Jan. 25, 1996. http://www.menagerie.net/ellison/ellihome.htm.

The Self on Trial:
Fragmentation and Magic Realism

Ellen Weil and Gary K. Wolfe

For all his stylistic and conceptual innovation, especially by the standards of the commercial fiction arenas of science fiction, fantasy, and horror, Ellison had never really been known as a structural experimentalist. Even when he incorporated typographical or visual effects in such stories as "Pretty Maggie Moneyeyes" (1967) or "The Region Between" (1970), these resulted as much from a 1960s passion for design as from any radical reinterpretation of form, and the stories themselves remain driven by fairly straightforward narrative arcs and character relationships. Much the same might be said of Ellison's most famous science fiction classics, "I Have No Mouth, and I Must Scream" and "'Repent, Harlequin!' Said the Ticktockman," which, for all their intense imagery and bravura manipulation of narrative voice, are fundamentally tales of rebellion and revenge, even though the latter was notably innovative for its time in its use of nonlinear chronology. Among writers trained in commercial storytelling venues, there has always been a vague mistrust of the "literary" short story, whether it be John Cheever in the 1950s, Ann Beattie in the 1970s, or T. Coraghessan Boyle in the 1990s, and this mistrust is even greater when it comes to avant-garde modes of fiction such as stream of consciousness, objectivism, the deliberately fragmented "cut-up" method of William Burroughs, or the French *nouveau roman*—all movements whose influence on genre fiction in the 1950s and 1960s proved to be short-lived. Ellison, too, has occasionally joined in the genre writer's criticism of stories in which nothing seems to happen or in which events seem unconnected by clear causality or are left deliberately unresolved, and when he speaks of story construction he often speaks in terms drawn from commercial fiction artisanship, such as the narrative "hook," the importance of clearly defined conflict, and the "payoff."

At the same time, he has often shown impatience with readers who demand unambiguous resolutions and explicit narrative exposition. "I've found more and more frequently these days that even fairly intelligent people reading good books come to the end of a story with a quizzical expression on their faces," he writes in *Strange Wine*. "Unless they have been told with nailed-down precision that John dies in the fire and Joan marries Bernice and the secret message in the codex was that we are all alien property, many readers have no idea what the point of the story may have been" (231). In his introduction to "Jeffty Is Five" in *Shatterday*, Ellison again complains that "the ending of the story somehow escapes the slovenly reader" (11). Although some readers have found such remarks gratuitous and even offensive—feeling that a story's subtleties ought not to be advertised by the author—the fact is that such comments are less an attack on readers than an expression of the frustrations of an author growing increasingly impatient with reader expectations engendered by the conventional protocols of popular narrative tradition. On occasion, this has led Ellison to mistake narrative subtlety or indirection for a kind of affected obtuseness, as when he concludes "The Boulevard of Broken Dreams" with an allusion that he clearly expects many of his readers to miss. In other cases, such as "The Deathbird," it is clear that the linear plotting of traditional popular fiction cannot sustain the kind of mythic resonance he wants to achieve.

We have already seen how, at key points in his career, Ellison almost fortuitously discovered ways of overcoming those frustrations by moving into new and more open markets: The men's magazines provided liberation from the tight formulas of the digest genre magazines; the atmosphere of experimentation during the period of the New Wave actively engendered narrative and stylistic innovation (such as J. G. Ballard's "condensed novels" and fragmented narratives); Ellison's own growing reputation and gradual escape from the restrictive label of science fiction writer offered even more freedom from genre expectations. Only in the mature phase of his career, though, has Ellison consistently and consciously begun to move beyond traditional means of structuring stories and to explore techniques of reinventing the short story by recombining its core elements in distinctly postmodern ways, fracturing and multiplying narratives and narrative units, exploring the intersections of the narrative and visual arts (and even, to a limited degree, computer gaming), and revisiting genre materials in new and more authoritative ways. Like a handful of other writers in the science fiction, fantasy, horror, and mystery fields, Ellison transformed himself from a writer whose works could be said to inhabit genre into a writer whose works were inhabited *by* genre: a writer whose authority finally exceeded that of his milieux.

Composite Stories and Vignettes

One such technique, which Ellison has refined for more than two decades, involves constructing a fiction from a series of smaller, semi-independent narrative units—sometimes vignettes or anecdotes, sometimes prose poems, sometimes interpolated comments or memoirs, sometimes complete short-short stories—which may be related only thematically or even stylistically. The episodic novel, of course, is a tradition of its own, with examples in American literature ranging from Melville's *The Confidence-Man* (1857) to Jerzy Kosinski's *Steps* (1968), but it is less common for a short story writer to use such a technique within a single story. In Ellison's case, this may well be a technique that initially evolved out of expedience, as a way of stringing together fragments or short pieces that might otherwise seem simply undeveloped ideas. As early as 1959, Ellison's "May We Also Speak?" in *Rogue* was subtitled "Four Statements from the Not-So-Beat Generation" and consisted of four brief sketches or vignettes intended to capture the tone of what Ellison later called the "hung-up generation." In 1962, also in *Rogue*, he gathered three of his more effective, if understated, character studies, "Robert Blake's Universe" (later retitled "The Universe of Robert Blake"), "Mona at Her Windows," and

"G.B.K.—A Many-Flavored Bird," under the collective title "Trio"; perhaps because the stories themselves were more substantial, the grouping achieves a sense of diffuse early-1960s alienation that none of the stories individually could likely have achieved. But in both of these cases, the stories seem to have been written independently of one another and assembled for magazine publication more as samplers than as thematic wholes.

In 1973, the same year in which he interpolated an autobiographical fragment in "The Deathbird," Ellison wrote a "Harlan Ellison Hornbook" column titled "The Day I Died," moving a step further toward the composite narrative by imagining different scenarios of his own death and writing brief dramatic anecdotes about each one: being knifed in New York in 1973, dying of pneumonia in a Scottish farmhouse while working on his magnum opus, losing a battle to stomach cancer in 1986, etc. None of the anecdotes in this "essay-fiction" last more than a paragraph, but the idea was clearly appealing, since Ellison would return to this approach again. "The Pale Silver Dollar of the Moon Pays Its Way and Makes Change" (1994; collected in *Slippage*) mixes real and fictional episodes of the narrator's life with historical events in key years from 1934 to 1992. In "Where I Shall Dwell in the Next World" (1992; collected in *Slippage*), Ellison uses the technique to address that annoying and incessant reader question regarding sources of ideas and inspiration. Here the conceit is that stories come from misheard remarks, and as illustration he offers short fantasy scenarios spun from simple misunderstandings: "Necro Waiters" (from Necco wafers), "Trees Rabelais" (from something his wife said that began with "Please"), etc. (Ellison has also commented that the title of "Jeffty Is Five" partly originated from mishearing a snatch of conversation at a party.)

Another factor that may have contributed to the evolution of the composite story was Ellison's occasional stunt of "performance writing," committing to write so many stories or pieces under tight circumstances, such as in the window of a bookstore, which tended to produce shorter and more fragmented work. The most famous of these stunts, attempting to write a story a week in the window of the Change of Hobbit bookstore in Los Angeles in 1976, resulted in a piece called "From A to Z, in the Chocolate Alphabet," made up of twenty-six short-short stories, pastiches, or one-liners in the tradition made popular in science fiction by Fredric Brown, whose pungent short-short stories, often turning on a bad pun, were popular in the 1950s. (The piece is included in *Strange Wine* and was adapted as a comic book in 1978, illustrated by Larry Todd.) Most of these are simply provocative but undeveloped ideas, such as the notion (under "E") that five hundred elevators in the United States are equipped with special relays to take them below the basement level into a frightening netherworld whose denizens are the anonymous, zombie-like riders so often seen in elevators. There is almost no deliberate attempt to maintain any sort of thematic or dramatic unity among the twenty-six parts of the "story," but patterns do seem to emerge: hidden or lost communities (Atlanteans, elevator people, mind readers, intelligent seals, troglodytes who live in city dumps and consume garbage), monsters of folklore and myth (vampires, golems, zombies, demons, rocs, werewolves, poltergeists), and allusions to favorite writers (Lewis Carroll, Philip K. Dick).

The first of Ellison's composite stories to seriously strive for some sort of cumulative aesthetic effect, "Eidolons" (1988; collected in *Angry Candy*), began in a manner similar to that of "The Chocolate Alphabet." "'Eidolons,'" wrote Ellison, "came from the assemblage of a congeries of misheard remarks, altered to form brief allegories or tone-poems. I did one each week as introduction to my stint as the host of a radio show" (*Slippage* 173). The story (whose title simply refers to an image or a phantom) consists of thirteen numbered but untitled sections wrapped in a frame story narrated by a Melmoth-like figure named Vizinczey, who introduces himself as an international pariah for reasons not made clear. In Australia, Vizinczey comes upon one of Ellison's ubiquitous mysterious little shops, this one selling miniature soldiers of astonishing detail and authenticity, which he gradually realizes are not models at all but actual soldiers snatched from the battlefields of history and somehow miniaturized and frozen in place. When the shop owner dies, apparently killed by a crossbow quarrel from one of his tiny prisoners, he passes on to the narrator an ancient scroll containing various secrets of life.

The segments that make up the bulk of the story are supposedly fragments from that scroll, though Ellison makes no real effort to present the episodes as consistent with any ancient European culture or even as consistent with the chronology of the scroll as outlined in the frame—there are, for example, quotations from Camus, allusions to Tinker Bell, the Hindenburg, and *The Sun Also Rises*, a brief memoir about growing up after the Great Depression. The segments begin with dreamlike meditations on friendship and responsibility, all set in the kind of spiritual twilight that Ellison calls "the hour that stretches" (or *djam karet*, an Indonesian phrase that Ellison has returned to repeatedly): a message from a dead friend is formed in dust motes on a forgotten book, winds from the top of the world unite separated lovers with "memories of those who have gone before," an anonymous authoritative voice announces a suspension "for the next few weeks" of irrational or hateful thinking (*Angry Candy* 205). An allegorical battle is joined between the forces of art and the forces of commerce, and a deformed singer becomes an image of the mystery and inaccessibility of art. Gradually, the segments begin to gain a more particularized focus, with brief character sketches of women who might once have been the narrator's lovers, an account of an apparent nightmare in which the narrator is threatened by "a billowing web" found in his kitchen at night, and finally a childhood memory in which a usually generous father refused a handout to a bum, leaving the adult narrator haunted by the mysteries of compassion. In the end, the frame narrator Vizinczey alludes to six more selections from the scroll, not included, which reveal such secrets as "the power to bend others to your will, or the ability to travel at will in an instant to any place in the world, or the facility for reading the future in mirrors" (212). The irony, of course, is that no such supernatural gifts are revealed in the thirteen segments which are included, unless we realize—as Ellison apparently wants us to—that what magic is available in the world is only the magic of memory, observation, art, and compassion.

For all its cumulative power, "Eidolons" never quite hangs together either as a unified narrative (which it makes only token attempts to achieve) or as an internally consistent suite of prose poems and memoirs (which is closer to its apparent goal). The frame narrative, in which Vizinczey learns from his experience with the scroll to become a secret doer of good deeds rather than a compulsive criminal, is a fairly clunky device which fails to add significantly to the power of the individual episodes, even though it makes for a characteristic Ellison redemption-fable on its own terms. A much more unified tale, "Scartaris, June 28th" (1990; collected in *Slippage*), organizes its episodes by means of a central godlike character who first appears as the victim of an Alabama lynch mob, calmly releasing himself from the noose two hours after his own hanging. Later, he shows up in Wisconsin to persuade a young man to attend the funeral of a bully who used to beat him, and then on an airliner where he challenges a fundamentalist minister's beliefs and, sympathizing with the aging and tired parents of a retarded woman, creates a fatal aneurysm in the woman's brain. He appears on the shore of the Aegean in Greece, murmuring the word *levendis* (a Greek term for one who enjoys life), and explaining to a local resident that his true home is far out in the sea and was mentioned by Plato. (This allusion to Atlantis is one of several in Ellison's recent work in which the legendary continent becomes a kind of magical Valhalla for lost gods or departed souls; see also "Midnight in the Sunken Cathedral" and "From A to Z, in the Chocolate Alphabet.") After a brief episode with a young woman in Zurich, the protagonist travels to Iceland, where, by following the clues of the characters in Jules Verne's *Journey to the Center of the Earth*, he prepares to depart the world by descending into the volcano described in that novel, to visit the Earth's hollow interior. Though any of these episodes might provide the basis for a separate story, the central role played by the protagonist, in his shifting guises, unites the various episodes into a cumulative thematic whole.

Easily Ellison's most successful experiment with the composite story is "The Man Who Rowed Christopher Columbus Ashore" (1991), which aggressively advertises its fluid nature not only by shifting its godlike main character freely through time and space but by changing titles four times in midstream—the text is periodically interrupted with announcements beginning "This is a story titled" followed by the new title: "The Route of Odysseus," "The Daffodils That Entertain," "At Least One Good Deed a Day, Every Single Day," and, at the very end, "Shagging Fungoes." As with "The Chocolate Alphabet," some of the thirty-five sections are no more than cynical one-liners, while others constitute short-short stories unto themselves. But more than with any of his other experiments with this form, Ellison now strives to find formal means of unifying a text whose narrative is deliberately fragmented. Each section, for example, begins by restating the name of the protagonist—"Levendis," the same Greek word as in "Scartaris, June 28th"—in boldface, then giving the date (the segments take place daily from October 1 through "the 35th of October"—a deliberate clue that the tale is moving from representation into myth), then almost always establishing where the action takes place and what Levendis's particular disguise is on this particular date. The effect is that of a catalog or chronicle whose entries occasionally erupt into partial narratives but which finally depends upon the cumulative effect of the various details that go to make up the episodes. Levendis is an enigmatic figure who sometimes seems no more than a bystander to history and at other times displays godlike powers by raising or lowering everyone's IQ, creating a cure for bone marrow cancer, or isolating Tibet with snowstorms. He is, in effect, a secret master, a kind of composite god whose function parallels the composite nature of the story, a god who is partly a figure of omnipotent will and partly an expression of the collective power of those anonymous individuals who transform history in profound but unrecognized ways—like the man who rowed Christopher Columbus ashore.

The story, which was the first of Ellison's to be selected for *The Best American Short Stories* annual (in 1993, with Louise Erdrich as editor), is essentially a series of moral-fantasy vignettes that initially seem almost random, until we realize that the central figure in each—Levendis—is a kind of renegade time traveler, a cosmic version of Ellison's more famous Harlequin. As he explains to a young boy in the ruins of a Greek theater in Turkey, "I am an unlimited person living in a limited world" (*Slippage* 8). Like the Harlequin, his actions are sometimes comically absurd, such as assuming the form of a Boy Scout to help an old woman across a street—against her will—and he is eventually caught and removed from his position by the faceless "Front Office" and something ominously called the "Master Parameter" (15). But his role is far more ambiguous than that of Harlequin. Sometimes his actions are simply cruel, like killing a cat; at other times they are bitterly ironic, such as sending a basket of fruit to parents who have given their son a gun as a present, even though it's the same gun that his older brother had used to kill himself. As if to underline the randomness of the forces that Levendis represents, Ellison has him silently watch skinheads savagely beat an interracial couple in Chicago, taking no action, but the very next day, in an almost identical incident in Pennsylvania (in one of the few cases where successive episodes are linked), he intervenes and murders each of the skinheads. In a thematically related later episode, Levendis spectacularly murders a former KKK leader running for office in Louisiana, but—with the irony typical of such acts in Ellison's universe—thus leaves the electoral field open to one of Joseph Mengele's former assistants, a child mutilator, and an "illiterate swamp cabbage farmer" (*Slippage* 15). Levendis, in fact, proves to be a fairly murderous character. He also kills a truck driver (for dumping toxic waste) and a group of surviving POWs in Cambodia (he spares one, who later becomes his own daughter's lover). On the other hand, he takes pity on a welfare mother who tries to save her children from rats, saves the life of a prostitute in New York in 1892 by providing her with penicillin (thus ensuring the birth of her child, who will grow up to save millions of lives), restores the Dalai Lama to the throne in Tibet, is present at the liberation of Buchenwald in 1945, and serves as attorney for a woman athlete in a lawsuit in which she seeks to be admitted to professional baseball.

While many of these episodes reflect Ellison's characteristic themes and preoccupations—racism, economic injustice, secret history (Levendis presents evidence that Marilyn Monroe actually murdered JFK, but destroys all remaining evidence that would reveal what happened to Jimmy Hoffa, Amelia Earhart, and Ambrose Bierce), one intervention that recurs in several venues involves proselytizing for quality in the arts, and in these episodes—which almost inevitably appear self-referential on Ellison's part—we gain perhaps the strongest clues to the story's governing rhetoric. Speaking before a "convention of readers of cheap fantasy novels," he says, "We invent our lives (and other people's) as we live them; what we call 'life' is itself a fiction. Therefore, we must constantly strive to produce only good art, absolutely entertaining fiction" (15). But, as if to underline the futility Ellison himself must have felt from time to time speaking before such groups, not a word of what Levendis says is understood, since he delivers his speech in Etruscan. He delivers a similar message to a group "representing the country & western music industry," arguing that the "one real evil in the world is mediocrity" (3). In Utah, he takes a group of "art-ignorant" Mormon schoolchildren to view Robert Smithson's famous environmental sculpture *Spiral Jetty*, and quotes Smithson's words: "Establish enigmas, not explanations" (9; the same quotation is later invoked in Ellison's *Mind Fields*, where it seems acutely apt for the surreal paintings of Jacek Yerka that accompany Ellison's words).

While such comments and quotations resonate with our own attempts to discern meanings in the very story we are reading, the most telling single literary allusion in the tale occurs on day twenty, when Levendis drives a rented van with a loudspeaker through the streets of

Raleigh and Durham, North Carolina, advising the residents that "perhaps they should ignore their bibles today, and go back and reread Shirley Jackson's short story, 'One Ordinary Day, with Peanuts'" (10). This 1954 story, in which an enigmatic figure named Mr. Johnson moves through his day helping strangers with seemingly random acts of kindness: helping a mother and son prepare to move, bringing a young couple together and paying for their lost wages if they take the day off on a date, sending another couple seeking an apartment to the one just vacated by the mother and son, paying for a veal cutlet lunch for a beggar, offering a racing tip to a cabdriver. At the end of the day, we learn that *Mrs.* Johnson has spent her day creating unhappiness and havoc that balances Mr. Johnson's kindnesses: accusing a woman of shoplifting, sending dogs to the pound, filing a complaint that may have gotten a bus driver fired. The two agree to change roles on the following day, and then they sit down happily to dinner. Mr. and Mrs. Johnson are Levendis's direct literary ancestors, wry personifications of the vicissitudes of daily fortune.

Jackson, a rare fantasist of her time whose work graced both the pages of the *New Yorker* and the *Magazine of Fantasy and Science Fiction* (where this tale originally appeared), might well be regarded as one of Ellison's literary godmothers, though the understated, elliptical fantasy of her short fiction (as opposed to her more traditionally Gothic ghost-novels) would not become a regular feature of Ellison's repertoire until fairly late in his career. One episode in particular of "The Man Who Rowed Christopher Columbus Ashore" could almost be a segment from the Jackson story, complete with its middle-class domestic mise-en-scène: Levendis, in a supermarket in Wisconsin, deliberately sets up a collision between the shopping carts of a lonely, aging homosexual and an equally lonely legal secretary, then causes them to become allies as he screams rudely at them. Outside, he lets the air out of the woman's tires, knowing that she will need a lift to the gas station and that a friendship will begin to blossom. Like most of the best segments of "The Man Who Rowed Christopher Columbus Ashore," this brief but touching vignette is the seed of its own unwritten tale, a small kindness that serves as an emblem of the randomness of life and of the fractal nature of the larger tale, with its fragments and anecdotes suggesting stories within stories within stories. In a strange way, "Columbus," with its rich catalog of unwritten story ideas, carries among its undertones an Ellisonian version of the sort of anxiety that a much younger Keats articulated in "When I Have Fears." Edging past middle age, his inventiveness showing no signs of flagging, Ellison has found in the composite tale not only a new form of discontinuous narrative structure but a kind of reservoir for unwritten tales, a hedge against silence, against the end of tales.

Mind Fields

Apart from "The Man Who Rowed Christopher Columbus Ashore," Ellison's most intriguing use of the very short fiction/prose poem/ meditation in the 1990s came via an unusual after-the-fact collaboration with Polish artist Jacek Yerka in a book titled *Mind Fields* (1994), which consists of thirty-four paintings by the surrealist artist, each accompanied by a brief story or prose piece by Ellison. Originally asked to write an introduction to a collection of Yerka's work, Ellison found the paintings—all acrylic on canvas, and all painted between 1981 and 1993—so compelling that, instead of the introduction, he offered to write original short fictions to accompany each one. The idea of writing stories to fit paintings wasn't entirely new to Ellison. He was, after all, one of those who suffered the indignities of trying to write stories to match prepurchased magazine cover illustrations back in the 1950s. But Yerka, whose imagination seems in its way as unpredictable as Ellison's own, provided considerably more fertile ground for Ellison's inventions, which have always had a strong visual aspect.

Throughout *Mind Fields*, Ellison seems to begin with a general emotional tenor suggested by his response to the painting, then imagines a scenario of his own that reflects this tenor, and finally (in most but not all cases) returns to the painting to find points of congruity with Yerka's images. It works more often than one might expect, especially given the strikingly different cultural sensibilities of the two artists. Most of Yerka's images derive from the fields and cottages of his native rural Poland, upon which he works delightful surrealist transformations showing the clear influence of the fantasy paintings of Bosch, Brueghel, and others: the wall of a stone cottage metamorphoses into a cave wall, which in turn becomes waves of water; a thatched-roof barn soars above the countryside on dragonfly wings; fields of grain hide whole villages or collections of strange objects; an apparent erupting volcano proves on closer inspection to be a vast cityscape at night. Ellison, on the other hand, has been accused of many things in his fiction, but pastoralism isn't one of them. Much of the fascination in the collection derives from the question of how Ellison's sharp-edged American urban imagination can interact with Yerka's ominous but essentially gentle dreamscapes. A painting called *The Agitators*, for example, shows five aging men standing or kneeling before a tiny forest church, which seems to transmute into an even tinier cathedral at its rear. Ellison's inventive conceit is that the church had indeed once been a cathedral, and the worshipers had numbered more than three hundred, but as the congregation shrank so did the size of the church. So far, the tale seems consistent with the kind of religious allegory that seems apparent in the painting, except for an odd reference to Erroll Garner-style music, heard when the church shrinks. But the five men in Ellison's story are not congregants but complainants, and their complaints are decidedly secular and American: Too much power to stop traffic is given to road construction flagmen in "those offensive Day-Glo orange vests," trading cards are a cheat with no bubble gum included in the package, Victor Mature was a completely talentless actor (46). Even in such cases as this, in which Ellison incorporates the exact scene of the painting into his fiction, he jarringly shifts the context and the characters from Yerka's world into his own.

But for the most part, the counterpoint works startlingly well. A painting called "Fever" (all the titles are Yerka's except two pieces called "Susan" and "Ellison Wonderland") shows a bedridden figure, only hands showing, cowering under menacing clouds. Ellison turns this into a Borgesian parable of an Icarus who survived the fall but suffered amnesia and still lives as a minor accountant in Switzerland who dreams each night about the sky. A crowded cupboard with hands peeking out of a drawer becomes an image of the afterlife of a Holocaust resistance fighter. Two of Ellison's strongest pieces have virtually no direct narrative relationship to the accompanying painting except for the title. "Base" is a bleak but sardonic anecdote in which the narrator is awakened in the middle of the night by police asking him to come downtown and identify a body. He provides them with all the positive identification they request, but then reveals to the reader that he has no idea who the body was, and that the police probably called a wrong number. The Yerka image is of two vaguely human-shaped mattresses resting under an outdoor canopy made up of junk. "Attack at Dawn" completely abandons any attempt to explain why a Volkswagen which is also half-lizard is being attacked by what appear to be biomechanical planes; instead, Ellison spins a tale of a daughter's well-planned righteous rebellion against her father in a corporate setting. Both the image and the tale touch upon themes of transformation and confrontation, but share little else in common.

In a few cases, Ellison turns to the resources of science fiction to find narrative analogues of the paintings. For Yerka's image of a printing press in a ramshackle shed, *Shed of Rebellion*, he evokes a nightmare postliterate future, suggestive both of Ray Bradbury's *Fahrenheit 451* and C. M. Kornbluth's "The Marching Morons," in which a thuggish and semiliterate video journalist boasts of using the latest technology to cover violent government reprisals against an underground movement called the "Resistance Readership Alliance." Yerka's two visions of fantasy-cities, "Eruption" and "Ammonite," become tales of the lost or hidden civilizations that might have built such structures, each of which reflects the recurring Atlantis theme in

Ellison's later work. "Under the Landscape"—the only piece to accompany two paintings, each depicting a small village hidden beneath fields of grass or wheat that serve as the villages' rooftops—returns to the composite narrative form, telling the stories of a half-dozen children brutalized in various ways in 1993, followed by three versions of what happens to them as adults, and how the world splits into two alternate possibilities in 2009, when a behavior control device called the Passion Inhibitor is either embraced or rejected by the medical and legal communities (in the world in which it is rejected, all the former abused children become great successes, but if the Passion Inhibitor is used, they are turned into anonymous drudges).

Other pieces, like episodes of "The Man Who Rowed Christopher Columbus Ashore," touch upon aspects of art or writing. "Metropolis II"—the painting shows a village street lined with old appliances and furniture instead of buildings—is narrated by a world-famous author lionized in a way even more excessive than that of Crowstairs of "All the Lies That Are My Life"; here even the names of the adulators are mentioned, and it is a litany of intellectual trendiness: Barzun, Kristeva, Paglia, Deran, Clute, Hardwick, Sontag, Gilder, Chomsky. But this brief vignette parallels that much longer story in another key way. The narrator reveals that all the elaborate stories he has told about his background over the years are complete fictions and that his real past is much closer to the seedy world depicted in the painting, "the shantytown that gave me birth" (16). Fearful that word of his inauspicious beginnings and various betrayals on his way to success might damage his reputation ("Somehow, I do not think the Literary Establishment would subsidize posters"), the narrator informs his listener that the two of them must duel to the death once this story has been told. Although few of the details of the narrator's real or imagined backgrounds suggest actual autobiographical elements, the notion of an invented past is more clearly delineated here than almost anywhere else in Ellison's fiction. In another tale, "Truancy at the Pond" (the image is of a crystal-clear pond beneath which can be seen an elaborate network of pipes, which may also be tree roots), Michelangelo invites art critics to view his latest masterpiece, a topiary garden with a clear pond at its center. At first, the critics are astonished: "'Perfection,' they said. And, 'Flawless'" (48). But they soon begin finding minute imperfections in the work, and Michelangelo promptly shoves them into the pond, where they sink without a trace.

Most of Ellison's fictions in *Mind Fields* can stand on their own and don't need the paintings to make sense. But in a few cases, a genuine synergy sets in, and the painting-plus-text becomes something entirely apart from either work individually. Of the three most personal pieces in the book, two are those for which Ellison himself chose the titles. "Ellison Wonderland" is vintage Ellison paranoia, made oddly appropriate to Yerka's desolate Antonio Gaudi-like buildings rising from muddy waters. In the story, the narrator reveals that he has at last unmasked the lifelong conspiracy that has kept his sense of being-in-the-world off-balance, and that the moment of revelation occurred when, at a Minneapolis airport, he read the departure time of his flight as 1:45 and his wife corrected him, saying it was 1:54. Looking again, he noted that the board did indeed say 1:54, but rather than assume a slight misreading on his part, he takes this as evidence of the conspiracy that controls his life by causing him to question his own judgment. He escapes from the world—and "the woman they had programmed to be my wife" (64)—and flees to the mysterious city of Yerka's painting. "Susan" is a sensitive and understated little romance of mortality—Ellison describes it as a valentine to his wife Susan—which, in its story of a husband who seeks to protect his new wife from his nightmares, which he says not only "come to life" but "killed and ate my first four wives" (26), resonates perfectly with Yerka's equally understated image of a bed and lamp in a wooded landscape. The final piece in the book, "Please Don't Slam the Door," may be the most affecting of all. It's not really Yerka's most original painting—by now we've grown accustomed to his floating landscapes, rural cottages, and volcanic structures—and it's not Ellison's strongest prose, verging on cloying sentimentality in its description of a beautiful child who sends dreams back into the world from his magical treehouse. But image and text combined work far more effectively than either alone, and they become a moving elegy to the young son Yerka lost during the preparation of the book, and to the child's sense of wonder.

Revisioning Genre

At the same time that Ellison was experimenting with fragmented, discontinuous, or miniature narratives, he was also increasingly engaged in revisiting many of the genre materials that he had worked with throughout his career, but with a new eye toward recombining these materials in increasingly complex ways. His 1997 collection *Slippage* included not only "The Man Who Rowed Christopher Columbus Ashore" and "Scartaris, June 28th," but tales of angry demons, vengeful gods, brutal killers, cannibals, psychic vampires, dryads, dragons, and other mythical beasts. "She's a Young Thing and Cannot Leave Her Mother" is a gruesome horror tale based on the legend of Sawney Beane; by taking its time to develop a character relationship it becomes far more effective than "Sensible City," whose plot is, as noted, about as sensible as that of an EC horror comic. Ellison's preoccupation with mythology is again evident in "Chatting with Anubis," "Darkness upon the Face of the Deep," and "The Lingering Scent of Woodsmoke." But in "Darkness upon the Face of the Deep," the Hittite god is little more than a Lovecraftian monster-in-a-vault (the story works better when it focuses on the testy relationship of the two old but slightly distrustful friends who unleash the beast), and "The Lingering Scent of Woodsmoke" is a slight tale involving dryads gaining a new kind of vengeance on Nazi war criminals. "The Dreams a Nightmare Dreams," about the extinction of the dinosaurs, and "Keyboard," about a vampire computer, are little more than underdeveloped one-joke tales, the latter of which might have fit seamlessly into *Mind Fields* had there been an appropriate dinosaur painting. One tale even harks back to the very early years of Ellison's career: "The Few, the Proud" is a science fiction story in the Kyben war sequence that dates back to the 1950s and is narrated in the same 1950s style of cocky dramatic monologue that now seems dated, but at its center is an act of passion and protest that is pure Ellison, and it reminds us that science fiction hadn't seen much of this until he came along. But the longest and most important story in the book is also the one that most clearly demonstrates Ellison's interest in transforming the genre materials of his past into denser, more complex, and more resonant narratives.

"Mefisto in Onyx"

"Mefisto in Onyx" (1993) is a rare Ellison story sustained principally by the ingenuity of its plotting, which in turn depends upon a careful manipulation of point of view. The tale is narrated by Rudy Pairis, a young black drifter and former Rhodes scholar who since childhood has possessed the gift of being able to enter the minds or "landscapes" of others, a skill which he calls "jaunting" (in an apparent homage to science fiction writer Alfred Bester, who in his classic 1956 novel *The Stars My Destination* used the term to refer to teleportation). Pairis uses the skill sparingly, however, because he finds the contents of most people's minds distressing. "If Aquinas had had my ability," comments Pairis, "he'd have very quickly gone off to be a hermit, only occasionally visiting the mind of a sheep or a hedgehog" (*Slippage* 127). Pairis's longtime friend and onetime lover, Allison Roche, a district attorney who has recently won multiple convictions against a famous serial killer named Henry Lake Spanning, now contacts him with an unusual request. She wants him to determine Spanning's guilt by "jaunting" into his mindscape, even though Spanning is already on Death Row and has been convicted on the basis of overwhelming evidence, including eyewitnesses. Roche, it seems, is not only now convinced of the innocence of the man she convicted but has fallen in love with him.

Despite considerable misgivings, Pairis eventually agrees and meets Spanning in prison, finding him good-looking ("even for a white guy") and extraordinarily ingratiating. When he "jaunts" into Spanning's mind, he is shocked to discover that the convicted man is innocent of all the crimes of which he has been accused and that the mutilated old woman with whom he was caught in a dumpster was simply a victim he had been trying to rescue and who died in his arms. Even more startling, perhaps prompted by reliving the death of the old woman, Pairis suddenly realizes that he *himself* is the murderer and that his memory of the crimes has been sealed off in what amounts to a separate personality. "The other Rudy Pairis had come home at last" (159). Pairis confesses, providing detailed accounts not only of the crimes of which Spanning had been accused but of more than a dozen other unsolved murders, and is himself sentenced to the electric chair. On the day of his execution, the now free Spanning shows up in the visitors' gallery together with Roche, and when Pairis attempts again to jaunt into his mind, he finds it blocked—an experience he had never before encountered. Then Spanning appears in *his* mind, and he realizes that Spanning, too, possesses the ability to jaunt. Spanning explains that he was in fact the murderer all along and that Pairis's apparent memories of committing the crimes were nothing more than elaborate constructions planted in his mind during the few minutes that he visited Spanning on Death Row.

Spanning, in fact, claims that not only is he able to enter other people's minds but he can transfer his entire consciousness into other bodies (an act which he calls "shriking"), and that he has survived for centuries by doing this, like a demon possessing a succession of victims. His various incarnations are a litany of such famous murderers, including Gilles de Rais, Vlad Tepes (the model for Dracula), Jack the Ripper, the Boston Strangler, Ed Gem (the model for Robert Bloch's novel *Psycho*), Charles Manson, and John Wayne Gacy. Now, inside Pairis's mind, he taunts him with racial slurs and with plans of butchering Allison Roche. But in a final reversal, Spanning finds that he cannot escape from Pairis's mind. During *his* time on Death Row, Pairis was able to deduce what had happened to him and to develop a strategy to trick Spanning in return. He berates Spanning for his naive egotism, accuses him of exaggerating or inventing most of his history, of failing the moral responsibilities of his talent, most of all of failing to learn. Pairis then transfers his mind into Spanning's body, leaving Spanning trapped just as the warden throws the switch of the electric chair. Pairis, now in the body of a white man, feels free to pursue his love of Roche, realizing that his lifelong failures have been due neither to his strange gift nor to his skin color, but because "I have always been one of those miserable guys who *couldn't get out of his own way*" (168).

When "Mefisto in Onyx" appeared in the October 1993 issue of *Omni* magazine, it was heralded as "Harlan Ellison's First Novella in 15 Years" and the longest piece of fiction *Omni* had ever published. It appeared as a separate specialty press book that same year, was quickly optioned for film adaptation (though the film plans later became stalled), and was generally well received by reviewers, with Eric P. Nash in the *New York Times*, for example, viewing it as "a reminder that Ellison has not lost has capacity to convey stark, staring psychosis." It received the Bram Stoker Award from the Horror Writers of America, the Locus reader's poll award from *Locus: The Newspaper of the Science Fiction Field*, and a nomination for the World Fantasy Award. No doubt part of the reason for the novella's popularity is the relative familiarity of its form, its twin climactic plot twists, and its use of recognizable genre materials, even though these materials are transformed somewhat by Ellison's ambitious use of a black narrator and his efforts to broaden the thematic base of the narrative to include questions of racism and personal responsibility.

One commentator, Darren Harris-Fain, wrote that the story "reads like a cross between Alfred Bester's science fiction classic *The Demolished Man* and Thomas Harris's *The Silence of the Lambs*" (Barron 369). Neither comparison is inappropriate: As we've already noted, Bester's novel gave Ellison the term *jaunting*, and *The Demolished*

Man (1953), widely recognized as one of the few successful science fiction/mystery hybrids, concerns a murderer in a future society in which the police force includes trained "espers," or mind readers. Thomas Harris's famous 1988 novel, on the other hand, is entirely lacking in overtly fantastic elements, and (together with its 1981 predecessor *Red Dragon* and its 1990 film adaptation) is credited by some critics with having shifted the focus of much horror fiction during the 1990s away from supernatural figures and toward the gruesome but all-too-recognizable figure of the serial killer. Harris's plot, in which a young and somewhat innocent figure with unresolved issues from the past is brought into a prison to aid investigators by establishing a kind of psychic link with a famously inhuman serial murderer, bears obvious parallels with "Mefisto in Onyx," although much of Harris's novel focuses on the procedural aspects of the ongoing criminal investigation, while in Ellison's case the pursuit and capture of Spanning is barely mentioned at all.

Essentially, then, the genre building blocks of "Mefisto" come from both science fiction, with its long catalog of telepaths (including many who seem as alienated and lonely as Pairis) and contemporary crime/horror fiction. But Ellison seeks to develop a more complex, character-based story as well: Why has Pairis been unable to profit, or even attain moderate happiness, from his extraordinary gift? And why is he unable to act on his abiding feelings for Allison Roche until he shifts into the body of a handsome blue-eyed white man? By the end of the tale—in an unexpected thematic reversal that comes on top of the climactic plot twists—we are told that it was neither telepathy nor racism that limited Pairis but his own inability to act without getting in his own way. By much the same token, Pairis suggests, Spanning's questionable career as a master criminal is less the result of grandiose evil than of simple mediocrity and lack of imagination. Spanning's tragedy is not merely that he is a psycho killer but that he can't think of much else to do. These major themes are introduced not as an integral part of the unfolding action but by means of tour de force narrative riffs and speeches by Pairis, who sometimes nearly even lapses into dialect in delivering them. "You so goddam stuck on yourself, Spankyhead," he says to Spanning just before leaving the killer to die in the electric chair, "you never give it the barest that someone else is a faster draw than you. . . . Know what your trouble is, Captain? You're old, you're *real* old, maybe hundreds of years who gives a damn old. That don't count for shit, old man. You're old, but you never got smart. You're just mediocre at what you do" (166).

For all its ambition of fusing familiar genre materials with broad themes of racial tension and the construction of identity, "Mefisto in Onyx" is not without its flaws. In order for the plot twists to work, Ellison has to concoct some fairly tenuous motives for Spanning to allow himself to be caught in the first place and then for waiting in prison three years before executing his plan to trap Pairis. Pairis, on the other hand, turns out to be an only semi-reliable narrator. Here Ellison faces the famous dilemma that Agatha Christie raised in her 1926 *The Murder of Roger Ackroyd* in which the narrator must carefully measure out what information is given to the reader since he himself, in the closing pages, will be unmasked as the murderer. Pairis must avoid telling us about the new psychic skills he learned while in prison, in order to spring them on us at the last minute, always an awkward moment in a first-person narrative. It is also unclear how Pairis knows that Spanning will be in the visitors' gallery at his scheduled execution. Finally, the evocative title of the tale is explained in a rather murky scene, unrelated to the main action, that seems to cast Pairis as both Faust and Mefisto in his relationship to Roche, and that tends to flatten the implicit Faustian theme involving Spanning. But as a whole, "Mefisto in Onyx" is the most successful of Ellison's mythical crime tales since "The Whimper of Whipped Dogs." An earlier crime story, "Soft Monkey" (1988), also featured a black protagonist, a homeless woman who becomes a hunted murder witness. It won an Edgar Award in short fiction from the Mystery Writers of America. But it's a far less substantial piece than either "Whimper" or "Mefisto." It develops a less ingenious plot and makes far less inventive use of genre materials, despite some scenes of extraordinarily dramatic realism.

After *Slippage*

At the end of the millennium, Ellison's fiction continued its evolving dialogue between the idioms of genre fiction and the possibilities of postmodern techniques, and he continued to inhabit an aesthetic and moral ground largely of his own making. The stylistic and narrative traditions that go to make up his fiction are traditions that are today found almost nowhere else. Echoes of the witty fantasy that John Collier or Shirley Jackson or Roald Dahl mix with the hard-boiled narrative economy of a Henry Slesar or Stanley Ellin, the mordant wit of Robert Bloch or Gerald Kersh (whom Ellison cites as his favorite writer), and occasional tonalities from Fritz Leiber, H. P. Lovecraft, and Alfred Bester (who may be Ellison's most immediate predecessor among science fiction writers, and who is paid subtle homage in "Mefisto in Onyx"). This is the region of the vernacular grotesque, a world in which (to take further examples from *Slippage*) an uneducated small-time hood can describe his demon pursuer as "a creature of stygian darkness" (in "Crazy as a Soup Sandwich") or a distinguished academic scholar of myths can narrate a whole story in a voice that sounds like Andy Griffith ("The Museum on Cyclops Avenue"). In each of these cases, the tale's basic premise is familiar—a deal with the demon and a variation on the disappearing-shop motif (which Ellison has used often)—but Ellison's characters and dialogue give each a distinctive, off-balance spin, and in almost every case the tale leads in unpredictable directions.

The questions that continue to haunt Ellison haven't changed that much over the years: How we choose to inhabit our lives, what our best and worst and most symbolic moments are and what they mean. In "Anywhere but Here, with Anybody but You," a husband whose wife has fled realizes he has defined himself only in terms of "my life till now," and he sets out in search of a desolate freedom. Another character recovers lost moments with a father he never really knew (in Atlantis, of all places) in "Midnight in the Sunken Cathedral." In "Pulling Hard Time," murderers are forced to relive, in infinite loops, the absolutely worst moments of their lives (this is a kind of counterpoint to Ellison's "The Cheese Stands Alone," in which characters could not escape the best moments of their lives). The best of Ellison's late fiction is fascinating because of its very liminality, its unmistakable provenance, its voice. If some readers find Ellison's frequent mythifying pretentious, and others view his genre work as too populist, it may be because he occupies a part of the literary landscape that is all but deserted except for him: a region where small-time hoods coexist with Anubis, pulp narrative hooks lead to postmodern fragmentation, high passion flows from tough technique.

In late 1999 and early 2000, only a few months separated the publication of two "historic" collectors' issues of leading science fiction magazines, each of which had featured many Ellison stories over the years: the six hundredth issue of the world's oldest science fiction magazine, *Amazing Stories*, founded in 1926, and the fiftieth anniversary issue of the *Magazine of Fantasy and Science Fiction*. In many ways, these two magazines symbolize two ends of the spectrum of Ellison's fiction. *Amazing Stories*, which had begun life as the original science fiction pulp only to see its role as the leading magazine in the field usurped by the more intellectual *Astounding Science Fiction* after 1937, had fallen on hard times with stunning regularity in the years since, and by the 1950s had become one of the secondary markets for young science fiction writers like Ellison; among the Ellison stories that first appeared there are such early hackwork titles as "Escape Route" (1957), "Gnomebody" (1956), "The Plague Bearers" (1957), and "The Vengeance of Galaxy 5" (1958). The *Magazine of Fantasy and Science Fiction*, in contrast, has generally been viewed as the most sophisticated of the digest magazines that supplanted the pulps in the 1950s, and it became one of the major outlets for Ellison's more ambitious or experimental stories, such as "Jeffty Is Five" (1977), "Adrift, Just off the Islets of Langerhans" (1974), "The Deathbird" (1973), and "All the Lies That Are My Life" (1980). It seems fitting, then, that for the celebratory anniversary issues of these two very different magazines, Ellison should contribute stories that reflect these contrasting aspects of his career. The story that appeared in the six hundredth issue of *Amazing Stories*, written as a tribute to Ellison's pulp ancestors, is titled "The Toad Prince; or, Sex Queen of the Martian Pleasure-Domes," and was originally written in 1991 for a small press called Pulphouse, edited by Kristin Kathryn Rusch and Dean Wesley Smith. The *Magazine of Fantasy and Science Fiction* story, on the other hand, titled "Objects of Desire in the Mirror Are Closer than They Appear," begins with the genre materials of the crime story but quickly evolves into an oblique narrative unlike almost anything Ellison had written before.

"The Toad Prince," accompanied in its original magazine appearance by a wonderfully lurid pulp illustration by Don Ivan Punchatz, is a lark, but a weighty lark, recasting the familiar fairy tale of the Frog Prince into a tale of an Earthborn prostitute named Sarna whose successful career on the Martian frontier—serving both human settlers and the oppressed Martians—is interrupted when a "yellow" (a halfbreed Martian descended from Martian women raped by Earth settlers) is murdered in her room, leaving behind a mysterious toadlike creature called only "one of the Six" (23). Forced to flee for her life when a long overdue Martian revolution threatens to kill all the human settlers, she learns that the toad-thing can communicate with her telepathically, offering to help save her and all the other humans on Mars, if she will help it reunite with its five siblings, from whom it has been separated for something like a million years. Skeptical but desperate, she agrees, and most of the story involves the quest to find each of the siblings—a glowing ball, a globule of water, a handsome, gray-haired man, and a "cloud of syrupy, milky effluvium" (31). Each adds a different function to the gestalt that is the Six—eyes, knowledge, legs, nerves, muscles—and as the being approaches wholeness, Sarna begins to realize that it is an insane ancient god, long ago banished into multiplicity, and that its reunification threatens the very survival of humans on Earth as well as on Mars. They (it?) give Sarna a glimpse of what the Earth will look like in a century, reduced to a fetid swamp full of strange beasts. To her astonishment, the five assembled segments inform her that she herself is the sixth and final component, and "suddenly the barriers shattered in her mind and a flood of memories poured back. . . . A million years of memories" (32). The human part of Sarna that remains, however, wills the entire entity to plunge into the sun, sacrificing herself but saving the universe—and, presumably, leaving Mars to the control of the native Martian revolution.

At its pulp-narrative level, this fast-moving tale of a plucky Earth girl who saves the universe from a senile, malevolent, Lovecraftian god is no more than a good-natured tribute to the magazines of Ellison's childhood, the magazines that died out only a few short years before his own professional career began. But it is not a parody or burlesque, and except for its initial situation, it is not particularly comic in execution. In its major subtext, it offers a sardonic critique of the sexist, capitalist, and imperialist values that were implicit in so many of the space operas of the 1930s and 1940s. Like Ray Bradbury's 1950 *Martian Chronicles*, it portrays an ancient race of golden-skinned Martians, whose survival is threatened by crass settlers from Earth. In Bradbury, the Martians eventually are killed off entirely by Earthborn diseases, in a manner that clearly seeks to evoke the genocide of native American populations in the United States. In "The Toad Prince," Ellison's Martians are compared to Pacific islanders: "Golden, as the Samoans, the Melanesian, had been . . . long ago on Earth. And as with the ancient peoples, the reavers had taken more than just the innocence of the alien culture: they had raped and dominated, savaged and strip-mined both Mars and its Golden people" (20). Instead of the military commanders and explorers who served as pulp heroes, Ellison chooses a prostitute who is herself a victim of the exploitation of what is only briefly referred to as the "New System" of commerce on Earth and

Mars. And when the violent Martian revolt threatens to butcher the entire human colony, Sarna's reaction is to realize that she has been brainwashed by imperialist values as surely as her true godlike nature has been hidden from her. "How I let myself be led by emotion into believing it was Terran property; by what right does Earth rule the planet Mars . . . ? By what right does any race enslave another?" (33). The story of an obscure individual who secretly saves the universe may have been a favorite plot of pulp science fiction writers, but the story of a hero reconstituted as a god who then *refuses* to save human colonists from aliens is far more unusual. Even as Ellison mimics the style and pacing of the old *Amazing Stories*, he critiques and revises the genre that gave him his earliest successes.

The much shorter and more poignant tale "Objects of Desire in the Mirror Are Closer than They Appear," with its title which evokes Luis Buñuel's 1977 film *That Obscure Object of Desire*, begins on nearly as familiar a note, but—like Buñuel's films—quickly shifts into a dreamworld where time is fluid and obsessions become real. While working on the case of a serial killer of prostitutes, homicide detective Francine Jacobs is called in to investigate a bizarre murder scene: three famous supermodels wailing hysterically over the corpse of an old man nearly decapitated in an alley next to a mission house. The only apparent witness, an alcoholic former aerospace worker, claims that he first heard the three girls laughing and singing, followed by the flash of a bright green light and "some kinda music" (26), and then the sound of the girls screaming. The witness admits to having returned later and stolen the old man's shoes and socks, as well as the murder weapon, a machete.

The case grows still stranger: The coroner estimates the age of the victim, who had appeared to be about sixty, at a hundred and two, and further reports that the body contains fully functional organs for two separate bodies—one male and one female—and that the female body was about three months pregnant. The three supermodels, too distraught to be useful witnesses, all claim that they loved the victim so deeply that they can't live without him. Shortly thereafter, they disappear from custody in another flash of green light. That night Francine, already distraught and withdrawn over an unspecified recent event involving someone named Andy, dreams that "the one real love of my life came to me" in the form of a woman appearing in a green light and offering to release Francine from "a life that was barely worth living" (30). The supermodels, she learns, have told this figure of Francine's beauty, and she makes love to Francine before taking her away "to a place where the winds were cinnamon-scented." In the story's conclusion, Francine says, "I am very old now," having lived long in the cinnamon-scented place and grown tolerant of her lover's moving back and forth in time, shifting sexual identities, but her discovery that the figure is now transferring her/his affections to an unborn child becomes unbearable. Equipped with the machete, Francine vows that "from this dream neither he nor she will ever rise. I am in the green light now, with the machete. It may rain, but I won't be there to see it" (30). In other words, Francine plots to commit the crime with which the story began, completing a cycle that shifts from reality through dream and back to reality.

Like "The Toad Prince," "Objects of Desire" was originally written for another venue than the magazine which first published it. It was, in fact, one of Ellison's performance stories, written in a window to match the unlikely premise of a hundred-year-old pregnant corpse, which had been supplied to Ellison on the spot. Unlike "The Toad Prince," however, the tale manipulates its genre materials and personal Ellisonian themes in thoroughly unexpected ways. The initial setting echoes the seedy, ominous urban backstreets of "Soft Monkey" and "The Whimper of Whipped Dogs" as well as of a generation of hardboiled police procedurals. The key fantastic element, a sexually dimorphic time traveler, will be familiar to science fiction readers from Robert A. Heinlein's famous 1959 story "All You Zombies," which constructs an elaborate scenario in which the male protagonist, originally born with both male and female reproductive organs, manages through time travel to both impregnate him/herself and give birth to himself, making him literally the only member of his entire family. The romantic notion of True Love made manifest, of course, echoes Ellison's own more sardonic "Grail." And the character of Francine, a lonely and embittered figure descended from a long line of Ellison's women-victims, from Mona at Her Windows and Jenny to Maggie Moneyeyes, offers some hints that the story may be in part another psychological portrait of a disturbed mind: She is unable to resume her life after Andy, she is envious of the supermodels, she believes—even though she herself is in her forties—that her boss is "twice, maybe three or four times, my age" (29), and at the end she becomes as vengeful as a Greek goddess.

What is most significant about the story in the context of Ellison's work, however, is its virtually complete interpenetration of dream and reality. Read purely as a mystery, it leaves major questions unanswered even though the initial murder is finally explained; read as science fiction, the time-loop remains unresolved because no rationale is offered to account for either the origins of the mysterious old man or the manner in which the dream world is made to fold back on the real world. In other words, the story does not permit, and does not reward, a one-dimensional reading. It is, like much of Ellison's more provocative work, radically uneven in tone, profoundly irrationalist at its core, and yet both psychologically and spiritually apt: Francine Jacobs, like almost all of Ellison's more memorable characters, is liberated from the entrapment of her life only to find herself in another trap, this one of her own making.

From *Harlan Ellison: The Edge of Forever* (2002) by Ellen Weil and Gary K. Wolfe. Copyright © 2002 by The Ohio State University Press. Reprinted with permission of The Ohio State University Press.

Works Cited

Barron, Neil, ed. *Fantasy and Horror: A Critical and Historical Guide to Literature, Illustration, Film, TV, Radio, and the Internet.* Lanham, Md.: Scarecrow Press, 1999.

Ellison, Harlan. *Angry Candy*. New York: New American Library, 1989.
_____. *Mind Fields: The Art of Jacek Yerka/The Fiction of Harlan Ellison*. Beverly Hills, Calif.: Morpheus International, 1994.
_____. "Objects of Desire in the Mirror Are Closer Than They Appear." *World Horror Convention Program Book*, 23-30. Denver: World Horror Literary Society, 2000.
_____. *Shatterday*. Boston: Houghton Mifflin, 1980.
_____. *Slippage*. New York: Houghton Mifflin, 1997.
_____. *Strange Wine*. New York: Harper and Row, 1978.
_____. "The Toad Prince; or, Sex Queen of the Martian Pleasure Domes." *Amazing Stories* 71, no. 5 (2000): 18-33.

RESOURCES

Chronology of Harlan Ellison's Life

1934	Harlan Ellison is born on May 27 to Louis and Serita Ellison in Cleveland, Ohio.
1949	Louis Ellison dies of a heart attack.
1951	Ellison enrolls at Ohio State University.
1952-1954	Ellison serves as editor of the fanzine *Bulletin of the Cleveland Science Fiction Society* (also known as *Dimensions*).
1953	Ellison attends the World Science Fiction Convention (Worldcon) in Philadelphia, where he meets Isaac Asimov and Robert Silverberg. He is expelled from Ohio State University after striking his English professor because the professor made contemptuous remarks about science fiction in general and Ellison's ability to write in particular.
1955	Ellison moves to New York City to pursue a full-time writing career, starting in science fiction.
1956	Ellison makes his first professional sale, the science fiction story "Glowworm." He marries Charlotte Stein.
1957	Ellison joins a Brooklyn gang to do research so that he can write about juvenile delinquency. He is drafted into the Army and serves until 1959. Ellison and his wife separate.
1958	Ellison's first novel, *Rumble* (later retitled *Web of the City*), is published.
1959	Ellison writes for and edits *Rogue* magazine in Chicago. He and his wife divorce.
1960-1961	Ellison works as an editor for Regency Books.
1961	The rock-and-roll novel *Spider Kiss* (also known as *Rockabilly*) is published. Ellison marries Billie Joyce Sanders; the marriage ends in divorce in a year. *Gentleman Junkie, and Other Stories of the Hung-Up Generation* is published and later favorably reviewed by Dorothy Parker.

Chronology **365**

1962	Ellison moves to Los Angeles, California, and begins selling his writing to Hollywood.
1962-1967	Ellison produces numerous screenplays for television, including such programs as *The Alfred Hitchcock Hour*, *Burke's Law*, *The Outer Limits*, *Star Trek*, *The Man from U.N.C.L.E.*, *Cimarron Strip*, and *The Flying Nun*. During this period he wins three of his four awards for outstanding teleplay from the Writers Guild of America.
1965	Ellison sells a screenplay for the film *The Oscar*. He marries Lory Patrick, whom he divorces within the year. He participates in a massive civil rights march from Selma to Montgomery, Alabama, led by the Reverend Martin Luther King, Jr. "'Repent, Harlequin!' Said the Ticktockman" is published; the story receives a Nebula Award and a Hugo Award the following year.
1967	The original anthology *Dangerous Visions*, edited by Ellison, is published. "I Have No Mouth, and I Must Scream" is published; the story receives a Hugo Award the following year. The story collection *I Have No Mouth and I Must Scream* is published.
1968	"The Beast That Shouted Love at the Heart of the World" is published; the story receives a Hugo Award the following year.
1969	The novella *A Boy and His Dog* is published; it receives a Nebula Award the following year.
1972	The original anthology *Again, Dangerous Visions*, edited by Ellison, is published.
1973	Ellison writes the television pilot *The Starlost*, winning another outstanding teleplay award from the Writers Guild of America, but withdraws from the television project. "The Deathbird" is published; the story receives a Hugo Award the following year. "The Whimper of Whipped Dogs" is published; it receives the Edgar Allan Poe Award the following year.
1974	"Adrift Just Off the Islets of Langerhans: Latitude 38° 54′ N, Longitude 77° 00′ 13″ W" is published; the story receives a Hugo Award the following year.

1975	The collection *Deathbird Stories* is published. The film adaptation of *A Boy and His Dog* is released.
1976	Ellison marries Lori Horowitz; they divorce within a year.
1977	"Jeffty Is Five" is published; the story receives both a Hugo Award and a Nebula Award the following year.
1980	The collection *Shatterday* is published.
1984	Ellison sues the production company of director James Cameron's film *The Terminator* for allegedly taking material for the film from two of Ellison's teleplays written for the television series *The Outer Limits*.
1985	Ellison serves as creative consultant and writes teleplays for episodes of the revived series *The Twilight Zone*. "Paladin of the Lost Hour" is published; it received a Hugo Award the following year.
1986	Ellison marries Susan Toth, whom he had met in Scotland the previous year.
1987	*The Essential Ellison: A Thirty-five Year Retrospective*, is published.
1988	The collection *Angry Candy* is published.
1993	Ellison begins serving as creative consultant for the television series *Babylon 5*. His 1992 short story "The Man Who Rowed Christopher Columbus Ashore" is selected for inclusion in the anthology *The Best American Short Stories*. The horror novella *Mefisto in Onyx* is published; it receives the Bram Stoker Award. *Mind Fields*, a collection of stories based on paintings by Polish artist Jacek Yerka, is published.
1994	Ellison undergoes quadruple coronary artery bypass surgery after suffering a heart attack. The book form of Ellison's unproduced screenplay for Isaac Asimov's *I, Robot* is published. An earthquake severely damages Ellison's enormous house, which is stocked with curios, books, and magazines.

1994-1997	Ellison appears regularly as a commentator on the *Sci-Fi Buzz* television program on the Sci Fi Channel.
1997	The collection *Slippage: Precariously Poised, Previously Uncollected Stories*, is published.
2000	Ellison sues Stephen Robertson and the Internet services and media company AOL for posting his stories online without authorization.
2001	*The Essential Ellison: A Fifty Year Retrospective* is published. *Troublemakers*, a reprint collection aimed at the young adult market, is published.
2005	Ellison has his name trademarked.
2006	The Science Fiction and Fantasy Writers of America name Ellison a Damon Knight Memorial Grand Master.
2008	An independent documentary about Ellison, *Dreams with Sharp Teeth*, is first screened in Los Angeles.
2009	Ellison is nominated for a Grammy Award in the category of Best Spoken Word Album for Children for his reading of *Through the Looking-Glass and What Alice Found There*. He sues CBS Paramount Television and the Writers Guild of America for income not received from the original *Star Trek* episode "The City on the Edge of Forever."

Works by Harlan Ellison

Long Fiction
Rumble, 1958 (also known as *Web of the City*, 1975)
The Man with Nine Lives, 1959
Spider Kiss, 1961 (also known as *Rockabilly*)
All the Lies That Are My Life, 1980
Run for the Stars, 1991

Short Fiction
The Deadly Streets, 1958, 1975
A Touch of Infinity, 1960
Gentleman Junkie, and Other Stories of the Hung-Up Generation, 1961
The Juvies, 1961
Ellison Wonderland, 1962 (also known as *Earthman, Go Home*, 1964)
Paingod and Other Delusions, 1965
From the Land of Fear, 1967
I Have No Mouth and I Must Scream, 1967
Perhaps Impossible, 1967
Love Ain't Nothing but Sex Misspelled, 1968
The Beast That Shouted Love at the Heart of the World, 1969
Over the Edge: Stories from Somewhere Else, 1970
Alone Against Tomorrow: Stories of Alienation in Speculative Fiction, 1971 (published in England as *All the Sounds of Fear*, 1973)
The Time of the Eye, 1971
Approaching Oblivion: Road Signs on the Treadmill Towards Tomorrow, 1974
Deathbird Stories: A Pantheon of Modern Gods, 1975
No Doors, No Windows, 1975
Partners in Wonder, 1975
The Illustrated Harlan Ellison, 1978
Strange Wine: Fifteen New Stories from the Nightside of the World, 1978
The Fantasies of Harlan Ellison, 1979
Shatterday, 1980
Stalking the Nightmare, 1982
The Essential Ellison: A Thirty-five Year Retrospective, 1987
Angry Candy, 1988
Footsteps, 1989
Dreams with Sharp Teeth, 1991
Mefisto in Onyx, 1993

Mind Fields: The Art of Jacek Yerka, the Fiction of Harlan Ellison, 1993
"Repent, Harlequin!" Said the Ticktockman: The Classic Story, 1997
Slippage: Precariously Poised, Previously Uncollected Stories, 1997
The Essential Ellison: A Fifty Year Retrospective, 2001
Troublemakers, 2001

Screenplay
I, Robot: The Illustrated Screenplay, 1994

Nonfiction
Memos from Purgatory, 1961
The Glass Teat: Essays of Opinion on the Subject of Television, 1969
The Other Glass Teat: Further Essays of Opinion on Television, 1975
Sleepless Nights in the Procrustean Bed, 1984
An Edge in My Voice, 1985
Harlan Ellison's Watching, 1989
The Harlan Ellison Hornbook, 1990

Edited Texts
Dangerous Visions: Thirty-three Original Stories, 1967, 2002
Again, Dangerous Visions: Forty-six Original Stories, 1972

Bibliography

Adams, Stephen. "The Heroic and Mock-Heroic in Harlan Ellison's 'Harlequin.'" *Extrapolation* 26 (Winter 1985): 289-99.

Aldiss, Brian W., with David Wingrove. *Trillion Year Spree: The History of Science Fiction*. New York: Atheneum, 1986.

Asimov, Isaac. *In Memory Yet Green: The Autobiography of Isaac Asimov, 1920-1954*. New York: Avon, 1980.

Barron, Neil, ed. *Fantasy and Horror: A Critical and Historical Guide to Literature, Illustration, Film, TV, Radio, and the Internet*. Lanham, MD: Scarecrow Press, 1999.

Clute, John, and Peter Nicholls, eds. *The Encyclopedia of Science Fiction*. New York: St. Martin's Press, 1993.

Cobb, Joann P. "Medium and Message in Ellison's 'I Have No Mouth, and I Must Scream.'" *The Intersection of Science Fiction and Philosophy: Critical Studies*. Ed. Robert E. Myers. Westport, CT: Greenwood Press, 1983.

Delap, Richard. "Harlan Ellison: The Healing Art of Razorblade Fiction." *Magazine of Fantasy and Science Fiction* July 1977: 71-79.

Dowling, Terry. Introduction. *Deathbird Stories*. By Harlan Ellison. Norwalk, CT: Easton Press, 1990.

_____. "Introduction: Sublime Rebel." *The Essential Ellison: A Thirty-five Year Retrospective*. Ed. Terry Dowling, with Richard Delap and Gil Lamont. Omaha, NE: Nemo Press, 1987.

Ellison, Harlan. "Ellison Wonderland: Harlan Ellison Interviewed." Interview by Joseph Francavilla. *Post Script: Essays in Film and the Humanities* 10.1 (Fall 1990): 9-20.

_____. Interview by Paul Walker. 1972. *Speaking of Science Fiction: The Paul Walker Interviews*. Oradell, NJ: Luna, 1978. 291-301.

Erlich, Richard D. "Trapped in the Bureaucratic Pinball Machine: A Vision of Dystopia in the Twentieth Century." *Selected Proceedings of the 1978 Science Fiction Research Association National Conference*. Ed. Thomas J. Remington. Cedar Falls: University of Northern Iowa, 1979. 30-44.

Francavilla, Joseph. "Mythic Hells in Harlan Ellison's Science Fiction." *Phoenix from the Ashes: The Literature of the Remade World*. Ed. Carl B. Yoke. Westport, CT: Greenwood Press, 1987. 157-64.

Frisch, Adam J., and Joseph Martos. "Religious Imagination and Imagined Religion." *The Transcendent Adventure: Studies of Religion in Science Fiction/Fantasy*. Ed. Robert Reilly. Westport, CT: Greenwood Press, 1985.

Gruber, Frank. "The Life and Times of the Pulp Story." *Brass Knuckles: The Oliver Quayde, Human Encyclopedia, Stories*. Los Angeles: Sherbourne Press, 1966.

Hart, Sue. "Theater as Informer to the Future in the Works of Harlan Ellison." *The*

Dark Fantastic: Selected Essays from the Ninth International Conference on the Fantastic in the Arts. Ed. C. W. Sullivan III. Westport, CT: Greenwood Press, 1997. 121-27.

Heldreth, Leonard. "Clockwork Reels: Mechanized Environments in Science Fiction Films." *Clockwork Worlds: Mechanized Environments in SF.* Ed. Richard D. Erlich and Thomas P. Dunn. Westport, CT: Greenwood Press, 1983. 213-34.

King, Stephen. *Danse Macabre.* New York: Berkley, 1982.

_____. Foreword. *Stalking the Nightmare.* By Harlan Ellison. Huntington Woods, MI: Phantasia Press, 1982.

McNelly, Willis E. Foreword. "I Have No Mouth, and I Must Scream." By Harlan Ellison. *The Mirror of Infinity: A Critics' Anthology of Science Fiction.* Ed. Robert Silverberg. New York: Harper & Row, 1970. 246-50.

Malzberg, Barry. *The Engines of the Night: Science Fiction in the Eighties.* New York: Doubleday, 1982.

Moorcock, Michael. Foreword. *The Fantasies of Harlan Ellison.* By Harlan Ellison. Boston: Gregg Press, 1979.

Nash, Eric P. Rev. of *Slippage*, by Harlan Ellison. *New York Times* 21 Sept. 1997: sec. 7, p. 25.

Nicholls, Phil. "On the Edge of Forever: The TV SF of Harlan Ellison." *Vector: The Critical Review of Science Fiction* 135 (Dec. 1986/Jan. 1987).

O'Brien, Geoffrey. *Hard-Boiled America: The Lurid Years of Paperbacks.* New York: Van Nostrand, 1981.

Ower, John B. "Manacle-Forged Minds: Two Images of the Computer in Science Fiction." *Diogenes* 85 (1974): 47-61.

Parker, Dorothy. Rev. of *Gentleman Junkie and Other Stories of the Hung-Up Generation*, by Harlan Ellison. *Esquire* Jan. 1962. Rpt. in "Book Reviews." *Gentleman Junkie and Other Stories of the Hung-Up Generation.* By Harlan Ellison. New York: Pyramid Books, 1975. 1.

Patrouch, Joseph F., Jr. "Harlan Ellison and the Formula Story." *The Book of Ellison.* Ed. Andrew Porter. New York: Algol Press, 1978. 45-64.

_____. "Harlan Ellison's Use of the Narrator's Voice." *Patterns of the Fantastic.* Ed. Donald M. Hassler. Mercer Island, WA: Starmont House, 1983. 63-66.

_____. "Symbolic Settings in Science Fiction: H. G. Wells, Ray Bradbury, and Harlan Ellison." *Journal of the Fantastic in the Arts* 1.3 (1988): 37-45.

Pielke, Robert G. "The Rejection of Traditional Theism in Feminist Theology and Science Fiction." *The Intersection of Science Fiction and Philosophy: Critical Studies.* Ed. Robert E. Myers. Westport, CT: Greenwood Press, 1983.

Platt, Charles. *Dream Makers: The Uncommon People Who Write Science Fiction.* New York: Berkley, 1980.

Poirier, Richard. *The Performing Self: Compositions and Decompositions in the Languages of Contemporary Life.* New York: Oxford University Press, 1971.

Porter, Andrew, ed. *The Book of Ellison*. New York: Algol Press, 1978.
Priest, Christopher. *The Last Deadloss Visions*. London: Author, 1987.
Roberts, Thomas J. *An Aesthetics of Junk Fiction*. Athens: University of Georgia Press, 1990.
Russ, Joanna. "*A Boy and His Dog*: The Final Solution." 1975. *To Write Like a Woman: Essays in Feminism and Science Fiction*. Bloomington: Indiana University Press, 1995. 65-78.
Silverberg, Robert. "Harlan." *Magazine of Fantasy and Science Fiction* July 1977: 63-70. Rpt. in *Reflections and Refractions: Thoughts on Science-Fiction, Science, and Other Matters*. By Robert Silverberg. Grass Valley, CA: Underwood Books, 1997. 299-306.
―――――. "The Jet-Propelled Birdbath." *The Book of Ellison*. Ed. Andrew Porter. New York: Algol Press, 1978.
―――――. "Sounding Brass, Tinkling Cymbal." *Foundation* 7-8 (1975): 6-37.
Slusser, George Edgar. *Harlan Ellison: Unrepentant Harlequin*. San Bernardino, CA: Borgo Press, 1977.
Stevens, Carol D. "The Short Fiction of Harlan Ellison." *Survey of Science Fiction Literature*. Ed. Frank N. Magill. Englewood Cliffs, NJ: Salem Press, 1979. 3:1978-88.
Sturgeon, Theodore. Introduction. *I Have No Mouth and I Must Scream*. By Harlan Ellison. New York: Ace, 1983. ix-xiii.
Sullivan, C. W., III. "Harlan Ellison and Robert A. Heinlein: The Paradigm Makers." *Clockwork Worlds: Mechanized Environments in SF*. Ed. Richard D. Erlich and Thomas P. Dunn. Westport, CT: Greenwood Press, 1983. 97-103.
Swigart, Leslie Kay. *Harlan Ellison: A Bibliographical Checklist*. Dallas: Williams, 1973.
Watson, Christine. "The Short Fiction of Ellison." *Survey of Modern Fantasy Literature*. Ed. Frank N. Magill. Englewood Cliffs, NJ: Salem Press, 1983. 3:1516-19.
Weil, Ellen, and Gary K. Wolfe. *Harlan Ellison: The Edge of Forever*. Columbus: Ohio State University Press, 2002.
Wendell, Carolyn. "The Alien Species: A Study of Women Characters in the Nebula Award Winners, 1965-1973." *Extrapolation* 20 (Winter 1979): 343-54.
White, Michael D. "Ellison's Harlequin: Irrational Moral Action in Static Time." *Science-Fiction Studies* 4 (July 1977): 161-65.
Williamson, Jack. "Science Fiction, Teaching, and Criticism." *Science Fiction Today and Tomorrow*. Ed. Reginal Bretnor. New York: Harper & Row, 1974. 309-30.
Wolfe, Gary K. "Rogue Knight: Harlan Ellison in the Men's Magazines." *Foundation* 44 (Winter 1988-89): 26-32.

CRITICAL INSIGHTS

About the Editor

Joseph Francavilla is Associate Professor of English at Columbus State University; he has been teaching film, science fiction and fantasy, and American literature since 1987. Twice nominated for Columbus State University Educator of the Year, he is a member of the Science Fiction and Fantasy Writers of America and the Science Fiction Research Association. He has published poetry, fiction, and film reviews in *Arden*, *Ethos*, *Leidght*, *New Dimensions 10*, and *Cinefantastique*. He has published criticism on authors such as Franz Kafka, Edgar Allan Poe, Ray Bradbury, Dorothy Parker, Woody Allen, William Carlos Williams, Harlan Ellison, Roger Zelazny, Thomas Disch, and Philip K. Dick, and on films such as *Bringing Up Baby*, *City Lights*, *Citizen Kane*, *Blade Runner*, and *This Is Spinal Tap*.

About *The Paris Review*

The Paris Review is America's preeminent literary quarterly, dedicated to discovering and publishing the best new voices in fiction, nonfiction, and poetry. The magazine was founded in Paris in 1953 by the young American writers Peter Matthiessen and Doc Humes, and edited there and in New York for its first fifty years by George Plimpton. Over the decades, the *Review* has introduced readers to the earliest writings of Jack Kerouac, Philip Roth, T. C. Boyle, V. S. Naipaul, Ha Jin, Ann Patchett, Jay McInerney, Mona Simpson, and Edward P. Jones, and published numerous now-classic works, including Roth's *Goodbye, Columbus*, Donald Barthelme's *Alice*, Jim Carroll's *Basketball Diaries*, and selections from Samuel Beckett's *Molloy* (his first publication in English). The first chapter of Jeffrey Eugenides's *The Virgin Suicides* appeared in the *Review*'s pages, as have stories by Rick Moody, David Foster Wallace, Denis Johnson, Jim Crace, Lorrie Moore, and Jeanette Winterson.

The Paris Review's renowned Writers at Work series of interviews, whose early installments include legendary conversations with E. M. Forster, William Faulkner, and Ernest Hemingway, is one of the landmarks of world literature. The interviews received a George Polk Award and were nominated for a Pulitzer Prize. Among the more than three hundred interviewees are Robert Frost, Marianne Moore, W. H. Auden, Elizabeth Bishop, Susan Sontag, and Toni Morrison. Recent issues feature conversations with Jonathan Franzen, Norman Rush, Louise Erdrich, Joan Didion, Norman Mailer, R. Crumb, Michel Houellebecq, Marilynne Robinson, David Mitchell, Annie Proulx, and Gay Talese. In November 2009, Picador published the final volume of a four-volume series of anthologies of *Paris Review* interviews. The *New York Times* called the Writers at Work series "the most remarkable and extensive interviewing project we possess."

The Paris Review is edited by Lorin Stein, who was named to the post in 2010. The editorial team has published fiction by Lydia Davis, André Aciman, Sam Lipsyte, Damon Galgut, Mohsin Hamid, Uzodinma Iweala, James Lasdun, Padgett Powell, Richard Price, and Sam Shepard. Recent poetry selections include work by Frederick Seidel, Carol Muske-Dukes, John Ashbery, Kay Ryan, Mary Jo Bang, Sharon Olds, Charles Wright, and Mary Karr. Writing published in the magazine has been anthologized in *Best American Short Stories* (2006, 2007, and 2008), *Best American Poetry*, *Best Creative Non-Fiction*, the Pushcart Prize anthology, and *O. Henry Prize Stories*.

The magazine presents three annual awards. The Hadada Award for lifelong contribution to literature has recently been given to Joan Didion, Norman Mailer, Peter Matthiessen, John Ashbery, and, in 2010, Philip Roth. The Plimpton Prize for Fiction, awarded to a debut or emerging writer brought to national attention in the pages of *The Paris Review*, was presented in 2007 to Benjamin Percy, to Jesse Ball in 2008, and to Alistair Morgan in 2009. In 2011, the magazine inaugurated the Terry Southern Prize for Humor.

The Paris Review was a finalist for the 2008 and 2009 National Magazine Awards in fiction and won the 2007 National Magazine Award in photojournalism. The *Los Angeles Times* recently called *The Paris Review* "an American treasure with true international reach," and the *New York Times* designated it "a thing of sober beauty."

Since 1999 *The Paris Review* has been published by The Paris Review Foundation, Inc., a not-for-profit 501(c)(3) organization.

The Paris Review is available in digital form to libraries worldwide in selected academic databases exclusively from EBSCO Publishing. Libraries can contact EBSCO at 1-800-653-2726 for details. For more information on *The Paris Review* or to subscribe, please visit: www.theparisreview.org.

Contributors

Joseph Francavilla is Associate Professor of English at Columbus State University; he has been teaching film, science fiction and fantasy, and American literature since 1987. Twice nominated for Columbus State University Educator of the Year, he is a member of the Science Fiction and Fantasy Writers of America and the Science Fiction Research Association. He has published poetry, fiction, and film reviews in *Arden*, *Ethos*, *Leidght*, *New Dimensions 10*, and *Cinefantastique*. He has published criticism on authors such as Franz Kafka, Edgar Allan Poe, Ray Bradbury, Dorothy Parker, Woody Allen, William Carlos Williams, Harlan Ellison, Roger Zelazny, Thomas Disch, and Philip K. Dick, and on films such as *Bringing Up Baby*, *City Lights*, *Citizen Kane*, *Blade Runner*, and *This Is Spinal Tap*.

Larisa Mikhaylova is a Russian philologist, literary critic, and translator. She received her Ph.D. at Moscow State University; her dissertation was titled "New Trends in British and American Science Fiction (1960-1980s)." She teaches courses on world literature of the twentieth century and on the history and translation of science fiction in the Department of Journalism at Moscow State University. A member of the Science Fiction and Fantasy Writers of America and the Science Fiction Research Association, she is chief editor of the Russian SF magazine *Supernova: F&SF*. She has translated fiction by many science fiction authors, among them Ursula K. Le Guin and Pat Cadigan.

Sam Costello lives in Providence, Rhode Island. His fiction and comics have appeared in *Punk Planet*, *Negative Burn*, *Cthulhu Tales*, and *Split Lip*. His journalism has appeared in *PC World*, *Rue Morgue*, and *Bitch*, and on CNN.com.

George Edgar Slusser is Professor Emeritus of Comparative Literature and was Curator of the Eaton Collection at the University of California, Riverside. He was a Harvard Fellow and has held two Fulbright teaching fellowships. He was awarded the Science Fiction Research Association's Pilgrim Award for lifetime achievement in the field of science fiction in 1986. He is the author or editor of thirty-five books and more than one hundred articles on American and European SF and science and literature. He founded and built the Eaton Collection to its present-day 125,000 volumes. In collaboration with Danièle Chatelain, he has produced two translations/critical editions of early French-language SF works: Honoré de Balzac's *The Centenarian* and *Three Science Fiction Novellas* by J.-H. Rosny. He has recently collaborated with Chatelain on a number of articles on SF as narrative, including an article on Jules Verne, Claude Bernard, and the creation of a sense of wonder in *Verniana* (2010).

Rob Latham is Associate Professor of English at the University of California, Riverside. A coeditor of the journal *Science Fiction Studies* since 1997, he is the author of *Consuming Youth: Vampires, Cyborgs, and the Culture of Consumption*, as well as numerous articles and reviews. He directs the biannual Eaton Science Fiction Conference and the annual Science Fiction Studies Symposium. Recently he has coedited *The Wesleyan Anthology of Science Fiction*, a historical overview of the genre designed for teaching.

Andrew J. Wilson is a writer, editor, and academic publisher. He graduated from the University of Edinburgh, one of the ancient universities of Scotland, as a Master of Arts with Honours. His essays, interviews, reviews, and obituaries have been published on both sides of the Atlantic. His short stories and poetry have also appeared all over the world, sometimes in the most unlikely places. With Neil Williamson, he coedited *Nova Scotia: New Scottish Speculative Fiction*, a critically acclaimed original anthology that was nominated for the World Fantasy Award.

Darren Harris-Fain is Professor of English and Chair of the Department of English and Philosophy at Auburn University Montgomery. Prior to joining the faculty at AUM, he taught British and American literature and popular culture at Shawnee State University in Portsmouth, Ohio, from 1995 to 2010. He is the editor of three volumes on British fantasy and science fiction writers for the *Dictionary of Literary Biography* and the author of *Understanding Contemporary American Science Fiction: The Age of Maturity, 1970-2000* (2005); he has also written on science fiction, fantasy, horror, comics and graphic novels, and the media for numerous books and journals.

Ellen R. Weil wrote on Holocaust literature and on the authors Jane Yolen and Joe Haldeman. In Chicago, she taught courses in Holocaust studies at Roosevelt University and the Newberry Library. She coauthored, with Gary K. Wolfe, *Harlan Ellison: The Edge of Forever*. She later became a consultant for the development of corporate retiree volunteer programs.

Gary K. Wolfe is Professor of Humanities at Roosevelt University and a columnist for *Locus* magazine. He is the author of *The Known and the Unknown: The Iconography of Science Fiction*, *David Lindsay*, *Critical Terms for Science Fiction and Fantasy*, and *Harlan Ellison: The Edge of Forever* (with Ellen Weil). His book *Soundings: Reviews 1992-1996* received a British Science Fiction Association Award and was nominated for a Hugo Award. He has received the Eaton Award, the SFRA Pilgrim Award, the Distinguished Scholarship Award from the International Association for the Fantastic in the Arts, and a World Fantasy Award for reviews and criticism. A second collection of reviews, *Bearings*, appeared in 2010, and an essay collection, *Evaporating Genres*, in 2011.

Fr. Charles J. Brady was Associate Professor in the Department of Religious Studies at the University of Dayton, one of the largest Roman Catholic universities in Ohio.

John Crow taught Victorian and modern British literature at Miami University starting in 1971 until he retired to California. In addition to his essay reprinted in this volume, he has published another article with colleague Richard Erlich, "Words of Binding Patterns of Integration in the Earthsea Trilogy," which appeared in *Ursula K. Le Guin*, edited by Joseph D. Olander and Martin H. Greenberg (1979).

Richard Erlich taught English and film at Miami University (Oxford, Ohio) from

1971 to 2006, retiring as a full professor. His large-scale study *Coyote's Song: The Teaching Stories of Ursula K. Le Guin* was issued in paperback in 2010. He currently lives in Ventura County, California, where he specializes in script analysis for film production.

Philip M. Rubens taught in the Communications and Rhetoric Department at Michigan Technological University and taught technical writing at East Carolina State University until his recent retirement. Among his published articles is "'Nothing's Ever Final': Vonnegut's Conception of Time," which appeared in *College Literature*.

Paul Di Filippo first met Harlan Ellison in 1976, although he had been reading Ellison's work for many years prior. He is the author of some twenty-five books of fiction and lives in Providence, Rhode Island, with his partner, Deborah Newton. He is the author of collections of short stories such as *Harsh Oases*, *The Steampunk Trilogy*, and *Ribofunk*, novels such as *Roadside Bodhisattva*, and the novella *A Year in the Linear City*.

Peter Malekin, after roaming the blacked-out wartime streets of London, went to grammar school and then Oxford. He taught in Scandinavian, German, and Middle Eastern universities, and at the University of Durham (England). He is interested in human intelligence as self-transcending, discursive thought/language as arising from ontologically prior holistic levels of mind, tappable by poetry and literature, and therefore in spiritual (not religious) theater and in the fantastic. He lives in Sweden with two ravens left by a one-eyed man.

Robert Thurston is the author of many novels, critical and historical essays, and short stories. His novels include *Set of Wheels* and *Q Colony*. He has coauthored several books, written shared-world novels for *Isaac Asimov's Robot City: Robots and Aliens* and *BattleTech*, and novelizations for the films *1492: The Conquest of Paradise* and *Robot Jox*. Currently he runs a tutoring program at New Jersey City University, where he also teaches courses in the humanities.

Oscar De Los Santos, Ph.D., is Chair of the Writing Department at Western Connecticut State University. His books include *Hardboiled Egg* (short stories), *Infinite Wonderlands* (science fiction, coauthored with David G. Mead), and *Reel Rebels*, an edited collection of film essays. His stories and essays have appeared in *New York Review of Science Fiction*, *Extrapolation*, *Connecticut Review*, *Saranac Review*, and other journals.

Acknowledgments

"The *Paris Review* Perspective" by Sam Costello. Copyright © 2012 by Sam Costello. Special appreciation goes to Christopher Cox, Nathaniel Rich, and David Wallace-Wells, editors at *The Paris Review*.

"The Annihilation of Time: Science Fiction" by Ellen Weil and Gary K. Wolfe. From *Harlan Ellison: The Edge of Forever* (2002) by Ellen Weil and Gary K. Wolfe. Copyright © 2002 by The Ohio State University Press. Reprinted with permission of The Ohio State University Press.

"Consumed by Shadows: Ellison and Hollywood" by Ellen Weil and Gary K. Wolfe. From *Harlan Ellison: The Edge of Forever* (2002) by Ellen Weil and Gary K. Wolfe. Copyright © 2002 by The Ohio State University Press. Reprinted with permission of The Ohio State University Press.

"The Computer as a Symbol of God: Ellison's Macabre Exodus" by Charles J. Brady. From *Journal of General Education* 28 (1976): 55-62. Copyright © 1976 by The Pennsylvania State University. Reproduced by permission of Penn State Press.

"Myth" by George Edgar Slusser. From "Introduction" in *Harlan Ellison: Unrepentant Harlequin* (1977) by George Edgar Slusser. Copyright © 1977 by George Edgar Slusser. Reprinted with permission of George Edgar Slusser.

"The Concept of the Divided Self in Harlan Ellison's 'I Have No Mouth and I Must Scream' and 'Shatterday'" by Joseph Francavilla. From *Journal of the Fantastic in the Arts* 6.2/3 (1994): 107-125. Copyright © 1994 by Joseph Francavilla. Reprinted with permission of Joseph Francavilla.

"Created in the Image of God: The Narrator and the Computer in Harlan Ellison's 'I Have No Mouth, and I Must Scream'" by Darren Harris-Fain. From *Extrapolation* 32.2 (Summer 1991): 143-155. Copyright © 1991 by The Kent State University Press, Kent, OH 44242. All rights reserved. Reproduced by permission.

"Mythic Patterns in Ellison's *A Boy and His Dog*" by John Crow and Richard Erlich. From *Extrapolation* 18.2 (May 1977): 162-166. Copyright © 1977 by The Kent State University Press, Kent, OH 44242. All rights reserved. Reproduced by permission.

"The Ellison Personae: Author, Storyteller, Narrator" by Ellen R. Weil. From *Journal of the Fantastic in the Arts* 1.3 (1988): 27-36. Copyright ©1988 by Ellen R. Weil. Reprinted with permission of Gary K. Wolfe.

"Descents into Private Hells: Harlan Ellison's 'Psy-Fi'" by Philip M. Rubens. From *Extrapolation* 20.4 (Winter 1979): 378-385. Copyright © 1979 by The Kent State University Press, Kent, OH 44242. All rights reserved. Reproduced by permission.

"Stripped Down Naked: The Short Stories of Harlan Ellison" by Paul Di Filippo. From *The New York Review of Science Fiction* 18.5 (January 2006): 1, 8-14. Copyright © 2006 by Paul Di Filippo. Reprinted with permission of Paul Di Filippo.

"The Factured Whole: The Fictional World of Harlan Ellison" by Peter Malekin. From *Journal of the Fantastic in the Arts* 1.2 (1988): 21-26. Copyright © 1988 by Peter Malekin. Reprinted with permission of Peter Malekin.

"Afterword" by Robert Thurston. From *The Fantasies of Harlan Ellison* (1979), by Harlan Ellison, edited by David G. Hartwell and L. W. Currey. Copyright © 1979 by Robert Thurston. Reprinted with permission of Robert Thurston.

"Clogging Up the (In)Human Works: Harlan Ellison's Apocalyptic Postmodern Visions" by Oscar De Los Santos. From *Extrapolation* 40.1 (Spring 1999): 5-20. Copyright © 1999 by The Kent State University Press, Kent, OH 44242. All rights reserved. Reproduced by permission.

"The Self on Trial: Fragmentation and Magic Realism" by Ellen Weil and Gary K. Wolfe. From *Harlan Ellison: The Edge of Forever* (2002) by Ellen Weil and Gary K. Wolfe. Copyright © 2002 by The Ohio State University Press. Reprinted with permission of The Ohio State University Press.

Index

Adams, Stephen, 98
"Adrift Just Off the Islets of Langerhans" (Ellison), 51-58, 94, 251, 253, 274
Again, Dangerous Visions (Ellison), 112-113
Aldiss, Brian W., 8, 77, 110, 122; definition of science fiction, 10; on the New Wave, 108; on Edgar Allan Poe, 10
"All the Lies That Are My Life" (Ellison), 277, 347
"All the Sounds of Fear" (Ellison), 182, 264
Alone Against Tomorrow (Ellison), 137, 270
"Along the Scenic Route" (Ellison), 42, 268
Angry Candy (Ellison), 278
Apocalyptic fiction. *See* Postapocalyptic fiction
Approaching Oblivion (Ellison), 138, 271, 319
Asimov, Isaac, 325
Autobiographical elements in Ellison's work, 238, 241, 243, 263, 267, 274, 336

"Back to the Drawing Boards" (Ellison), 261
"Basilisk" (Ellison), 40, 69, 274
"Beast That Shouted Love at the Heart of the World, The" (Ellison), 130, 184-185, 287, 290-291
Berger, Harold L., 97
Biblical allusions, 71, 128, 177, 221-222, 226, 240
"Bleeding Stones" (Ellison), 39, 43
Borges, Jorge Luis, 238
Boy and His Dog, A (Ellison), 17, 70, 78, 82-83, 93, 130-135, 230-235, 269, 287-289; controversies, 133; critical responses, 97; film version, 132, 163, 232, 234-235
Brady, Charles J., 95, 221, 224, 380
"Bright Eyes" (Ellison), 265, 302
Bullying, 61, 161, 339

"City on the Edge of Forever, The" (Ellison), 149-151
Clark, Michael, 97
Clarke, Arthur C., ix, 94
Cobb, Joann P., 95, 224
Conformity and nonconformity, 83, 118, 163, 178, 293, 299, 301, 307, 310
"Corpse" (Ellison), 44
Costello, Sam, 379
"Crackpots, The" (Ellison), 120, 293, 301
"Crazy as a Soup Sandwich" (Ellison), 161
Crow, John, 95, 134, 380

Dangerous Visions (Ellison), 25, 67-68, 109-111, 265, 325; controversies, 67, 110; critical responses, 110
"Daniel White for the Greater Good" (Ellison), 63; review by Dorothy Parker, 91
Deadly Streets, The (Ellison), 30, 61, 259, 286
"Deathbird, The" (Ellison), 42, 47, 71, 94, 240, 255-256, 274, 290, 317, 319; critical responses, 96; Ellison on, 318; structure, 327
Deathbird Stories (Ellison), 38, 48, 72, 240, 273; introduction, 39, 317; thematic structure, 39-41
De Los Santos, Oscar, 96, 381
"Delusion for a Dragon Slayer" (Ellison), 46, 190, 249-250, 253, 305

"Demon with a Glass Hand" (Ellison), 17, 148
Di Filippo, Paul, 381
Disch, Thomas M., 15
Displaced realism, 121
Djam karet, 121, 187, 338
Doppelgängers, 11, 194, 249, 253, 277
Dreams, 45, 47, 52, 57, 189-190, 252, 305, 307, 349, 360
Dreams with Sharp Teeth (documentary film), 23, 102

"Eggsucker" (Ellison), 76, 131, 136
"Eidolons" (Ellison), 279, 337
Ellison, Harlan; atheism, 26; awards and honors, 3, 5, 28, 60, 64, 67, 98, 115, 265, 352; critical reception of works, 4, 19, 91-95; early life, 23, 90, 258; literary legacy, 5; on the New Wave, 109; comparison with Edgar Allan Poe, 4-21; on popular and critical success, 7; public persona, 3, 37; social activism, 25, 62; on speculative fiction, 66; on writing, 24; writing career, 4, 24, 27, 30, 38, 60, 64, 259, 263, 334; writing for television, 142-147, 149-151, 153-162; *Ellison Wonderland* (Ellison), 264
Erlich, Richard D., 95, 97, 134, 380
"Ernest and the Machine God" (Ellison), 52, 270
"Eyes of Dust" (Ellison), 304

"Facts in the Case of M. Valdemar, The" (Poe), 16
Female characters, 97; as narrators, 260; as victims, 361
"Forces that Crush, The" (Ellison), 264
Francavilla, Joseph, 95, 220, 225, 376
Frankenstein (Shelley), 8, 15, 77
Franklin, H. Bruce, 123, 127, 152

Freud, Sigmund, 194, 200
Frisch, Adam J., 96
"From A to Z, in the Chocolate Alphabet" (Ellison), 276, 337

"GBK—A Many-Flavored Bird" (Ellison), 244
Gentleman Junkie, and Other Stories of the Hung-Up Generation (Ellison), 262; review by Dorothy Parker, 64, 91
"Glowworm" (Ellison), 20, 259, 310
"Goodbye to All That" (Ellison), 284

"Harlan Ellison's Movie" (Ellison), 163
Harris-Fain, Darren, 96, 125, 317, 352, 380
Hart, Sue, 141
Hartwell, David G., 323
Hatred, 48, 96, 123, 161, 186, 189, 216, 219, 289, 291
Heinlein, Robert A., 7, 59, 94, 118, 121, 158, 360
Heldreth, Leonard, 95
"Hitler Painted Roses" (Ellison), 27, 276
Horror fiction, 272, 326, 353
"Hour that stretches," 121, 187, 338

"I Have No Mouth, and I Must Scream" (Ellison), 17, 31, 65, 86, 92, 94, 96, 122-129, 175-179, 186-188, 203-206, 214-227, 266, 302-304, 317; differing versions, 215; narrator, 215, 217
I, Robot (Asimov), 166
I, Robot (Ellison screenplay), 166-168
"I'm Looking for Kadak" (Ellison), 239, 272
Implied author, 239, 241, 243-244

Jackson, Shirley, 343
"Jeffty Is Five" (Ellison), 24, 31, 94, 242-243, 276, 334

"Kid Killer" (Ellison), 61, 260
"Knife in the Darkness" (Ellison), 154
Kyben war stories, 137, 148, 261, 281, 350

Last Dangerous Visions, The (unpublished), 101, 113
"Last Question, The" (Asimov), 173
Latham, Rob, 379
"Lonelyache" (Ellison), 266, 306, 308
Love, 41, 44, 49-50, 59, 83, 134, 157, 185, 189, 225, 232, 235, 266, 272, 276, 280, 287-288, 359

McBride, Debra L., 224
McCarthy, Cormac, 76
McHale, Brian, 326
McNelly, Willis E., 95, 125, 221, 227
Magic realism, 100, 246, 333
Malekin, Peter, 381
"Man Who Rowed Christopher Columbus Ashore, The" (Ellison), 27, 101, 281, 320, 323, 327, 340, 343
Martos, Joseph, 96
Mefisto in Onyx (Ellison), 282, 350-354; critical responses, 352
"Memo from Purgatory" (Ellison), 142
Memos from Purgatory (Ellison), 37, 61, 142, 286
Mikhaylova, Larisa, 379
Mind Fields (Ellison), 280, 342, 344-348
Misogyny, 133
"Monster in the Clearing, The" (Fayette), 174
Moorcock, Michael, 107, 120, 130, 241
"MS. Found in a Bottle" (Poe), 18
Myths, 53, 95, 134, 148, 181, 191, 221, 227, 230, 240, 248, 272, 284, 290, 305, 349

Narrative of Arthur Gordon Pym, The (Poe), 18
Narrators and narration, 70, 86, 96, 216, 226; first person, 98; implied author, 239, 241, 243-244; omniscient, 260; self-conscious, 328; unreliable, 187, 217, 354
"Neither Your Jenny Nor Mine" (Ellison), 244, 267
"Neon" (Ellison), 43
New Wave in science fiction, 15, 68, 107-108, 110, 116, 324, 334
"Night of Delicate Terrors, The" (Ellison), 62
Nonconformity. *See* Conformity and nonconformity
Nye, David E., 12

"O Ye of Little Faith" (Ellison), 45
"Objects of Desire in the Mirror Are Closer than They Appear" (Ellison), 283, 357, 359-360
"On the Downhill Side" (Ellison), 49, 56, 274
"One Life, Furnished in Early Poverty" (Ellison), 243, 272
"One Ordinary Day, with Peanuts" (Jackson), 343
Ower, John B., 94, 218, 221, 223

"Paingod" (Ellison), 50, 183, 265, 297
Paingod and Other Delusions (Ellison), 116, 264
"Paladin of the Lost Hour" (Ellison), 162, 279
Parker, Dorothy, 63, 91, 263
Patrouch, Joseph F., Jr., 98, 226
Pielke, Robert G., 96
Pierce, Hazel Beasley, 98
"Place with No Name, The" (Ellison), 46, 192, 254
Plank, Robert, 251
Poe, Edgar Allan; comparison with Ellison, 4-21; and science fiction, 10

Pohl, Frederik, 65, 111, 214
Postapocalyptic fiction, 71, 75, 85, 93, 122, 132, 136, 174, 230, 255, 281, 310, 315
Postmodernist literature, 94, 323, 325, 328
"Pretty Maggie Moneyeyes" (Ellison), 48, 188, 266, 306
Priest, Christopher, 101, 107, 110, 114
"Prowler in the City at the Edge of the World, The" (Ellison), 128, 155, 270

Quest stories, 45, 47, 51-52, 182, 190, 192, 278, 282, 318

Racism, 70, 91, 154, 161, 263, 269, 321-322, 341-342, 351-352, 354
Rebellion, 11, 65, 118, 130, 272, 282, 302, 307, 315, 319, 333, 346. *See also* Conformity and nonconformity
"Region Between, The" (Ellison), 279, 315-316, 325
Religion, 95, 171, 215, 221, 225-226, 240, 290
"'Repent, Harlequin!' Said the Ticktockman" (Ellison), 64, 92, 117-121, 265, 299-300, 313-314; critical responses, 98
"Resurgence of Miss Ankle-Strap Wedgie, The" (Ellison), 245, 267
Revenge, 31, 43, 61, 63, 83, 124, 188, 203, 262, 333, 349
Road, The (McCarthy), 76, 78-82, 84-87
"Rock God" (Ellison), 43
Rubens, Philip M., 95, 381
Rumble (Ellison), 9, 24, 30, 37, 61
"Run for the Stars" (Ellison), 148, 261
"Run, Spot, Run" (Ellison), 76, 131, 136
Russ, Joanna, 97, 113, 134

"Santa Claus vs. S.P.I.D.E.R." (Ellison), 98, 268
"Scartaris, June 28th" (Ellison), 281, 339

Science fiction genre, 326; British authors, 77; computers in, 172; definitions, 9-11; development, viii, 5; the grotesque in, 11, 16, 296, 355; lack of respect for, 7, 14, 66; New Wave, 15, 68, 107-108, 110, 116, 324, 334; satire in, 296; the sublime in, 11-12, 16, 19; on television, 145; tropes, 14
Sexuality, 93, 124, 175, 205, 218, 231-232, 287-288
"Shatterday" (Ellison), 207-211
Shatterday (Ellison), 100, 276
"Shattered Like a Glass Goblin" (Ellison), 69, 72, 130, 269, 287; as horror fiction, 69
Shelley, Mary Wollstonecraft, 8, 15, 77
Show business, 141
"Silent in Gehenna" (Ellison), 272, 286
"Silver Corridor, The" (Ellison), 158, 264, 279
"Sky Is Burning, The" (Ellison), 262
"Sleeping Dogs" (Ellison), 301
Slusser, George Edgar, 93, 96, 217, 219, 379
"Soft Monkey" (Ellison), 279, 354
"Soldier" (Ellison), 146, 266
Spanos, William V., 326
Speculative fiction, 3, 31, 67, 99, 110, 269, 310, 324, 326; urban fantasy, 273. *See also* Science fiction genre
Spinrad, Norman, 112, 324
Stevens, Carol D., 95, 221
Sturgeon, Theodore, viii, 266
Suicide, 49, 86, 203, 272, 304, 315
Sullivan, C. W., III, 94
Swigart, Leslie Kay, 98

Technological sublime, 12
Themes and motifs; bullying, 61, 161, 339; conformity and nonconformity,

Acknowledgments **387**

83, 118, 163, 178, 293, 299, 301, 307, 310; doppelgängers, 11, 194, 249, 253, 277; dreams, 45, 47, 52, 57, 189-190, 252, 305, 307, 349, 360; hatred, 48, 96, 123, 161, 186, 189, 216, 219, 289, 291; "hour that stretches," 121, 187, 338; love, 41, 44, 49-50, 59, 83, 134, 157, 185, 189, 225, 232, 235, 266, 272, 276, 280, 287-288, 359; misogyny, 133; myths, 53, 95, 134, 148, 181, 191, 221, 227, 230, 240, 248, 272, 284, 290, 305, 349; questing, 45, 47, 51-52, 182, 190, 192, 278, 282, 318; racism, 70, 91, 154, 161, 263, 269, 321-322, 341-342, 351-352, 354; rebellion, 11, 65, 118, 130, 272, 282, 302, 307, 315, 319, 333, 346; religion, 95, 171, 215, 221, 225-226, 240, 290; revenge, 31, 43, 61, 63, 83, 124, 188, 203, 262, 333, 349; sexuality, 93, 124, 175, 205, 218, 231-232, 287-288; show business, 141; suicide, 49, 86, 203, 272, 304, 315; trickster figures, 98, 118, 281, 310, 312, 322; violence, 39, 41, 45, 48, 59, 62-63, 70, 93, 154, 175, 184, 193, 200, 207, 220, 225, 232, 262, 286-287, 290; war, 40, 69, 79, 124, 148, 152, 186, 219, 261, 274, 350

Thurston, Robert, 381

"Toad Prince, The" (Ellison), 283, 357-358

Trickster figures, 98, 118, 281, 310, 312, 322

Troublemakers (Ellison), 282

2001: A Space Odyssey (Clarke), 94

Vengeance. *See* Revenge

"Very Last Day of a Good Woman, The" (Ellison), 264

Violence, 39, 41, 45, 48, 59, 62-63, 70, 93, 154, 175, 184, 193, 200, 207, 220, 225, 232, 262, 286-287, 290

War, 40, 69, 79, 124, 148, 152, 186, 219, 261, 274, 350

Web of the City. See *Rumble*

Weil, Ellen R., 5, 17, 62-63, 78, 81, 91, 93, 380

Wendell, Carolyn, 97, 133

"Whimper of Whipped Dogs, The" (Ellison), 41, 62, 155, 245, 273

White, Michael D., 120

Williamson, Jack, 108

Wilson, Andrew J., 380

Wolfe, Gary K., 5, 17, 62-63, 78, 81, 91, 93, 380

Women characters. *See* Female characters

"World of the Myth" (Ellison), 305

Yerka, Jacek, 280

Zelazny, Roger, 265, 271

PS
3555
.L62
Z64
2012